PSYCHIATRISTS—
the Men Behind HITLER

The Architects of Horror

PSYCHIATRISTS

.

THE MEN BEHIND HITLER

THE ARCHITECTS OF HORROR

DR. THOMAS RÖDER • VOLKER KUBILLUS • ANTHONY BURWELL

FREEDOM PUBLISHING
LOS ANGELES

The Original Edition of this book appeared under the title DIE MÄNNER HINTER HITLER in the German language in 1994. Published by Pi-Verlag für Politik und Gesellschaft, Postfach 346, CH-6102 Malters / Switzerland.
Authors: Dr. Thomas Röder, Volker Kubillus
Co-Author: Peter-Karl Talkenberg
Research: Hans Deimel, Wilhelm Koopmann, Dominik Hochstetter

German Original Edition © 1994 Pi-Verlag für Politik und Gesellschaft, 1994
Die Deutsche Bibliothek—CIP Einheitsaufnahme
Die Männer Hinter Hitler: Wer die geheimen Drahtzieher hinter Hitler Wirklich waren...; und unter welchem Deckmantel sie noch immer unter uns weilen / Thomas Röder; Volker Kubillus (Hrsg.)—Malters: Pi-Verl. für Politik und Gesellschaft, 1994
ISBN 3-9520639-0-8
NE: Röder, Thomas (Hrsg.)

This English Edition by Freedom Publishing, Los Angeles, CA 90028

First Edition

Authors: Dr. Thomas Röder, Volker Kubillus, Anthony Burwell
Translators: Rolf and Sybil Rentmeister
Cover art: Peter Green and Carrie Cook

Psychiatrists—the Men Behind Hitler

Exposé
Includes Index
       1. Psychiatry   2. Human rights
       3. Social issues   4. Holocaust
       5. Nazis   6. Hitler   7. World War II

ISBN: 0-9648909-1-7

Photo credits: FPG International, pages 5, 304; The Descent of Man; page 13; KVPM Archive, pages 29, 163, 213; AP/Wide World Photos, pages 127, 161; DPA, page 191; Photo Archive, page 54; The Big Encyclopedia of the Third Reich, page 48; Bettmann Archive, pages 224, 237, 240; UPI/Bettmann, pages 266, 268, 270, 294, 303, 336; Reuters/Bettmann, page 360; German Publishers House Ltd., page 34.

Manufactured in the USA by the Courier Companies, Inc.

CONTENTS

∎

PART TWO
THE SUPPRESSED PAST

PART THREE
"THE MEN BEHIND HITLER" IN AMERICA?

ACKNOWLEDGEMENTS

The staffs and supporters of the Citizens Commission on Human Rights International, United States and Germany are especially acknowledged for their long-term dedication in preserving and restoring human rights and dignity to those who have been violated by psychiatry. Their research, documentation and expertise have been invaluable in the preparation of this book.

Anthony Burwell

This publication has been made possible through the unwavering support of the United States INTERNATIONAL ASSOCIATION OF SCIENTOLOGISTS *Members' Trust in freeing mankind from the damaging practices of psychiatry and restoring human rights and dignity to psychiatry's victims. The membership of the IAS is gratefully acknowledged for its continued vigilance.*

The Publishers

Dedicated to all those who fight for freedom and human rights—including all the writers, journalists, critics and activists, past and present, who have labeled these horrors for what they are—in the profound hope that such atrocities might one day cease to exist.

PREFACE OF THE EDITORS

Hitler's "Thousand Year" Reich lasted just twelve years—in historical terms a relatively short period of time. Yet, the residue of the Nazi terror is still present today, half a century later and after the unification of the former West Germany and East Germany.

Hitler's wars of conquest and the Nazi Holocaust left an indelible legacy which has been inherited, and will continue to be inherited, by every succeeding German generation. But holding future generations answerable for the atrocities of their ancestors is not a solution to the problem. It is more important to expose the causes of the Nazis' crimes and ensure that those causes are readily recognizable. In that fashion, if the seeds of genocide ever begin to appear, they can be identified and eradicated before they ripen. Only then can we feel secure that the atrocities of the Third Reich will never happen again.

There have been a multitude of attempts to explain how the unthinkable catastrophe of Nazi Germany could have happened. Many questions have been answered, but many others have evaded adequate explanation. To this day it is still a mystery how a country of poets and thinkers could be transformed so quickly into one of hatred and genocide.

In the first half of the twentieth century there was certainly no shortage of right-wing dictators who came to power or seized it in Europe—Mussolini in Italy, Franco in Spain, Salazar in Portugal, Pilsudski in Poland, just to name a few. Certainly, there was discrimination based on race or religion in places other than Germany, as were there violations of basic human rights, political murders, persecutions, war and mass executions. But nowhere else was so extensive a genocide so systematically and thoroughly executed as it was in Hitler's Germany. Nowhere else must today's generation still bear the shame and responsibility that Germans must as a result of the murderous excesses of their fascist past.

Despite all the research into the Nazi era, the true cause of the genocide has remained elusive. This puzzle will at last be solved in the following pages, and the solution is disturbing because many of those who bear responsibility for the Holocaust escaped unscathed, avoiding the

Nuremberg War Crimes Trials and the Denazification Program. Even more disturbing is the fact that to this day, their adherents and their philosophical descendants pursue the same sordid theories and practices, on a smaller scale, in a new guise and in new places.

With that in mind, this book is intended as a warning to be vigilant, as a call to the defense of freedom. Freedom is not without costs. It demands our constant alertness and our willingness to rise against its enemies and defeat them.

This book, *Psychiatry—the Men Behind Hitler,* is the result of years of extensive research and investigation. The number of people who helped in its writing, either through investigations or the tabulation of results, is very large. But even larger is the number of people who have been anxiously awaiting this book. We are happy to be able to present the book that solves the riddle of who the men behind Hitler really were and who made his reign of terror possible.

Read on and find out who the men behind Hitler were and where they are now.

The Editors
October 1995

PREFACE OF THE AUTHORS

"To bury the truth, many shovels are needed."
Proverb

WHAT THIS BOOK WILL REVEAL

The men behind Hitler. Certainly an emotional topic, and a controversial one, too. But it is controversial for only one reason—until now the men behind Hitler have never been publicly identified and documented.

In fact, these sinister characters have successfully camouflaged their real role in the Nazi horror for decades. Despite the most careful and probing investigation, they have remained largely unnoticed and undiscovered. However, these invisible people are the ones who ultimately made the Third Reich's genocide possible.

Until now, their role, shrouded in mystery, has never really been microscopically examined. Until now, they have never been scrutinized in the harsh light of all the evidence or offered for the collective judgment of mankind.

To many knowledgeable historians, Hitler remains a mystery. How could one man by himself rise to such power and commit such atrocities? How could one madman so captivate and seduce an entire nation so thoroughly that it embraced such barbarism for his glory? These mysteries might never have been solved if the heretofore hidden "catalyst" in the reaction had not been identified.

We do not mean to minimize Hitler's responsibility for the inhuman crimes that the Third Reich committed. The fact remains that Adolf Hitler deservedly was, is and always will be adjudged the ultimate criminal of the Reich. There never can be any justification, rationalization or defense for what he did.

But our focus here is his unseen "advisors"—the ones who escaped punishment after the war and whose role in the Reich's reign of terror has never been exposed adequately. In this volume we name the men behind Hitler who managed to conceal their actions and even their identities from the public and from history so effectively.

In Part One of this book we identify the men behind Hitler and explore the sources of their philosophies and powers.

Without identifying and exposing these people and what they did, neither Hitler nor his atrocities can be adequately understood. This subject has never been addressed as thoroughly as it is in this book.

In Part Two of this book, we document how so many of the men behind Hitler disappeared after the war, only to re-emerge thereafter. We will also document what honors they have received, what teachings they espouse and what influence they have exerted since the war, both personally and through their students.

But this story is even more dramatic. We will also demonstrate that the men behind Hitler are very much with us today. Their ideas and methods are still in vogue today and their philosophical descendents vividly echo the teachings and practices of the Nazi past.

In Part Three of this book, we demonstrate that the influences, theories and practices that so centrally contributed to Hitler and his Nazi agenda did not confine themselves to Germany either before or after the war. It offers the facts that portend a chilling realization that the demise of the Third Reich was not an invitation to apathy.

This book has all the makings of a ready-made scandal. We have not been afraid to name names, to point fingers, to tell the truth. The daily abuse of human rights simply cannot continue to be ignored, because people around the world are still being maimed and injured today in much the same way as the races Hitler deemed "inferior" were targeted and abused.

A wide variety of historians, scholars, journalists, prosecutors and social activists have managed to follow the trails of Hitler's henchmen and have succeeded in exposing many of their misdeeds and atrocities. The discoveries of those researchers, which are a basis for this book, are detailed and substantiated. However, it is certain that this book will provoke controversy because much of what has been reported elsewhere as isolated incidents has been pieced together for the first time in these pages. The result is a frightening jigsaw with a new, more profound, and ultimately more disturbing portrait than seen elsewhere.

In essence, this book addresses two types of readers. The first is the professional—the sociologist, the doctor, the historian, the scholar and the like. The other is the general reader who is interested in history and seeks to be enlightened. Thus we had to confront the age-old problem of having to serve two masters. On the one hand, science demands precision, unshakable sources and a detailed study of the subject matter. We have satisfied those demands and complied with that rigor.

On the other hand, clear, easily understood terminology had to be a requirement, along with sufficient explanation of technical terms which are familiar to experts but not to the general reader. Additionally, drawings had to be produced and photographs included which would facilitate understanding of the material.

Scholars and scientists are invited to forgive our reader-friendly style. In turn, the layperson is invited to forgive us for the occasional compromises we had to make with simplicity and for the exactitude, documentation and citation of sources necessary to satisfy the empiricist.

Just one last note. This book contains several descriptions of brutalities that, by their inherent depravity, are difficult to imagine, let alone to comprehend. We assure you that nothing was exaggerated and nothing was embellished. Just as nothing has been blown out of proportion, nothing has been swept under the carpet. This book thus is not for weak stomachs. Even though various incidents have been described as clinically as possible, they will and should be upsetting to many readers. Therefore, forgive us if from time to time we show our sadness or our outrage.

The Authors
October 1995

PART ONE

THE ARCHITECTS OF THE HORROR:

WHO REALLY STOOD BEHIND HITLER?

"A man said once to me: 'Listen, if you are going to do this, all of Germany will go to pieces within six months.' I said: 'What do you mean by that?' 'That Germany will cease to exist.' I answered: 'The German people survived the wars with the Romans. The German people survived the mass migration. Later on, the German people survived the great wars of the early and late Middle Ages. After that, the German people survived the Thirty Year War. Even later the German people survived the Napoleonic Wars, the freedom wars. They survived even a World War, even the Revolution—they will survive me as well!'"
Adolf Hitler

THE MISSING PIECE IN THE PUZZLE

A ny exploration of how Hitler's Third Reich came to be and how it mutated into a machine for the commission of atrocities must ultimately address the "whos" and "whys" of a dark history.

To do that, we have to penetrate that darkness, remove the lingering shrouds that conceal the truth, and piece together the disparate elements of a puzzle containing thousands of jagged pieces. It is a critical analysis, one that must be completed because the concern that it may happen again is as real as the horror that it ever happened at all.

The search for the answers to the "whos" and the "whys" begins with events that preceded the Holocaust.

By January 30, 1939, Hitler—who came to power in 1933—had announced openly that he was planning the "extermination of the Jewish race in Europe." His stance was that stark and that unequivocal. Countless documents reveal that well before that time, Hitler's profound anti-Semitism had been very much in evidence.[1] Later, in a dinner conversation on May 29, 1942, Hitler actually demanded that Europe be "free of Jews."[2]

The pursuit of his avowed intentions were ruthlessly executed in 1939 in Poland, in the very first military campaign on which Hitler embarked. In Warsaw, Lodz and other Polish cities, the Jewish population was herded into ghettos. Near Lublin, a "territory of 35 to 40 square miles was declared as a reservation for Jews."[3] The list of atrocities takes its reader's breath away: arrests, incarcerations, torture, murders—any crime, injury, or brutality that could be inflicted, any atrocity that could be imagined, was suddenly the norm. Hitler's hatred and prejudices, his madness and brutality, had all become facts of life beyond Germany's borders.

The same scenario was replayed in 1940 in Denmark, Norway, Holland, Belgium, Luxembourg and France. Anti-Jewish legislation, based on the German model, became law in France, Rumania, Italy and Hungary. Suddenly, across the continent, and in virtually every Jewish enclave, order and peaceful coexistence were replaced by chaos and violence. Blackmail, synagogue desecrations, involuntary deportations, theft, and executions became matters of daily routine.

By 1941, wherever German authority extended, extermination by gas chamber had become commonplace. By December of that year, when the United States finally joined the war after the Japanese attack on Pearl Harbor, the concentration camps at Auschwitz, Chelmno, Belec, Sobibor, Treblinka and Maidanek had become sites of unspeakable horror. The Nazis had, in fact, developed a grotesque refinement in the extermination of innocent men, women and children. At one point, for example, the Auschwitz gas chamber was re-tooled so that instead of using the lethal exhaust fumes from a diesel engine, it used the more efficient toxic gas called Zyklon B, a poison manufactured by Degesch, a subsidiary of the infamous I.G. Farben industrial empire.[4]

Zyklon B was ultimately the agent of millions of deaths. The Jewish death toll alone, according to the Nuremberg Tribunal, was estimated at 5,721,800. All told, more than six million people were exterminated.

Viewed from another perspective, there were approximately 15 million Jews worldwide in 1939. By 1945, that number was reduced to 9 million. In 1939, because of Hitler's policies and unprecedented emigration, there were only 200,000 Jews in Germany; by 1945, there were barely 12,000.[5]

Unfortunately, there is much more to recall, because the Third Reich's horror assumed many forms. Hitler's euthanasia program was a separate, but parallel chapter in this sordid story. Euthanasia, despite its literal and relatively benign meaning—"assistance to die"—is a misleading term, particularly when it is filtered through the prism of Nazi hate. All pretense aside, Nazi euthanasia programs were systematic mass murders. Camouflage organizations like the "Reichsarbeitsgemein-schaft Heil- und Pflege-anstalten" ("Work Association of Sanitariums and Nursing Homes of the Reich") were on the lookout not only for certain "health symptoms,"

Adolf Hitler

but also for people's work records and race. Characteristics such as that could target a person for execution in the guise of "euthanasia."

Other front groups like the "Gemeinnützige Krankentransport-gesellschaft GmbH" ("Public Utility Ambulance Service Ltd.") channeled between 100,000 and 200,000 purportedly "ill" and "inferior" people to the death camps' transit stations. Through euthanasia, the Third Reich rid itself of its troublesome prison population, those incapable of working and a variety of political and racial undesirables. It also was in the Nazi euthanasia programs that alarming human experiments were conducted. Testing was done with subatmospheric pressure, supercooling, spotted fever and sulfomides—all on live human beings who had the misfortune of displaying one or more of the designated "symptoms" that qualified them for the program.

Of course, beyond the Nazis' murder and torture, there was world war. The naked statistics of World War II are bloodcurdling: of 110 million soldiers, 27 million died. On top of that, 25 million civilians perished and 3 million others disappeared. The Soviet Union alone lost 20 million people, China at least 10 million, Poland 5.8 million, Germany 4.6 million (another 2.5 million either fled the country or were deported or expelled), Japan 2 million, Yugoslavia 1.7 million, France 600,000, Great Britain 400,000, and the United States 300,000 people.

The numbers, of course, are only a portion of the many sobering facts about World War II and the events surrounding it. However, it is viewed, World War II was the largest organized mass murder in recorded history.

Since then, armies of scholars have attempted to piece together the puzzle that would explain how such slaughter could have happened. Many lines of investigation have been followed. Historians, social scientists, scholars of all description have all examined a variety of factors which suggest themselves as contributing causes to the Holocaust, the euthanasia, the war and the carnage.

Among their inquiries was the question of how come Hitler came to power. On that subject, there is no shortage of theories: a prolonged and unprecedented economic crisis; unspeakable inflation; Germany's crushing defeat in World War I; the Treaty of Versailles and unlivable terms of surrender; virtually nonstop food shortages and unemployment from the war's end into the thirties; a basic unfamiliarity with, and lack of confidence in, the democratic process; virulent ideological crises and the emergence of extremist political philosophies; a trend toward fascism across the continent; the failure of traditional church leaderships to bolster the faithful.

To one extent or another, each of those factors was instrumental in Hitler's rise to power, though distilled to their essential core, the catalogue of causes reduces to a single, fundamental proposition. Hitler came to power because he was able to exploit an opportunity created by a prolonged period of political, social and economic turmoil.

It is curious, at least, to note that the circumstances that made a Hitler regime possible in Germany were by no means unique to Germany. By the early 1930s, even the nations which had been victorious in World War I and which had prospered during the Roaring Twenties were, by the end of that decade, in the grips of an unprecedented global economic depression that would last for at least another decade.

Hard times bred bad leaders in a number of nations, but none so horrific as Hitler. So the conundrum persists—how was it that Hitler's peculiar and perverse demagoguery was possible in Germany but seemingly not elsewhere?

Logic dictates that the inquiry must begin with Hitler's own personal history. His life has been analyzed, dissected and examined as no other person's life ever has been, before or since. Hitler biographies, Hitler analyses, and Hitler interpretations abound.

Probably the best Hitler biographer in the German-speaking world, the noted historian Joachim C. Fest,[6] researched and analyzed every conceivable aspect of Hitler's life in an effort to identify even the slightest potential influence on the man and his madness. Other eminent scholars have written books with self-explanatory themes like *The Man Who Inspired Hitler*,[7] in which Wilfried Daim concludes that Hitler's anti-Semitism traces back to the writings of Jörg Lanz von Liebenfels (publisher of a series of anti-Semitic writings). There can be little doubt that Liebenfels was a major influence on the future Führer just as there is little doubt that Liebenfels' virulent hatred of Jews occupied a niche in Hitler's racial mania.

There is not one corner of Hitler's life that had not been thoroughly researched. While it is certainly enlightening to study these investigations and to retrace Hitler's life through the interpretations of scholars and thinkers, it is also frustrating to dwell even temporarily in Hitler's life. It was a life, in which, according to Fest, "states of great elation abruptly changed to moods of deep depression, where he saw only injustice, hate and hostility, and where he all by himself stood against all of mankind."[8]

Through these biographies, it is possible to gain some understanding of his hatred, the anti-Semitic literature that he consumed, the importance he placed on German culture and customs, and his own maniacal supernationalism. However, after all the scholarship and research, after all the theorizing, after the most exhaustive scrutiny to which any person has ever been subjected, Hitler remains an essential enigma. We can study his social surroundings and get some insight into a great deal of trivia, but we cannot penetrate the essential core of the house painter-turned-mass murderer.

So we dug deeper. Using available historical documents, retracing steps that could be reconstructed, analyzing every shred of evidence, sifting through rumor in search of a particle of truth, we came to the realization that for all that had preceded us, part of the puzzle was still missing. The part that makes it possible to recognize what the puzzle actually is. Part of the puzzle was buried—inadvertently or perhaps even purposely—because even the most comprehensive scrutiny of a life ever undertaken left the ultimate question unanswered. Until now.

One possibility had been raised again and again, but never proven conclusively or pursued to a conclusion. That possibility is that all the atrocities and mass murders that Hitler inspired can only be understood if the researcher starts with the assumption that behind Hitler stood certain manipulators who not only encouraged the brutalities, but actually "justified" them. The philosophy of Hitler, his world view, his concept of man and the people who shaped his life and thoughts all played a major role in the creation of history's most abhorrent character. So, too, must those who espoused those theories, advocated those philosophies, justified indefensible brutalities and acted with him in pursuit of common ends.

From there flows the fact—now documented and not open to dispute—that Hitler's philosophy and his concept of man in general was shaped to a decisive degree by psychiatry. Read on and learn how psychiatry, an influential cluster of psychiatrists and their frightening theories and methods collectively form the missing piece in the puzzle of Hitler, the Third Reich, the atrocities and their dreadful legacy. It is the overlooked yet utterly central piece of the puzzle. It also offers real insight into the sources of history's most sinister chapter and answers the questions that have lingered.

CHAPTER 2

"Definition of 'Ideology': A vaccine which immunizes against thinking."

> Ron Kritzfeld
> German merchant, born 1921

THE HISTORY OF THE POLITICS OF HATE

We begin with Nazi ideology and seek to trace it back to its sources. It is a subject of both interest and importance, but it is also an inquiry that follows essentially a virgin pathway, because it has been the subject of surprisingly little scrutiny in the earlier investigations that historians and social scientists have performed.

In this historical autopsy of a political philosophy of hate, innocence must be temporarily abandoned and susceptibility to shock must be put to one side. Those are the demands of maintaining perspective while researching the most consuming political vehicle for hate ever devised.

The names and theories of five historical figures emerge again and again in researching the historical antecedents of the Nazi movement in Germany—Malthus, Darwin, Nietzsche, Gobineau and Chamberlain. Those five names keep appearing in every corner of the investigation, like dust in every room of a grotesque house. An examination of their writings yields some surprising clues to the Hitler enigma and the Nazi shame. One by one their ideologies have contributed to the mosaic of hate that Hitler and his accomplices embraced as a social and political philosophy. They were truly catalysts in a chemistry of hate.

THOMAS ROBERT MALTHUS

Despite some rather glaring stretches of logic in his analyses, Thomas Robert Malthus (1766-1834) is regarded in many circles as an influential and far-sighted British economist, demographer and social philosopher who gained renown for his controversial "population theory."[1] In essence, Malthusian population theory postulates that nations grow too fast. Indeed, his view was that populations grow so rapidly that they outdistance the food supply making poverty natural and virtually inevitable.

While in the abstract, such a notion does not necessarily present itself as a cause for alarm, consider what Malthus identified as necessary implications of his theory. Accepting that theory as a given, conflict, epidemics and famines that occur and impede growth ultimately serve a useful function by thinning out the population which unchecked, grows too fast. As a result, according to Malthus, devastating human tragedies—war, pestilence and famine—actually serve as survival mechanisms of the human race by preventing overcrowding. Therefore, he continued, demonstrating astounding elasticity of logic, we should not tamper with this normal— and, to Malthus, natural and beneficial—course of events.

In 1798, Malthus presented his ideas to the public anonymously in the book *An Essay on the Principle of Population as it Affects the Future Improvement of Society*. The book became a much-discussed topic of the day, and, in fact, became the 18th century version of a bestseller. Later editions expanded on the theories of the unsigned first edition and identified Malthus as the author.

The great popularity of the book was neither a surprise nor a coincidence. Malthus' theory was very welcome in some circles, as it was viewed as offering supposedly plausible and philosophically sound political and social options to a British aristocracy that watched with alarm as the population of the lower classes burgeoned. That aristocracy perceived the population boom of the lower classes as a direct threat to their historical power and dominance through wealth and position, and Malthus gave them an outline of self-preservation at the expense of the underclasses.

Malthusian population theory is based on the assumption that food supply increases arithmetically while population grows exponentially. This growth imbalance produces an ever-widening gulf between food production and population. According to Malthus, it was theoretically conceivable that the quantity of food would ultimately be insufficient to feed everyone—to Malthus, "everyone" meant the English population—and that such catastrophe would likely happen sooner rather than later. His conclusion was that the English population could not be allowed to con-

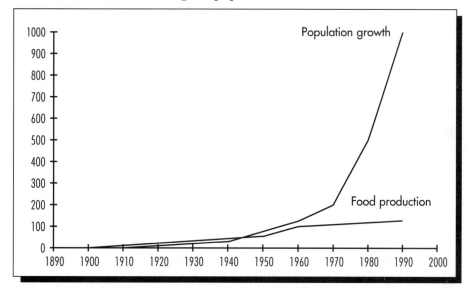

Malthus' alarming prediction about population growth and food production.

tinue to grow as it was doing. The poor and the lower members of the social scale were, according to Malthus, to be discouraged to have children. An end had to be put to their "sexual mania."

Malthus also concluded that the wages of the working population were not to be raised. Otherwise, he adduced, the worker would feel encouraged to produce too many offspring. Additionally, welfare for the poor would be totally abandoned in a Malthusian world, as it might produce laziness and an increase in the size of the families.

Thus, Malthus viewed unchecked disease, starvation and organized national murder—i.e., war—as agents of a socially beneficial purpose. Likewise, Malthus argued that lower wages were necessary for disciplined work, for obedience and for the elimination of the "reckless fertility of the poor." Malthus also believed that, if necessary, a nation should "subject itself to the periodically recurring shrinking of the population surplus

11

through famine, pestilence or war."[2]

From today's perspective, Malthus' theories cannot be supported scientifically, even though they linger nowadays, albeit with reservations, as considerations with respect to the population explosion in Third World countries. Nonetheless, Malthus' assumptions and attitudes are fundamentally unsound.[3] The Malthusian legacy is an atmosphere of excuses, where need is subordinated and comfort is exalted. It is a strange and artificial world where exploitation of the weak and the poor is characterized as "good" and logical.

Malthus was received in certain circles "like a divine revelation," writes American historian Will Durant. But Malthus was less visionary than he was the father of a new kind of witch hunt—the pursuit of the expendable inferiors. It was Malthus' influence that caused William Pitt, then the British Prime Minister, not only to withdraw the legislation which he had introduced to improve the welfare of the poor, but also to call for cuts in the wages of working people.

In 1834, Malthus achieved one of his biggest successes. The British Parliament passed legislation that provided for the establishment of poor houses in which men and women would be strictly separated—to check the "unstoppable population surplus." Malthus' idea of introducing moral barriers to limit the population growth had been legislatively implemented in tangible form.

With Malthus' theory we have the first cornerstone of the Nazi political philosophy. As we recognize today, Malthusian theory was based entirely on unscientific assumptions and the prejudices of the economically privileged among whom Malthus correctly placed himself. Bias, fear and irrationality were actually responsible for this population theory. It was those evils that Malthus wrapped in a couple of mathematical formulas and offered as "science" and "philosophy."

It is also of great significance that Malthus directly and substantially influenced the man who provided the second cornerstone of the philosophy of Nazi Germany.

CHARLES DARWIN

Charles Darwin (1809-1882) made the following observation in his autobiography:

"On October 1838...I happened to read for amusement Malthus on Population...it at once struck me that under these circumstances favourable variations would tend to be preserved & unfavourable ones to be destroyed...Here then I had at last got a theory by which to work..."[4]

Published in 1859, Darwin's seminal book, *The Origin of Species*, was probably the most influential book of the nineteenth century. In many respects it completely changed the way that people view and understand the world.

Darwin's research initially related to the animal world. His basic theory was that various animal species he had studied were generated through natural selection. According to Darwin, animals adapt themselves to the

Charles Darwin (1809–1882)

given environmental conditions at hand and, through natural selection, only those who were the strongest and the best equipped to survive would actually survive. It is in this way that Darwin explains how some mutations accidentally survive and from where new species come.

Darwin, like Malthus, assumed that "too large a number of offspring from organisms" would decimate themselves through "natural selection." The strongest would propagate, the weakest would perish, and thus a gradual restructuring of the species—which until Darwin had been considered to be immutable—would occur, leading automatically to a higher development. A better beast.

If Darwin had confined his theories to the animal kingdom—which, as a naturalist, was the province he best understood—it is likely that the controversy that has trailed his name to this day would have been substantially diminished. But Darwin went much further. He hypothesized his notion of natural selection through to mankind, with disastrous results.

Darwin entangled his theory of natural selection with the assumptions of Malthus' population theory. The result was a strange, incongruous marriage of Darwin's observations of the animal world with Malthus' emotional assumptions about the uncontrollable population growth and social solutions to preserve the British aristocracy.

In other words, Darwin's biological interpretations of physically observed events of the animal world were grafted onto Malthus' social speculations on human survival and society. In effect, Darwin applied biological hypotheses derived from observing creatures such as tortoises to human social conditions, and the supposedly beneficial effects of war, disease and starvation.[5] Darwin's own words reveal the perilous implications of expanding biological Darwinism to embrace Social Darwinism:

"With the savages, the weak in body or mind are soon eliminated; and those that survive commonly exhibit a vigorous state of health. We civilised men, on the other hand, do our utmost to check the process of elimination; we build asylums for the imbecile, the maimed and the sick; we institute poor-laws; and our medical men exert their utmost skill to save the life of every one to the last moment. There is reason to believe that vaccination has preserved thousands, who from a weak constitution would formerly have succumbed to small-pox. Thus the weak members of civilised societies propagate their kind. No one who has attended to the breeding of domestic animals will doubt that this must be highly injurious to the race of man. It is surprising how soon a want of care, or care wrongly directed, leads to the degeneration of a domestic race; but excepting in the case of man himself, hardly any one is so ignorant as to allow his worst animals to breed."[6]

Later Darwin wrote a letter to William Graham, a Professor of Jurisprudence in Belfast:

"Looking at the world at no very distant date, what an endless number of the lower races will have been eliminated by the higher civilised races throughout the world."[7]

Whatever he may or may not have intended, Darwin—with his words and his chilling observations—had plainly laid the purportedly philosophical and scientific foundation for the Holocaust, its disgraceful racial purity platitudes, for Hitler's euthanasia and the consequent murder of Germany's feeble-minded, the crippled and the sick.

If Darwin had confined his speculations to the studies of the history of the evolution of the animals he observed, and confined his hypotheses to the animal kingdom instead of extrapolating them into the social aspects of mankind, he might well have made a significant and relatively non-controversial contribution to scientific research. What controversy might still be generated could be addressed by reference to Darwin's actual research and the persuasive force of empirical observation. But by combining his own research with the antisocial population doctrine of Malthus, a new theory of how a society should be established was formed by a naturalist who seemed insensitive at best to the implications of his own encroachment into social and political philosophy of the most indefensible sort.[8]

At times, Darwin himself insisted that he did not want to address theories of human society, preferring instead to limit himself to his zoological studies. But the fact is that he wrote the statements quoted above, and within a very short time, hordes of scientists began to preach the "virtues" of Social Darwinism. Darwin's statements, which today are rightly condemned, were hardly decried at all in his day. In fact, they attracted enthusiastic followers who labeled these hair-raising hypotheses as a "science."

Darwin's theory has been offered as scientific support for all sorts of twisted sentiments and hateful intentions. Ideology seized what science had perverted, and phrases like "natural selection," "preservation of the favorite race," "struggle for existence," "survival of the fittest" and other such empty slogans became the justifications for sick hatred and social bias.

Laws of evolutionary development of the animal kingdom were swiftly transplanted into social processes without regard for their source or their rather obvious limitations. Man came to be regarded as just another animal, higher on the evolutionary scale than others, but an animal nonetheless. According to the theorists who embraced pure Social Darwinism, Beethoven (who was deaf), Bach (who was blind late in life) and Toulouse-Lautrec (whose stunted growth was due to a congenital calcium deficiency), were candidates for extermination.

Bluntly stated, Social Darwinism was perhaps the central theoretical foundation of German Nazi ideology. Very soon after Darwin, dangerous new ideas began to emerge, among them the concept of "social hygiene" (literally, "cleanliness of society") the brain child of German philosopher Wilhelm Schallmayer,[9] and, as we will see later, a recurrent theme in Nazi ideology and practice.

Social Darwinism certainly has not escaped condemnation as the supposed philosophical model for the killing programs of Nazi Germany.[10] But Social Darwinism alone does not completely explain the Third Reich's brutalities. After all, Social Darwinism, was embraced all over Europe.[11] Nevertheless, Darwin's influence on Hitler's and his accomplices' perverse world view is undeniable, particularly when two particular observations are noted:

1. The literal application of animal research and observations to people and human society has led to disastrous results because such direct application is inherently unsound and unwarranted; and

2. The word "science" was misused then and now to disguise faulty and unethical conclusions—often based on prejudices—and to impart undeserved "legitimacy" to them.

Beyond that, it is valuable to recall that it is sometimes foolish to equate "science" with "good." We do not have the luxury to give uncritical credence to something just because it has been uttered under the banner of science. Countless errors and atrocities have been committed in the name of science, and unthinking acceptance of a notion only because it's expressed in scientific terms is dangerous. Think of certain drugs whose side effects are worse than the disease they were meant to treat. Think of non-antiseptic surgery, which prevailed until late last century.

In Darwin, who contributed so greatly to the formation of the Nazi philosophy, we should see a warning sign. We must learn to temper our respect for science with the harsh and unforgiving glare of hot lights and cool assessment. We have seen throughout history, as we see with Darwinian theory and Nazism, that science can be a cover under which immorality, misanthropy and murder can prosper.

FRIEDRICH WILHELM NIETZSCHE

Another prominent name in the development of Nazi ideology is that of Friedrich Wilhelm Nietzsche (1844-1900). It is undisputed that Nietzsche is one of the most influential modern philosophers, but it ought to be equally clear that his theories often warrant condemnation and his praise is often undeserved. Detached from handsome rhetoric and examined with the attitude of a critic rather than a disciple, it is clear that

Nietzsche forwarded some of the most absurd, antisocial ideas that anyone ever has espoused. Nevertheless, Nietzsche is another cornerstone in the foundation of the Nazi philosophy.

It is plainly beyond the scope of this book to undertake a complete analysis of Nietzsche's philosophy. To some, that in itself is virtually a life-time's undertaking. Nevertheless, we must reach behind his elegant craftsmanship and momentous rhetoric to unveil some of the corrosive beliefs that fired Nazi furnaces and propelled the world into war and slaughter.

The statements at the core of his philosophy, as enumerated by one of the most important researchers of Nietzsche's works, Karl Schlechta, can be reduced to some basic ideas:

1. Ideas of values and virtues (like kindness and charity) are pure non-sense.[12]

2. The world is in actual fact without purpose; it is nonsense[13] and cannot be comprehended.

3. A woman is an inferior being.

4. The only type of person to be admired is the "superhuman," who is marked by power, love for war, eagerness to fight and the will for power.[14] The superhuman loves force and is physically and mentally strong. Nietzsche favored an aristocracy of the refined, who accept the offerings of the weak and the slaves.

5. War is good, positive, and to be embraced.[15]

6. Certain races are superior to other races.

Nietzsche wrote:

"Christianity, rooted in Jewish tradition and nothing more than a plant from its soil, is a counter-movement against any morals of the breeding, the race, the privileges—it is the anti-Aryan religion par excellence: Christianity, the transformation of all Aryan values...the evangelism of the poor, the inferior, the complete rise of all the down-trampled, the wretched and the poor against the 'Race'...."[16]

That is the quintessential Nietzsche, who is still revered in some quarters. We can read through all of his works and never find any qualifying or moderating statements. Nietzsche was blunt and unequivocal when discussing the "governing race,"[17] the "cleansing of the race,"[18] and the "cross-bred races."[19] In addition, he spoke of the "industrious race"[20] and distinguished between "strong races"[21] and "deteriorated races."[22]

Nietzsche not only made a contribution to the Nazi politics of hate—he is virtually synonymous with it.

JOSEPH-ARTHUR, COMTE DE GOBINEAU

Before we examine the role of psychiatry—the heretofore missing piece of the puzzle of Hitler and his tyranny—we need to focus on the remaining two philosophical cornerstones of German Nazism.

Gobineau (1816-1892), a French diplomat and writer, was a pioneer in poisoning minds with prejudice and coating his venom with veneer—thin and cheap as it is—of science. In his four-volume work, entitled *Essay on the Inequality of Human Races*,[23] Gobineau virulently contested the notion of equality of the various human races. In a feverish outburst meant to demonstrate the superiority of the "Aryan" race, he provided both the inspiration and ammunition for the race fanaticism of Nazis. He glorified the idea of an "exceptional human" or "superhuman," leading some historians to label him the first important race ideologist.[24]

In his warped and universally discredited concept of racial purity and a natural racial hierarchy, Gobineau saw a guarantee of superiority and domination. By contrast, in racial mixtures, he saw inferiority. Blood mixtures would improve the lower races, but dilute the higher ones, he thought, making them less creative, more corrupt and more immoral. In a romanticized gushing of impassioned words, he envisioned a race, superior to all other races. Gobineau was convinced that survivors of that race could still be found in several countries of Europe trying to keep their Aryan aristocracy intact under the oppressive intrusions of the inferior races.

However, Gobineau never claimed to prefer German Aryans over anyone else, nor did he specifically denigrate any other races by name. In truth, he was perhaps more concerned about the differentiation between the social classes. Gobineau wrote at length about the relationship between the aristocracy and the proletariat. The conflict between them he described later spread to the middle class, who saw in Gobineau's ideology an opportunity to draw a line between themselves and the working class, which they despised and considered riff-raff. Out of the philosophy that pitted the aristocracy against proletariat emerged the idea of "civilized man" versus "carnal man."[25]

In many ways, Gobineau was a perfect precursor to Hitler, who openly embraced "Gobinism," as Nietzsche did earlier. Gobineau was an opponent of democracy, an opponent of welfare, and an opponent of the lower classes—a social Darwinist of the first order, with absolute confidence, like Nietzsche, in the superiority of a nebulous Aryan race and a Malthusian distaste for the lower classes.[26]

HOUSTON STEWART CHAMBERLAIN

British-born philosopher H.S. Chamberlain (1855-1927), who later married the daughter of composer Richard Wagner (who was himself a confidant of Nietzsche and a virulent anti-Semite), became a German citizen in 1916. He defended Gobineau's supremacist philosophy—his own philosophical inspiration—in his principal work, *The Foundations of the Nineteenth Century*, a two-volume tract that appeared in 1911. Published in German, Chamberlain's treatise also asserted the superiority of the Aryan race and heavily promoted the "Aryan world philosophy." He also portrayed Jewish influences as negative and inferior. Chamberlain's remarkably faulty understanding of European history is reflected in his interpretation of it as a history of racial battles in which only one race deserves to survive. To Chamberlain, the most damaging occurrences were foreign infiltration and miscegenation of the Aryan race:

"Moderate talent…is frequently a character of bastards; one can easily observe this daily in cities where, as in Vienna, the various peoples meet each other: at the same time one can also notice a particular laxity, a lack of character, in short, the moral degeneration of such people."[27]

Those five—Malthus, Darwin, Nietzsche, Gobineau and Chamberlain—deserve a significant share of the blame for what ultimately came from the darkest prejudices and barbarism of the Third Reich. But as will now be seen, another culprit was afoot—psychiatry—better concealed than racial supremacists, Aryan philosophers and pseudoscientific hate mongers. Psychiatry's role in the Third Reich's atrocities begins with its own tortured history.

In the following chapters, which focus on the pivotal part psychiatry played in Hitler's bloodbath, the philosophies discussed in this chapter will cast their shadows again and again. The difference between philosophy and psychiatry in this examination is that while the words and thoughts of five twisted minds influenced those who committed the horrors of the Third Reich, these philosophers never flicked a switch, gave an injection or tapped a gas valve in pursuit of their prejudices.

"With the exception of the clergyman, there exists no profession in which silence plays as big a part as with us, and by this I mean silence with respect to everything."
Hans Bürger-Prinz
German psychiatrist,
1897-1976

A SHORT FOCUSED HISTORY OF PSYCHIATRY IN GERMANY

There is so much that is not generally known about the history of psychiatry that grudging admiration is due to someone for managing to keep so many sordid secrets from public exposure.

The focus of this book is German psychiatry, its role in the Third Reich and therefore, this compressed history of psychiatry primarily addresses the practice in Germany and its development through and after World War I and makes no effort to plumb antiquity.

Psychiatry actually began as the purported care for the insane in German penitentiaries late in the eighteenth century. Those who cared for the insane at that time performed gruesome "cures" which, in reality, were little more than torture. Such cures consisted of giving electric shocks, removal of the clitoris, severing penile nerves, chloroform "therapy," tearing out of the patient's hair and applying caustic substances to burn the patient's skin.[1] These doctors—the original psychiatrists—had no experience whatsoever in the causes or cures of insanity. With their techniques and remedies, they could never realistically be regarded as healers.[2]

Despite this inauspicious beginning, psychiatry established itself as a science.[3]

The term "psychiatry" itself was not coined until 1808 by Johann Christian Reil. Prior to that, the term "psychic medicine" was used to describe the practice. "Psychiatry" literally means "doctor of the soul," from the Greek "psyche" (soul) and "iatros" (doctor). It is therefore both ironic and revealing that such "doctors of the soul" were actually preoccupied not with spiritual matters, but with the human brain.

In 1758, even before the term came into use, the first textbook on psychiatry appeared. It was *Treatise on Madness*, by W. Battie. In 1811, a professorship in "psychiatric therapy" was established at Leipzig, followed by a similar chair in psychiatry at Berlin. It was not long thereafter that a fierce dispute arose about the real causes of mental illness and the sadistic methods that had been part and parcel of psychiatric "therapy" from its inception. In reality, that dispute was among the earliest protests against psychiatry. Debate continued and in 1882, prominent individuals, parliamentarians, journalists and scientists published a sensational appeal against psychiatrists and their controversial techniques.

In the face of all the controversy and protests, the early psychiatrists' defiant arrogance was remarkable. In a famous speech on January 16, 1897, legislator Julius Lenzmann attacked the psychiatric community before the German Reichstag:

"Worst of all is…every physician for the insane believes himself…to be more infallible than the Pope in Rome.…Most if not all of the doctors for the insane are extremely nervous individuals. I have knowledge of trials where all of the participants were of the opinion that the only insane one was the doctor."[4]

Even then, late in the nineteenth century, Lenzmann and others had enough courage to denounce psychiatry publicly and, to recognize and decry the utter failure of the ideology that purported to operate as a medical science. But psychiatry would not disappear.

One of the most basic problems that we find in psychiatry is its lack of understanding of just what constitutes an illness. Obviously it is impossible to hope to cure something that cannot first be adequately defined. Psychiatrists never fully identified what it was that was to be cured, and the approaches were many and varied, and almost continually conflicted with each other.

For example, in 1850, psychiatrist C. T. Groddeck was awarded a doctorate for his dissertation entitled "The Democratic Disease—A New Form of Insanity." In Groddeck's view, every democratically inclined person was insane. In 1854, his colleague, C. J. Wretholm, "discovered" the "Sermon Disease." Psychiatrist P. J. Möbius lectured shortly thereafter on the "psychological feeble-mindedness of the woman."

Not long thereafter, the leading proponents of psychiatry in Germany were advocating the theory that anyone who refused military service for religious reasons was abnormal and "sick." A psychiatrist named Adolf Hoppe characterized conscientious objection to military service as an "unmistakable expression of ethical inferiority." One of psychiatry's leading figures, Richard von Krafft-Ebing, added to his list of varieties of mental disorders "political and reformatory insanity"—meaning any inclination to form a different opinion from that of the masses. An excellent tool was thus created for politicians to denounce opponents. With the help of psychiatric classifications, it was now possible to perform the character assassination of a political enemy in the wink of an eye—anyone who disagreed was obviously insane.

According to Krafft-Ebing in 1892:

"In history as well as now, one encounters individuals who, unsatisfied with the social institutions, get the idea to improve the world or, at least, put something new in place of the old....They appear in the roles of leaders of revolutions, founders of political parties...and they make themselves and others unhappy. The incubation phase of the disease is long, often reaching back to childhood."[5]

It is chilling to recognize that those sentiments, so profoundly ridiculous and dangerous on their face, are the products of a legendary psychiatrist, lionized by his profession to this day, whose theories, especially in the area of sexual-psychopathology, are still considered state-of-the-art by psychiatrists today. But such nonsense is often taken seriously in psychiatric circles.

Another doctor of the insane, one named Carl Stark, published a treatise in 1871 entitled "The Psychical Degeneration of the French People." In this remarkable document, the psychiatric scholar argues that the mental condition of the French people had deteriorated to the point where the entire nation was stricken with megalomania and was living in a delirious condition. In other words, being French was a mental illness.

Now consider this. At the beginning of World War I, a Munich psy-

chiatrist named Löwenfeld published a paper about "the national character of the French and its sickly excesses," in which he wrote:

"The kind of mental abnormalities that are emerging nowadays belong to
a borderline area which I label as psychopathy, psychopathic inferiorities,
psychopathic conditions and so on. I believe therefore that it is justified now
to talk about a 'psychopathia gallica' which should by now be obvious."[6]

Thus "psychopathia gallica"—literally "French psychosis"—wasn't out-
rightly ridiculed in 1871. Adherents persisted as supposedly respectable
medical practitioners for nearly half a century. There is more to the story
of psychopathic gallica than merely psychiatry's tolerance of silliness.
Psychopathia gallica is prejudice—prejudgement and hatred because of
race or ethnicity. Labeling membership in a race or an ethnic group as a
mental illness will resonate throughout this story, and there is nothing
funny about psychiatry's willingness to indulge in such hate in the guise of
science.

A similar foreboding notion in psychiatry's past is found in its affinity
to glorify the related concepts of war and nationalism while at the same
time condemning as mental illness the twin antitheses of pacifism and tolerance. The rising tide of nationalism as somehow a determinant of mental health or illness is also cited in the 1916 comments of a medical consultant in Emmerdingen:

"The war, until now an affair of honor and a means to an end, now
becomes an end in itself! From now on, all those unredeemed German
souls, down to the last pacifist, will recognize their sins—that their ideals
are relics. The whole nation should demand as one the eternal war."[7]

Similarly glorifying war was Dr. Johannes Bresler, editor-in-chief of the
Pychiatrisch-Neurologische Wochenzeitschrift (*Psychiatric Neurological Weekly*)
in 1926:

"The world war was sacred to us and will remain sacred to us for all
eternity. It was and is our just cause."[8]

The psychiatric literature of the era is nothing short of amazing. It is plain
that in the opinion of the leading psychiatrists of the age, everybody who
loved peace or sought it as an end was mentally abnormal. World War I psychiatry had created a new term, the "war neurotic," when AWOLs became
more and more frequent and whole units experienced fits of crying, began to
vomit or otherwise exhibited "war-hysterical" symptoms. According to psy-

chiatric theory, entire battalions had been afflicted by war neurosis "epidemics," thus posing major problems for the military leadership.

Soldiers whose extremities or whole bodies were trembling and who thus were of no further use to the armed forces, were common sights in Germany during World War I. Increasingly, these patients arrived in psychiatrists' offices where they became evidence for the bizarre theories of disease. But in an even more sinister and dangerous vein, they were exposed to the gruesome therapies—such as electroshock therapy—that the psychiatrists developed to make the war-hysterical soldier war-usable again. Hamburg-based psychiatrist, Max Nonne described this "hysteria of the man" during World War I as follows:

"The war brought us in Eppendorf a tremendous workload. We soon got to see sad pictures of men who were amputated, half-paralyzed through head wounds, paralyzed down to the legs, the bladder and the rectum because of bullets in the spine, of epileptics who had seizures because of head wounds. But after a few months we saw a sight that we had rarely seen before—the sight of hysteria virilis, the 'manly hysteria,' which had once been described to us by Charcot in Paris. We had said then: 'This happens only to the French. In Germany, hysteria of the men does not exist.' But now we saw it often and in all forms: as paralysis of the vocal cords, as dumbness, as paralysis of the upper and lower extremities, as trembling in all parts of the body, as spasms of single muscles and muscle groups, as deafness, as inabilities to see and walk, and as dislocations in the most confounded forms."[9]

Sometimes in place of war neurosis German psychiatrists used terms like "traumatic neurosis,"[10] "fright neurosis," "grenade shock" or "war hysteria." In other countries, this hysteria was described as "shell shock," "concussion neurosis," "exhaustion neurosis," "gas neurosis" or "battle fatigue." However, in 1915, the German army medical services forbade the use of the term "hysteria" in military psychiatric diagnosis because it was contrary to the noble concept of honor befitting a warrior. In the eyes of the army, the diagnosis of an hysterical reaction was dishonorable and, therefore, banned. No doubt the German army was offended in part by the suggestion that its soldiers might be less than "manly." After all, "hysteria" comes from the Greek "hyster," meaning "uterus," and connotes a woman's suffering, not the illness of a soldier. At the same time, however, the military

25

reaction serves to highlight the lack of any sensible thought behind the psychiatric theories, therapies and labels of the era. Diagnosis was subject to non-medical factors.

But it is equally true that by denying that the symptoms, however labeled, were a valid complaint, the military could keep soldiers on the front lines longer regardless of their condition. From 1917 onward, in order to prevent the "tremblers" or the "hysterically reacting" from being sent home from the front, it was forbidden to make a diagnosis of "nerve shock."[11]

So what at first blush appears to be a fundamental conflict between psychiatry and the military actually turned out to be among the earliest alliances between them, and a deadly trend was inaugurated. Psychiatry proved to be the ideal partner for the German military. With the help of "therapies" like electrification, soldiers unfit for active duty were promptly made "fit" to return to the front again, combat-ready.

Out of the many outrageous experimental procedures tested to accomplish that end, the most effective was deemed to be the "Kaufmann Therapy," which was fast, cheap and practical, despite the fact that several deaths had occurred during its development.

Kaufmann Therapy was based on the premise that war neurosis was a chemo-biological dysfunction, and that anyone experiencing it simply had a "constitutional, psychopathic inferiority."[12] In other words, for systemic reasons, the patient was too weak to endure the beauty of the war.

The developer of this therapy, Fritz Kaufmann, a neurological medical officer in a military reserve hospital, summarized his restorative procedure as follows:

"From life's experience we know that the transportation of a stimulus by the nerves, once thrown off the right track through a mental shock, will very frequently be thrown back onto the right track by another shock. We are now in the position to produce in a sick person…such a shock through treatment with a strong electrical current, artificially produced…in conjunction with the help of appropriate verbal suggestions in the form of commands. Our process is made up of four components:

"1. Preparing the patient with pre-shock suggestions.

2. The application of a strong alternating current combined with plentiful verbal suggestions.

3. Suggestions in the form of military-style commands.

4. The strict enforcement that they must be healed in one session."[13]

In other words, Kaufmann's therapy was to treat a shock with an even stronger shock and to order the patient to get well. Even in the psychiatric community this was considered a radical approach. At a conference of neurologists in Baden-Baden, it was pointed out that Kaufmann had no medical research whatsoever to back up his claims, and that his therapy had never been scientifically tested. In fact, critics pointed out, the damage that electric shock could do was already documented. Even to the psychiatrists of the day, it must have been plain that Kaufmann Therapy was nothing more than old-style torture in modern dress.

Nevertheless, at the military's urging, psychiatrists regarded war neurotics as nothing more than fakers and psychopathic personalities who literally had to be made to jump out of their neurosis and get back to the front. Working together, psychiatry and the military were dedicated to maintaining troop strength and in covering up the damage that the war had inflicted on Germany's soldiers. There was also no reason to respect or ever sympathize with a patient who had proven himself to be clearly "inferior." From the beginning, electroshock was a method of discipline and a means to cover-up embarrassing breaches in the nobility and honor demanded of German military service. It was used on soldiers for the simple reason that they believed that everyone who suffered psychological problems caused by the war had to be inferior.

As a result, psychiatry created a "therapy" doused in medical terminology and claiming a pseudo-scientific result. In reality, Kaufmann Therapy was nothing more than the forced imposition of extreme military discipline on soldiers unable to cope with the rigors and demands of military discipline.

Today's so-called "electroconvulsive therapy"—"ECT" or "electroshock" for short—is based on precisely the same principle. It is a direct descendant of World War I era German military and psychiatric techniques such as Kaufmann Therapy which were nothing more than examples of medicine surrendering to the military.

Even though these horrific methods were criticized at the time by the scientific community as "sinking back into the barbarism of the Middle Ages,"[14] they were widely used. However, in the trial of Professor Julius

Wagner von Jauregg, a University of Vienna professor[15] and one of the most active World War I era proponents and practitioners of electricity as "medical" treatment, no less a figure than Sigmund Freud, the founder of psychoanalysis, gave his expert opinion about the use of electricity on war neurotics. In his testimony, Freud was very clear about the consequences:

"The strength of the initial current as well as the additional treatments have been consistently increased to intolerability in order to make money from the war neurotics. No one denied that deaths have occurred during treatment in German hospitals as well as suicides thereafter."[16]

Wagner was acquitted.

It took considerable courage to denounce the psychiatric movement of the era because critics were liable to be labeled with an unfavorable diagnosis by the very subjects of their criticism. That was no idle fear. In 1927, a professor of psychiatry from Hamburg named Ernst Ritterhaus actually came up with the diagnosis of "mass psychosis of hostility toward psychiatry" for all critics of the psychiatric movement. In other words, "if you disagree with us or challenge our methods, you are insane."

The same diagnosis was also applied to a large number of journalists, doctors, officers, legislators, manufacturers and law professors as well as the victims of psychiatry who had dared to challenge the utility and ethics of inhuman therapies. By then, it was almost impossible to argue logically against psychiatry—psychiatry was too irrational to allow for it.

As early as 1899, P. J. Möbius had shown just how arrogant psychiatry already had grown when he wrote:

"The psychiatrist should be the judge about mental health, because only he knows what ill means. If one views psychiatry in this way, then it turns from a servant into a ruler, and becomes what by nature it should be. The psychiatrist then becomes a judge of all human things, a teacher of the lawyer and the theologian, a leader of the historian and the writer."

Later, in 1918, Emil Kraepelin, probably the most influential psychiatrist of his time, announced that the psychiatrist was:

"An absolute ruler who, guided by our knowledge of today, would be able to intervene ruthlessly in the living conditions of people and would certainly within a few decades achieve a corresponding decrease of insanity."[17]

An interesting statement, considering that there were already countless victims of psychiatry. In a 1911 case, a psychiatrist named August Forel wrote a letter about a lawyer who represented victims of psychiatric abuse who was seeking compensation for damages caused by unjustified institutionalization:

"Psychiatric science demands empirically that such people are rendered powerless."

The formula was as simple as it was chilling in its implications. Beneath a shroud of a few impressive-sounding Greek- and Latin-based words and cloaked with the presumed authority of a medical science, to shut up your critic, simply pronounce him or her insane and do so from the point of view of the omniscient expert.

The most important conclusions to be drawn from the infancy of German psychiatry are obvious. Of signal importance is the recognition that from its earliest days, psychiatry deemed "sick" those who were in disagreement either with psychiatrists or with the existing authorities. Since its

Emil Kraepelin (1856–1926)—Founder and director of the German Research Institute for Psychiatry.

inception, psychiatry had worked for and with the state, and was, in essence, charged with the responsibility of keeping order and setting the norms of society demanded by those in power. It rewarded compliance and punished disobedience as a matter of politics, not medicine.

More fundamental conclusions are easily derived from an examination of German psychiatry's history. Cost-cutting—beneficial to the state but often harmful to the patient—was also one of the earliest signatures of the psychiatric community. In addition to protecting the state against anyone who might disagree with it, psychiatrists were also expected to render patients harmless as cheaply and economically as possible. To this day, psychiatry has never fully rid itself of this historical obsession.

Even in the psychiatry practiced in asylums for the criminally insane, in everything from therapeutic assessment to the actual procedures, consideration of cost played and still plays a deciding role. Later on during the Third Reich, psychiatry would accomplish its ends through sterilization and mass murder under government auspices, and even then, psychiatrists identified cost as the main justification for their lethal "therapies."

At the same time, psychiatry branched out in new directions—especially in the direction of medicine. In an 1891 commencement address at the University of Jena, Professor of Psychiatry Otto Binswanger stated that a primary duty for psychiatrists was to weed out the fakers from the truly sick. The evaluation of illness thus became another of psychiatry's self-proclaimed specialties. From the military to the society at-large, a campaign was launched to expose all the fakers in order to save the state the expense of paying for unnecessary treatment. As a result, the alliance formed between the state and psychiatry continued and flourished.

Binswanger also fought long and hard for the establishment of psychiatry as a recognized medical discipline. Finally in 1901, it was accredited as an official medical subject for which one could be called a doctor.

But before that accreditation could occur however, a major obstacle had to be overcome. As late as the 1870s, psychiatry and neurology were two separate and distinct disciplines. In 1865, however, psychiatrist Wilhelm Griesinger left his job as head of a medical clinic in Zürich to accept a similar position at a psychiatric clinic in Berlin where he could pursue a combination of psychiatry and neurology. The result was a new and profound idea. Since most of the nerves converge in the brain, then all mental illnesses must be diseases of the brain.[18]

This "discovery" was celebrated by the noted medical consultant, Professor C. Wernicke, who wrote in 1889:

"For the first time and supported with full conviction…the clinician who had already proven himself in another field had recognized the principle that mental illnesses are illnesses of a very particular organ, the cerebrum, thereby blazing a trail for certain success in the future. We should think of the cerebrum as a destination and rendezvous point of all nerves. It was therefore essential to address the anatomy and physiology of the nervous system before anything else, as a fundamental of future psychiatry."[19]

With this step, a new type of doctor was born who had little in common with the old doctor of the insane. Research and study suddenly turned in a totally new direction. The asylums of the era provided a constant stream of human guinea pigs for educational and research purposes. The object of research was the human brain, specifically people with brain damage and its resulting conditions. The study of genetically caused illness became the other important area of research that the new neuropsychiatrists explored.

Neuropsychiatry was vigorously promoted, and it boomed. Neuropsychiatric clinics sprang up in universities, producing more and more neuropsychiatrists. These clinics quickly spread through the general hospitals of Vienna and Innsbruck in Austria, and Berlin, Frankfurt, Cologne and Hamburg in Germany, as well as Switzerland and elsewhere. Universities opened department after department, specifically designed to train neuropsychiatrists and offer them facilities in which to conduct their research.

From the beginning, neuropsychiatry was the natural and open enemy of all the other psychologies, such as psychoanalysis, clinical psychology and psychosomatology. Those practices were decried by the neuropsychiatrists and ridiculed as quackery. Psychoanalysts were never accepted by neuropsychiatrists.[20] By this time psychoanalysis, however, had become its own discipline despite everything possible that neuropsychiatry did to prevent its taking root. The establishment of psychiatry within medical circles was, in short, a struggle for recognition. In the end, it won out and gained the recognition of the other medical fields.

It is not unlikely that the medical community was happy that the neuropsychiatrist would take over part of what they themselves were unable to cure. The end result, however, was disastrous both for medical and social development. A patient who visited a neuropsychiatrist to cure a nervous system disorder such as an inflammation of a nerve could be categorized as having any one of any number of disorders, and have any number of tortuous psychiatric "treatments" imposed.

Moreover, through its traditional and ongoing servitude with the government, psychiatry became exceptionally successful in establishing itself as an indispensable, yet utterly obedient minion of the state. Contrary opinions were branded as "sick," and ways were found for dissidents to be neutralized and money saved for the state. Even though bizarre "illnesses" continued to be defined and diagnosed, and even though not one workable therapy was developed as a cure, psychiatry still managed to establish itself as the absolute authority on what was "normal" in human behavior.

CHAPTER 4

"The past is not dead, it's not even over with yet."
Epitaph of Nazi victims

THE SECRET PACT WITH THE DEVIL

THE ALLIANCE BETWEEN RACIAL THEORISTS AND PSYCHIATRY

Thus far we have outlined the philosophic underpinnings of Nazism and the development and growth of psychiatry in Germany. In the period following World War I, parallels of racist theory and psychiatry would merge and eventually develop into a deadly hybrid. That hybrid was the confluence of Nazism's racist ideology and psychiatry's compatible theories and therapies, both of which were born in Hell. It was the Nazis' racist ideology that led to the extermination of "life unworthy of living," as the Nazis called their victims. It was that racist ideology that promoted the persecution of the Jews, gypsies and others. It was also that racist ideology that made World War II "necessary" as the Aryan peoples became more and more deluded that they needed more room in which to expand.

Some highly volatile questions result from such a stark statement of reality. What really were the features of this racist ideology that resulted in such widespread persecution and extermination of so-called racial inferiors? Was it limited to Hitler and his political and military cronies or was it deeper and wider? More particularly, where precisely did the Nazi racist and the psychiatrist find common ground?

The answers to these questions lie within Gobineau's hateful propaganda of racial superiority and psychiatry's ugly theory of "racial hygiene" and eugenics.

As noted in Chapter 2, Gobineau neither claimed to prefer the German Aryans nor did he denigrate other races by name. His racist ideology was not so much concerned with racial lines as it was with class lines. However, Gobineau unabashedly espoused the loathsome theory, long since discredited in every meaningful quarter, that the destiny of a civilization depends on racial composition, and that Aryan societies are the most advanced. While he was superficially more interested in the relationship between the aristocracy and the proletariat, his concepts were expansive and flexible, and they embraced the theory that society pits superior "civilized man" against inferior "carnal man."

Arthur Comte de Gobineau (1816-1882)

It is precisely at this point that psychiatry enters the picture and the Nazi/psychiatric courtship begins.

As noted in Chapter 3, German psychiatry developed and advocated a variety of methods of managing and treating war neurosis or any of the other labels affixed to that condition. One psychiatrist involved in that work was Gustav Liebermeister, who, with Gobineau's odious axioms as an obvious theoretical basis, formulated a therapy, establishing a therapeutical differentiation based on class hatred. Indeed, in his essay on so-called war neurosis, Liebermeister insisted on the importance of distinguishing between "civilized man" and "carnal man." According to Liebermeister's interpretation of Gobineau's classification, "carnal man" (the foot soldiers) was to be treated as close to combat as possible, while the "civilized man" (the officers) was to heal completely at home and not to return too early to the front.[1]

Psychiatry thus embraced Gobineau, and by immediate and necessary implication, Nietzsche and Chamberlain as well. But Liebermeister and certain of his contemporaries already had embraced Malthus and Darwin through their racial hygiene theories. Indeed, psychiatry performed the unholy marriage by uniting hateful racist theory with the racial hygiene horror of isolating and eliminating undesirable human traits. Racial hygiene literally means "cleanliness of the race." Eugenics is composed of the Greek words "eu-," meaning "well" or "good," and "-gennan," or "to reproduce." Literally translated, it means "well reproduced" or, in more scientific terms, "the study of hereditary health." In time, these two terms came to be used interchangeably. The theory of eugenics states that certain genetic traits are good, others bad. Of course, the theory of the racist ideologue was that the Aryan race is good, others bad.

This alliance of racism and eugenics would reshape history. Indeed, eugenics and racial hygiene formed the theoretical basis for the cult of the Aryan master race.

In 1895 in his book *The Fitness of Our Race and the Protection of the Weak*, Dr. Alfred Ploetz, called by some the founder of the psychiatric breeding technique, articulated the "scientific" basis for what would be the Nazi racial hygiene program. In order to avoid the painful "rooting out" of inferiors by the natural Malthusian elements of war, pestilence and famine, Ploetz concluded that, for humanitarian reasons, the quality of human progeny should be improved:

"If we could research the conditions under which parents create children who have better tendencies than themselves and study the laws of variability, we could bring their manifestations under our control. We already know a sizable amount about animals. Progress would thus be assured, the fight for survival, and the conscious and unconscious competition of the individual for food for the children would be unnecessary for the maintenance and perfection of the power and beauty of our race."[2]

Ploetz's notion of controlling and directing genetic characteristics toward what he and his colleagues defined as "perfection" and "beauty" inspired a generation of psychiatrists to create certain genetic criteria to assess the biological "value" of human beings and thus what measures needed to be taken to perfect the race quickly and efficiently.

It was in precisely that fashion that what ultimately took the form of the systematic murder of designated segments of society began to take theoretical shape in the twisted notions of turn of the twentieth-century medical literature. In the sick world of racist theory and eugenics, a perfect synthesis of two worlds had been created. Articles in the distinguished *Ärztlichen Vereinsblatt* (*Medical Association Paper*) document this development thoroughly:

"The future belongs to that nation that has the highest birth rate and possesses the least sympathy not only toward other countries, but toward its own people....Anyone who doesn't care for anything, who lives so unrestrained and is so maladjusted that he is a burden to the public at large has to bear the same consequences as if he were under natural circumstances. The fight for survival is, after all, a natural law."[3]

In this ugly climate of intellectual justification for selective manipulation of humans in society, psychiatry had found its new calling. A new definition for "normality" was created, and it was pristinely simple—the healthy Aryan was normal; others were not.

This classic example of defining prejudice as philosophy and cloaking hatred in the presumed prestige of science was the precursor of a generation of murder and suffering unprecedented in human annals. Yet it was spawned in short-sighted, hate-laden clinical intellectualism, stained by the self-exalting notions of pseudo-thinkers like Gobineau, and spread through the arrogance of psychiatry and its vaunted self image as the ultimate authority on all it chose to address.

The first important step taken to get rid of "life unworthy of living" was compulsory sterilization. The entire German medical community, the local authorities, teachers and welfare institutions were instructed to take part in the implementation of this cultural mission. Walther Auer of the University of Cologne psychiatric clinic, whose director was the prominent psychiatrist Gustav Aschaffenburg, noted one problem that would have to be solved before the plan for compulsory sterilization could be implemented. The problem that Auer noted was the fact that there were laws against it.[4]

Throughout his life, Auer's mentor, Gustav Aschaffenburg[5], advocated the sterilization of what he called the "vermin of the nation." Aschaffenburg's "vermin" included the physically sick, the "incomplete" (such as tuberculosis sufferers, the handicapped and the elderly) and persons who either burdened or damaged society, such as the homeless, the chronically ill and alcoholics. A student of Emil Kraepelin—who was a leading advocate of unfettered psychiatric intervention to decrease what he defined as insanity—Aschaffenburg vigorously espoused extermination of society's inferiors until fate and his intellectual bedfellows caught up with him and his theoretical atrocities. Aschaffenburg, alas, was Jewish, and while Aschaffenburg did not define Jews as being among the racial inferiors, his colleagues in the psychiatric and political communities unequivocally did. Aschaffenburg became the target of anti-Semitic attacks as early as 1932. To avoid being fired, he retired on March 31, 1934. Shortly thereafter he was officially forbidden to give lectures. His successor, in October 1934, was Austrian psychiatrist Max de Crinis, who would play a central role in the Nazis' euthanasia program, which we address later.

The fourth member of this seminal group of eugenics proponents—joining Liebermeister, Ploetz and Aschaffenburg—was Fritz Lenz. A "human geneticist," Lenz was extremely active between 1919 and 1933 for the *Archiv für Rassen und Gesellschaftbiologie (Archive for Racial and Social Biology)*, the name of which, standing alone, is chilling. With Erwin Bauer and Eugen Fischer, he wrote *Menschliche Erblehre und Rassenhygiene (Human Genetics and Racial Hygiene)*, which was published in 1921. Lenz's ghastly words convey the attitude that ultimately paved the way for Hitler:

"I have heard that Hitler had read the second edition of Bauer-Fischer-Lenz during his incarceration in Landsberg. Some parts of it are mirrored in Hitler's phrases. In any case, with great mental energy, he had made the basic ideas of racial hygiene and their importance his own, while most of the academic authorities still look upon these issues rather unappreciatively."[6]

On July 4, 1933, the Sterilization Act was enacted and became the law of Germany.

Clubs and associations dedicated to influencing national politics and debate on this issue sprang up all over Germany. One such association, Gesellschaft für Rassenhygiene (Society for Racial Hygiene), was the driving force behind a racial hygiene and eugenics program:

"As particular reactions toward World War I, propagandistic elements became more and more prominent; racial hygienical lifestyles became totally unimportant. In 1931, statutes were changed to substitute the concept of 'races' for catch phrases like 'family' or 'nation.' In addition to the steady demands for a 're-evaluation' of the nation, demands for [compulsory] sterilization of so-called 'inferiors' joined the program."[7]

It took the racial hygienists less than thirty years to import their ideas into science, politics and even the law. It was psychiatry that first married eugenics to the racist ideology of the Third Reich.

"Since sterilization is the only sure thing to prevent the further transmission of mental illness and serious hereditary afflictions, it must therefore be viewed as an act of charity and precaution for the upcoming generation."

Professor Ernst Rüdin
German psychiatrist, 1936

"We should make a law which helps nature have its way. Nature would let a creature which is not equipped starve to death. It would be more humane for us to give it a painless mercy killing. This is the only option which is proper in such cases and it is a hundred times more noble, decent and humane than the cowardice which hides behind the idiocy of humanitarianism and which burdens both the creature with its own existence, and the family and the society with the burden of supporting it."

Das Schwarze Korps
(The Black Corps)
on March 18, 1937

HOW PSYCHIATRIC IDEAS INFILTRATED SOCIETY

While history documents how psychiatry's eugenics and the racist ideology of Aryan domination combined to form the foundation from which the Third Reich's horrors would grow in post-World War I Germany, we do not yet have the answers to how such racially unappealing ideas came to seep so deeply into society and gain such widespread acceptance. How did so many physicians, nurses and others turn into advocates and even practitioners of mass murder? How did an entire nation embrace such elitist and racist ideals and pursue them as a matter of public policy?

Unfortunately, there were many reasons. The first was that the psychiatrists played upon the preexisting and deep-seated prejudices of the time, especially anti-Semitism, and promoted popular fantasies of a troubled time, such as the supposed superiority of the Aryan race. The psychiatrists, advocating sterilization, eugenics and racist theory, also allied themselves with a totalitarian system which had at its disposal a well-tuned propaganda machine to drum this message of hate weekly, daily—even hourly—into the minds of the people. Still, even with growing public sentiment in their favor, the Nazis and their psychiatric cohorts needed a precise plan to implement.

Shortly after the turn of the century, psychiatry began its fixation with genetics as the key to redefining the human race. Practically every abnormality—mental, spiritual, criminal and sexual—could, to the psychiatric way of thinking, be explained away by genetic traits. Therefore, the theory went, what was discovered to be genetically abnormal had to be diagnosed early in life and eradicated to prevent its proliferation. It was in this context that the notion of "life unworthy of living" was concocted.

In 1920, two scholars—one a psychiatrist, the other a doctor of jurisprudence and philosophy—published a short, focused paper in which they advocated that, in certain cases, the arrival of death should be assisted. Years before, as a young psychiatrist, Alfred E. Hoche, then a clinical assistant in Heidelberg, had been called to the deathbed of a nine-year-old girl. Years later, Hoche described his thoughts:

"We were extremely interested as scientists in performing an autopsy to see the progress of the disease. If she were alive at her father's return, which was set for the next hour, I would have to hand her over; but if she were to die before, we could do the autopsy. I...played with the thought of completely extinguishing the flickering light of her life with a small injection of morphine. While the surgical nurse was having her dinner, I sat on the small bed with a full syringe in my hand and wavered—should I or shouldn't I? I covered this issue later... in a very controversial paper; I refuse to accept the viewpoint that the physician has the unconditional duty to prolong life."[1]

Only the fact that the father demanded the release of his daughter and the fact that the law still made euthanasia a crime prevented the murder Hoche contemplated. Ironically, but not surprisingly, Hoche changed his mind abruptly on this issue in 1940 when he was sent an urn with the ashes of a relative murdered in the Holocaust. He suddenly and violently denounced euthanasia. By then, of course, it was too late. Hoche had already become a victim of the Nazis' use of his own teachings.

Hoche's co-author of that landmark paper on euthanasia—entitled "The Permission to Destroy Life Unworthy of Living"—Karl Binding, was born in 1841, the son of a Frankfurt lawyer. He ascended to the post of Chief Justice of the Reich, but died before the paper went to press in 1920.

The major points of their 62-page tract are these:[2]

1. The suffering of a sick or wounded person who is about to die can be shortened through the use of a medical drug.

2. This acceleration of the death process is not an act of murder but "in truth a pure act of healing." (This justification was later used specifically by the Nazis in defense of their extermination programs).

3. A doctor should be able to employ euthanasia on any unconscious person without legal consequences.

4. There are people who are worthless to society. Primary among these are the inmates of the "idiot institutes," who are "not only worthless, but of absolutely negative value."

5. The incurably dumb who can neither agree to survive or to be killed should be killed. "Their death will not be missed in the least except maybe in the hearts of their mother or guardian...When we become more advanced, we will probably be saving those poor humans from themselves." This was intended to be the scientific justification for the murders being advocated. Ethical matters were to be figured out later.

In twenty years, in the hands of Hitler and the Third Reich, the grotesque advocacy of Hoche and Binding would reach its horrible climax. It is also instructive, considering psychiatry's historical obsession with low-cost handling of the mentally ill described above, to note that Hoche and Binding also offered economic justifications for the medical murders:

"The inevitable expense for these dead-weight characters was justified for all kinds of reasons, and was not a problem when we had prosperity; it is different now and we have to do something about it."[3]

There is no doubt that 1920 Germany was in financial shambles. There is equally no doubt that hard times elevate economics and subjugate ethical restraints. In a time of virtually universal economic ruin, it was far easier to sell an ideology which supported the extermination of the social and political—and inevitably, economic—"dead-weight." If anyone foresaw the disastrous consequences of this way of thinking—the systematic extermination of six million people—their protests were overwhelmed by the time and tide of politics, economics and prejudice.

FROM RACIAL HYGIENE TO NAZISM

Contemporaneously with the publication of Hoche and Binding's seminal work on euthanasia, another theory seeped through to the surface—namely, the notion of "mental hygiene." Originally meant to denote preventative mental care, its definition changed very rapidly to "racial purity" and the "eradication of all inferior genotype." Ultimately, it meant the same as the definition into which "eugenics" evolved—the eradication of inferiors.

It was also at that point in time that a decisive leap had been made, and that leap was in the definition of the "inferior."

To understand how the ultimate definition of "inferior" came to be, we must address the principles articulated by another prominent psychiatrist of the day—a true pioneer in the psychiatric-Nazi death machinery—Ernst Rüdin. Unlike his predecessors, Rüdin was more practical than theoretical; it was he who developed the uses of psychiatric genetics and racial hygiene which the Nazis embraced so thoroughly.

It was also Rüdin who, in May, 1930, gave a lecture at the First International Congress of Mental Hygiene in Washington, D.C., on the subject, "The Importance of Eugenics and Genetics in Mental Hygiene."

It was also Rüdin who made racial hygiene as socially acceptable a concept as possible and who, in 1933, was one of the three scientists who composed the legal argument for the Sterilization Act of 1933, the law that cleared the path for wholesale euthanasia.

It was also Rüdin who transferred Mendel's laws of genetic transmission into the human arena and created what passed for a practical basis for the compulsory sterilization programs that resulted. He did so almost three decades before the Nazi party's assumption of power and more than a decade before Hitler publicly declared any thoughts of this kind whatsoever.

In 1911, Rüdin and Max von Gruber published a study on population called "Fortpflanzung, Vererbung, Rassenhygiene"[4] ("Procreation, Transmission, Racial Hygiene"), which stated:

"All nations have to haul around with them an extraordinary large number of inferiors, weaklings, sickly and cripples...The demand for the organization of systematic data is the next item that racial hygiene has to put on the state administration."[5]

Bear in mind that by this time, psychiatry had already become active in politics, lobbying for its racial hygiene programs:

"It is not enough to have a moral reawakening...of a truly national sentiment and lifestyle. ...Hopefully, the time is not far away when lawmakers will realize that the people (are rewarded) ...for this service by the procreation of a strong next generation. Only in this way will it be possible to stand up to the destructive evil of the so-called 'women's emancipation movement.'[6]

"Through a wise legislation along this line...we would also be able to pursue rationally the best avenues for breeding. Voluntary sterility of physical and moral inferiors would then go without saying!"[7]

Eugenics legislation was thus suggested for the first time in 1911 by psychiatry. It would take a mere twenty-two years for the eugenicists' wish to be fulfilled in Germany.

For many years, German psychiatry had been trying to find a legal basis for breeding a "master race." It had finally found a "scientific" tack which would influence legislators and get their ideas implemented broadly into society. All programs in the Nazi era to promote favorable genetic traits and to suppress unfavorable ones can be traced back to racial hygiene or eugenics.

The ideal type of human being could be produced through "positive" and "negative" eugenics, terms that had already been used by the eugenicists and racial hygienists for quite a while. "Positive eugenics" promoted favorable genetic traits using such governmental programs as marriage counseling, state subsidies of large families with a healthy genotype, and so on.

"Negative eugenics," on the other hand was nowhere near benign. It meant the extermination of all people who had undesirable and unfavorable genetic traits, mainly by eliminating procreation. Since marriage counseling by itself was not enough—the government tried unsuccessfully to convince people with unfavorable genetic traits to voluntarily sterilize themselves—a legal means had to be found that would allow the compulsory sterilization of genetically damaged men and women.

Genetics and racial hygiene now began to cover a wider spectrum, and psychiatry proved to be the ideal sphere of activity for both fields.

Rüdin wrote in 1930:

"...We have to do something about the positive and negative eugenics before it is too late. For the negative, the sterilization of the genetically sick has to be closely looked at....It would be a blessing to know that genetically incompetent, unhappy people would not be produced anymore. Much more national expansion would be created through positive eugenics than we can imagine.

"The fertility rate of the genetically undesirables is so great today that we have every reason in the interest of humanity to address ourselves to the prevention of the genetically weak. The increase of the hereditarily healthy that is so necessary to us as a nation today will cause us less of a headache in the future."[8]

From this we can see plainly that it was not the Nazis who were at the forefront of this cause—it was the psychiatric racial hygiene movement, led by Rüdin three years before the Nazis even came to power. We can also see that they knew that only through a law would it be possible for them to realize their evil dreams. They tried to accomplish this by advancing economic arguments to win over the lawmakers in the Reichstag. Despite working for many years to pass this legislation, the psychiatrists continued to fail. But with the seizure of power by the Nazis, all that changed. Both halves of the sinister equation were finally in place.

How much psychiatry welcomed the Nazis' ascension to power is very obvious, as the legal brief arguing for the Law for the Prevention of Genetically Diseased Children shows:

"With the passing of the Law for the Prevention of Genetically Diseased Children, the German Nazi government took an important step for the future of our nation. Because of their nature, our previous governments could not come to a decision, since German parliamentarianism has generally shown itself to be incapable of innovative steps for the salvation of our nation....Only the Nazi world view has reoriented us to the future, we have again remembered the meaning of our lives, the purpose of the state, the fight for survival and life of our families, the species and the race! Hitler writes in his book *Mein Kampf*: 'Who is not healthy bodily or mentally is not allowed to perpetuate his malady in the body of his child....'

"Therefore, this Act is a complete break from the small-mindedness of an outdated philosophy of life and the overblown and suicidal charity of the past centuries."[9]

CHAPTER 6

*"This is not about the extermination of 'life unworthy of living,'
but about the freeing of heavy and very heavy sufferers and
their relatives from their pain."*

> *From the minutes of a secret
> meeting concerning euthanasia
> on April 23, 1941, written by
> Dr. Alexander Bergmann*[1]

THE SECRET ACTIVITIES OF THE THIRD REICH

T4—THE KILLERS GO TO WORK

On January 30, 1933, Austrian-born Adolf Hitler was elected Chancellor of the Reich. Two months later, in the Reichstag elections of March 5, the Nazi party received less than a 44 percent plurality of the vote. By forming an alliance with another political party, the Kampffront, the Nazis were able to solidify a majority in parliament and secure Hitler's position. By mid-March—barely two weeks later—Minister of the Interior Hermann Goering declared a war against "filth." This was followed quickly by the establishment of the first concentration camp at Dachau on March 22, 1933, where the homeless, once collected off the streets, would be housed and educated. Meanwhile, in front of his generals, Heinrich Himmler, the head of the Schützstaffel—better known as the SS, or state security police—ordered the "inferiors" eliminated.

Less than four months later, on July 14, 1933, the Law for the Prevention of Genetically Diseased Children was passed, to go into effect on January 1, 1934. The main proponent of this legislation was Ernst Rüdin, who was the Director of the Kaiser Wilhelm Institute for Psychiatry in Munich.

Sterilization under that law was no small or isolated program. The estimated number of sterilizations performed in Germany between 1934 and 1945 fluctuates between 100,000 and 350,000. It is likely that many of those who were forcibly sterilized later became victims of euthanasia institutes. In

Werner Heyde—One of the chief organizers of the euthanasia program

1934, the first year of compulsory sterilization, 62,000 sterilization orders were issued by the Court for the Elimination of Hereditary Disease—a chilling name for a ghastly tribunal—while only 4,814 applications were declined. The following year, 1935, more than 71,000 sterilization orders were granted while only 9,000 were rejected.[2] Only the hopelessly naive would doubt that many sterilization orders were issued for purely political reasons.

In early March 1933, the ward physician of the psychiatric clinic of Würzburg and one of the chief organizers of the euthanasia program, psychiatrist Werner Heyde, (who after the war would escape justice and continue to practice psychiatry under the alias of "Dr. Sawade") released a mental patient named Theodor Eicke as fit for discharge. Eicke, who was sent to prison as a hardened, violent criminal, was classified by Heyde as no longer dangerous. Yet Eicke became the first commandant of Dachau and in 1934 was promoted to Inspector General and Chief of all concentration camps. By 1936, he had become the leader of the SS "Deathhead" units. Heyde joined the Nazi party in 1933 and by 1935 had become an Associate Judge of the Court for the Elimination of Hereditary Disease—the ultimate arbiter of sterilization requests. Finally, on July 1, 1936, Heyde himself became a member of the SS "Deathhead" units and a consultant to the Gestapo.

In his resume dated January 1, 1939, Heyde wrote:

"In 1936, I had…been urgently requested to establish and direct the psychiatric-neurological and genetic surveillance of the concentration camps and to take over a psychiatric-neurological advisory function for the Secret State Police (Gestapo) in Berlin."[3]

Starting in 1937, criminals and repeat offenders were systematically relocated to KZs, the German abbreviation for concentration camps (Konzentrationslager). That practice was followed by orders for "welfare units" to arrest "vagrants, alcoholics, work dodgers, welfare recipients and even already-sterilized, feeble-minded women."[4] Eventually, the Law for the Prevention of Genetically Diseased Children laid the foundation for a large-scale witch hunt, culminating in the euthanasia program.

Demands became more and more radical. Hitler and his trusted and powerful aide, Himmler, were obsessed with "cleansing the nation's body." Driven by their own projection of all manner of evil onto the Jewish population and inspired by the racial hygiene teachings of Lenz, Rüdin and others, they escalated their solution. In psychiatry, they found willing accomplices to enforce their insane ideas. This is not surprising, since it was psychiatry that had created and developed the concept of racial hygiene to begin with. In this endeavor, the Nazis found psychiatry to be a willing, eager and compliant bedfellow.

New conditions were defined to fit the political agenda of the Reich. Professor Werner Villinger, a psychiatrist and physician in the German town of Bethel, first introduced the term "endogenous work-shyness" and traced this "condition" back to genetic origins. The name is foreboding—endogenous means "depending on the traits." Lazy or unemployed people thus were in jeopardy of removal from society. Friedrich Stumpfl, a colleague of Rüdin's at the Kaiser Wilhelm Institute, theorized that tramps are much more psychopathic and feeble-minded than the average person. That made them prime candidates for extermination. The Nazi psychiatrists also coined the term "camouflaged feeble-mindedness" to describe a form of feeble-mindedness that carries "the mask of cleverness."[5] The designation was particularly nefarious. In similar terms, even people who were not feeble-minded could be classified as "camouflaged feeble-minded" if they were politically or otherwise undesirable. Anyone who was normal but troublesome could be labeled "feeble-minded"—camouflaged, but feeble-minded nonetheless—and subject to removal and elimination.

Playing perilous games with language and concocting transparently political psychiatric illnesses, the Nazi psychiatrists extended genetic theories on feeble-mindedness to include completely normal people and to justify eliminating them for political reasons. Communists, pacifists and democrats were branded "camouflaged feeble-minded" and disposed of by the Nazis. It is terrifying to ponder what psychiatry in Germany was able to do in the 1930s. It is a ghoulish historical fact that when those psychiatrists were free to define their own rules and operate within their own boundaries, the diagnosis of normal and abnormal became a matter of politics and prejudice, and treatment was sterilization or death at the hands of a totalitarian regime.

Political dissidents and members of the wrong religion or ethnic group were far from the only victims. The law allegedly designed to preserve the future was turned against all "work dodgers," "offenders," alcoholics, vagrants, beggars and "asocials." Practically everybody who was a burden to society, in someone's bias or someone's aspirations, was arrested.

By 1936, at the beginning of Heyde's tenure as psychiatric head of all of the concentration camps, the first systematic transfers of the mentally ill out of various mental institutions and into the KZs began. Then in 1937, the Reich embarked upon a systematic cleansing of churches and charitable establishments. Inmates were relocated first into state institutes, and ultimately to the death camps. At about the same time, the public was deluged with propaganda attempting to legitimize the political process of elimination of undesirables, massaging public opinion, and paving the way for public tolerance of the euthanasia to come. Visitors were given tours of psychiatric institutions to demonstrate the necessity of eugenics and euthanasia. Students in secondary schools were encouraged to write final examination essays about the value and benefits of euthanasia. The principal theme of the pro-euthanasia propaganda was the claim that the extermination of "life unworthy of living" would free up scarce public funds for other, more important things for the good of healthy, productive members of society.

The first documented euthanasia killing occurred in 1939. The practice escalated into an avalanche of killing that would not end until Germany's surrender in May of 1945. In that first case, Dr. Karl Brandt, Hitler's personal physician, was given the responsibility of dealing with the petition of a father to euthanize his own child who was born handicapped. In no uncertain terms, Hitler commanded his Justice Department to look the other way, since laws against the killing were still on the books. Dr. Brandt then carried out the vile process in the incident that is now known as the "Child Knauer case."

Hitler then ordered Dr. Brandt and Philipp Bouhler, the head of the Chancellery of the Führer "to deal with cases of a similar nature analogous to the case of the Child Knauer."[6] Thus was hatched a diabolical plot against the weakest and most vulnerable of all children. Child euthanasia was conceived and plotted in the inner circles of the Chancellery of the Führer. Among the architects of the program to slaughter handicapped children were Dr. Karl Brandt, who was a physician and surgeon; Dr. Helmut Unger, an ophthalmologist; Dr. Ernst Wentzler, a pediatrician; Dr. Hans Heinze, a psychiatrist; and Professor Werner Catel, a child specialist at the University of Leipzig Clinic.

On August 18, 1939, a confidential decree was issued which required notification to the government of the birth of any deformed or handicapped child. That was bad enough, but the decree also commanded the registration of all deformed or handicapped children up to the age of 3 years old. Midwives and physicians were obligated to report all children who were mentally or physically handicapped or paralyzed who were born in the future or who had been born in the preceding four years.

In July of 1939, Hitler summoned State Secretary of the Ministry of Interior, Leonardo Conti, Chief Officer of the Party Office Martin Bormann and Minister of the Reich and Head of the Reich's Chancellery Hans Heinrich Lammers to a conference in which Conti was given responsibility for administrating the euthanasia program. Soon thereafter, however, he was relieved by Bouhler and Dr. Brandt, who had been working on the Reich's adult euthanasia program as well. Together they searched for reliable physicians to help them—Max de Crinis then of Berlin, Carl Schneider of Heidelberg, Berthold Kihn of Jena and Werner Heyde of Würzburg, who by this time had been promoted to a full professorship at the university there. Others who came to be involved were Dr. Ernst Wentzler of the child euthanasia committee, his committee colleagues, Drs. Helmut Unger and Hans Heinze, and the directors of the asylums, Dr. Hermann Pfannmüller of Eglfing-Haar, Dr. August Bender of Berlin-Buch and later, Professor Paul Nitsche of Sonnenstein-near-Pirna.

The euthanasia program for the handicapped and mentally ill was organized exactly as prescribed in Alfred Hoche's and Karl Binding's notorious 1920 treatise. Hoche had also suggested in 1920 that a commission be appointed to order the euthanasia of "dead-weight characters," and Binding provided ideas for the removal of legal hindrances.[7] Nearly twenty years later, the euthanasia program was established exactly as Hoche and Binding and others had imagined it a generation earlier when Germany was a republic rather than a dictatorship and when law, not hate, ruled. Theory in a republic had become an unspeakable reality in the twisted minds of totalitarian demagogues.

This extermination campaign against the "inferiors" had as its principal strategist Phillipp Bouhler, who was the Hitler confidante who had assisted Dr. Brandt in formulating the policy born out of the Child Knauer case. He was aided and abetted by hand-selected, politically reliable psychiatrists and physicians. This campaign became known as the "Aktion Gnadentod" ("Operation Mercy Killing"). Mercy, of course, had nothing to do with it.

The physicians Bouhler chose to assist him were invited to Berlin at the end of July of 1939, to devise, define and implement Operation Mercy Killing. The stated, official purpose of this meeting was to create hospital space for the wounded of the fast-approaching war. Hitler, sensitive to foreign policy concerns, had rejected any solution involving legalization. At the same time, however, he promised those who participated in the euthanasia program that they would be exempt from legal prosecution for their service. Except for de Crinis (who would later support euthanasia anyway), all the invitees agreed to give their support and assistance. Several methods of killing were proposed and discussed by the physicians, but ultimately they reached a consensus: carbon monoxide was to be used for the extermination. I. G. Farben Industries, the large German chemical manufacturer, would be given the contract for the production of the gas.

On September 1, 1939, the same day that German troops invaded Poland and precipitated World War II, an official halt to sterilization was ordered and an executive order was issued authorizing Bouhler and Dr. Brandt to "expend the authority of the as yet unnamed physicians" to perform mercy killing. From that day on, sterilization was to be used only in unusual cases. In addition, marriages no longer had to be officially sanctioned. The euthanasia program, as designed by those who had gone to Berlin in July, was not yet fully in place when the first mentally sick were gathered from institutions in Meseritz, Pomerania (now Poland). They were summarily executed in a forest by SS firing squads, a process difficult to imagine as having any characteristic of euthanasia. The corpses were secretly buried in mass graves. Only at the approach of the Russian troops in 1945 were these mass graves opened by German soldiers to burn the remains. Approximately 3,500 mentally ill persons from Pomeranian insane asylums were executed in this fashion.

Barely a month later, on October 9, 1939, an edict was issued requiring all institutions throughout the Third Reich to categorize all of their patients and inmates according to stated criteria. Issued by Dr. Conti, the head of the Reich's Interior Health Ministry's Services Office, this decree was deliberately crafted to give the misimpression that the purpose was to allow for better organization of patient care, supposedly necessitated by the war.

Leonardo Conti's decree required reports to be compiled and submitted on all those in care or custody who suffered from a variety of stated symptoms, among them: schizophrenia, epilepsy, senility, paralytic diseases, feeblemindedness and psychiatric diseases. Also to be reported were all persons who have been imprisoned for five years or more or who are "criminal" or who are "not of German or related 'species' blood."

Meanwhile, preparations for formal, government-authorized mass executions proceeded apace. Three days after Conti's edict, on October 12, 1939, Castle Grafeneck was appropriated and the refurbishment began under the direction of Dr. Viktor Brack and Dr. Werner Heyde. The first "test gassing" with carbon monoxide took place at Brandenburg in January 1940. Euthanasia had been more or less legalized by Hitler's September 1 executive order, and the plan to exterminate segments of German society continued to be refined under the auspices of the German government.

It is somewhat surprising that except for this secret order, no legal basis for euthanasia would have existed in any form whatsoever. "Everyone involved knows that Hitler rejects a legal ruling for political reasons."[8] In other words, everyone involved understood that what was going to happen in the Reich's death camps, and everyone involved knew that what actually happened was authorized by Hitler but apparently illegal under the existing laws of the Third Reich.

More particularly, however, the wording of Hitler's secret authorization—even with the most liberal interpretation imaginable—could not, on its face be interpreted as an approval to murder anyone who is unproductive, incurably insane or merely bothersome. Obviously, then, one of two possibilities explains the genocide that followed. Either it was Hitler's intent all along that exactly what happened actually happen, or Hitler's authorization was interpreted by the leading psychiatrists of Germany as the green light to make reality out of a generation of sadistic psychiatric theories. Or both.

Clearly, both. This is precisely where the politics of power and the psychiatry of hate merged with unspeakably horrible results.

The Reichsarbeitgemeinschaft Heil- und Pflegeanstalten (Working Association of Sanitariums and Caretaking Facilities of the Republic) was founded in Berlin. Its sole purpose was to gather and kill "inferiors." Initially located in the Columbushaus at the Potsdamer Platz, it was moved in April of 1940 to new quarters at Tiergartenstrasse 4. Hence the infamous code name "T4." Nothing about the outside of the building even hinted at the fact that inside was a chamber of horrors more terrible than any imagined in gothic fiction. By the beginning of October of 1940, the number of people the operation planned to murder was set at 70,000. A morbid quota, to be sure, but T4's business was murder.

T4 headquarters

Psychiatrist Werner Heyde moved from Würzburg to Berlin to become T4's medical director and to supervise its consulting staff of approximately 30 physicians, most of whom were psychiatrists. Three physicians were chosen to decide the fate of each case on the basis of the stacks of questionnaires which arrived daily at a post office box, to avoid revealing the secret location. The Reichsarbeitgemeinschaft (RAG)—better known as T4—was financed by the Treasurer of the Nazi party.

It was all carefully organized and very well planned. The Gemeinnutzige Krankentransport GmbH (Public Utility Ambulance, Inc.—named "Gekrat" for short) was incorporated to pick up the patients who had been selected by consultants to be killed. Such relocations—save for the intended outcomes—were official and thus known to the general public. This was effected through legal channels, such as Ordinance X 4792 of Wuerttemburg's Ministry of the Interior and other similar ordinances of other Interior Ministries throughout the Reich:

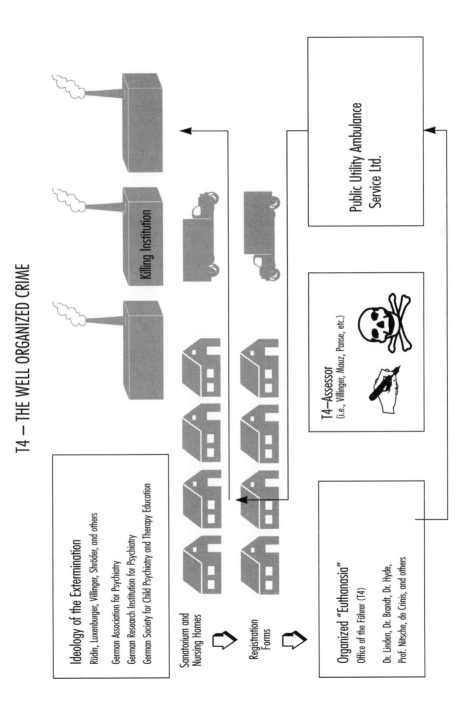

T4 – THE WELL ORGANIZED CRIME

Ideology of the Extermination
Rüdin, Luxenburger, Villinger, Shröder, and others

German Association for Psychiatry
German Research Institution for Psychiatry
German Society for Child Psychiatry and Therapy Education

Sanatorium and Nursing Homes

Registration Forms

Organized "Euthanasia"
Office of the Führer (T4)

Dr. Linden, Dr. Brandt, Dr. Hyde,
Prof. Nitsche, de Crinis, and others

Killing Institution

T4–Assessor
(i.e., Villinger, Mauz, Panse, etc.)

Public Utility Ambulance Service Ltd.

KILLING INSTITUTIONS

"The present situation makes the relocation of a large number of patients who are housed in sanitariums and caretaking facilities of a similar nature necessary."[9]

The relocation programs were designed to leave the legitimate caretaking facilities and church welfare institutions guessing about the true nature of the government's operation, although it is clear in retrospect that a significant number of directors of such private institutions either had been quietly let in on the secret or had figured it out on their own. Like livestock the patients were herded by soldiers onto the railway platform and given what was described as an "injection with sedatives," but which was, in reality, an overdose of Scopolamine, a powerful muscle relaxant. One eyewitness reported that many patients were injected with the same needle.

"...the sick went after a few minutes into shock that manifested itself through foam on the lips, interruption of the ability to respond, the eyes popping out and the inability to move the extremities..."[10]

It got worse. Those who were being transported were executed in gassing trucks especially built for the purpose. The deadly gas was fed into the hermetically sealed interior of the truck. When the screaming stopped, the soldiers would drag the dead and the half-dead out of the truck and bury them in mass graves in a nearby forest. Whoever was not killed by the gas was dispatched by a bullet in the head. It is likely, though, that many were actually buried alive.

There was nothing resembling mercy in Operation Mercy Killing.

In the meantime, the preparations for transferring the insane from their sanitariums to extermination institutes were feverishly underway in the euthanasia headquarters in Berlin. Special crematorium furnaces were under construction for the extermination institutes. Scheduled first were Brandenburg and Grafeneck. Ironically, only the Christmas holiday of 1939 interrupted these outrageous preparations, of which the German public knew nothing.

It was in January of 1940 that the first test killings with carbon monoxide gas took place in the Brandenburg sanitarium, where Viktor Brack and Dr. Heyde were in charge of the pilot project. Several physicians were also there, as were a variety of others who would later take part in human extermination in other institutes. Everyone was sworn to secrecy. For the purpose of the demonstration, a special "shower room" was constructed into which the unsuspecting inmates were led, supposedly to clean up. In the water pipes along the wall were tiny holes through which the deadly gas could spew into the hermetically sealed room. In the door was a peephole.

"In this first gassing approximately 18 to 20 persons were led into the 'shower room' by the nursing staff. These men had to undress in the anteroom so that they could be completely naked. The door was closed behind them. These men walked quietly into the room and showed no signs of being upset. Through the peephole I saw that after approximately one minute the men just collapsed or lay on the benches. There were no scenes or commotions. After another five minutes the room was aired. SS personnel took the dead on special stretchers out of the room and brought them to the crematorium furnaces."[11]

The "special stretchers" were especially constructed so that they could be placed directly on top of the furnaces and the bodies could then be shoved into the furnace the same way a baker shoves a loaf of bread into an oven. According to this same eyewitness, the victims did not undergo any medical examination at all. They were assumed—but not known for certain—to be dead. It is thus not unlikely that some people were actually cremated alive.

The apparent success of this test killing hastened the production of killing facilities. More death institutes sprang up around occupied Poland, equipped with "shower rooms," machine guns and gassing trucks. To avoid arousing suspicion, the trucks were painted to look like "Kaiser's Coffee" trucks. The pure carbon monoxide gas was fed from steel canisters directly into the van of the truck.

Obviously, this activity was concealed from the general public. The authorities were careful to ensure that the cause of death in every case was attributed to "natural causes" of one sort or another. Relatives were notified of their loved one's sudden death by the institute into which the deceased had been relocated. All the letters of notification were virtually identically worded, identifying one of a variety of plausible causes of death—heart failure, stroke, or some other fatal disease.

Because the war was so much on everybody's minds, the euthanasia effort was able to come into being without arousing any suspicions, let alone much attention at all. But once the numbers of the killings increased and stated causes of death began to accumulate that were completely inimical to the physical condition of the deceased, notice and suspicion were unavoidable. Relatives started to ask questions and lodge complaints. Employees of the asylums from which the patients originally came caught on quickly, since the clothing of the victims was always returned by the Gekrat to the original institution, but the patients never came back. Eventually the general population caught on, too, but by then it was too late. "Evacuation" or "disinfection," as euthanasia was called in the lingo of those who engaged in it, was the business of Operation Mercy Killing, and business was booming.

Questionnaires from state and private sanitariums and caretaking institutes began arriving in larger and larger numbers to euthanasia headquarters. The questionnaires were copied and sent to three consultants, and after that to a chief consultant. The three consultants—psychiatrists and other physicians who made the decisions—marked those who were to be killed with a red "+" sign, and those allowed to live were marked with a blue "-" sign. The chief consultant had the last word and would make the final decision if there was any doubt. One of the chief consultants was Dr. Heyde, another was Dr. Herbert Linden, who was later replaced by professor Nitsche, who was a psychiatrist. The ultimate decision was up to Brack (who had by that time assumed the alias of Jennerwein). He was an economist by training and knew nothing about either medicine or psychiatry.

Killing institutions, modeled after the original one at Brandenburg, complete with a gas "shower" room and cremation furnaces, were built at Grafeneck, Sonnenstein and Hartheim, which is in Austria. Late in 1940, Grafeneck and Brandenburg were closed, but additional facilities at Hadamar and Bernburg-an-der-Saale continued their work.

Guidelines abounded in the Third Reich's bureaucracy, and even when the official business was murder, administrative protocols had to be observed. For example, there were guidelines to select which victims would be killed, however it is clear that such bureaucratic niceties did not deter the psychiatrists who stayed very active, guidelines or not. When euthanasia was officially stopped by Hitler in August of 1941, T4 had already reached its original quota of 70,000 persons euthanized. Indeed, T4 had exceeded its quota—by 273 persons.[12] All this killing was done because

Germany's leaders were concerned about their victim's "usefulness," as this internal T4 document shows:

"Elimination of all those who are unable to work productively, therefore not just of the mentally dead."[13]

The consultants who operated the killing institutes made quite a bit of money from their work. In October of 1940, a psychiatrist working as a euthanasia consultant received 100 marks per evaluation, up to a total of 500 questionnaires. But there were bonuses to be earned. Any especially fast administrator could make 200 marks per evaluation for the 2000 questionnaires, 300 marks for each additional questionnaire for up to 3000, and 400 marks for all questionnaires above that. It is, therefore, not surprising that the consultants churned out death sentences like they were working on an assembly line.

For example, a psychiatrist named Dr. Hermann Pfannmüller completed 2000 registration forms in only three weeks, while another one, Dr. Schreck, "very conscientiously" cranked out 15,000 forms in nine months, according to his own testimony.[14] One witness reported that a consulting physician even worked "while drinking wine in a public restaurant."[15] The physicians and psychiatrists needed only to suppress any residue of humanity that may have lingered in them to make a fortune by merely shuffling paper. And killing people.

The people who worked at the death factories made better livings than they could have virtually anywhere else in the Reich. Not only because they were better paid—which they were—but also because they were able to take and use the food stamps of those they had killed. The patients who had gold teeth had a cross inscribed on their backs before extermination, and the cremators were instructed to pull the gold teeth and send them on to the front office.

During the Reich's euthanasia campaign, three out of every four schizophrenic patients were sentenced to death by euthanasia consultants, despite the fact that then, as now, the definition of schizophrenia is extremely elusive. On many registration forms, "schizophrenic" appears to have been something of a catch-all code word for "unwanted patient." Another obvious target was patients housed in the church-managed institutions, where the percentages of those removed from church institutes for euthanasia was: 34 percent feeble-minded, 23 percent idiots, 16 percent epileptics, 12 percent schizophrenics.[16]

So while the rest of Europe and the world debated the relative merits and morality of capital punishment for crimes such as murder and treason, the German government was actually putting people to death for being ill or slow-witted or an economic burden.

It is also remarkable to note that patients were never transferred from the psychiatric mental hospitals or clinics operated by universities. According to Dr. Linden, "except for a few demonstration cases...no long-term patients are kept" in those clinics.[17] The "demonstration material" of the university clinics thus was spared. Ironically, capital criminals who were committed to asylums as insane, thus escaping the death penalty, ended up being executed anyway. Their "judges" were the T4 consultants, whose income was directly proportional to the volume of death sentences issued. Their executioners were the physicians who opened the gas valves. Much later—in 1961—Dr. Heyde himself would admit that they were under orders that "criminals are to be judged especially harshly."[18]

Humans being humans, errors occurred. Now and then mix-ups happened, especially with people sharing the same name. For identification purposes, an adhesive strip with the person's name written on it was stuck to the back of the victim. But with common names like Keller or Müller, mistakes can and did happen:

For example, a bureaucratic error caused the papers of a patient named Keller to be transferred with the papers of another patient named Keller to a death camp. The Keller whose papers had accidentally been sent (but who was still alive) was reported as dead to his relatives, even though they knew he was still alive. Later, the innocent Keller, a harmless, slightly neurotic painter, was sentenced to euthanasia solely to correct the error in the filing system.[19]

It is a matter of significant controversy whether the killings actually were as peaceful as they were described during the trial run. Remember that the only eyewitnesses were biased in the extreme. All the reports about the trial killings came from the killers, who had little sympathy for the suffering of their victims and little reason to implicate themselves in what might rightly be viewed as an atrocity.

A witness from Hadamar gave a very different account of the killing process from that offered by the executioners: "Through (the spyhole)...I saw about 40 or 45 men who were tightly packed into an anteroom dying slowly. Some lay on the floor, others had collapsed, many had their mouths open as if they couldn't get enough air. This kind of death could not be called humane. I observed this process for about two or three minutes, and then I left because I couldn't bear the sight any longer and got sick."[20]

All personnel who took part in the killing were sworn to silence, sometimes under the threat of death. Nevertheless, rumors got out. It is amazing, however, that no uproar was raised by the friends and relatives of the victims. An angry German populace might have been enough to stop the carnage, since at the time, Hitler feared internal political problems more than external ones, and he was still sensitive to image and public relations concerns.

The psychiatrists who participated in these programs performed their official duties very thoroughly. Every murdered person had a file. The registry office was always duly notified when bureaucratic snafus like the one involving the two Kellers, had to be rectified. Sometimes strange administrative contradictions would surface, as in the case of a prisoner named Werner W., who was scheduled to be released from an asylum on June 15, 1940, but who had been put to death on March 26 of that year "as a result of pleuritis." In another case, Dr. Friedrich F., who was being prosecuted for libel, was acquitted but placed under psychiatric care. A little while later, he passed away "because of a heart attack" just after he had been transferred from the institute in Waldheim to the Brandenburg facility. His wife became suspicious after receiving conflicting information about the cremation site.[21]

As is the case with any ugly secret that's known by more than one person, the secrecy surrounding the killing program eroded. Bureaucratic blunders and administrative errors kept contributing to the suspicion, until enough snippets of information leaked out to permit people to begin to piece together what was really going on. In one case, two urns were shipped to the same family; in another, parents received the news of the "death" of their mentally ill child along with an urn. Their suspicions were aroused because only a few days earlier, they had brought their son home from the asylum. To show how careless the paperwork and administrative details had become, in another case, "appendicitis" was given as the cause of one death, even though the appendix of the deceased had been removed many years before.[22]

Meanwhile, T4 officials found yet another financial windfall in the business of mass executions. The scam was ridiculously easy. Those officials quickly recognized that between the day the patient was euthanized and the day the relatives would have to be notified, there was a significant time gap during which the cost of providing accommodations at the death institute could be billed and collected. By delaying the actual recording of the official date of death, they could gather a lot of money by merely invoicing as though the patient were still alive. By the time that he turned his job over to his successor, the head of the clearing office, Hans-Joachim Becker (nicknamed, appropriately enough, "Million Becker") had managed to accumulate 14 million marks in his personal bank account, although Becker would later be caught in his embezzlement and the money was transferred to the Treasury arm of the Nazi party. The crime was not fraud; the crime was failing to turn the proceeds of the fraud over to the Nazi party.

There were numerous other examples of corruption and brutality during the first wave of exterminations by the psychiatrists and the rest of the T4 staff. It only got worse. After all, it was after the supposed end of euthanasia by Hitler's decree in 1941 that the killing actually escalated to staggering proportions with which we are all now familiar.

It has already been noted that some propaganda efforts were undertaken to garner public support for the programs that were offered as economic benefits while, in reality, they were investments in death. Indeed, orders were placed in October of 1939 for two propaganda films to be made. One was "Dasein ohne Leben" ("Existence Without Life") by Dr. Kampfer. The other was simply entitled "Geistekrank" ("The Mentally Ill").

In "Existence Without Life," mental illness was portrayed as a genetic defect and the mentally ill as grotesque creatures. The objective was to convince the population that the care for the sick was much too expensive and that therapy was useless, since the diseases were genetically generated.

In "The Mentally Ill," the incurability of the insane is "scientifically" proven by failed "cures" of electroshock and insulin treatments. This film actually showed T4 psychiatrists—members of the selection committee—at work in their Tiergartenstrasse headquarters. Incredibly, the closing scene of the movie even shows the gassing process.[23] This film, however, was never released; nor was a 1941 movie, in which there was a huge blunder discovered before release. Of all the patients they could have filmed, a female patient whose only defect was multiple sclerosis was used as an example of a classic case of someone who should undergo euthanasia.

There is room for debate about whether Hitler knew or understood the actual breadth of the euthanasia campaign he had approved. What we do know is that in 1941, less than two years after he made it possible, he stopped it. Why Hitler changed his mind may never be fully explained. We can only guess based upon what various witnesses have said about it. One such witness was a psychiatrist named Menneckes, who was involved in the euthanasia program in the Rhenish Eichberg Institute:

"One day when Hitler was traveling on his special train from Munich to Berlin, it had to make a stop at a station at Hog. To find out why, he went to the window and was spotted by a crowd standing outside that had been witnessing the shipment of mentally ill patients. When the crowd saw Hitler at the window, they became irate, as they knew what would happen with the patients. This demonstration of dissatisfaction against Hitler prompted him to call off what had been going on until then."[24]

Another document substantiates that Hitler made an effort to distance himself from the program:

"The discontinuation of extermination was skillfully exploited, according to a physician of the Weissengau Institute, by spreading a whisper campaign that it had happened because of Adolf Hitler, who prior to that had not been aware of the killings."[25]

There is a third possibility which appears to be the most plausible. The original target figure of patients to be exterminated had been reached in August 1941, the precise time that Hitler ended the program. The original campaign apparently had accomplished its purpose and was shut down. But that did not mean that a new euthanasia program wasn't waiting to begin.

Plans had existed since early 1941 to exploit the deadly expertise of T4 for weeding out what the Nazis regarded as the "dead weight" from the overcrowded concentration camps. This "cleansing action" was coded "14f13," but it was actually the preliminary stage of the "Endlösung"—the so-called "final solution"—the extermination of the Jews.

By 1941, T4 psychiatrists were well-schooled and their personnel well-trained in the art and science of mass human extermination. Hitler and the rest of the Nazi hierarchy were anxious to have them apply their lethal techniques on a grand scale in the KZs. Starting in April of 1941, eminent physicians and psychiatrists began to visit the concentration camps, among them Heyde and Nitsche, the leading T4 consultants. Nitsche himself would later admit that "the killing in the KZs went along the exact same lines and with the same registration forms as in the insane asylums."[26]

In fact, it ran like a well-oiled machine because the sick and the infirm of the asylums had served as a ghoulish dress rehearsal. First, there was the registration of the "sick" KZ inmates, followed by transfer through Gekrat to the institutes in Bernburg, Hartheim and Sonnenstein. There the transferred prisoner was gassed.

Especially targeted were Jews, Poles, criminals and pacifists. The killing institutes now had more than enough business, despite the cessation of the euthanasia program that Hitler had ordered in August of 1941. From that point on, however, no condolence letters were mailed out to the relatives, and no more death certificates were issued. The official date of death was now considered to be the date of the inmate's incarceration in the concentration camp.

Beginning in September of 1941, a campaign using T4's methods was launched to exterminate the Jews being held in Poland. Shipping canisters to the east was deemed too expensive; the gas had to be produced on location. Prussic acid gas, also known as Zyklon B, was manufactured by DEGESCH, an acronym for German Corporation for Pest Control and a subsidiary of I.G. Farben, for the express purpose of exterminating the "vermin" in the concentrations camps. Two dozen Russian prisoners of war, lured into the truck under the pretense that they would be deloused, were the first victims of the gassing. The Commander of the Auschwitz camp, Rudolf Hoess, gave a report on the first "test runs" of the mass murdering that was to follow:

"The Russians...after being told that they would be deloused, all calmly went to the mortuary...As they were being thrown in, some cried, "Gas!" This was followed by an enormous amount of screaming and pushing for the two exits, which of course would not open. Not until after several hours had passed were the doors opened and air was let in. It was then that I first saw the crowd of corpses. An uneasy feeling overcame me, a kind of trembling…"[27]

There were many different euthanasia operations after Hitler had ordered a stop to it in August 1941. The existing extermination institutes continued to operate at a capacity level, fed a continuous stream of victims by the KZs. In Poland and the captured territories of the USSR, systematic T4-style killings were carried out on a daily basis. As to Jewish extermination, all of the experience and personnel of T4 were put at the disposal of the Third Reich. The "Aktion Reinhard" (named after Reinhard Heydrich and consisting of assigning euthanasia personnel for the extermination of Jews) began almost precisely after the euthanasia program was stopped in 1941.

Then three extermination camps modeled after the German killing institutes were constructed in Poland—at Belzec, Sobibor, and Treblinka. According to reliable estimates, at least 1.7 million people were put to death in these three camps alone. The gas chambers proved too small to accommodate the incoming masses of people and expansion was deemed necessary. The gas chambers were eventually built so that approximately 500 people at a time could be led to what some sarcastically referred to as the "peaceful sleep." Sometimes, however, authorities crammed up to 1500 people into the death chambers.

"The faster the gassing was completed, the shorter was the suffering and fears of the Jews that were soon to be killed. They had aroused his sympathy especially during a strong frost in winter when they had to wait naked and freezing in the waiting room, sometimes at temperatures of minus 20 degrees Celsius. He had then strongly insisted on a quick and economical filling of the gas chambers in order to shorten the wait for the naked people in the bitter cold."[28]

The extermination of the Jews was an exact replica of T4's earlier euthanasia program. In a letter to the Reich's Commissioner for the East, it is very clear that Dr. Viktor Brack, the head of all of the euthanasia programs, was all too willing to make men and materiel available. "As things stand now, I would be perfectly happy if those Jews who were not able to work are eliminated with Brack's methods."[29] Approximately 100 experienced staff were transferred from T4 headquarters and the German killing institutes to the Polish extermination centers. Their headquarters, however, was still T4.

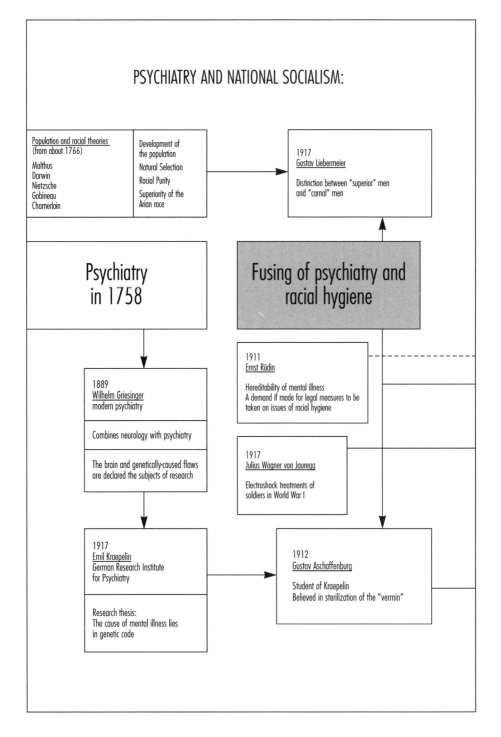

PSYCHIATRY AND NATIONAL SOCIALISM:

Population and racial theories (from about 1766)

Malthus
Darwin
Nietzsche
Gobineau
Chamerlain

Development of the population

Natural Selection

Racial Purity

Superiority of the Arian race

1917
Gustav Liebermeier

Distinction between "superior" men and "carnal" men

Psychiatry in 1758

Fusing of psychiatry and racial hygiene

1911
Ernst Rüdin

Hereditability of mental illness
A demand if made for legal measures to be taken on issues of racial hygiene

1889
Wilhelm Griesinger
modern psychiatry

Combines neurology with psychiatry

The brain and genetically-caused flaws are declared the subjects of research

1917
Julius Wagner von Jauregg

Electroshock treatments of soldiers in World War I

1917
Emil Kraepelin
German Research Institute for Psychiatry

Research thesis:
The cause of mental illness lies in genetic code

1912
Gustav Aschaffenburg

Student of Kraepelin
Believed in sterilization of the "vermin"

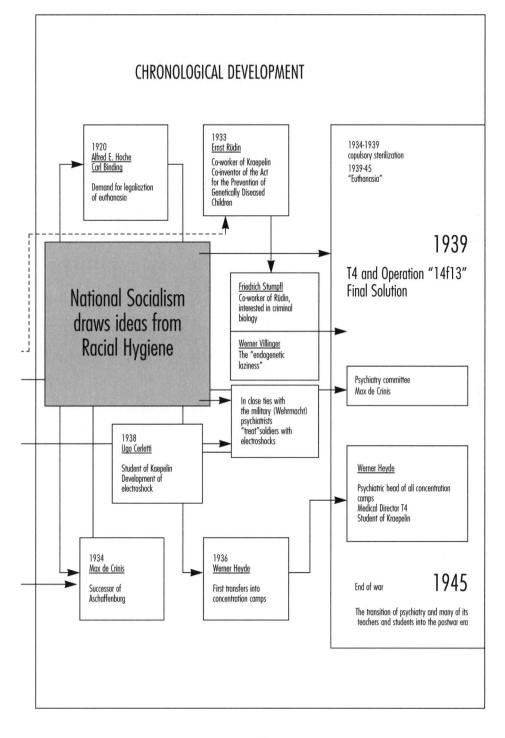

CHRONOLOGICAL DEVELOPMENT

1920
Alfred E. Hoche
Carl Binding

Demand for legaliaztion
of euthanasia

1933
Ernst Rüdin

Co-worker of Kraepelin
Co-inventor of the Act
for the Prevention of
Genetically Diseased
Children

1934-1939
copulsory sterilization
1939-45
"Euthanasia"

**National Socialism
draws ideas from
Racial Hygiene**

1939
T4 and Operation "14f13"
Final Solution

Friedrich Stumpfl
Co-worker of Rüdin,
interested in criminal
biology

Werner Villinger
The "endogenetic
laziness"

Psychiatry committee
Max de Crinis

In close ties with
the military (Wehrmacht)
psychiatrists
"treat"soldiers with
electroshocks

1938
Ugo Cerletti

Student of Kaepelin
Development of
electroshock

Werner Heyde

Psychiatric head of all concentration
camps
Medical Director T4
Student of Kraepelin

1934
Max de Crinis

Successor of
Aschaffenburg

1936
Werner Heyde

First transfers into
concentration camps

End of war   **1945**

The transition of psychiatry and many of its
teachers and students into the postwar era

The stage was set for the systematic extermination of "life unworthy of living"—Jews, Gypsies and others deemed "inferior." Numerous eyewitness reports attest to the barbaric cruelty inflicted upon the Nazis' helpless victims:

"After the arrivals were taken to the location next to the crematorium, they had to undress entirely because they were told they would have a shower. They then were chased—often with beatings—by the SS into the so-called bath, which in reality was a gas chamber...." [30]

"[In the dressing room of the crematorium] people's blood-stained and battered heads and faces proved that there was scarcely anyone who had been able to dodge the truncheon blows in the yard. Their faces were ashen with fear and grief.... Hope and illusions had vanished. What was left was disappointment, despair, and anger.

"They began to bid each other farewell. Husbands embraced their wives and children. Everybody was in tears. Mothers turned to their children and caressed them tenderly. The little ones...wept with their mothers and held on to them....

"After a while I heard the sound of piercing screams, banging against the door, and also moaning and wailing. People began to cough. Their coughing grew worse from minute to minute, a sign that the gas had started to act. Then the clamor began to subside and to change to a many-voiced dull rattle, drowned out now and then by coughing...." [31]

This is the tragic climax of the racial hygiene program that had been devised by Rüdin and the other psychiatrists. This was the intolerable legacy of the psychiatric philosophy—to show the world how the healthy and the sick, the normal and the abnormal, the racially pure and the racially impure, were to be separated from one another by extermination.

And make no mistake—euthanasia continued in the German institutes after Hitler ordered it stopped. The psychiatrists themselves were the ones holding the reins, apparently in direct contradiction to Hitler's orders.

When, on August 24, 1941, Hitler ordered that euthanasia be discontinued immediately, the psychiatric institutes continued their work in secrecy. This is recorded in history as the so-called "wild euthanasia," although it is not clear whether it represents catching up with a huge backlog of designated victims that still had to be processed, or whether an unofficial continuation of an officially prohibited act had been undertaken on a large scale.

The fact remains that a request for the continued killing was issued. The Counselor of State of the Thüringian Ministry of the Interior, Professor Karl Astel, visited the euthanasia clinic there.

"At the time, Dr. Astel asked us physicians to continue with the euthanasia. He did not actually mention the word 'euthanasia,' but his words clearly indicated that he expected this from us."[32]

Astel had been reprimanded several times before by his superior for the use of euthanasia in his area of responsibility:

"As you know, the Führer wishes that all discussions about euthanasia are to be avoided."[33]

From then on, those who persisted in the murderous onslaught did so without government sanction or involvement. Psychiatrists, wedded as they were to their own eugenic theories, continued their murderous activities, with silent approval from the Nazi regime. This approval no longer came from Hitler or the T4, which would have been much too high-profile, but from the Reich's Interior Ministry and its national medical subdivision.

The extensive gassing program was replaced by other various but equally deadly methods: food poisoning, lethal injections, or starvation. Unfortunately, the official end to the euthanasia program did nothing to stop the mass murdering of children; in fact, it made it worse. The age limit that defined who was a "child" was raised to sixteen years, qualifying a whole new age group of unfortunates for extermination. There were even cases of juveniles who managed to stay alive through the end of the adult euthanasia program, only to be reclassified as a child and marked for death.

The pediatric department of the killing institution at Brandenburg-Goden, under the aegis of Professor Hans Heinze was an especially prolific example of the murderous abuses of power by the Nazi psychiatrists. Other prominent child-killing institutes were located at Kalmenhof in Idstein and at München-Haar. An eyewitness at the latter, which was run by the notorious Dr. Hermann Pfannmüller, reported that:

"I remember the gist of the following general remarks by Pfannmüller: These creatures (he meant the children) naturally represent for me as a National Socialist only a burden for the healthy body of our Volk. We do not kill (he could have here used a euphemistic expression for this word kill) with poison, injections, etc.; then the foreign press and certain gentlemen in Switzerland would only have new inflammatory material."[35]

Psychiatrists took a special interest in the brains of those they killed. The University of Heidelberg worked closely with the killing institutes to get such "material." The Kaiser Wilhelm Institute for Brain Research in Berlin received nearly 700 brains of murdered victims from the Gekrat for research.

At the Eichberg in the Rhinegau, they were not interested in brain research alone. Human experiments with medical drugs were performed on behalf of I. G. Farben, the chemical manufacturer. At this institute, both children and adults (many among them workers from the East) were killed on a regular basis until the end of the war. An argument over the brains eventually erupted between the Eichberg and Heidelberg research departments. Professor Carl Schneider in Heidelberg demanded part of the so-called "material" for his own research.

At the center of this research effort was the euthanasia headquarters, which organized personnel and facilities for killing and offered its know-how and administrative resources. T4 was, in fact, the nerve center of the extermination campaign and was not just the forerunner of the ensuing mass extermination of the Jews, Gypsies, Poles and other human beings "unworthy of life." T4 was actually the organizer, education center and spiritual and administrative focal point that would continue in its criminal activity for another six years. All that T4 did was quietly performed behind the scenes.

On May 8, 1945, the war ended in Germany. In the extermination institutes, they either kept on killing, or let the patients starve to death. As late as May 29, 1945, a four-year-old feeble-minded boy was murdered in Kaufbeuren, and on July 7 a Munich newspaper made a horrifying discovery which proved that the loss of World War II had had no effect on the overall intentions of those who still operated the human slaughterhouses.

On July 2, 1945, Robert E. Abrahams walked into the district hospital of Kaufbeuren to find the warm, swinging body of a physician who was junior only to the director. He had hanged himself. Twelve hours earlier, the last adult had died. In Irsee, soldiers found the bodies of men and women who had died just hours earlier, most of them through starvation.

The most horrible chapter of German history has long since passed, yet many questions remain unanswered. The exact number of those killed by euthanasia may never be discovered, as many of the killing institutes destroyed all of their records immediately after the war. Many of those who took part in the carnage escaped punishment and remained hidden to this day or have died. One thing is certain: there was a veritable army of psychiatrists and their followers who worked directly for T4 or voluntarily did T4's bidding. In addition, there are countless numbers of their disciples who fervently believed in their racist and eugenic rhetoric and who worked within the Nazi party and Hitler's bureaucracy. Unfortunately, a great many of the psychiatrists who worked for T4 escaped detection altogether.

The propaganda machinery of the Nazi regime successfully impeded the full discovery of all those who worked within T4. It is only with great difficulty that the connections have now been reconstructed and the full dimensions and significance of T4 completely identified and assessed. The secret euthanasia campaign of the psychiatrists within the Nazi regime was carried out with very little public outcry during the war and was well-hidden afterward. Uncovering this tragic episode of history did not begin until the mid-seventies, and still has a way long to go. This much, however, is certain: Psychiatry under the Nazis was more than an obedient servant and an executioner. It was a co-conspirator and co-initiator, if not the major force behind a staggering portion of genocide.

This does not exonerate Adolf Hitler in the least. He was and is still the monster that we know him to be. The same is true of Heinrich Himmler, Alfred Rosenberg, Martin Bormann and all the other Nazi racists and killers history will forever condemn. But we must also point a finger at the other guilty party whose real role to this day has never been completely exposed—the psychiatrists who cold-bloodedly carried out the ethnic cleansing program, and have barely been called to account for themselves.

Why this profession has had difficulty with active repentance is beyond the scope of this book. The only conclusion that can be reached is that self-criticism is not an activity in which they indulge, especially those who were actively engaged in the planning and execution of extermination psychiatry.

Without a doubt, Hitler was the main culprit; it was he who was the catalyst on the political level for the years of unrelenting murder. But without his co-conspirators, without the godless inhumanity with which the horrible murdering was systematized and "mechanized," it is questionable if millions of Jews and other minorities would have been slaughtered in such numbers and in such an organized, perfunctory and brutal fashion.

Übersicht :   Aufstellung der Beratenden Psychiater im Ersatzheer

Übersicht : Einsatz der Beratenden Psychiater im Ersatzheer im Jahre 1942
(nicht vollständig)
Quelle: BA/MA RH12-23 H20/475 (div. Korrespondenz)

Wehrkreis	Dienstgrad	Titel und Name
I..............Königsberg	Oberarzt; Stabsarzt	Prof. Mauz
II.............Stettin	Oberstarzt	Dr. Franckenberg
III............Berlin	Oberstarzt später Oberfeldarzt	Prof. de Crinis
		1945 Beratender Psychiater
		beim Heeressanitäsinspekteur
IV............Leipzig	Oberarzt	Prof. Wagner
IV............Dresden	Oberstarzt	Dr. Butter
V.............Straßburg	Oberfeldarzt	Prof. Bostroem
VI............Ensen/Köln	Stabsarzt	Prof. Pohnisch; Nachfolger
		Dr. Panse
VII..........München	Oberstarzt; Oberkriegsarzt	Prof. Bumke
VIII		
IX............Marburg	Oberstabsarzt	Prof. Kretschmer
X.............Hamburg	Stabsarzt	Prof. Bürger-Prinz
XI............Braunschweig	Stabsarzt	Prof. Ernst
		später Beratender Psychiater
		der Heeresgruppe F
XII...........Heidelberg	Oberstabsarzt	Prof. Carl Schneider
XIII..........Erlangen	Marine-Oberstabsarzt	Prof. Meggendorfer
XVII.........Wien	Oberfeldarzt	Dr. Fuchs
XVIII.......Innsbruck	Stabsarzt	Prof. Scharfetter
XIX		
XX...........Riesenburg	Oberstabsarzt	Prof. Otten
XXI.........Posen	Oberarzt	Prof. Weigl
Koordinationsstelle	Oberstarzt	Prof. Wuth bis Anfang 1945
Militärärztliche Akademie		dann bis Kriegsende
Berlin		Prof. de Crinis
Berater 1939	Generaloberarzt a.D.	Prof. Stier

The above is a summary of the formation and employment of the consulting psychiatrists in the Reserve Army in the year 1942.

So far we have seen the development of the philosophy of eugenics up to the large-scale extermination of minorities in Germany as well as the interlinking and intertwining of psychiatry and Nazi politics. Up until now, the development of psychiatry followed the same route as Hitler's Third Reich.

We come now to the second part of this book. What happened to the psychiatric instigators of the Holocaust after 1945? How did so many of them manage to remain in high positions until the end of their lives? How was it possible for psychiatry to escape completely unscathed after the war? How could it have gone undetected as jointly responsible for the Holocaust, as the principal architects of the institutional, assembly line killings, and as the crucible of an ideology that purported to justify these murders in the first place?

In the second part of this book, we will also name names, sometimes of esteemed and celebrated psychiatrists. But we will go even further than that by documenting how little psychiatry has changed since 1945. In its methods, which are still seen today in modern "therapy," we can see results that are at best questionable and, as we have seen in the events that took place before 1945, results which are uniquely despicable in their cruelty.

Map of the euthanasia institutes (X), extermination camps (□), concentration/extermination camps (◼) that were mentioned in these documents. Germany and Austria within the borders of 1937.

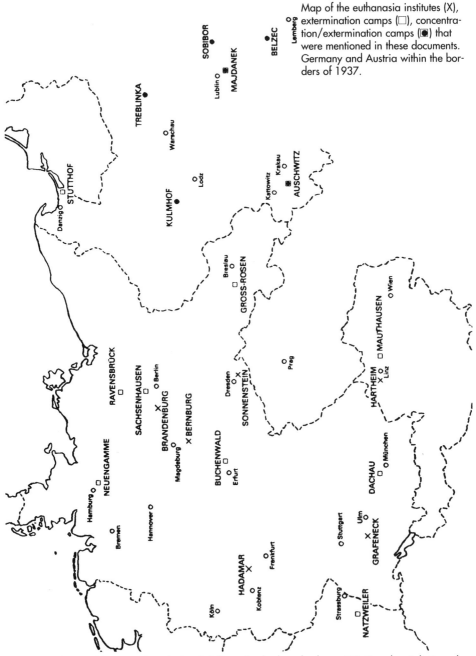

Eugon Kogon, Hermann Langbein, Adalbert Rückerl and others: "Nationalsozialistic=sche Massentötungen durch Giftgas."

District map 1943. (Map of the political sections of the German Reich. Published by Richard Schwarz. Armament inspection status 1.8.1943. This map was kindly made available by the federal and military archives in Freidburg.)

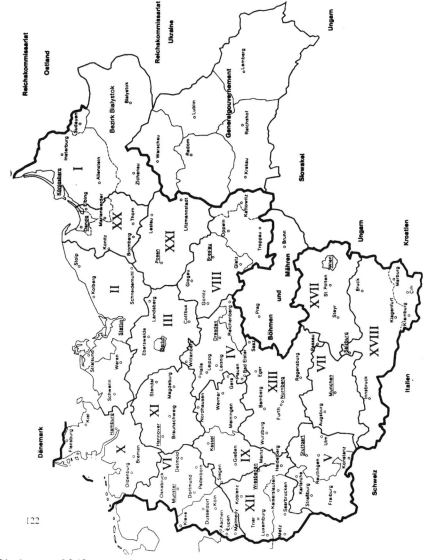

District map 1943. During the greatest expansion of the German Reich.Source: Günter Komo: "Für Volk und Vaterland" ("For People and Fatherland"), Military Psychiatry during World War I and II, Hamburg, 1991.

PART TWO

THE SUPPRESSED PAST

"The criminal court...is not of the opinion that the extermination of the mentally dead and the 'empty human husks,' as Hoche has called them, is absolutely immoral per se. There can be extremely different opinions about this. Long ago, the removal of 'life unworthy of living' went without saying.... All these details...lead us to the conclusion that the question of the shortening of life unworthy of living is, of course, a highly contested problem, but that its execution can in no way be called a measure which conflicts with the general moral code."

Criminal Court 1 of the District
Court of Hamburg on the issue
of child euthanasia on
April 19, 1949[1]

HOW THE TRANSITION WAS ENGINEERED

It is hard to conceive, much less understand, what happened in Germany after World War II. Many of the war criminals and their accomplices, advocates and sympathizers not only managed to keep their positions, but they were celebrated, honored and glorified—some even to this day stand as apparent or perceived heroes. Just as astonishing, and certainly just as disturbing, is the fact that rather than distancing itself from its Third Reich disgraces, psychiatry was and is today, at best, only equivocal about the psychiatric teachings and doctrines that were foundational elements of the Nazi horrors.

Where the world has the right to demand instant condemnation, psychiatry responds by hedging. Hesitation, where condemnation is required, is tantamount to a confession of guilt.

Of course, some of the Nazi psychiatric war criminals were caught, tried, convicted and sentenced as murderers. Some were executed, such as Professor Paul Nitsche, who was sent to the guillotine on March 25, 1948 in Dresden, and Carl Schneider, who was executed as a result of the Nuremberg trials. Others opted for self-executions, such as Dr. Leonardo Conti, the Third Reich's Minister of Health from 1939 to 1945, who committed suicide. Others seemed determined to practice murder as a supposed "solution" to the very end. While fleeing from the authorities, Max de Crinis took his own and his family's lives with potassium cyanide. Other Nazi psychiatrists, such as Professor Heinze, were sentenced to long prison terms for their war crimes. Many others fled, escaping arrest, trial and sentencing, and perhaps even execution.

What is much more disturbing is that many of the Third Reich's most savage and most culpable psychiatrists continued on after the war as if nothing had happened. Professor Heyde, once the head of T4, for example, not only fled after his 1947 arrest, he managed to resume his work as a psychiatrist under the alias of "Dr. Sawade." He was also active as a psychiatric consultant in the Courts of the Schleswig-Holstein district of Germany, "even though numerous professors, the Director of the Social Court, the Chief Justice of the provincial Social Court, a district court counselor, a Social Court counselor, two presidents of the Senate and even a federal judge all knew that Professor Heyde was also Dr. Sawade."[2] Obviously, there were still many in official positions in Germany who felt it appropriate to maintain a "code of silence." Sadly, it is plain that apparently no crime was sufficient to deprive the criminal of the shelter of that cowardly code.

Silence is indeed a highly prized attribute among psychiatrists. Dr. Hans Bürger-Prinz, who is thought to have been aware of "Dr. Sawade's" true identity, told the Schleswig-Holstein parliament's 1961 investigation into the case of Heyde/Sawade:

"With the exception of the clergyman, I do not believe that there exists a profession in which silence plays as big a role as with us, and by this I mean with respect to everything…Silence is very important to us and is not limited to the legal requirement concerning confidential medical communication…."[3]

It is troubling enough that war criminals such as T4's Dr. Heyde was able to assume a new identity and continue his psychiatric practice after the war, but the truth is even worse than that. Many psychiatrists who had held positions of responsibility—and therefore, culpability—during the Nazi era didn't even have to hide after World War II. Nobody brought them to justice. Nobody even really tried. Ernst Rüdin and Ernst Kretschmer are two of the most outrageous examples of psychiatrists whose transition into the postwar era, like other Nazis cloaked with the mantle of "scholar," was painless and free from the recriminations that justice demanded.

A great deal of the blame for such omissions is found in the way that justice was administered during and pursued after the Third Reich. Even today, fifty years later, there are still gaping holes in the investigation of Nazi war crimes. For example, the activities of what the Nazis called "special courts" have scarcely been examined.

"The main duty of the special courts was to criminally prosecute the political resistance to the Nazi regime. During the Second World War, they gradually took over the duties of ordinary justice and from 1942 on, most of the sentencing. Experts estimate that the special court of Hannover alone, one of several in today's Saxony, sentenced 4,000 defendants, about 170 of them to death. Approximately fifty judges and prosecutors who were employed at the special courts were later taken on by the legal administrative body of lower Saxony."[4]

Thus in Hannover and elsewhere, the prewar judges and prosecutors became the postwar judges and prosecutors, making for a unified administration of injustice, but allowing for the acts of those people to be safe from official scrutiny. Not surprisingly, many postwar verdicts reflected an unwillingness to punish war crimes, possibly because of wartime complicities and crimes of the prosecutors and judges:

"The shortening of 'life unworthy of living,' stated the district court of Hamburg on April 19, 1949, could in no way 'be called a measure which conflicts with the general moral code.' Dr. Lotte A., who admitted to killing 14 children, was 'exempt from prosecution.' That decision was pronounced by a judge who had formerly been the head of a district of the Nazi party in Bielefeld. Dr. Lotte A. practiced until 1986."[5]

Apparently, the confessed murder of 14 children did not conflict with the general moral code of the Nazis who endured in positions of power.

Evasion of justice was so rampant in the German postwar era that surviving patients sometimes fell again into the hands of their own former captors and torturers. In one case, a female patient, who had been transferred by Dr. Hans Bürger-Prinz into the death institute at Meseritz, and who survived only by pure luck, saw herself once again exposed to Bürger-Prinz as her consulting physician by assignment after the war. This was not just an isolated incident—it was, sadly, relatively commonplace according to survivors and records which were not destroyed.

Significant elements of postwar Germany remained receptive to the theories and hypotheses of racial hygiene. In fact, extensive research did not reveal a single academic advocate of racial hygiene and compulsory sterilization since 1945 who had been called upon officially to account for such advocacy. This includes Dr. Bürger-Prinz, who carried on after the war. He was the same Bürger-Prinz who was quoted in a 1988 article of *Der Spiegel*, reminding his psychiatric colleagues in 1935, "To 'register' young children 'afflicted with a hereditary disease' before 'fertility' in order to 'pick them out and exclude them from procreation.'"

The 1988 *Der Spiegel* article continues, "[Bürger-Prinz] became an ordinary professor in Hamburg! Konrad Lorenz, who would later win a Nobel prize, stood up in 1940, demanding the 'more stringent eradication of ethical inferiors,' only to concern himself after the war with writing bestsellers, only generally about the 'so-called evil,' not about his own past.

"Johannes Heinrich Schulz, the father of 'autogenic training' and a nononsense expert on hereditary disease and homosexual behavior, sent homosexuals to the concentration camps if they could not have intercourse with a woman while he watched. After 1945, he became one of the most popular medical educators in the country. The professor died in 1970, as old as Methuselah and highly honored.

"Hans-Joachim Rauch, who as court psychiatrist was very active in Stammheim, was for decades afterward a full professor in Heidelberg. During the Nazi era, he was a pathologist who dissected the brains of gassed children. The small patients were brought to the killing institute of Eichberg, near Heidelberg. This institute thus satisfied Rauch's desire for their freshly slaughtered organs."[6]

Academia in particular was riddled with people with blood on their hands. Denazification programs undertaken after 1945 within German colleges and universities were generally thwarted before they assumed meaningful proportions, and those that managed to get off the ground were soon shot down. There was simply too much resistance from those in power to allow for significant scrutiny, let alone for rooting out and expelling Nazis. One of the few dedicated apostles of denazification who persisted in the face of such obstacles was a pediatrician named Dr. Rudolf Degkwitz. His ultimate failure—despite his laudable dedication—symbolizes the frustration of those who felt both the need and the moral duty to make amends for the past by bringing culpable Nazis to justice and freeing the nation as much as possible from history's stain.

After the war, Dr. Degkwitz was the Dean of the Medical Faculty and President of the Health Department in Hamburg. Professor Hendrik van den Bussch, one of the most knowledgeable experts on the history of Nazi medicine described in his book what happened to Degkwitz:

"…According to his opinion, every physician who had been a member of the Nazi party should be dismissed from state service. With this opinion, Degkwitz stood very much apart. Neither the British military authorities nor the Hamburg Senate, not to even mention the senate of the university of the faculty, shared this viewpoint in the least. When Degkwitz tried nevertheless, all by himself and not always in orthodox ways to push this intention through, he became very quickly in medical circles the most hated man in Hamburg."[7]

Ultimately, his stamina eroded in the wake of bureaucratic, medical, and academic opposition, and Degkwitz gave up and emigrated to the United States. He did not, however, go silently or compliantly.

"With his letter of May 25, 1948, Degkwitz resigned his service. He did not, however, refrain from publicly presenting the reasons for his resignation in the political arena."[8]

In a paper to the senate of the University he wrote:

"Almost all of the former Nazis, the bearers and preachers of Hitler's gospel of violence, have been reassigned back to the universities, with the excuse that they had just been 'nominal members'…. Would it be possible under such circumstances to educate free thinkers and democrats? Or hasn't the same old situation that is to blame for the German catastrophe of modern times been resurrected: to endure superiors whom one cannot respect by humbling oneself and by secretly cursing them, ultimately to resign oneself to leaving the responsibility to 'those up there'? And who is to impress upon the academic youth that the era of Hitler was an era of shame, if those who come back to our universities are personally responsible for it? They would gather their old fellow party members around them and the few lecturers who were anti-Nazi from the beginning would form just as powerless a minority as they did in Hitler's time....They will not stand up for Hitler, of course, but their nationalism, out of which Nazism was born, will remain unchanged and will come to the surface whether they want it to or not."[9]

Given the amount of complicity in high positions in Germany, the postwar halls of justice were every bit as polluted with Nazis as were the halls of academia. The courts held a plethora of judges and prosecutors whose tenures were interrupted, but not concluded, by military defeat. It is, therefore, not surprising that Germany's justice system did little to overcome Germany's bloody past in the days following the Third Reich's decline. The truth is that many Nazis returned to positions as judges and prosecutors with little or no scrutiny from those supposedly responsible for supervising the administration of justice.

"Most of the murderers were only overcome through the advance of time, through their own old age. After the founding of the Federal Republic of Germany, they advanced again to the ranks of head physicians, medical officers and professorships, respected as academics and college teachers, and finally woven back into the political fabric of justice, bureaucracy and archives, protected by their old comrades....The Nazi idea...was forgotten, suppressed and glossed over, right from the start."[10]

The remarkably cold-blooded, yet relatively typical quotation at the beginning of this chapter, is illustrative. It is part of a written court decision that exempted twenty Nazi criminals from trial and thus insulated them from justice. Note that the court refers explicitly as justification for its decision to Binding and Hoche's 1920 tract espousing and defending eugenics and weeding out "empty human husks" and "life unworthy of living." The importance of this philosophy's persistence in official Germany after the war can neither go unnoticed nor ignored. The court's opinion represents the postwar marriage of the psychiatric and official authorities who had initiated and advocated mass extermination being quoted as justification of why the mass extermination could not automatically be condemned even in retrospect. It was, in fact, the only official reason why the court of Hamburg exempted the twenty accused Nazis from prosecution for war crimes, four years after Hitler was defeated.

The purpose here is not to dwell on individual miscarriages of justice regardless of how blatant. This book's focus is the real scandal—that so many truly guilty people avoided detection and capture. When Nazism met its gruesome, but well-deserved fate, psychiatry was able to continue on virtually unimpeded in the advocacy and the dissemination of much of its vile doctrine. Many of the psychiatric pioneers of the Nazi genocide programs and their sympathizers were able to instill new generations of students with their ideology. Their research activities continued as if nothing had happened. They were, of course, careful not to utter any racist ideological statements, but the theoretical and philosophical continuum continued virtually unchanged.

Certainly the Reich's sociopolitical philosophy persisted in the Nazis who avoided punishment immediately after the war. One notable example is Professor Werner Catel, of the "Reichsausschuß zur wissenschaftlichen Erfassung schwerer erb- und anlagebedingter Leiden" ("Reich's Committee for the Scientific Registration of Serious Genetic and Inherent Sufferings"), the committee of consultants on child euthanasia. After the war, Catel enjoyed a very good reputation in Europe as a "professor of child therapy." The International Biographical Archive wrote of him in 1964:

"Catel had, of course, nothing to do with the euthanasia operation against adults during the Nazi period. However, as head of the children's clinic in Leipzig, he had worked from 1940 to 1944 as a consultant in the so-called 'Reich's Committee for the Scientific Registration of Serious Genetic and Inherent Sufferings.' Based on these expert opinions, a number of infants, all complete idiots, had been killed in certain hospitals....

"In an interview in *Der Spiegel*, the professor, who since then had proposed in a book that lawmakers should give the physician a free rein in the killing of completely idiotic children, had declared that he stands firm in this opinion just as before."[11]

Catel—a children's doctor who advocated killing children—was a paradox indeed. Catel is also said to have worked in a clinic until 1945 against the directives of the Nazi regime, treating numerous Jewish children on his own and at his own risk. He is also said to have admitted several hundred sick babies from Poland, Russia and France into his clinic and reared them with the milk from German mothers.[12]

Klee remarks that, after that war, nobody had talked as hypocritically about Nazi child murder as Catel. In Catel's own words, one did not euthanize; rather one used a "soothing therapy" with the aim of "putting to sleep" handicapped children who were therefore "soothed to death."[13]

Just as heinous sociopolitical philosophy persisted after the war, so too, did acceptance of psychiatry's antisocial traditions and potential for enormous suffering and harm. That conclusion is bolstered by an analysis of texts that document the transition from the Third Reich to the postwar era. For example, from the psychiatric journal *Der Nervenarzt*, comes a 1948 paper written by Werner Villinger and Hermann Stutte which is replete with antisocial psychiatric terms like:

"Human material," (meaning "patients")

"social biological inferiority,"

"the locating, screening and directing of this flotsam of neglected and disassociated youth,"

"social troublemakers and enemies of society."[14]

Another remarkable postwar quote comes from psychiatrist Gerhard Kloos who, in 1942, had taken over the special children's department in Kiel and, in 1952, was named an associate professor of psychiatry:

"With bothersome psychopaths, especially the unstable ones, those that are devoid of feeling, the criminals, the sexually perverse and the troublemakers, neutralization is very important through the preventative means of society (placement into institutions, workhouses, preventative detention, etc.).[15]

The most chilling aspect of Kloos' disturbing quote is that it was written in 1968. The Nazi ghosts continue to haunt subsequent generations.

Such loathful sentiments certainly reveal an elitist and Nazi-type attitude. As we have mentioned earlier, Werner Villinger was not a minor figure, but rather a leading adolescent psychiatrist and a professor of Psychiatry and Neurology at the University of Marburg. After the war, Villinger worked hard "on a 'New Sterilization Act' that was compiled by the Health Committee of Stuttgart's Council of the Länder from 1947 to 1949, with the permission of the American occupation force."[16]

How did some of psychiatry's most vile practitioners accomplish this virtually Teflon-coated escape from punishment and feel free to continue to preach a "science" of hate? For one thing, the postwar German justice system simply wasn't interested in bringing any skeletons out of the closet. Nor was the German public well enough informed about what really occurred to do much about it, even if there had been much call for justice, which there was not. The allies also let most of the perpetrators go free or excused their involvement as "nominal membership." Many questions remain unanswered, and may remain so forever.

What we do know, however, is what happened to many of the psychiatrists involved in the Nazi horrors, what happened to their ideology, and what has become of their methods.

CHAPTER 2

*"We feel responsible for shaping and perfecting the convention-
al according to new experiences, discoveries and possibilities in
order to contribute with our modest means to the preservation
and augmentation of the striking power of our armed forces and
thus to the victory of Germany."*

> Werner Villinger in 1941,
> President of the German
> Society for Psychiatry and
> Neurology, 1952-54.

GERMAN PSYCHIATRY AFTER THE WAR:

ECHOES OF THE PAST

The best way to understand the reach of Nazism's residue in psychiatry is to examine what became of some of the most prominent German psychiatrists after the war. We have already noted that many of them were able to continue their activities with little or no interruption. Some who spearheaded the Reich's murderous policies were captured and convicted or escaped punishment by committing suicide. Other collaborators in the Holocaust found, however, that Nazi stormtroopers could serve as a very useful alibi. They reasoned that it was very easy to blame everything on them. If this alibi was successful, they reasoned, then their own past could be forgotten, too, because—according to their defense—they were also victims.

Still, for these significant, often central, figures in the Nazi campaigns of sterilization and murder to escape punishment, common sense dictates that there had to be a significant cover-up. Research and analysis confirms that intuition, and demonstrates that well-known organizations and institutions that played a major role in rebuilding Germany after the war were involved.

This examination necessarily begins with the "Deutsche Gesellschaft für Psychiatrie und Nervenheilkunde" ("German Society for Psychiatry and Neurology"—GSPN for short). Its history, membership, leadership and activities as psychiatry's national society eloquently demonstrates the resilience of prewar psychiatry after World War II.

The GSPN sprang from the ruins of the "Gesellschaft Deutscher Neurologen und Psychiater" ("Society of German Neurologists and Psychiatrists"), which in turn was created in 1935 as the successor to the "Deutscher Verein für Psychiatrie ("German Association for Psychiatry"), which traced its roots back to 1864. It cannot be denied that both of these seminal organizations endorsed eugenics, racist biology and the refinement of the Aryan genotype. In 1925, psychiatrist Robert Gaupp, Sr. spoke to the German Association for Psychiatry on "The Sterilization of the Mentally Ill and the Inferior":

"When one speaks about combating the degeneration of a people by the eradication of its inferior members through sterilization, then of course one thinks in the first place about...the bulk of the degenerates and psychopaths who live in freedom, cause lots of disasters and even then, when they are morally not inferior but represent a heavy burden to state and nation...without their sterilization the eugenic idea of the cleansing of the whole nation from its inferior elements can never be realized."[1]

It was precisely this sort of thinking and advocacy that inspired the 1935 formation of the Society of German Neurologists and Psychiatrists, which became the GSPN in 1955. Even today, Professor Gaupp is featured among the roster of distinguished members and past presidents published by the GSPN. A cursory look at this list reveals it to be a veritable Who's Who of eugenicists and racial hygienists, many of whom played major roles in the Nazi excesses that culminated in genocide and global war.

It is chillingly revealing to review some of the past presidents of the GSPN and it's predecessor organization.

ERNST RÜDIN (1874-1952): PRESIDENT FROM 1935 TO 1945

As noted above, Ernst Rüdin was among the psychiatrists who were most intimately involved with both the Nazi movement, and the Third Reich's criminal programs that were based upon psychiatric theories. Long before then, however, in 1904, Rüdin founded an organization called "Archiv für Rassen- und Gesellschaftspsychologie" ("Archive for Racial and Social Psychology"). It was an ignoble start to a malevolent career. Rüdin's resume is virtually an indictment for crimes against mankind.

Rüdin was appointed a full Professor of Psychiatry (1916,

Ernst Rüdin—"Father" of Racial Hygiene.

then Director, 1919), of the Department of Genealogy of the "Deutsches Forschunginstitut für Psychiatrie" ("German Research Institute for Psychiatry") in Munich. In 1933, he was promoted within the Third Reich to Commissioner of the "Deutsche Gesellschaft für Rassenhygiene" ("German Society for Racial Hygiene") and named Chairman of the Advisory Board of experts on population and racial politics.

On his 65th birthday in 1939, Rüdin was awarded the Goethe Medal for Art and Science by Adolf Hitler himself. Five years later, the Führer personally honored Rüdin with a bronze medal embossed with a swastika and with the honorary title of "Pioneer of Racial Hygiene."[2] Rüdin, besides being a racial hygenicist and the principal drafter of the Sterilization Act, was also the co-author of the treatise which was relied upon as the Nazis' justification for the Law for the Prevention of Genetically Diseased Children. His co-author, Falk Ruttke, was also the author of the Nuremberg Race Act, which essentially legalized the persecution of Jews.

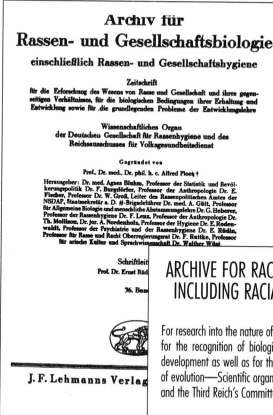

ARCHIVE FOR RACIAL AND SOCIAL BIOLOGY INCLUDING RACIAL AND SOCIAL HYGIENE

For research into the nature of race and society and its interrelationships, for the recognition of biological conditions for their conservation and development as well as for the fundamental problems about the theory of evolution—Scientific organ of the German Society for Racial Hygiene and the Third Reich's Committee for the National Health Service

Founded by
Prof., Dr. med., Dr. phil. h. c. Alfred Ploetz

Publisher: Dr. med. Agnes Bluhm; Professor of Statistics and Population Policy, Dr. F. Burgdorfer; Professor of Anthropology, Dr. E. Fischer; Professor Dr. W. Gross, Director of the Racial Politics Department of the National Socialistic (Nazi) Party; State Secretary (retired), SS Brigade Leader Dr. med. A. Gutt; Professor of Biology and Theory of the Origin of the Human Species, Dr. G. Heberger; Professor of Racial Hygiene, Dr. F. Lenz; Professor of Anthropology, Dr. Th. Mollison; Dr. jur. A. Nordenholz; Professor of Hygiene, Dr. E. Rodenwaldt; Professor of Psychiatry and Racial Hygiene, Dr. E. Rüdin; Professor of Race and Law, Senior Executive Director, Dr. F. Rattke; Professor of Aryan Culture and Linguistics, Dr. Walther Wüst

Editorship
Prof. Dr. Ernst Rüdin, Munich

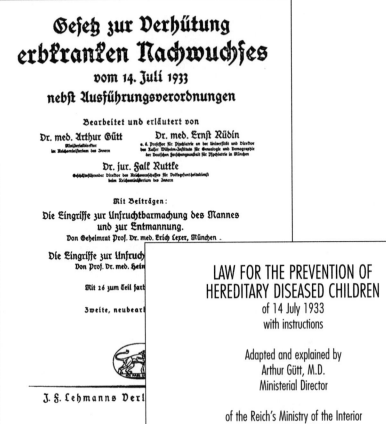

**Gesetz zur Verhütung
erbkranken Nachwuchses**
vom 14. Juli 1933
nebst Ausführungsverordnungen

Bearbeitet und erläutert von

Dr. med. Arthur Gütt
Ministerialdirektor
im Reichsministerium des Innern

Dr. med. Ernst Rüdin
o. ö. Professor für Psychiatrie an der Universität und Direktor
des Kaiser Wilhelm-Instituts für Genealogie und Demographie
der Deutschen Forschungsanstalt für Psychiatrie in München

Dr. jur. Falk Ruttke
Geschäftsführender Direktor des Reichsausschusses für Volksgesundheitsdienst
beim Reichsministerium des Innern

Mit Beiträgen:

Die Eingriffe zur Unfruchtbarmachung des Mannes
und zur Entmannung.
Von Geheimrat Prof. Dr. med. Erich Lexer, München .

Die Eingriffe zur Unfruch...
Von Prof. Dr. med. Hein...

Mit 26 zum Teil farb...

Zweite, neubear...

J. F. Lehmanns Verl...

LAW FOR THE PREVENTION OF HEREDITARY DISEASED CHILDREN
of 14 July 1933
with instructions

Adapted and explained by
Arthur Gütt, M.D.
Ministerial Director

of the Reich's Ministry of the Interior
Ernst Rüdin, M.D.
Professor of Psychiatry at the University and Director of the
Kaiser Wilhelm Institute for Genealogy and Demography of the
German Research Institute of Psychiatry in Munich

Falk Ruttke, J.D.
Executive Director of the Reich's Committee of National Health
Services at the Reich's Ministry of the Interior
with the contributions of:

The Intervention for the Sterilization and Castration of Men
by Privy Counselor, Erich Lexer, M.D., Munich
The Intervention for the Sterilization of Women
by Heinrich Eymer, M.D., Munich
with 26 illustrations, partially colored
second revised edition

Aufgaben und Ziele der Deutschen Gesellschaft für Rassenhygiene.
Von Prof. Ernst Rüdin.

Die Gründung der Deutschen Gesellschaft für Rassenhygiene geht zurück auf das Jahr 1905, als Alfred Ploetz, der Begründer der deutschen Rassenhygiene und heute Ehrenmitglied der Gesellschaft, zusammen mit wenigen Freunden, zu denen auch ich gehörte, den ersten Versuch in Deutschland wagte, dem rassenhygienischen Gedanken durch eine Vereinsorganisation weitere Verbreitung zu verschaffen. Aber trotz unserer beständigen Anstrengungen, die Öffentlichkeit darauf aufmerksam zu machen, daß endlich auch für die Rasse etwas zu geschehen habe, trotz unserer Hinweise schon am Anfang dieses Jahrhunderts, auf den kulturschöpferischen Wert der nordischen Rasse, auf die ungeheure Gefahr des Sinkens der deutschen Geburtenrate und auf die naturwidrige Aufpäppelung alles Erbschwachen, Kranken und Minderwertigen, konnten unsere Ideen keine Anerkennung bei den maßgebenden Stellen erzielen. Wenn es unserer geistigen Bewegung auch gelang, im Stillen und ganz allmählich die Köpfe und Herzen unserer besten Deutschen zu gewinnen, so sorgten doch die bekannten damals herrschenden Strömungen dafür, daß keine rassenhygienischen Maßnahmen getroffen werden durften. Die Bedeutung der Rassenhygiene ist in Deutschland erst durch das politische Werk Adolf Hitlers allen aufgeweckten Deutschen offenbar geworden, und erst durch ihn wurde endlich unser mehr als dreißigjähriger Traum zur Wirklichkeit, Rassenhygiene in die Tat umsetzen zu können.

Die gegenwärtige Kundgebung soll darum unserm Führer den tiefen Dank dafür vor aller Welt zu[...]

Heute ist die Bahn f[...]
ersten Schrittchen auf ih[...]
bis wesentliche Ziele de[...]
Modesache, sondern sie [...]
Höhe bleibt. Und diesen [...]
rassenhygienischen Gesi[...]
werk, all dem geistigen [...]
schicksalsbestimmende [...]
und mit der Gesetzgebu[...]
hygiene, die durch das V[...]
schen Sinne neu organis[...]

THE AIMS AND PURPOSES OF THE GERMAN SOCIETY FOR RACIAL HYGIENE

by Prof. Ernst Rüdin

The formation of the German Society for Racial Hygiene goes back to 1905, when Alfred Ploetz, the founder of German racial hygiene and today an honorary member of the society, set out with a few friends (to whom I also belong) to create a wide dissemination of the ideas and principles of racial hygiene. Despite our continual attempts to call the public's attention to the fact that something had to be done for our race, and despite our revealing the degenerating quality of the Nordic race which had been going on since the beginning of this century, the immense danger of the declining birthrate and the unnatural nursing back to health of the genetically weak, sick and inferior, our ideas could not gain recognition at the upper echelons of government. Even when our spiritual movement succeeded in quietly and gradually winning over hearts and minds of our best Germans, the powers that be ensured that no racial hygiene measures could be taken. Only through the Führer did our dream of over thirty years, that of applying racial hygiene to society, become a reality.

This present proclamation will therefore express our deepest thanks to our Führer in front of the entire world.

Today, racial hygiene has been given the green light. Yet we have only made a few small steps and there are many, many more steps to go until the essential goals of racial hygiene are attained. Racial hygiene is not a fad—it has to accompany a nation constantly so that it constantly remains at the top. In conjunction with other organizations and legislation, the mapping out of the future path for our nation and our race according to racial hygienical viewpoints, the furnishing of the nation with all the tools and mental and moral provisions that it needs for its fateful journey is the duty of the German Association for Racial Hygiene, which, due to the efforts of the Minister of the Reich, Dr. Frick, stands here newly organized.

94

It is difficult to overstate Rüdin's influence on the Third Reich's atrocities. It was through Rüdin that psychiatry enjoyed what amounted to carte blanche to research, develop and even practice its most deadly and inhumane theories and methods. Even after the war, German psychiatry never bothered to distance itself from either its brutal legacy or its pioneers of racial hygiene, among them, Rüdin. Certainly there has been sporadic criticism of Rüdin within his own community, but it pales in comparison to praise for his "following his own convictions in 'racial hygienic' measures, cooperating with the Nazis as a psychiatrist and helping them legitimize their aims through pertinent legislation."

It would be bad enough if the foregoing quotation was from Nazi-era propaganda, lionizing Rüdin as a fine mind and a good soldier. However, it was written in February 1992. The prestigious Max Planck Institute included this acknowledgement in the publication "75 Years of the Max Planck Institute for Psychiatry, Munich 1917-1992."

If he were alive to read this 1992 praise, Rüdin might have responded much as he did to the GSPN in March, 1939:

"It should be noted first of all that it was above all the psychiatrist who pointed out to the state and the party the immense genetic dangers that certain mentally and neurotically sick people represented to the future of our nation, and it is a great achievement by the German state and its people that they did not close their eyes to this insight but proceeded vigorously to combat this danger."[3]

ERNST KRETSCHMER (1888-1964): PRESIDENT FROM 1948 TO 1951

Prominent in both the pre- and postwar psychiatric communities, Ernst Kretschmer was renowned internationally for his research regarding "constitutional biology," a subset of psychiatric eugenics that studied the build of the body and any conclusions to be drawn from it. Kretschmer coined terms like "leptosome," "pyknic" and "athletic" to classify types of human beings. He also developed the Kretschmer-Hohn Test for college students.[4] Kretschmer was a student and disciple of Professor Robert Gaupp, Sr., the patriarch of organized German psychiatry. He was also a military district psychiatrist and an active racial hygienist.

In 1934, Dr. Kretschmer spoke out pointedly on what he perceived to be the need to sterilize the feeble-minded, whom he depicted as "most

TIMETABLE: DR. ERNST KRETSCHMER

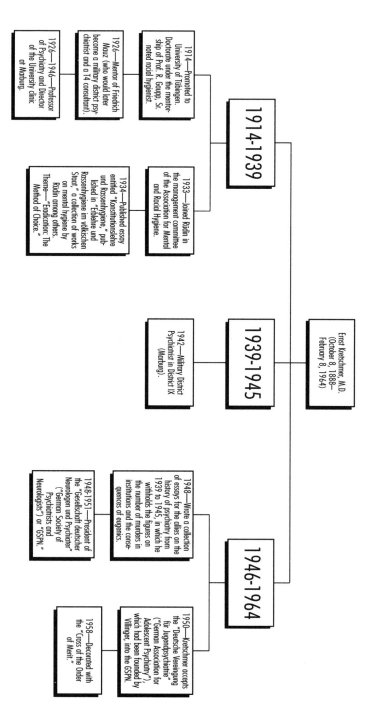

Ernst Kretschmer, M.D.
(October 8, 1888–
February 8, 1964)

1914-1939

1914—Promoted to University of Tübingen. Doctorate under the mentorship of Prof. R. Gaupp, Sr., noted racial hygienist.

1926—Mentor of Friedrich Mauz (who would later become a military district psychiatrist and a T4 consultant).

1926–1946—Professor of Psychiatry and Director of the University clinic at Marburg.

1933—Joined Rüdin in the management committee of the Association for Mental and Racial Hygiene.

1934—Published essay entitled "Konstitutionslehre und Rassenhygiene," published in "Erblehre und Rassenhygiene im völkischen Staat," a collection of works on mental hygiene by Rüdin among others. Theme—"Eradication: The Method of Choice."

1939-1945

1942—Military District Psychiatrist in District IX (Marburg).

1946-1964

1948—Wrote a collection of essays for the allies on the history of psychiatry from 1939 to 1945, in which he withholds the figures on the number of murders in institutions and the consequences of eugenics.

1948-1951—President of the "Gesellschaft deutscher Neurologen und Psychiater" ("German Society of Psychiatrists and Neurologists") or "GSPN."

1950—Kretschmer accepts the "Deutsche Vereinigung für Jugendpsychiatrie" ("German Association for Adolescent Psychiatry"), which had been founded by Villinger, into the GSPN.

1958—Decorated with the "Cross of the Order of Merit."

96

dangerous for procreation." According to Kretschmer, they: "can best and safely be handled by the simple sterilization process... (this is) therefore the greatest and hygienically most worthwhile course of action."[5]

On top of this, Kretschmer also included "drunkenness, criminality and epilepsy" within the "more or less unspecified lot of degenerations" which are the "actual great sphere of action for eventual eradication."[6] Kretschmer even recommended that "the healthy, nervous and psychopathic" undergo the especially careful examination of a medical marriage counselor trained in "constitutional biology."

Kretschmer was also active in the organized psychiatry of the Nazi regime.

"On July 29 of [1933], there was a session of the managing committee of the 'Deutscher Verein für Psychiatrie' ('German Association for Psychiatry') at which Kretschmer participated. A closer link was formed between the psychotherapy movement, the 'Verband für Mental Hygiene und Rassenhygiene' ('Association for Mental and Racial Hygiene') and the 'Deutscher Verein für Psychiatrie.' Voted into the management committee were Rüdin, Kretschmer and Roemer; Rüdin was elected vice-chairman."[7]

Before the end of the war, "Zeitschrift für psychische Hygiene" ("Journal for Mental Hygiene"), edited by Kretschmer and Rüdin among others, was on its last legs. In actuality, though, the journal was a supplement to the official publication of the Society of German Neurologists and Psychiatrists, so Kretschmer's editorial duties lent him prominence and prestige among his colleagues.

While it has never been substantiated that Kretschmer was directly involved with the euthanasia program, he must have observed what was happening but neither spoke out for nor against it. In either event, his basic attitude toward racial hygiene suggests that he had no reason to protest.[8]

In a collection of essays he wrote on what psychiatry did between 1939 and 1945, which was compiled after the war on the order of the Allies, Kretschmer did not mention a word about the killings in the institutes.[9] Years later, however, in a 1966 published work called *Mensch und Lebensgrund* (*Men and Reason for Living*), he wrote rather hypocritically:

"An odd teachings of the race...tried...with extremely ruthless methods to conquer the soul of the German people. Appearing under a seemingly scientific cover, it stands out…in sharp contrast to the results of thorough and serious research in this field."[10]

That cryptic observation raises several critical questions: Just what was it that appeared "under a seemingly scientific cover?" And who is "engaged in serious research in this field?" Why was Kretschmer denouncing racial hygiene as if he had nothing to do with it, and with the same passion with which he once espoused the "eradication?"

Kretschmer managed to raise serious doubts about his own sincerity when only a few pages later he writes:

"That the genes inherited from one's forefathers must harmonize healthily…(this) corresponds correctly to practical experience. Therefore in many modern nations…(there are) so-called eugenical movements …which using careful research want to prevent the rampant increase of genetic diseases.…Well, that is very commendable."[11]

A few pages later, Kretschmer shares with the reader how this prevention process is accomplished. As you read the following words remember that psychiatrists regard Dr. Kretschmer as one of the preeminent psychiatrists of the twentieth century:

"In the breeding of genius in a legal manner, we should first look at incest, which enriches certain special skills, and then crossbreeding, which brings about mental expansion and increases the resiliency of the personality. The best results do not therefore occur through constant incest and even less so through continued random mixing, but quite obviously through a certain rhythm in the change of incest and crossbreeding."[12]

WERNER VILLINGER (1887-1961): PRESIDENT FROM 1952 TO 1954

One of mental hygiene's most outspoken advocates, Werner Villinger is one of psychiatry's most controversial figures both during and after the Third Reich. Dr. Villinger was the chief physician of the Bodelschwingh Institutes in Bethel from 1934 to 1939 and a professor at Breslau from 1938 to 1945, while also serving as a consulting physician in Military District VIII. After the war, he was a professor at the University of Marburg from 1946 to 1955. In 1953 he received the Cross of the Order of Merit from the Federal Republic of Germany and an honorary Doctor of Law degree from the University of Hamburg.

On May 1, 1937, while serving as an associate judge of the High Court

TIMETABLE: DR. WERNER VILLINGER

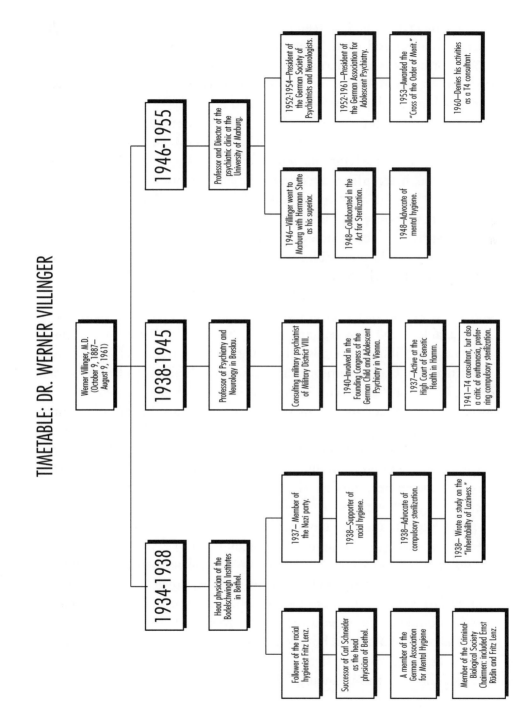

Werner Villinger, M.D. (October 9, 1887 – August 9, 1961)

1934-1938

Head physician of the Bodelschwingh Institutes in Bethel.

- 1937— Member of the Nazi party.
- 1938—Supporter of racial hygiene.
- 1938—Advocate of compulsory sterilization.
- 1938— Wrote a study on the "Inheritability of Laziness."

- Follower of the racial hygienist Fritz Lenz.
- Successor of Carl Schneider as the head physician of Bethel.
- A member of the German Association for Mental Hygiene
- Member of the Criminal-Biological Society Chairman: included Ernst Rüdin and Fritz Lenz.

1938-1945

Professor of Psychiatry and Neurology in Breslau.

Consulting military psychiatrist of Military District VIII.

1940—Involved in the Founding Congress of the German Child and Adolescent Psychiatry in Vienna.

1937—Active at the High Court of Genetic Health in Hamm.

1941—T4 consultant, but also a critic of euthanasia, preferring compulsory sterilization.

1946-1955

Professor and Director of the psychiatric clinic at the University of Marburg.

- 1952-1954—President of the German Society of Psychiatrists and Neurologists.
- 1952-1961—President of the German Association for Adolescent Psychiatry.
- 1953—Awarded the "Cross of the Order of Merit."
- 1960—Denies his activities as a T4 consultant.

- 1946—Villinger went to Marburg with Hermann Stutte as his superior.
- 1948—Collaborated in the Act for Sterilization.
- 1948—Advocate of mental hygiene.

99

for Genetic Health in Hamm and Breslau, Villinger joined the Nazi party. That was a year and a half after the time that official records show that 2,675 notifications for sterilization were reported, 600 applications for sterilization were filed and 460 sterilizations were actually performed all under Villinger's direction.[13] Villinger also relied upon the guidelines of the Sterilization Act to justify sterilizing what he deemed to be "asocials."[14] As a military district psychiatrist in 1941, Villinger is listed in official Nazi records as a T4 consultant and thus was involved in the euthanasia program, although according to witnesses, he had doubts about it:

Villinger became a T4 consultant in March, 1941. He participated in this with hesitation. According to T4 staff member Meumann, "the registration forms that were processed by him came back to us with considerable delays." In addition, Villinger came "almost exclusively" to the conclusion that "the sick are not to be sent for extermination."[15]

Villinger was certainly not as convinced about the necessity for euthanasia as Max de Crinis or Carl Schneider, yet he certainly made himself available to the Nazi regime to do as they asked in T4.

Reviewing Villinger's published writings, we also learn that it is folly to think that psychiatry's antisocial attitudes were limited to the Nazi era. Villinger's prose teems with degrading characterizations of the human race. As a child and adolescent psychiatrist, Villinger leaves little doubt about his true feelings regarding his young patients when he refers to them (as late as in 1948) as "human material." Those under his care who were impaired by environmental influences were, to him, the "flotsam and jetsam of the neglected and dissociated youth." Or more simply, "social troublemakers" and "psychopaths."[16]

By all accounts and appearances, Villinger was such an elitist that he represents the practical antithesis of a humanitarian. Given his preference, sterilization would have been practiced on a grand scale in Germany. The handicapped would have been rendered infertile, down "to the last man, and the last woman," thus causing their physical impairments to be "eradicated" as burdens of the genotype.[17] Moreover, what "hesitations" he may have had about euthanasia, he was involved in its practice, and acts such as that are far more revealing than any supposed theoretical hesitations.

After the war, the Hamburg Medical Faculty described Villinger as follows:

Nationalsozialistische Deutsche Arbeiterpartei

Gauleitung   Weßfalen-Süd

Gaupersonalamt, Hauptst. III.

Bochum, den 17.7.37.

Politisches Führungszeugnis!

Streng vertraulich!

Pg. (n) _____ Professor Villinger _____ Beruf: _____ Dr. med. _____
Wohnung: _____ Bethel bei Bielefeld _____
Mitglied einer Gliederung _____ seit: _____

Über Obengenannte (n) ist in politischer Hinsicht Nachteiliges nicht bekannt geworden. Er — sie bietet die Gewähr, sich auch in Zukunft für den national-sozialistischen Staat einzusetzen.

NATIONAL SOCIALIST GERMAN LABOR PARTY

SERVICE RECORD
strictly confidential

Civilian: Professor Villinger Profession: Doctor of Medicine
Address: Bethel near Bielefeld
Member of an organization: ___ ___ since ___ ___

Nothing negative with regard to politics has become known about the above mentioned. He/she also pledges to support the Nazi state in the future.

Heil Hitler!
(stamp and signature)

"Above all as the leading adolescent psychiatrist in the country, it has seldom been mentioned that Villinger is also one of the most active advocates for the application and broad-minded interpretation of the Sterilization Act and as a consultant he contributed also to adult euthanasia."[18]

Villinger was prominently involved in the design of the postwar Sterilization Act that was enacted with the approval of the American occupation forces by the Health Committee of the Stuttgart Council of the Länder.

Villinger's long-term connections with Hamburg did not end, even after his appointment to his professorship at Marburg in 1946. On July 20, 1959, the faculty of the Hamburg University Department of Jurisprudence awarded him an honorary doctorate because Villinger had contributed "important ideas on how to organize care for the mentally ill and other persons who need assistance."[19]

Villinger's name arose again in *Der Spiegel* in 1961, in a report referring to the consulting he had done for T4 during the Third Reich.[20] In an angry response, Villinger wrote to the editor:

"The attempt to contribute to the investigation of this horrible event is very much appreciated. You did, however, make an error when you listed me as an active participant in this process. This was not possible in view of my well-known professional attitude toward euthanasia, in view of my activity over the past decades as chief physician in Bethel and my basic personal attitude, especially since I myself have been affected by this process in my family."[21]

Villinger's denials did not stop there. In front of prosecutors, Villinger also denied any involvement in T4. That denial was, of course, nonsense.

On August 9, 1961, while walking near Innsbruck, Villinger fell down a mountain and was found dead. He was in Innsbruck to preside over the seventh conference of the German Society for Adolescent Psychiatry.

In summary, the least we can say is that Villinger was guilty of remaining generally silent about the atrocities committed by the Nazis both during and after the war, although records and some witnesses attribute greater involvement in the atrocities to him. By contrast, Fritz von Bodelschwingh was one of the few directors of an institute who actively resisted the Nazi terror programs. He even went so far as to petition the top Nazi authorities to save his patients from extermination. Unfortunately, he was successful only to a small degree. When Bodelschwingh sought Villinger out as an ally, he was met with deaf ears. This is documented in their correspondence which is quoted by Achim Thorn among others in the book *Medizin unterm Hakenkreuz* (*Medicine under the Swastika*).

JÜRG ZUTT (1893-1980): PRESIDENT FROM 1954 TO 1956

Jürg Zutt, a university professor, cannot be accused of any connections to Nazi psychiatry. In fact, just the opposite is true. It is Zutt's straightforward statement of his position that thoroughly impeaches the psychiatric excuse that the doctors had no choice but to succumb to Hitler's will and carry out his evil programs.

In an article which appeared in the August 1942 edition of the *Zentralblatt für die gesamte Neurologie und Psychiatrie*, a publication of which he was the editor-in-chief, Dr. Zutt was highly critical of Nazi psychiatry:

"When one nowadays…views that psychiatry, definitely not rarely, sees certain people as inferior and superfluous, and degrades the genetically sick and very often the mentally ill too, and even advocates the extermination of difficult cases…this is a great injustice."[22]

Publishing such sentiments in 1942 in an official scholarly organ that was strictly monitored by the censors of the Third Reich was an act of courage, not to mention a rare display of honesty and integrity within Dr. Zutt's professional community. He was the human evidence that there were opposing voices active during Nazi Germany who were not reticent about lodging their protests against the psychiatric practices of the state. Dr. Zutt's example plainly refutes the favorite justification of the psychiatric war criminals that their obedience was enforced by the threat of execution. By his resistance to Nazi politics, Dr. Zutt is proof that the psychiatrists' self-forgiving assertions were lies.

FRIEDRICH MAUZ (1900-1979): PRESIDENT FROM 1957 TO 1958

In contrast to Dr. Zutt, his immediate predecessor, Friedrich Mauz was a former Military District Psychiatrist, a T4 consultant and a strictly traditional mental hygienist. This is not surprising, since his mentor was Ernst Kretschmer, under whom he became a university lecturer in 1928.

Mauz never deviated from the paths blazed by the Nazi eugenicists. In a commemorative article published in the psychiatric periodical *Der*

Nervenarzt in 1980, tribute was paid to the accomplishments of Robert Gaupp, Kretschmer and Mauz. Years later, in Mauz's obituary, psychiatrist Rainer Tolle refers to Mauz's tenure as a T4 consultant as follows:

"In 1932 Mauz and Kretschmer were called to Bern. If this plan had not fallen apart, Mauz might have been spared a few troubles during the following years and the war, which also left a stain on his record." [23]

Notwithstanding that little nugget of understatement, the fact remains that Mauz was one of the T4 psychiatrists, and yet he died in 1979, highly honored and esteemed within his profession. Klee commented:

"In the list of consultants for the T4...some famous people are recorded. Besides professors Heyde and Nitsche, we can also find the names of professors Polisch and Panse (Bonn), Carl Schneider (Heidelberg), Erich Straub (Kiel), Friedrich Mauz (Konigsberg), Berthold Kihn (Jena), professors Zucker and (probably only for a short while) Reisch, while Villinger (Breslau), as we have seen, was involved for much longer." [24]

In 1948—only three years after the end of his tenure as an accomplice to the Nazi regime—Mauz was the German delegate to the Third International Congress of Mental Hygiene in London. It was during this congress, that the World Federation for Mental Health was founded as a successor organization to the International Committee for Mental Hygiene. The work of the World Federation for Mental Health will be examined later in this book.

Psychiatry in postwar Germany has never critically assessed its role in the Third Reich's horrors. Indeed, to gloss over the past and avoid confronting the truth, psychiatrists would not talk about "euthanasia," but instead would use the euphemism "disinfection." Be that as it may, "disinfectors" continued to occupy niches of distinction in psychiatric circles long after the war, and Mauz is a primary example. Here is an excerpt from an article that appeared in the *Münsterische Zeitung* on May 17, 1980:

"The medical faculty of the University of Münster commemorates today their member of long-standing and Director of the University Clinic, Prof. Dr. Robert Friedrich Mauz....He has helped, as hardly any other psychiatrist of his generation has, to shape the thoughts and actions of German medicine....(Let us) then pay tribute to the special accomplishments of Friedrich Mauz." [25]

This is the same Friedrich Mauz who was intimately involved in the development of a law "ending the suffering" of the incurably ill. Klee establishes this in "Was sir taten—was sie wurden: Ärzte, Juristen und andere Beteiligte am Kranken- oder Judenmord" ("What They Did and What Became of Them: The Physicians, Lawyers and Other Participants in the Murder of the Sick and the Jews").[26] The final session of the planning of the law took place in August 1940. The resulting draft no longer exists, but is documented by a collection of several statements by the participants. The physicians involved were mostly concerned with finding an incontrovertible legal basis for euthanasia. Hitler rejected the draft and left it in a drawer. Legalization of euthanasia was probably scheduled for sometime after Germany had won the war. However, legalization would have brought with it a lot of unnecessary public relations complications that the psychiatrists would have preferred to avoid. In the end, then, the psychiatric murders continued unhindered and outside of the law.

That legacy is among "the special accomplishments of Friedrich Mauz."

HANS BÜRGER-PRINZ (1897-1976): PRESIDENT FROM 1959 TO 1960

As noted earlier, Bürger-Prinz was the military district psychiatrist who was in charge of the Neuropathy Clinic in Hamburg from 1937 to 1970. While the dimensions of his role in the euthanasia movement are obscure, it is certain that he knew about euthanasia. It is also clear that Dr. Bürger-Prinz never distanced himself from what happened during the Nazi era. According to a 1988 *Der Spiegel* article:

"No academic propagandist of racial hygiene, compulsory sterilization and extermination has been brought to justice. Hans Bürger-Prinz, who had strongly admonished his psychiatric colleagues in 1935 to 'register the hereditarily afflicted' when they were still children before fertility in order to 'pick them out and eliminate them from procreation,' became a professor in Hamburg."[27]

Bürger-Prinz was a student of Paul Schröder, the founder of the Deutsche Gesellschaft für Kinder- und Jugendpsychiatrie (German Society for Child and Adolescent Psychiatry). After Hitler had given his authorization to perform euthanasia, Bürger-Prinz spoke with the Minister of Health from Hamburg about what he planned to do:

"One evening, during the time of the Poland campaign, the Hamburg psychiatry professor Hans Bürger-Prinz chatted a little while with the Hamburg

Psychiatrische und Nervenklinik
der Hanfischen Universität

Hamburg 22, den 7. April 1942.
Eingang: Elbeckal
Fernspr.: 28 10 01

Akten-Nr. _____

Es wird gebeten, alle Zuschriften nur
an die Direktion zu richten und dabei
obige Akten-Nr. anzugeben.
Bei Anfragen Rückporto beifügen.

Herrn

Oberstarzt Prof. Dr. Wuth
Militärärztliche Akademie

Berlin NW 40
Scharnhorststr.35

Betr.:Schüttelzitterer oder Kriegsneurotiker.

Sehr verehrter Herr Kollege !

Ich habe bis jetzt hier nur einen Fall von
Schüttelzittern gesehen, der auf keinerlei Therapie (Elektrizi-
tät, Cardiazolschocks) angesprochen hat, sondern in demselben
Ausmaße wie bisher weiter schüttelt. Ich erwischte ihn auf
einer Heeresentlassungsstelle und ließ ihn hier nach Hamburg
bringen, wo ich ihn in einem Lazarett einem sehr guten Psychiater
und Neurologen, der auch lange an der Front war, Oberarzt
Dr. Müller, anvertraut habe. Wir wollen in den nächsten Tagen
versuchen, ihn in eine Dauerschlafbehandlung zu nehmen, oder ihn
für therapeutische Maßnahmen geeigneter und reifer zu
machen. Be...

Psychiatric and Neurological Clinic
of Hanseatic University Hamburg,

the 7th of April 1942

Document # _____

Assistant Medical Director, Prof. Dr. Wuth
Medical Military Academy
Berlin, NW 40
Scharnhorststrasse 35

Re: Tremblers and war neurotics

My most distinguished colleague!

Up until now, I have seen only one case where a trembler did not respond to any kind of therapy (electricity, Cardiazol shock) but continued to tremble as much as before. I found him in
an army discharge office and had him brought to me here in Hamburg, where I entrusted him
to a military hospital with a very good psychiatrist and neurologist, Assistant Medical Director
Dr. Müller, who had also been at the front for a long time. In the next few days, we wanted
to try to give him deep sleep treatment in order to make him more suitable for psychotherapeutic treatment. As with others I have seen, I very strictly confronted them with the choice
either of recovering or continuing to undergo ruthless punishment for feigning neurosis. With
further therapeutic treatment using the usual methods, they would recover well enough (considering that they were dead-weight characters to begin with) to rejoin our civilian work force
for our utilization. I am also of the opinion that one should become quite ruthless if all therapeutic attempts should fail. A transfer back to civilian life represents, after all, just a way out
that could turn from a small trickle into a big stream. I believe that one should not give a
damn about patients' complaints about our methods of treatment. Whatever happens, we can
always count on the readiness of the therapists to stand up for their practices. I know many
suitable men in the military district who would do this, even though, as in any field, the sheer
workload can gradually overload the individual. I could name Assistant Medical Director Dr.
Löffler, assistant (resident) physician Dr. Hoffmann, Reserve Hospital XI, Assistant Medical
Director Dr. Müller, Reserve Hospital V, Hamburg.

With my best respects, I remain
As always
Your most humble servant
(Prof. Bürger-Prinz)

Oberstarzt Prof.Dr.Wuth
Beratender Psychiater
beim Heeres-Sanitätsinspekteur
Dienstliche Militärärztliche Anschrift
Nr. 1371/42

Berlin NW 40, den 24.April 1942
Scharnhorststr. 35

Herrn
Stabsarzt Prof.Dr.Bürger-Prinz
Psychiatrische und Nervenklinik
der Hansischen Universität
H a m b u r g 22

Betr.: Schüttelzitterer oder Kriegsneurotiker.

Sehr geehrter Herr Stabsarzt !

Ich bestätige mit Dank den Empfang Ihres Schreibens vom 7.d.M.
und ersehe daraus, daß einzelne Fälle von Schüttelzitterern im Wehrkreis
X behandelt werden können. Was etwaige Beschwerden der betreffenden zu
Behandelnden

Assistant Medical Director Prof. Dr. Wuth
Consulting Psychiatrist
Berlin NW 40,   the 24th of April, 1942
at the armed forces inspection Scharnhorststrasse 35
Agency of the Medical Military Academy
No. 1371/42
Document # _____
Capt. Prof. Dr. Bürger-Prinz
Psychiatric and Neurological Clinic
of the University of Hamburg
Hamburg 22
Re: Tremblers and War Neurotics
Most Distinguished Captain!
With great thanks I would like to confirm the receipt of your letter of the 7th of this month. I have gathered from it that individual cases of tremblers can be treated in Military District X. With regard to eventual complaints by the patients in question, the situation is not as simple as you might think. The O.K.W. (high command of the army) has issued orders about allowing "interventions." Circumstances are also different than during the last war—the complaints are now forwarded through party channels to much higher authorities who are not physicians, and then one is forced to come up with specific statements.
Strictness certainly applies, but among war neurotics there certainly are only a few fakers since, once the reflex has set in, it can no longer be suppressed voluntarily.
If you talk about "feigning neuroses" to the judges, the patient can be sentenced to death according to paragraph 83 of the MStGB (Military Criminal Law Book), despite the fact that he suffers from a curable disturbance.

Heil Hitler
I am
quite humbly yours
(signature)
(Correspondence between Hans Bürger-Prinz and Head Physician Prof. Dr. Wuth in 1942)

Minister of Health after a reception in the Hotel Atlantic in the presence of five or six of his colleagues. It was here that the physicians found out that the patients of Hamburg would soon be picked up for 'euthanasia.' Bürger-Prinz exclaimed to the Minister of Health: 'Just look at it from a practical side!' He had thought that getting this done would be impossible."[28]

No objections or countermeasures by Bürger-Prinz are known to have been lodged or undertaken.

In 1951, Bürger-Prinz—along with Villinger and others—participated in the first postwar meetings of the "Europaische Liga für psychische Hygiene" ("European League for Mental Hygiene"). It is interesting yet disturbing to note this, since we now have evidence that Bürger-Prinz, who came originally from the prewar Nazi school of racial hygiene, obviously had not been sobered by the war which had ended only six years earlier, remaining instead faithful to his philosophy and helping to carry the legacy of mental hygiene forward in an unbroken tradition to the postwar era.

Some apologists defend Bürger-Prinz, saying that he turned a blind eye toward evil and tried to repress his own Nazi past. He claimed not to have known anything about the transportation of inmates from the Hamburg asylums. He even contested that it happened at all, both in front of a Hamburg investigations committee and in his own autobiography. Klee, however, demonstrates that Bürger-Prinz was not being forthright. "Especially from Hamburg, inmates of institutes were transported *en masse* to Hadamar, Vienna, Meseritz, Tiegehof, etc. to be murdered."[29]

Here again are the words of Bürger-Prinz, uttered to the committee investigating the case of the notorious Heyde/Sawade case. In this new light, his somewhat characteristic comments give us plenty of reason to doubt the credibility of his protestations:

"With the exception of the clergyman, I do not believe that...there exists a profession in which silence plays as big a role as with us, and by this I mean silence with respect to everything....Silence is very dear to us; it is not limited to the 'legal requirement' concerning confidential medical communication...."[30]

HEINRICH KRANZ (1901-1979): PRESIDENT FROM 1961 TO 1962

As a researcher specializing in twins, Dr. Kranz generated significant research results for genetic science. Researching twins was a favorite

TIMETABLE: DR. HANS BÜRGER-PRINZ

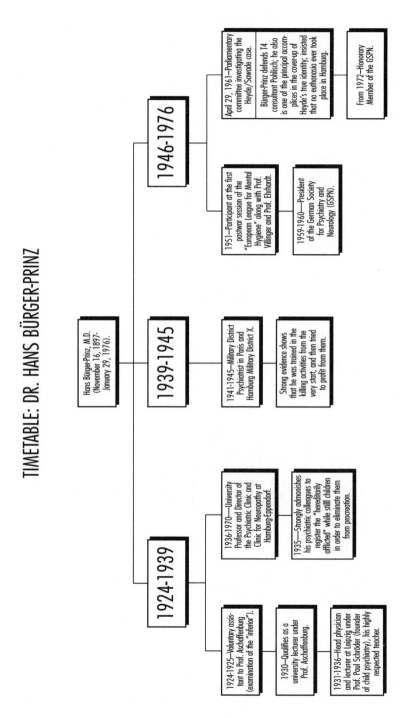

Hans Bürger-Prinz, M.D. (November 16, 1897-January 29, 1976).

1924-1939

1924-1925—Voluntary assistant to Prof. Aschaffenburg (examination of the "inferior").

1930—Qualifies as a university lecturer under Prof. Aschaffenburg.

1931-1936—Head physician and lecturer at Leipzig under Prof. Paul Schröder (founder of child psychiatry), his highly respected teacher.

1936-1970—University Professor and Director of the Psychiatric Clinic and Clinic for Neuropathy at Hamburg-Eppendorf.

1935—Strongly admonishes his psychiatric colleagues to register the "hereditarily afflicted" while still children in order to eliminate them from procreation.

1939-1945

1941-1945—Military District Psychiatrist in Paris and Hamburg Military District X.

Strong evidence shows that he was trained in the killing activities from the very start, and then tried to profit from them.

1946-1976

1951—Participant at the first postwar session of the "European League for Mental Hygiene" along with Prof. Villinger and Prof. Ehrhardt.

1959-1960—President of the German Society for Psychiatry and Neurology (GSPN).

April 29, 1961—Parliamentary committee investigating the Heyde/Sawade case.

Bürger-Prinz defends T4 consultant Pohlisch; he also is one of the principal accomplices in the cover-up of Heyde's true identity; insisted that no euthanasia ever took place in Hamburg.

From 1972—Honorary Member of the GSPN.

endeavor of genetic and racial hygienists; they were looking for insights into the transmissibility of mental illnesses from the development of monovular twins.[31] Ernst Rüdin and Hans Luxenburger in particular singled Kranz out for his work in their book *Erblehre und Rassenhygiene im völkischen Staat* (*Genetics and Racial Hygiene in the Ethnic State*).

Personally, Dr. Kranz appears to have held a far less radical genetic viewpoint than colleagues such as Rüdin and Luxenburger, as Kranz recognized that social influences were at work as well. Consequently, he was the target of criticism from hard-line racial hygienists. In the end, however, Kranz bowed to the pressure, and during World War II, he joined in the lobbying for such radical measures as dissolving the marriages of the feeble-minded, putting feeble-minded children into reformatories and enforcing compulsory sterilization laws and commitments to asylums.[32] It is impossible, therefore, to state that Kranz, even with his less radical stances, was not a solid advocate and participant in this ugly tradition of torture and death.

Sixteen years after the war, he was named president of the national society.

HANS MERGUET: PRESIDENT FROM 1963 TO 1964

Dr. Merguet was a mental hygienist before assuming the presidency of the GSPN.

"After Merguet became probably the first German psychiatrist in the postwar era to publicly endorse the resumption of mental hygiene work…in 1949…the "Deutsche Arbeitgemeinschaft für psychische Hygiene" ("German Research Foundation for Mental Hygiene") was established, which was incorporated into the WFMH (World Federation for Mental Health) during the WFMH's fifth international conference in Brussels in 1952."[33]

In addition, Merguet, while Director of the Landesanstalt Lengerich, wrote a very positive article about institutional psychiatry in which he strongly endorsed brain surgery. Merguet lamented the small role in Germany of an extremely controversial therapy called "leucotomy," a barbarous surgical procedure performed upon the white matter of the human brain:

"In some institutes it [the leucotomy] has been applied more frequently.…The high percentage of patients who became dischargeable afterwards should give us reason to rethink our position on this weighty matter."[34]

Rethink, to be sure. What really is "psychosurgery" or "leucotomy" or a "stereotactic operation?" According to experts, what we are describing is a fancy euphemism for the slaughterhouse method of modern "healers of the soul." That these procedures are not only brutal but unworkable is all too graphically illustrated by the case of Bernd L.

"The 24-year-old Bernd L. underwent brain surgery after several indecent assaults on some boys. He was not concerned about the risks to himself...He let himself be operated on in Hamburg by Prof. Dr. Dieter M. in order to be freed from his abnormal compulsion. The psychosurgeon charred, of course, part of his brain. The success was, however, only of short duration. After the surgery, Bernd L. assaulted the 10-year-old son of his neighbor, strangling him with an electric cable."[35]

In addition to being a strong and outspoken advocate of psychosurgery, Dr. Merguet fought hard against the legal provisions and measures that were designed to protect the patient from his psychiatrist.

FRIEDRICH PANSE (1899-1973): PRESIDENT FROM 1965 TO 1966

Dr. Panse was also a military district psychiatrist and a T4 consultant.

Before that, however, he was the assistant medical director at the Wittenauer Heilstatten and an associate judge at the High and Common Courts for Freedom from Hereditary Diseases, collaborating in sterilization matters with Heyde, among others. In 1935, Panse, along with Kurt Pohlisch, created the "Rheinische Provinzialinstitut für psychiatrisch-neurologische Erbforschung" ("Rheinish Provincial Institute for Psychiatric and Neurological Genetics"). He was admitted into the GSPN's predecessor group in 1937, and was present with Pohlisch at a secret euthanasia conference in Berlin. The propaganda film about euthanasia that was produced by the Reich was based on an idea by Panse, and the treatment and "cure" of war neurotics, the so-called "Pansen," was named after him.

As the war progressed, Panse came to regard more and more people with neuroses caused by the war or war-related trauma as fakers, or as he put it, with "psychopathy with the purpose of surreptitiously obtaining pensions and compensations." In other words, Panse believed that people who

TIMETABLE: DR. FRIEDRICH PANSE

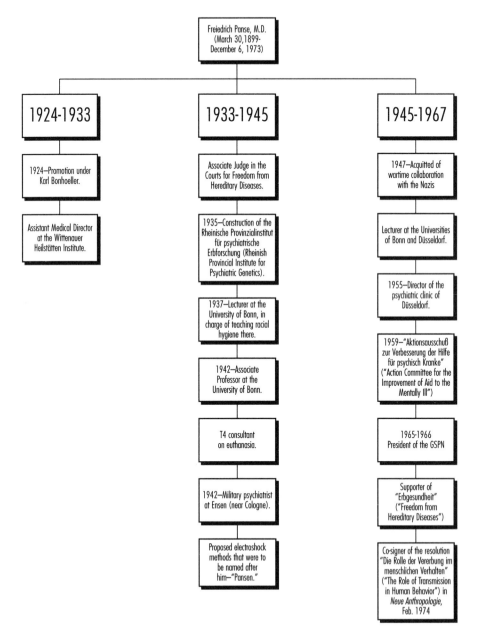

Freiedrich Panse, M.D.
(March 30,1899-
December 6, 1973)

1924-1933

1924—Promotion under Karl Bonhoeller.

Assistant Medical Director at the Wittenauer Heilstätten Institute.

1933-1945

Associate Judge in the Courts for Freedom from Hereditary Diseases.

1935—Construction of the Rheinische Provinzialinstitut für psychiatrische Erbforschung (Rheinish Provincial Institute for Psychiatric Genetics).

1937—Lecturer at the University of Bonn, in charge of teaching racial hygiene there.

1942—Associate Professor at the University of Bonn.

T4 consultant on euthanasia.

1942—Military psychiatrist at Ensen (near Cologne).

Proposed electroshock methods that were to be named after him—"Pansen."

1945-1967

1947—Acquitted of wartime collaboration with the Nazis

Lecturer at the Universities of Bonn and Düsseldorf.

1955—Director of the psychiatric clinic of Düsseldorf.

1959—"Aktionsausschuß zur Verbesserung der Hilfe für psychisch Kranke" ("Action Committee for the Improvement of Aid to the Mentally Ill")

1965-1966 President of the GSPN

Supporter of "Erbgesundheit" ("Freedom from Hereditary Diseases")

Co-signer of the resolution "Die Rolle der Vererbung im menschlichen Verhalten" ("The Role of Transmission in Human Behavior") in *Neue Anthropologie*, Feb. 1974 returned from the war mentally ill were feigning the condition for money:

"A further fact which has contributed very much to the understanding of the 'pension-neurosis' was my observation that the neuroses healed after final settlement of the compensation proceedings by monetary reimbursement."[36]

In other words, based on the observation that war neurotics showed improvement after receiving the compensation to which they were entitled, Panse came to the conclusion that such neuroses were malingering for the purpose of obtaining money.

Research also reveals Panse to have had a curious involvement in modern electrotherapy:

"On the basis of the 'Kaufmann Therapy' of World War I, Professor Panse...has developed a 'therapeutic process,' which was called in the armed forces 'to be Panse'd.' Unlike the Kaufmann Therapy, the stimulation of motor nerves with alternating currents is not done. Instead, very painful stimulations of electrical currents up to 300 milliamperes are applied to large sections of the skin with a roller."[37]

What Panse claimed to have developed was, in reality, a very old "therapy" indeed. It was a direct descendant of the "direct-current therapy" that military psychiatrists had used in World War I supposedly to cure but in reality to discipline. No one disputes that such a strong electrical current is a very traumatic experience in itself, one which shakes the entire body. The Panse certainly proved useful in neutralizing its patients, making them more manageable, and several centers were established toward that end. Friedrich Panse enjoyed such success that his military hospital became known as the foremost "treatment center for even the most obstinate cases of war neurotics."[38]

In 1947, Friedrich Panse was acquitted of all criminal charges, including collaborating in Nazi war crimes. He was never even called upon to explain his actions as a psychiatrist or to account for his antisocial methodology. In fact, he had little or no trouble advancing to some very high posts and receiving major honors after World War II. By 1959 he was an active participant in the "Aktionsausschuss zur Verbesserung der Hilfe für psychisch Kranke" ("Action Committee for the Improvement of Aid to the Mentally Ill"), and by the mid-1960s his prominence led him to the presidency of the GSPN.

HELMUTH E. EHRHARDT (1914-   ): PRESIDENT FROM 1969 TO 1971

Ehrhardt was the secretary of the GSPN from 1952 to 1968 before finally ascending to its presidency in 1969. His connections to German military psychiatry are clear and documented. In his doctoral thesis prepared in 1940 at the University of Breslau, Ehrhardt offered special tokens of gratitude to his "academic teachers," and to the military district psychiatrists Oswald Bumke, Max de Crinis and Werner Villinger.[39]

Ehrhardt also avidly advocated electroshock.

In fact, he made a name for himself within the psychiatric community because of his research into the changes in eyeball pressure during and after the administration of electroshock. Erhardt's overall findings were that under the effects of electric shock, the eyeball will sink anywhere from 25 to 55 percent below normal conditions. The "investigation was performed on 20 patients undergoing shock treatment..."[40]

In 1948, Ehrhardt went a step further when he proposed applying the "simple and technically elegant procedure" of electroshock to the ambulatory in order to empty the valuable beds in the institutes, which were in short supply after the war, and to allow more patients than ever before to "benefit" from electrical current being fired through their brains.

"In view of the lack of room as well as for general economic reasons, the ambulant treatment of certain mental forms of diseases is a question of practical importance. Electroshock gives us the opportunity to treat ambulatorily a whole lot of mental and psychological disturbances with good chances of success. The ambulatory electroshock treatment opens the way to fast and effective help for many of those who until now have been neglected or for patients who had insufficient means to be fully treated. ..."[41]

On the surface, the racial hygiene program of the Third Reich and the mental hygiene advocated by Ehrhardt and his colleagues mischaracterized their methods as "help" and their purpose as the welfare of the individual. They propagandized the barbarism they passed off as therapy. It should come as no surprise, therefore, that Ehrhardt had been an ardent apologist for the Sterilization Act of 1933. Testifying along with Villinger in 1961 before the 34th session of the Reparations Committee which was debating whether to compensate victims of compulsory sterilization, Ehrhardt voiced a strongly negative opinion:

"The Committee had invited experts to its 34th session to discuss the theme more closely. Among the attendees were Hans Nachtsheim, the psychiatrists Lauber, Villinger and Lewenstein, as well as the penologist Ehrhardt. During the day-long negotiations, Nachtsheim, supported by Villinger and Ehrhardt in particular, insisted that the Sterilization Act was legal and he justified his opinion with the standard eugenical argument...that one should take into consideration the population explosion and with it the deterioration in the quality of the human species: 'It will snowball from generation to generation—Where will we be when all is said and done?'"[42]

During this Committee's session, Ehrhardt was hopeful, even optimistic, that a new sterilization act would be enacted.

It is also noteworthy that when he was questioned by the municipal court of Marburg on July 26, 1961 about Villinger's activities as a T4 consultant, he said, "It is obvious that Prof. Villinger has given expert opinion on this matter."[43] This is the same Ehrhardt who, a decade and a half later, referred to euthanasia in the *Deutsches Ärzteblatt* (*German Medical Paper*) this way:

"With reference to euthanasia...I am no longer interested anymore in whoever, under what circumstances and to what extent, had participated in the fundamentally condemnable Nazi extermination measures."[44]

Probably the most remarkable of Ehrhardt's statements are the conclusions he drew about what happened during the Third Reich in his article "Euthanasie und Vernichtung 'lebensunwerten' Lebens" ("Euthanasia and the Extermination of Life 'Unworthy of Living'"), which appeared in the *Forum der Psychiatry*, published by none other than Hans Bürger-Prinz in 1965:

"There were attempts to obtain various professors of psychiatry as 'consultants,' which were successful only in isolated cases, and even then only partially; not counting the few who were already active in the 'leading group'.... The university clinics and their directors lay very far away from the actual front lines of the activities.... This also applies to the overwhelming majority of institutional psychiatrists...."[45]

That assertion, of course, is a blatant lie, as T4 records and reports reveal. In fact, the universities fought hard for their patients, their "demonstration material." But what would one really expect from Ehrhardt, a student of T4 psychiatrist Max de Crinis and T4 consultant Werner

TIMETABLE: PROF. HELMUTH E. EHRHARDT

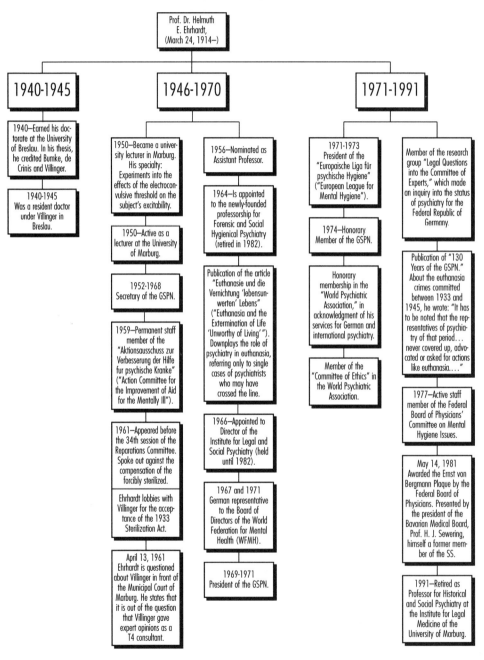

Prof. Dr. Helmuth
E. Ehrhardt,
(March 24, 1914–)

1940-1945

1940—Earned his doctorate at the University of Breslau. In his thesis, he credited Bumke, de Crinis and Villinger.

1940-1945
Was a resident doctor under Villinger in Breslau.

1946-1970

1950—Became a university lecturer in Marburg. His specialty: Experiments into the effects of the electroconvulsive threshold on the subject's excitability.

1950—Active as a lecturer at the University of Marburg.

1952-1968
Secretary of the GSPN.

1959—Permanent staff member of the "Aktionsausschuss zur Verbesserung der Hilfe fur psychische Kranke" ("Action Committee for the Improvement of Aid for the Mentally Ill").

1961—Appeared before the 34th session of the Reparations Committee. Spoke out against the compensation of the forcibly sterilized.

Ehrhardt lobbies with Villinger for the acceptance of the 1933 Sterilization Act.

April 13, 1961
Ehrhardt is questioned about Villinger in front of the Municipal Court of Marburg. He states that it is out of the question that Villinger gave expert opinions as a T4 consultant.

1956—Nominated as Assistant Professor.

1964—Is appointed to the newly-founded professorship for Forensic and Social Hygienical Psychiatry (retired in 1982).

Publication of the article "Euthanasie und die Vernichtung 'lebensunwerten' Lebens" ("Euthanasia and the Extermination of Life 'Unworthy of Living' "). Downplays the role of psychiatry in euthanasia, referring only to single cases of psychiatrists who may have crossed the line.

1966—Appointed to Director of the Institute for Legal and Social Psychiatry (held until 1982).

1967 and 1971
German representative to the Board of Directors of the World Federation for Mental Health (WFMH).

1969-1971
President of the GSPN.

1971-1991

1971-1973
President of the "Europaische Liga für psychische Hygiene" ("European League for Mental Hygiene").

1974—Honorary Member of the GSPN.

Honorary membership in the "World Psychiatric Association," in acknowledgment of his services for German and international psychiatry.

Member of the "Committee of Ethics" in the World Psychiatric Association.

Member of the research group "Legal Questions into the Committee of Experts," which made an inquiry into the status of psychiatry for the Federal Republic of Germany.

Publication of "130 Years of the GSPN." About the euthanasia crimes committed between 1933 and 1945, he wrote: "It has to be noted that the representatives of psychiatry of that period... never covered up, advocated or asked for actions like euthanasia...."

1977—Active staff member of the Federal Board of Physicians' Committee on Mental Hygiene Issues.

May 14, 1981
Awarded the Ernst von Bergmann Plaque by the Federal Board of Physicians. Presented by the president of the Bavarian Medical Board, Prof. H. J. Sewering, himself a former member of the SS.

1991—Retired as Professor for Historical and Social Psychiatry at the Institute for Legal Medicine of the University of Marburg.

Villinger—a condemnation of his own scientific mentors?

"Based on my critical analysis of the extermination action against the mentally ill between 1939 and 1945, we should note that some psychiatrists were, of course, prominently involved in the preparations and execution of the action. However, neither 'German psychiatry' nor the majority of German psychiatrists had ever accepted—even hypothetically—the demands for a 'legally limited extermination of life unworthy of living.' At the time of the extermination, 'German psychiatry' had never had the opportunity to form a free opinion, to create a binding expression of its opinion or to make the preparation of a joint statement.... Thus the question of guilt and responsibility in the extermination activities under discussion is posed much 'more collectively' to the judiciary than to psychiatry...."[46]

It would not be unfair to label Ehrhardt as one of German psychiatry's greatest apologists for the killing that psychiatry conceived, conducted and condoned both actively and passively.

RUDOLF DEGKWITZ (1920-1990): PRESIDENT FROM 1971 TO 1972

The son of the Rudolf Degkwitz, to whom we referred earlier, Degkwitz followed in his father's courageous footsteps to become one of the sharpest postwar critics of German psychiatry and its collaboration with the Nazis. During the war, the younger Degkwitz also publicly protested psychiatric crimes and was arrested and sentenced for it. Degkwitz's example buttresses that of his predecessor Dr. Zutt and his father, that those whose consciences would not allow them to do the Nazis' bidding did not have to pay for it with their lives.

HANNS HIPPIUS (1925-   ): PRESIDENT FROM 1973 TO 1974

A student of both Villinger and Helmut Selbach,[47] and the director of the University of Munich's neurological clinic, Dr. Hippius made headlines in 1989 with his "anti-fear pill." Hippius sought and was awarded a grant of a quarter of a million German marks by the German Interior Ministry to investigate the effects of anti-anxiety pills on mentally ill patients. Out of this, he contended, important conclusions were to be drawn regarding human behavior in time of catastrophe, such as nuclear war, or in time of panic, such as the deadly stampede in a Brussels soccer stadium.

Hippius' methodology was simple. First, horror movies ("Alien" and similar films) were shown to specially selected patients. Afterwards, they were given various mood-altering drugs and their effects on the subjects' psychological behavior were measured. The idea was to find a way that if an emergency occurred, the rational abilities of the army and the population to defend themselves would not be impaired by uncontrollable fear and panic reactions. That is, to identify the drugs that would make people braver. In his request to the German Federal Department for Civil Defense (an agency within the Ministry of the Interior), Hippius wrote:

"The overcoming of 'fear' plays a particularly big role in one's efficiency in extremely stressful situations.... The knowledge of the maximum stress level of the individual, as well as the psychological and somatic ability to recover quickly and sensibly respond to these dangers makes a prediction of individual fear reactions possible in threatening situations of various intensity.

"Of particular importance is a possible modification of the maximum stress level of a person through pharmacological or behavior-modifying drugs." [48]

Only after several indignant articles appeared in the media did the Minister of the Interior cut off the grants to Hippius. Hippius is even rumored to have personally ordered his staff not to say a word about anything they had done to anyone outside his office. As one publication reported: "Like opium or LSD, the pill for our civil defense will also bless us with euphoric hallucinations." [49] Happy and relaxed in the face of the apocalypse—that was the objective of "Hippi," as the Munich psychiatrist was affectionately called by his colleagues. After this debacle, Hippius' image and repute suffered mighty setbacks, especially since his activities had been conducted in such secrecy and toward such a preposterous end.

Secrecy seems to have been a significant and recurrent theme in Hippius' modus operandi. While he personally originated and instituted these studies, he intentionally tried to make it appear that an official research request by the Federal Department of Civil Defense had led to the program.

Panic research was a long-term infatuation for Hippius. His fascination with this branch of military psychiatry dates back at least to 1971, when he co-founded the Expert Committee VII on Psychobiology (a "science" of behavior in high-stress situations) within the framework of the so-called "protective commissions" of the Federal Ministry of the Interior.

Hippius' research focused on biological factors as matters of primary interest, since mood-altering chemical remedies were at the heart of the research. Fear and panic were assumed to be biochemical reactions, processes which—according to the logic of the "doctors of the soul"—could be changed by chemicals into a mood of happiness. What Hippius was essentially attempting to do was to create still another, new, illicit liaison between psychiatry and politics. [50]

That Hippius took on such major studies is hardly surprising. He was (and is) a strong advocate of psychopharmacological treatment. He appears to favor electroshock as well.

Hippius' characteristic arrogance, which also appears to be a frequent component of the methodology of psychiatric research, surfaced as early as 1955, during his experiments with Reserpin, an alkaloid of the herbal root "Rauwolfia," also called "madness weed." Under the heading "Application on the Sick," he wrote:

"When psychotically sick patients refused to take the medication, Serpasil was injected intramuscularly until the patient had calmed down to a point where he didn't resist oral medication any longer."[51]

Hippius apparently could not tolerate this notion that a patient might have a say in what happens to his body.

According to investigations done by Hippius' clinic at the University of Munich, "almost every fifth citizen of the Federation is mentally ill." This was published by the *Oberhessische Presse* in Marburg on June 9, 1981. Another 20 percent, his study went on to say, suffer from occasional disturbances which, however, need no treatment. If those inflated numbers had any merit at all, Hippius would venture that fully 40 percent of the populace was in need of his service.

According to available information, Hippius was a close friend of some of his colleagues we have already profiled or referenced: Gerhard Harrer (a Nazi psychiatrist), Hans Bürger-Prinz (a military district psychiatrist), Hans-Werner Müller (a student of de Crinis), L.B. Kalinowsky (a student of Cerletti who brought electroshock to the United States), Joachim-Ernst Meyer, a psychiatrist at "Aktion Psychisch Kranke" ("Operation Mentally Ill") said to have collaborated with de Crinis and Hallervorden,

Oswald Bumke (a military district psychiatrist), Max Mikorey (a panic researcher and racial hygienist) and Kurt Kolle (an avid follower of Rüdin).

In fairness, Hippius' criticism of the uncontrolled dissemination of psychiatric drugs is to be commended, as are his protestations about the broad use of Methadone as a substitute drug during heroin withdrawal.[52] Despite those random flashes of responsibility, one look at his record reveals Hippius' dedicated advocacy of the mental hygiene movement. For example, in 1973, Hippius served as vice president of the European League for Mental Hygiene, an association whose goals and purposes are self-evident merely by reading the names of its directors, all of whom were students of Villinger, de Crinis, Rüdin or Bürger-Prinz. It is not coincidental that Hippius held this particular office at the exact same time that he became president of the GSPN. Just prior to that time, in 1972, he had become assistant chairman of the Psychiatry Inquiry Committee, whose ideological origin and purposes will be examined more closely in a later chapter. At the time Hippius was also a member of the World Federation for Mental Health.

In Hippius we see a psychiatric philosophy that seems to be at war with itself. On the one hand, it advocates more openness and a broader, more people-oriented service that is opposed to the isolation of the mentally ill (which Hippius put into effect in his model of an open psychiatric clinic). On the other hand, however, he slavishly adheres to a rigorous devotion to solve everything on a biochemical level—i.e., with pharmacological drugs. Hippius' pill against fear, his "Happiness Pill as a defense against catastrophe" is the perfect example of what Hippius worked at so actively and how ludicrous his theories were and are.

HANFRIED HELMCHEN (1933-   ): PRESIDENT FROM 1979 TO 1980

Helmchen was a student of Julius Hallervorden, a brain specialist who supported the autopsy of euthanized children for research purposes. Hallervorden once said: "…I heard that they would do it and so I went there and said to them, 'Look here, boys, if you kill the people anyway, then at least remove the brains so that the material can be used…'"[53]

In a 1956 paper about his teacher, Hallervorden, Dr. Helmchen wrote: "I am indebted to Dr. med. Julius Hallervorden for his critical advice and references to literature." No ideological closeness should necessarily be deduced here from this polite language, since such veiled references are commonly used in such dissertations. Helmchen likewise praised Friedrich Mauz, the military district psychiatrist and T4 consultant "for the advancement of psychiatry on a national and international level."[54] That observation is similarly cryptic.

It is very difficult to summarize the scientific undertakings of a psychiatrist like Helmchen in a few sentences. The examples that follow are merely a glimpse of a small portion of a multi-faceted career.

For example, in its July 1, 1982 edition, *Die Tagezeitung* of Berlin reported that:

"To this day he has distinguished himself in particular through his fight against the few remaining rights of patients; after all, it is scientifically much more interesting to try out new chemicals and immobilizing drugs on humans than on rats, which are boring. However, the laws that regulate experiments on humans have gotten in Helmchen's way...Hanfried Helmchen said in response, 'Practically speaking, these legal barriers are not always adequate and not always compatible with our understanding of medical behavior.'"[55]

A few years earlier, Helmchen wrote an article in the psychiatric periodical Der *Nervenzart* about "D-Penicillamin in the treatment of schizophrenia" after which, he thanked the Berlin-based Heyl company for the "generous donation of experimental portions."

In this case history, female patient Ragna M. is 24 years old and suffers from "hebephrenia," a form of "juvenile-schizophrenia":

"On Day Six, the patient wets the bed while sitting. On Day Seven, she eats...soap and toothpaste....On Day Eight, the patient becomes very verbally aggressive, refuses to accept the medication, is very agitated....Finally, in a state of extreme agitation and high behavioral disorder, the patient eats the flowers, including cacti in the ward. The treatment with Penicillamin was then discontinued....

"Thus it appears desirable and well-founded now to perform systematic investigations of the psychopathological effects of D-Penicillamin."[56]

Die Tagezeitung also reported a July 1, 1982 case involving a 61-year-old female patient who had been thrown out of her sister's apartment after living with her for a year. The woman was described as very depressed. She

Ehrenmitglieder

A Deutscher Verein für Psychiatrie

Geh. Rat Dr. H. Laehr, Zehlendorf (1905)
Prof. Dr. L. Bianchi, Neapel (1906)
Prof. Dr. V. Magnan, Paris (1906)
Prof. Dr. A. Tamburini, Rom (1906)
Geh. Med.-Rat Prof. Dr. E. Hitzig, Halle (1907)

Geh. Med.-Rat Dr. G. Ludwig, Heppenheim a. B. (1908)
Geh. Med.-Rat Prof. C. Pelman, Bonn (1909)
Geh. Rat Dr. G. Weber, Sonnenstein (1909)
Geh. Rat Dr. H. Schüle, Illenau (1910)
Hofrat Prof. Dr. H. Obersteiner, Wien (1918)
Geh. Rat Prof. Dr. E. Kraepelin, München (1920)
Geh. Med.-Rat. Dr. F. Siemens, Lauenburg (1920)
Geh. Med.-Rat Prof. Dr. F. Tuczek, Marburg (1920)
Geh. Sanitätsrat Dr. H. Laehr, Wernigerode (1924)
Geh. Rat Dr. A. Mercklin, Treptow a. d. R. (1925)
Prof. Dr. J. Wagner von Jauregg, Wien (1926)
Prof. Dr. E. Bleuler, Zürich (1928)
Justizrat Prof. Dr. W. Kahl, Berlin (1931)
Oberreichsanwalt Prof. Dr. L. Ebermayer, Leipzig (1931)
Prof. Dr. K. Rieger, Würzburg (1933)
Obermed.-Rat Dr. H. Simon, Gütersloh (1933)
Obermd.-Rat Dr. G. Kolb, Erlangen (1934)
Geh. Med.-Rat Prof. Dr. E. Schultze, Göttingen (1934)
Geh. Rat Prof. Dr. G. Ilberg, Dresden (1934)

B Gesellschaft Deutscher Neurologen und Psychiater

Geh. Rat Prof. Dr. K. Bonhoeffer, Berlin (1935)
Geh. Rat Prof. Dr. R. Sommer, Gießen (1935)
Prof. Dr. Dr. h. c. K. Schaffer, Budapest (1935)
Dr. med. Dr. phil. h. c. L. Binswanger, Kreuzlingen (1953)
Prof. Dr. R. Gaupp sen., Tübingen (1953)
Prof. Dr. K. Jaspers, Basel (1953)
Prof. Dr. J. Klaesi, Bern (1953)

The lists above and on the facing page show the honorary members of:
A. The German Association for Psychiatry,
B. The Society of German Neurologists and Psychiatrists and
C. The German Society for Psychiatry and Neurology (GSPN).   (Source: GSPN, 1993)

Ehrenmitglieder

C Deutsche Gesellschaft für Psychiatrie und Nervenheilkunde

† Prof. Dr. Dr. v. von Gebsattel, Bamberg (1964)
† Prof. Dr. F. Kehrer, Münster (1964)
† Prof. Dr. M. Reichardt, Würzburg (1964)
† Prof. Dr. Dr. Dr. h. c. K. Schneider, Heidelberg (1964)
† Prof. Dr. J. H. Schultz, Berlin (1964)

† Prof. Dr. P. H. Baan, Utrecht/Holland (1968)
Prof. Dr. M. Bleuler, Zürich/Schweiz (1968)
† Dr. med. Drs. h. c. Henri Ey, Paris/Frankreich (1968)
† Prof. Dr. H. Hoff, Wien/Österreich (1968)
Prof. Dr. L. B. Kalinowsky, New York/USA (1968)
Prof. Dr. J. J. Lopez-Ibor, Madrid/Spanien (1968)
† Prof. Dr. M. Müller, Bern/Schweiz (1968)
† Prof. Dr. E. Stengel, Sheffield/GB (1968)
† Prof. Dr. E. Straus, Lexington/Kentucky/USA (1968)

† Prof. Dr. J. S. Aksel, Istanbul/Türkei (1970)
† Prof. Dr. F. J. Braceland, Hartford/Connecticut/USA (1970)
Prof. Dr. M. Kaila, Helsinki/Finnland (1970)
Prof. Dr. E. Lindemann, Palo Alto/California/USA (1970)
Prof. Dr. C. Redlich, New Haven/Connecticut/USA (1970)
Prof. Dr. J. Ruesch, San Francisco/California/USA (1970)
Prof. Dr. R. Sarro, Barcelona/Spanien (1970)
† Dr. R. Schimrigk, Dortmund (1970)
† Prof. Dr. E. T. Slater, London/England (1970)
† Prof. Dr. Y. Uchimura, Tokyo/Japan (1970)
† Prof. Dr. H. Z. Winnik, Jerusalem/Israel (1970)
† Prof. Dr. E. Wittkower, Montreal/Kanada (1970)

† Prof. Dr. Dr. h. c. H. Bürger-Prinz, Hamburg (1972)
† Prof. Dr. H. Kranz, Mainz (1972)
† Prof. Dr. F. Mauz, Münster (1972)
† Med.-Dir. Dr. H. Merguet, Münster (1972)
† Prof. Dr. F. Panse, Düsseldorf (1972)
† Prof. Dr. J. Zutt, Frankfurt/Main (1972)

† Prof. Dr. W. von Baeyer, Heidelberg (1974)
Prof. Dr. Dr. Dr. h. c. H. E. Ehrhardt, Marburg/Lahn (1974)
Prof. Dr. R. K. Freudenberg, Reigate/Surrey/GB (1974)
† Prof. Dr. W. Skalweit, Berlin (1974)
Prof. Dr. E. Strömgren, Risskov/Dänemark (1974)

† Prof. Dr. L. Kanner, Baltimore/Maryland/USA (1976)
Prof. Dr. Dr. P. Pichot, Paris/Frankreich (1976)

† Med.-Direktor Dr. Dr. H. E. Schulz, Schondorf (1978)

† Prof. Dr. H. Schulte, Bremen (1984)

was first prescribed the stimulant Tofranil and then the deadening neuroleptic Taxilan. Helmchen himself described what happened:

"The patient was in a delirium and completely disoriented, did not recognize the surroundings, talked confusedly and was in an extremely agitated state. Her face was deep red...and she perspired profusely. After the patient regained some coherency under Decortin (a drug that counteracts the swelling of the brain), on the third day she fell into a catatonic stupor with a clear improvement in temporary memory loss. On the fifth day, however, the stupor gradually changed back into an excited delirious hallucination that couldn't be controlled. Especially impressive were the involuntary and rhythmic twisting movements of the hands at periodic intervals. On the seventh day, the patient met her death by circulatory collapse."[57]

What's especially frightening about that description was the unwillingness of the psychiatrist to do anything about the adverse reaction to the drug that he himself gave the patient except to chronicle the course from medication to death. It is as if he were merely a spectator, with little or no influence over or responsibility for the outcome of his own patient's reaction to his own treatment regimen. It is not a clinical dispassion we observe, but rather an inhuman neutrality that suggests an unarticulated hope that the reaction will actually conquer the patient instead of the reverse.

Helmchen acknowledged as much about "the problems of therapy research in psychiatry."

"He (the physician) has almost never had a complete and far-reaching knowledge about all elements and their respective importance in a particular case that could influence his choice of therapy. Therefore every decision regarding the treatment and its results is full of uncertainty about one's personal assessments, which are decided basically on probability. So every routine therapeutic decision could also be technically called an experiment."[58]

In conclusion, we can only observe that the history of modern German psychiatry sprang from tainted roots indeed. Most of Germany's leading and most honored postwar psychiatrists did much they never answered for and managed, from their positions, to perpetuate their legacy among the generations that followed.

"Regarding euthanasia...today it is no longer of any interest who had participated, under what circumstances and to what extent, in the basically condemnable Nazi extermination measures." [1]
Professor Helmuth E. Ehrhardt,
German psychiatrist, 1977

THE REMARKABLE SECRET CONNECTIONS OF GERMAN CHILD AND ADOLESCENT PSYCHIATRY

In examining the status and influence of German child and adolescent psychiatrists since the end of World War II, the inescapable result is a sense of outrage rendered especially unpalatable because the objects of their attention are kids. Recall, though, that the first people killed under the influence of Nazi psychiatry were defenseless children. It is, as will now be seen, a matter of pure disgrace, that postwar German psychiatry for children largely has been shaped by persons who have embraced the theoritical ends to which their Nazi mentors aspired.

From the very beginning of the specialty, the elite of German child psychiatry shared a radical, racist and state-oriented point of view. After the war, the same psychiatrists—among them the top man of T4—were entrusted with the responsibility for giving expert advice about children. They considered themselves the "reorganizers of child and adolescent psychiatry" and continued on with their activities.

It is remarkably revealing to put the subject of child and adolescent psychiatry under a microscope, because under such careful scrutiny we can identify the true structure and composition of a field of endeavor whose practitioners claim to pursue the best interests of the most defenseless of all defenseless patients. The real story is different from what the psychiatrists want you to believe.

Child psychiatry, from its very origin, has devoted itself to thoroughly racist objectives. Its Nazi background has already been documented in detail by several authors; the unbroken flow of theory and practice within the child psychiatric movement from then to now, however, has never been clearly documented until now. One disturbing fact to note at the start of this inquiry is that in the last twenty years the number of child and adolescent psychiatrists in Germany has climbed from about twenty to around five hundred. This rapid expansion of psychiatrists focusing on children has brought Germany a far-reaching mental hygiene policy, as it is still called even today. It also has flooded the German populace with prescriptions for psychiatric drugs for children, about which critics continuously raise their voices in alarm. A direct connection to Nazi war crimes cannot be established by this pill-pushing alone, but some very shocking alliances of child and adolescent psychiatry with the Nazis are found in the available documents.

This inquiry begins in 1939, when the Deutsche Gesellschaft für Kinderund Jugendpsychiatrie (German Alliance for Child and Adolescent Psychiatry) came into being. It was also then that Hitler gave his go-ahead to the psychiatrists to euthanize mentally handicapped children.

On March 27, 1939, the Arbeitgemeinschaft für Kinderpsychiatrie (Cooperative for Child Psychiatry) was founded in Wiesbaden by Dr. Paul Schröder, a professor of psychiatry and neurology at the University of Leipzig. This association participated in the First Conference of the German Society for Child Psychiatry and Therapeutic Education in Vienna on September 5, 1940. That society would change its name after the war to the German Society for Child and Adolescent Psychiatry. The founding congress was anything but apolitical:

"Present were about five hundred participants, among them representatives of the Ministry of the Interior of the Reich and the Ministry of the Reich for Public Enlightenment and Propaganda, the president of the Reich's Ministry of Health and its officials, numerous representatives of the Reich's administration of the Nazi teachers' association, the Office for Health Guidance and the Reich's Youth Guidance and other organizations of the party...."[2]

Present also were the elite and the patriarchs of Nazi psychiatry, including Professor Wagner von Jauregg, who barely escaped sentencing in a military court after World War I for applying electric current to soldiers. The lectures at the conference followed the theme, popular at that time, that the unworthy genotype had to be filtered out and eliminated from the nation's gene pool. This conference is of great historical interest, not only because of its content, but also for learning about the future by examining who spoke about what and what roles these eminent people play in postwar psychiatry.

At the convening session, Dr. Schröder began his speech by saying:

"Child psychiatry has to...help to integrate (her-

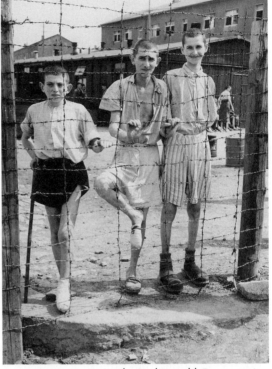

Young inmates in the Buchenwald Concentration Camp after the Allies arrived

editarily) damaged or inadequate children for their own and the public's good (each according to his ability) into the community and the general economic process. This, however, cannot happen at random and to the same degree with all 'difficult cases,' but instead under constant expert selection of the valuable and educable ones with just as strict and resolute a sacrifice of those deemed predominately worthless and uneducable."[3]

In his speech, Schröder also claimed that psychiatry had the knowledge to achieve the earliest possible recognition of an existing disorder or possible harm to society. That is an interesting perspective, indeed, in a world where the patient can rightfully expect a physician's first instinct to be the welfare of the patient rather than society-at-large. Schröder was subse-

127

quently elected to serve as the first president of the Deutsche Gesellschaft für Kinderpsychiatrie und Heilpädagogik (German Society for Child Psychiatric and Therapeutic Education).

Werner Villinger, whom we discussed earlier, was at the 1940 founding congress, too. Villinger shared this pithy observation with his colleagues:

"Our educational success…is not so much dependent on our educational willingness and skill but rather on the clay we have to mold, the wood we have to carve."[4]

The psychiatrists proved themselves to be especially talented masters of this "educational activity" and had already proven it by the time the congress convened. Villinger was an enthusiastic follower of the racial hygienist Fritz Lenz whom he quoted (among others) in his 1940 lecture. Holding strongly that "no doubt was possible" about the inheritance of personality, Villinger came to the dubious—but considering his ideology, logical—conclusion that:

"The individual traits of the character's structure and his emotional and animalistic life are extensively predestined and fixed through the genetic code, and are probably even the final imprint of his personality."[5]

Villinger became even more explicit in his opinions later in his speech when he railed against the "unprincipled" of the democratic Weimar Republic in Germany. He said:

"A whole nation can go bad when the people at the reins of government and the example they are supposed to set are missing. We therefore see…in the unprincipled twenties an especially large number of the maladjusted…. They are virtually extinct, those unruly ruffians, who once populated the public and private welfare institutions."[6]

In view of the carnage that was occurring at that time in Germany, that is an unforgivably cold assessment of the then state of affairs. But remember, those were not the words of a mad politician—they were the words of someone who was purportedly practicing medicine. It is even worse to remember that Villinger is still celebrated to this day as an enlightened voice within his profession. It is the same Villinger who, more than twenty years later, in 1961, defended himself in a letter to *Der Spiegel* against accusations of his T4 involvement :

"There was, however, an error made by you when you listed me as an active participant in that process."[7]

Villinger was not literally an "active participant" in the act of euthanasia. After all, he never opened a gas valve or gave a lethal injection. But he was not an innocent bystander, not in practice—he was a T4 consultant—and not in sentiment. "They are virtually extinct, those unruly ruffians...," he told those gathered in Vienna, before concluding: "The eyes of the world are on Germany; let us do our best!"

Another member of the founding congress of the German Society of Child Psychiatry and Therapeutic Education, was Dr. Anna Leiter, a genetic researcher from Dresden. In her remarks, she referred to the "unusually high hereditary taint" of the "children-material" that she had examined which were "to a very high degree asocial and antisocial," and "odd in character." She had studied approximately 3000 children, leading her to this remarkable conclusion:

"Therefore we demand that as soon as a careful and responsible analysis shows an extremely unusual lack of emotions in connection with other criminogenic reactive tendencies, we detain these children as early as possible, since they represent an unbearable burden and danger for the entire country."[8]

A remarkable thought, and one embraced by the child psychiatrists she addressed. Childlike stoicism and criminal "tendencies" should endanger children to being separated from society right away, "since they represent an unbearable burden and danger." It was not specifically articulated, but it was the psychiatrists who were to decide who was to be placed into custody. Although unarticulated, it was exactly the purpose for which this new professional association of child psychiatry had been established. It follows then that from the start, child psychiatry was oriented toward racial hygiene and selection—from society as psychiatry viewed it, and at the expense of the patient. But the conference went beyond that:

"The screening of school dropouts" was explained in detail by principal E. Lesch, describing dropouts literally as "bad student material." They were then classified in the following categories:

1. Actual and potential repeaters of the lower public school grades

2. Students from higher grades who have been recommended for special school, as well as "drawn-out, borderline and questionable cases"

3. Uneducable children

4. Children with special educational difficulties

5. Schoolchildren whose brothers and/or sisters or relatives are or have been in a special school; "genetic and national health considerations recommend their preventative registration."[9]

According to Lesch, "consideration toward parents, kindness, mercy or good-naturedness are not appropriate here."[10]

A comparison of these 1940 categories with modern psychiatric/mental hygiene shows some horrifying parallels. In the upcoming chapter on the modern mental hygiene movement, we will elaborate quite a bit on those themes. But it is not only the political climate in which these demands were posed that should alarm us; it is also the arrogant aim of psychiatry to use categories it had arbitrarily defined to screen, isolate and detain—and ultimately, treat—children.

No less demeaning of the human race were the words of Dr. K. Tornow of Magdeburg:

"The new Germany has the most advanced animal protection laws in the world. How could it not bestow upon its weak and harmed national members protection and help?"[11]

Only a few lines after this do we find out what kind of mentality was really at work:

"Despite all the considerable successes in special education we have achieved, a Germany without 'special students' would be much more to our liking than a Germany with them."[12]

Lesch continues, "The establishment of a central office for the whole field of special education which covers all the problems of special schooling would seem to me most important....In the field of special schooling, Germany will outstrip its ideological opponents and will blaze a trail for the welfare of nations. May the new founded Society for Child Psychiatry and Special or Therapeutic Education help in this important new quest, above all to solve our country's current ethnic problems. Therefore, I work in the interest of a racial recovery according to the principle: 'Nothing for us, everything for Germany, loyalty to Adolf Hitler!'"[13]

We conclude our review of the founding congress with a few observations. Its first president, Paul Schröder and its first secretary Werner Villinger, were prominently involved in this racial-ideological movement. Later on, its successor group's long-standing president , Hermann Stutte (more on whom will come later) reminisced nostalgically about the founding conference in a 1970 article :

"The official founding of the German Society for Child Psychiatry and Therapeutic Education occurred...on September 5, 1940 in Vienna. This founding conference took place under the aegis of the former professor of psychiatry, Prof. Wagner von Jauregg, the renowned Nobel prize winner. Representatives of the Reich's Ministry of the Interior, the Reich's Health Department, the Reich's Youth Guidance...directed their happy birthday greetings to the founding group which consisted mostly of men in uniform...The lectures at this first German congress for child psychiatry were given at a considerably high academic level...I was so impressed that right then I decided that this is what I wanted to do professionally."[14]

Certainly no one can accuse Hermann Stutte of exaggeration—his subsequent career reveals just what an impression this founding congress made on him. The original quotes from this congress, however, suggest that Stutte possessed a selective memory.

As was true of the GSPN, it is the publications and careers of the leaders of psychiatry for children which light the path toward truly understanding motives and actions. Its first leader, Paul Schröder, had made a name for himself in psychiatry even before the founding Congress. He acknowledged that he was an eager student of Kraepelin and Karl Bonhoeffer, "teachers whom he revered all his life," according to Bürger-Prinz. In 1933, Schröder published an article in a weekly medical journal called the *Münchener Medizinischen Wochenschrift* about psychopaths and abnormal people, in which he defined a "psychopath" as a person "outside of the playing range of the average and normal." To Schröder, psychopaths were not only those who have, compared with the average person, "more or less self-esteem, an ability to love, an urge to be recognized, a temperament and a responsiveness,"[15] but also people who are extremely talented, able to love, temperamental and the like. It is chilling that anyone with a heightened sense of purpose could be labeled a "psychopath." It is even more chilling that Schröder's teachings are still widely disseminated in the psychiatric community.

A sense of how lethal Schröder's research and theories may have been and what impact they may have had on more than 3,000 juvenile patients in the Nazi era can be drawn from the fact that his so-called "character research" was the basis for determining "hereditary ability" and whether or not the person should be exterminated. Schröder did not live long enough to see the fruits of his theories. He died on June 7, 1941 in Leipzig. His obituary states: "Often tormented by migraines and its accompanying disgruntlements…. Schröder had many difficulties with others."

Schröder's designated successor was the ubiquitous Werner Villinger, although he had to settle for the title of secretary; "because the government appointed somebody else to be the chairman."[16] At least that's what Hermann Stutte states in a 1970 memorandum about the society, but who that "somebody" might have been Stutte does not disclose. The Society's official annals identify Dr. Villinger as chairman after 1941.

Villinger was, however, only a figurehead. The real leader was the controversial Dr. Hans Heinze, the director of the Laender Institute of Brandenburg-Gorden and the chief consultant of child euthanasia, who gained prominence on the Reich's Committee for the Scientific Registration of Hereditary and Inherent Sufferings"—the "cover organization for the murder of handicapped children and youth."[17] The Reich's Committee was practically affiliated with T4. The only difference was that it was responsible for child euthanasia. But Heinze was versatile; he was also a T4 consultant for adult euthanasia. Heinze's teachings and connections to child and adolescence psychiatry thus warrant close scrutiny.

In 1931, while Dr. Heinze was a physician at the children's outpatient department at Leipzig, he collaborated with Paul Schröder on a book called *Kindliche Charaktere und ihre Abartigkeiten* (*Child Personalities and Their Abnormalities*).[18] In the very first paragraph of the introduction, Heinze and Schröder define what they mean by the word "degenerate" in much the same way that Schröder would define "psychopath" two years later:

"Degenerate means deviating from the species, from the norm, or from the wide range of the average. 'Degenerate' is not equal to 'sick'. 'Degenerate' also includes the oversized or undersized person, the athlete, the highly talented, the genius. A degenerate in the psychological area is someone who…deviates above and below the average."[19]

Such a definition, elastic and sweeping, confined only by the bounds of imagination is transparently self-serving. The obvious purpose is flexibility—to embrace an extremely large proportion of the population and make them eligible for psychiatric examination and treatment. It ensures psychiatric intervention in any given situation at the psychiatrist's sole discretion as a "corrective action," and according to psychiatry's own arbitrarily designated definitions.

From the beginning, Dr. Heinze was dedicated to defining, segregating and exterminating certain classes of people, following the dictates of the state economy, Nazi doctrine and the precepts of "racial hygiene psychiatry." According to Klee and others, Heinze was involved with the planning and design of the adult euthanasia program as well as a chief consultant in the child euthanasia movement.[20]

In 1938, Heinze became the director of the Brandenburg-Görden sanitarium. By 1940, Brandenburg-Görden was functioning as a halfway house for T4 "supply transports." During this time, Heinze instituted a special children's department, the function of which was to kill handicapped children. Some of the sanitarium's children were, however, sent to the gas chambers of the former prison at Brandenburg. According to T4 physician Bunke:

"Some of the children's corpses were dissected by Prof. Hallervorden in Berlin and were taken along for scientific evaluation...I believe there was a total of two shipments. At that time, Prof. Heinze himself was in Brandenburg."[21]

Brandenburg-Görden was essentially a training center—in Nazi lingo, a "Reich's Schooling Station"—for the physicians who were to be in charge of the killing at other facilities. Klee quotes the example of physicians from Stuttgart named Lempp and Schütte who had been brought to Berlin "so that they could be indoctrinated at the Reich's Schooling Station in Gorden by Heinze regarding how to perform the task in question."[22] This perspective is horrific. Heinze, among the most prominent of child and adolescent psychiatrists, was not only a key consultant in the euthanasia program, but he was also the Nazi trainer of choice for some of its euthanasia physicians. Hallervorden was Heinze's senior consultant; he also collaborated closely with de Crinis.

"In 1939, the Kaiser Wilhelm Society (now called the Max Planck Society,) bestowed upon the institute director Heinze the unusual honor of a seat on its Board of Trustees of their Brain Research Institute, at the same time that Max de Crinis has entered the ranks of this committee. It is extremely likely that a child-killing department had been installed in this very same Kaiser Wilhelm Institute for Brain Research."[23]

Thom goes even further:

"According to investigations by Aly...it can even be assumed that in certain cases children were not killed because of the severity of their handicap but because of the doctor's interest in comparable brain specimens for experiments on brain conditions, progress and age groups."[24]

Heinze, then, is a central figure of Nazi psychiatry, with an especially active research interest in children and young people, and a function as a trainer in the art of murder. Heinze was one of the diabolic Nazi psychiatrists who was eventually brought to justice. In comparison to the crimes he committed, however, his punishment was quite mild. He was tried and convicted in 1946 by a Russian military tribunal which sentenced him to seven years' hard labor. He served his term in various prisons until 1952, whereupon he returned to Germany, and became an assistant physician at a sanitarium near Münster in Westphalia.

During his interrogation, Dr. Heinze claimed that he acted on orders from the Nazi hierarchy which he carried out "under threat of extermination in a KZ." He also claimed that through his activities as a consultant, he actually saved the lives of hundreds of children. It has already been seen by the example of psychiatrists like Zutt and Degkwitz that prominent psychiatrists could and did resist the politics of euthanasia without incarceration or execution. Heinze denied any connection to the experimental hospital in Heidelberg, despite numerous documents linking him to the Heidelberg euthanasia research center. In 1962, a preliminary inquiry into Heinze's wartime activities was begun, but several medical opinions certified him as unfit to be questioned and unable to understand the proceedings. In his 1963 testimony, the medical examiner said:

"After initially logical answers, his train of thought strayed alarmingly...after a short while he answered back, his hypersensitivity about the series of questions regarding 'euthanasia' surfaced clearly again...to relapse later into a kind of explosive aggression...."[25]

At later investigations he even burst into tears—and the hearing was finally discontinued. In 1966, Heinze was deemed unfit to stand trial because he was a "mental wreck." When he died, nearly two decades later, the following obituary appeared:

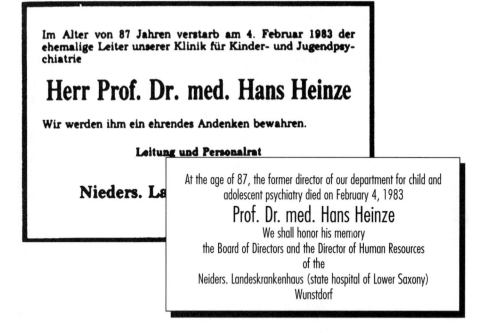

Im Alter von 87 Jahren verstarb am 4. Februar 1983 der ehemalige Leiter unserer Klinik für Kinder- und Jugendpsychiatrie

Herr Prof. Dr. med. Hans Heinze

Wir werden ihm ein ehrendes Andenken bewahren.

Leitung und Personalrat

Nieders. La

At the age of 87, the former director of our department for child and adolescent psychiatry died on February 4, 1983

Prof. Dr. med. Hans Heinze

We shall honor his memory
the Board of Directors and the Director of Human Resources
of the
Neiders. Landeskrankenhaus (state hospital of Lower Saxony)
Wunstdorf

A very high honor indeed for probably the lead consultant in the child euthanasia program, and a man who was directly responsible for signing the death warrants for innumerable children and adults.

Small wonder that the Society for Child and Adolescent Psychiatry has deleted Heinze's name from its records and has inserted Werner Villinger's name in his place. One can only speculate about the wisdom of substituting Villinger considering his own Nazi and T4 past. At the re-establishment of the society in 1952 during the conference of the Gesellschaft deutscher Neurologen end Psychiater (Association of German Neurologists and Psychiatrists), it was Villinger who reemerged as the new president of the "Deutsche Vereinigung für Jugendpsychiatrie" ("German Association for Adolescent Psychiatry").

Villinger continued as the society's president until 1961, dedicating his efforts toward getting child and adolescent psychiatry recognized as an independent medical specialty. That recognition ultimately was bestowed by the federal medical society in 1968 when that society's leadership included physicians named Ernst Fromm and H. J. Sewering, both of whom were identified by *Der Spiegel* as former SS members.[26]

Daten zur Geschichte der Vereinigung

1939	Gründung einer kinderpsychiatrischen Arbeitsgemeinschaft auf Veranlassung von Prof. Dr. P. Schröder (Leipzig).
1940	Gründung der «Deutschen Gesellschaft für Kinderpsychiatrie und Heilpädagogik» in Wien. Vorsitzender: Prof. Dr. P. Schröder, Schriftführer: Dr. W. Villinger.
1949	Erstes Nachkriegssymposium einiger Kinderpsychiater in Marburg.
1950	Neugrü
	Jugend
1973	Änderu
	und Ju

Vorsitz

1940—41	Prof. D
1941	Prof. D
1950—61	Prof. D
1961—67	Prof. D
1967—70	Prof. D
1970—72	Prof. D
1972—74	Prof. D
1974—	Prof. D

Periodi

Bis 1944	(51. Jah
ab 1952	«Praxis
ab 1934	«Zeitsc
	«Acta
1956—72	«Jahrbu
ab 1973	«Zeitsc

Kongre
Die De
in zweijährigen Abst
gen statt.
Die «U
ihrer Gründung im
1975 in Wien.
Die «I
seit ihrer Gründung
delphia (USA) statt.

THE HISTORY OF THE ASSOCIATION:

1939: Founding of a child psychiatric association by Prof. Dr. Paul Schröder.

1940: Founding of the "Deutsche Gesellschaft für Kinderpsychiatrie und Heilpadägogik" ("German Society for Child Psychiatry and Therapeutic Education") in Vienna. Chairman: Dr. Paul Schröder; secretary: Dr. Werner Villinger.

1949: First postwar symposium of child psychiatrists in Marburg

1950: Re-establishment of the society, changing its name to "Deutsche Vereinigung für Jugendpsychiatrie" ("German Alliance for Adolescent Psychiatry"), at the convention of the GSPN in Munich.

1973: Changed its name again to "Deutsche Vereinigung für Kinder- und Jugendpsychiatrie" ("German Alliance for Child and Adolescent Psychiatry")

Chairmen

1940-1941: Dr. Paul Schröder (Leipzig)

1941: Dr. Werner Villinger (Bethel, Breslau)

1950-1961: Dr. Werner Villinger (Marburg)

1961-1967: Dr. G. F. von Stockert (Frankfürt)

1967-1970: Dr. Hermann Stutte (Marburg)

1970-1972: Dr. H. Harbauer (Frankfürt)

1972-1974: Dr. G. Nissen (Berlin)

1974-present: Dr. R. Lempp (Tubingen)

Periodicals

until 1944: "Zeitschrift für Kinderforschung" ("Periodical for Child Research")

since 1952: "Praxis für Kinderpsychologie und Kinderpsychiatrie" ("Practical Application of Child Psychology and Psychiatry")

since 1934: "Zeitschrift für Kinderpsychiatrie" ("Periodical for Child Psychiatry"), renamed in 1953 "Acta Paedopsychiatria")

1956-1972: "Jahrbuch für Jugendpsychiatrie" ("Adolescent Psychiatry Yearbook")

since 1973: "Zeitschrift für Kinder- und Jugendpsychiatrie" ("Periodical for Child and Adolescent Psychiatry")

Conventions:

The German Alliance for Child and Adolescent Psychiatry holds biannual conventions. The 14th congress was held in 1975 in Göttingen.

The "Union Europaischer Padopsychiater" (UEP, "Alliance of European Child Psychiatrists") holds its foundation congresses once every four years. The last one took place in 1974 in Philadelphia.

(from: the Deutsche Vereinigung für Kinder- und Jugendpsychiatrie Statutes and Membership Directory, June 1, 1975 edition)

Another leading figure in child psychiatry during the postwar era was the aforementioned Hermann Stutte who, from 1967 to 1970, was the president of the Society.

Stutte received his doctorate under Sommer, the founder of the Deutscher Verband für psychische Hygiene (German Association for Mental Hygiene), which will be examined later. Dr. Stutte played an important role in the development of the specious field of criminal biology, and his research and publications contain numerous references to major Nazi authorities and psychiatrists like Helmut Ehrhardt and Max Eyrich—a pediatrician involved in killing activities starting in 1940—as well as his mentor, Dr. Villinger.

Another of Dr. Stutte's teachers was the notorious Fritz Hoffmann, the same Hoffmann who had announced "large-scale investigations of offspring" in the 1934 anthology "Erblehre und Rassenhygiene im völkischen Staat" ("Genetics and Racial Hygiene in the Ethnic Nation"), which was published under Dr. Rüdin's supervision. Dr. Stutte was appointed as a member of those investigations.

Stutte had witnessed the development of the German Society for Child and Adolescent Psychiatry from its inception, and he may well have known about extermination and euthanasia activities. At the time the society was founded in 1940, at least 14,000 people had already been gassed in the Nazi euthanasia institutes, among them many classified as "feebleminded and useless" children.

Hermann Stutte himself was neither a member of T4 nor a Nazi military psychiatrist. He was, however, a member of the SA (a military policing unit similar to the SS under Hitler's direct control since 1934) as well as a member of the Nazi party since 1937. Like his mentor Villinger, Stutte was a scientist thoroughly versed in genetic doctrine. In 1941, he welcomed the "subdivision of the educational reforms according to biological and prognostic viewpoints." To fully understand this comment, it is necessary to know that education was viewed by the Nazis as a "genetic filter" through which to neutralize and eradicate the "diseased" hereditary flow.

With the fall of the Third Reich in 1945, the terror of the brown shirts stopped, but the research activities of the Nazi psychiatrists did not. As noted earlier, after the war, Dr. Villinger became a professor in Marburg and director of the university clinic. He brought his disciple, Dr. Stutte,

TIMETABLE: PROF. HERMANN STUTTE

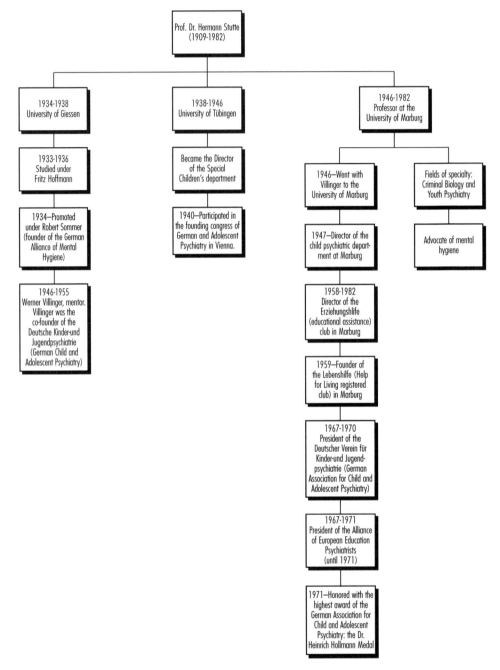

Prof. Dr. Hermann Stutte
(1909-1982)

1934-1938
University of Giessen

1933-1936
Studied under
Fritz Hoffmann

1934—Promoted
under Robert Sommer
(founder of the German
Alliance of Mental
Hygiene)

1946-1955
Werner Villinger, mentor.
Villinger was the
co-founder of the
Deutsche Kinder-und
Jugendpsychiatrie
(German Child and
Adolescent Psychiatry)

1938-1946
University of Tübingen

Became the Director
of the Special
Children's department

1940—Participated in
the founding congress of
German and Adolescent
Psychiatry in Vienna.

1946-1982
Professor at the
University of Marburg

1946—Went with
Villinger to the
University of Marburg

1947—Director of the
child psychiatric depart-
ment at Marburg

1958-1982
Director of the
Erziehungshilfe
(educational assistance)
club in Marburg

1959—Founder of
the Lebenshilfe (Help
for Living registered
club) in Marburg

1967-1970
President of the
Deutscher Verein für
Kinder-und Jugend-
psychiatrie (German
Association for Child and
Adolescent Psychiatry)

1967-1971
President of the Alliance
of European Education
Psychiatrists
(until 1971)

1971—Honored with the
highest award of the
German Association for
Child and Adolescent
Psychiatry: the Dr.
Heinrich Hollmann Medal

Fields of specialty:
Criminal Biology and
Youth Psychiatry

Advocate of mental
hygiene

along with him as assistant medical director. Stutte, whose 1944 university thesis "Über Schicksal, Persönlichkeit und Sippe ehemaliger Fürsorgezöglinge" ("About Fate, Personality and Kinship of Former Wards") had earned him the qualifications necessary to lecture. After the war, both Stutte and Villinger made a point not to mention what they had done to help the German adolescent psychiatry movement under the Nazis:

In 1948, Stutte and Villinger collaborated on an article entitled "Contemporary Tasks and Problems With Youth Care" in the periodical *Der Nervenarzt*. In it, they discussed the reformatory education of the "social-biological inferiority of the people-material" and demanded that "the examination, screening and guidance of this flotsam of juvenile delinquents be a medical psychiatric task." One possible solution was "the establishment of a Labor Service (with supervision from the psychiatric side)."[27]

It is difficult to imagine anyone informed of his background would trust Dr. Stutte to draw up sensible doctrines in psychiatry. This is so especially since he has never critically distanced himself from his teachers of the Nazi era.[28]

In 1956, Dr. Stutte issued a call for even more drastic measures in his *Handbook for Institutional Education*. "The infectious core group of chronically asocial (should) as early as possible 'be introduced to' a suitable special treatment."[29] The question of why a psychiatrist with his history was still in a position to be practicing more than a decade after the fall of the Nazis is both troublesome and unanswered. His suggestion was eerily predictable.

In 1959, Dr. Stutte co-founder of "Lebenshilfe, e.V." (Help for Life Club, Inc.), an institution purportedly dedicated to the welfare of handicapped children and their families. He called his institution the "greatest mental hygiene achievement of the postwar era."[30] Historians can correctly regard it as a cause for alarm, as it wraps itself in the euphemism of "mental hygiene," which raises the specter of the students of Nazi psychiatrists preparing to penetrate German society once again with their mentors' and teachers' doctrines and methods.

That perception was buttressed when Dr. Villinger was brought in to assume the chairmanship of the scientific council of the Lebenshilfe. "The admission of Villinger and Stutte, means that in the next few years, the Lebenshilfe will be demanding what has just been abandoned: the steril-

FROM RACIAL HYGIENE TO AN OFFICIALLY RECOGNIZED MEDICAL SPECIALTY:
THE HISTORY OF THE DEVELOPMENT OF CHILD AND ADOLESCENT PSYCHIATRY IN GERMANY:

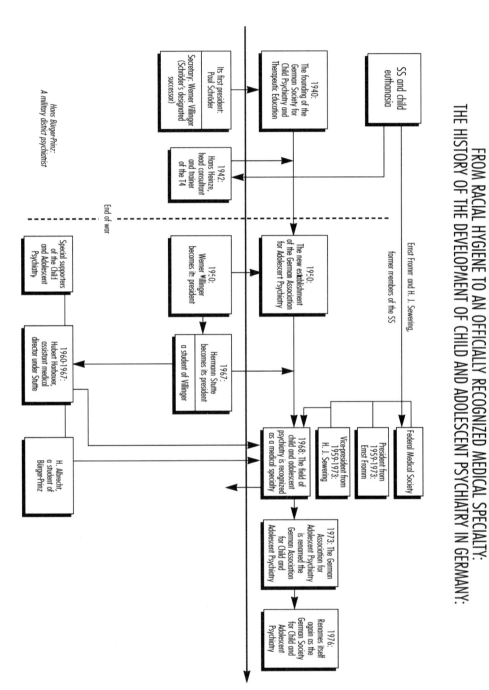

Its first president: Paul Schröder

Secretary: Werner Villinger (Schröder's designated successor)

1940: The founding of the German Society for Child Psychiatry and Therapeutic Education

SS and child euthanasia

1942: Hans Heinze, head consultant and trainer of the T4

Hans Bürger-Prinz: A military district psychiatrist

End of war

1950: The new establishment of the German Association for Adolescent Psychiatry

1950: Werner Villinger becomes its president

Special supporters of the Child and Adolescent Psychiatry

1967: Hermann Stutte becomes its president a student of Villinger

1960-1967: Hubert Harbauer, assistant medical director under Stutte

H. Albrecht, a student of Bürger-Prinz

Ernst Fromm and H. J. Sewering, former members of the SS

Federal Medical Society

President from 1959-1973: Ernst Fromm

Vice-president from 1959-1973: H. J. Sewering

1968: The field of child and adolescent psychiatry is recognized as a medical specialty

1973: The German Association for Adolescent Psychiatry is renamed the German Association for Child and Adolescent Psychiatry

1976: Renames itself again as the German Society for Child and Adolescent Psychiatry

ization of handicapped people,"[31] commented *Die Zeit*. Immediately afterward, Dr. Stutte proposed the "reimplementation of protective supervision," referring to such dubious sources as *Volk und Rasse* (*Nation and Race*—1937) and *Handbuch der Erbbiologie* (*Handbook of Genetics*—1939), and the odious "characterological investigations" of Dr. Heinze.

It is difficult to imagine anyone who espoused such ideals and advocated such heinous methods to be the subject of accolades. Nevertheless, in 1971, the German Society of Child and Adolescent Psychiatry conferred upon Dr. Stutte the Heinrich Hollmann Medal, the society's highest honor.

In the period since 1971, child and adolescent psychiatry developed completely along the theoretical and methodological lines developed by its Nazi-era founders. In 1972, Dr. Hubert Harbauer who had served on the Kommission zur Untersuchung der Lage der Psychiatrie (Commission for the Investigation of the Situation of Psychiatry), succeeded Dr. Stutte at the helm of the Society for Child and Adolescent Psychiatry. Harbauer had been an assistant medical director under Dr. Stutte, and thus was one of his students and proteges.

In his publication *Modern Erziehen* (*Modern Educating*), here is what Müller-Küppers wrote about schizophrenia:

"On the basis of twin research, we must all admit that there is a transmissibility of certain dispositions. Through the introduction of modern medicinal treatment methods that can also be applied to children, their prognosis has become markedly better. The so-called 'electroconvulsive treatment' can still be used but only in special cases if there are no other therapeutic possibilities."[32]

In Müller-Küppers' world, no official action of any kind was to be taken with respect to a child without the psychiatrist: "No adoptions, no sending to reform school, no provisions for school attendance without child psychiatric examinations."[33]

Helmut Remschmidt, a student of Dr. Stutte, directed the Society from 1983 to 1984. He eulogized his mentor, as follows:

"His works embody in their thoroughness and originality, their farsightedness and richness in perspective, an extensive set of dogmas regarding child and adolescent psychiatry that was highly effective and will remain so in the future, too."[34]

What an extraordinary way to characterize the Nazi theories that "justified" exterminating children.

Dr. Remschmidt extensively studied the phenomenon of hyperactivity in children. It was, in part, his research that lead to hyperactivity becoming one of the favorite diagnoses of child psychiatry. It is a fluid diagnosis, to be sure. A child can be deemed to be "hyperactive" if he showed the following symptoms more frequently than "the norm":

1. Restless, overactive
2. Excitable, impulsive
3. Disturbs other children
4. Starts something and doesn't finish it, short attention span
5. Fidgets constantly
6. Easily distracted
7. Wishes have to be fulfilled immediately; easily frustrated
8. Cries often
9. Quick, extreme mood shifts
10. Tendencies toward angry fits and unpredictable behavior

Similar criteria for hyperactivity can also be found in standard psychiatric and psychological manuals such as the current issue of the *Diagnostic and Statistical Manual of Mental Disorders*. This is not an unusual or isolated diagnostic method, despite the obvious flaw that it is difficult to imagine a child who doesn't exhibit most, if not all, of the "symptoms." What those ten characteristics reflect is an effort to embrace virtually every child—all "child-material" as the early child psychiatrists referred to young human beings—and to subject them to psychiatric "treatment." For "hyperactivity," the "treatment" is especially horrifying because it is the widely applied use of drug therapy, particularly Ritalin, a drug which can produce a very heavy dependency and serious side effects.

Remschmidt, then as now, advocates the new "genetics," which assumes a genetic cause for hyperactivity:

"...after there had been indications that organic factors could not satisfactorily explain the cause for the disturbance, genetic research experienced an upswing. The strongly disproportionate relationship (9 to 1) between normal and hyperactive children hints at a genetic answer, also the fact that hyperactivity has also been found among the subjects' biological parents."[35]

Grave dangers are clearly discernible in the jargon and the "scientific" practice of child psychiatry, especially when, in the same breath, the "authorities" assert that ten percent of all children are psychiatrically ill, and are therefore in need of treatment.[36] It is by no means shocking for Remschmidt to be a prominent advocate of horrible things. After all, he is a disciple and protégé of Nazis, and co-editor of the periodical *Psycho* with former Nazi psychiatrist Gerhart Harrer.[37]

What is equally frightening and obvious is that the racist and elitist theories of the original child psychiatrists—as documented in 1940 at the First Congress—have not only survived but flourished. It has been a natural passage of poison from teacher to student from the Nazis to subsequent generations of child and adolescent psychiatrists. The efforts "to spot and screen"—that is, to distinguish between the valuable and less valuable human beings—are more than dubious—they are indefensible. But that is precisely what still is advocated, along with a proclivity to treat children with psychotropic drugs that alter moods but cure nothing.

The society's president from 1988 to 1990 was Joest Martinius, a prominent advocate of the use of psychotropic drugs on children. In 1984, Dr. Martinius, along with Gerhardt Nissen and Christian Eggers, published a paper in which he examined the results and side effects of mood-altering drugs on children.[38] In this paper, Martinius and his colleagues developed, articulated and advocated some astonishing points of view.

Proceeding from the observation that "The number of mood-altering drugs presently in use is considerable and show enormous progress,"[39] the legacy that the authors drew upon becomes all too evident when they quote one of their sources of inspiration—Dr. Kraepelin—who was, as mentioned earlier, one of the earliest promoters of radical imperialism and totalitarianism. Observe the subtle scientific method of how discoveries are made:

"Kraepelin had already seen the future when he coined the term 'pharmacopsychology' in 1892, by writing: '…that we will arrive at a point where we can see more clearly from a particular effect that a remedy that is already better known can influence the thought process in the same way."[40]

It sounds even more outrageous when it is plainly stated: medication should be given to people so that the psychiatric community can study the reactions and side effects it causes in order to learn more about mental illness. Cart-before-the-horse does not begin to describe that sort of convoluted logic.

It is not necessary to elaborate much further on this remarkable and dis-

143

turbing study that delves deeply into the "hyperkinetic syndrome," an observable set of conditions which accompany an overly active and therefore (according to the psychiatrist) "disturbed child." This much, though, must be said: The study admits that the "placebo effect" ranges to about 40 percent. In other words, 40 percent of the test children's "behavioral disturbances" decreased after taking a sugar pill with no medicinal character whatsoever. In view of the enormous addictive potential of mood-altering drugs, and in view of documented dangers of a panoply of side effects associated with those drugs, it is incredible that such drugs are ever prescribed when a percentage of patients approaching one-half improve without medication at all. This is all the more so when it is remembered that the experimental subject matter is the brains of children.

Martinius and his colleagues also observed that:

"Mood-altering drugs are frequently being used on children and youth, even though knowledge about the effects of these substances in the developing organism is still full of holes."[41]

Then:

"Observations on children do not necessarily mirror the patterns of animals, and therefore were conducted as attempts to treat the patients…"[42]

One thing seems to be certain: To these child psychiatrists, drug therapy represents an easy "solution," to be used in the absence of any real knowledge or understanding of the causes for the child's health and behavioral changes, in the absence of any understanding of long-term effects, purely in an experimental fashion, and even though 40 percent of the children responded positively without medication. In the end, they retreat to the psychiatrist's excuse of last resort: it's all in the genes.

What is also apparent is the recurrent theme that psychiatry defines disorders to embrace as much of the populace as it can, and that psychiatrists who treat children are among the worse offenders. In this context, a document called "A Memorandum About the Situation of Child and Adolescent Psychiatry in the Federal Republic of Germany" furnishes a lot of insight. Originally published by the board of the directors of the German Society for Child and Adolescent Psychiatry in March 1984, a quote from its 1990 edition demonstrates psychiatry's fondness for all-inclusive definitions in the following discussion of "psychiatric illnesses:"

"The incidence of psychiatric illnesses and peculiarities in non-selected populations varies. In the third year of life it is around 20 percent, falls toward the sixth year of life to about 15 percent, then it climbs to 16 percent with 8-year-olds, and to about 20 percent with 13-14 year olds....

"In rural areas the range of the figures is somewhat lower. The average for 3 to 13 year olds is around 18 percent. A good third of them have more serious illnesses that are definitely in need of treatment. For the other two-thirds, a frequent consultation with the child and their families is enough. For all of West Germany this amounts to about 2.5 million mentally peculiar and sick children and juveniles, of whom 800,000 are in urgent need of treatment."[43]

Later it states:

"Underlying numerous psychiatric illnesses and peculiarities there are genetic influences...."[44]

Note that the language—but not the theory—has changed. Instead of talking about a "genetic burden," there are references to genetic "influences"—an incomparably more elegant phrase designed not to stir up unpleasant memories. Their demands today are, however, the same as yesterday—more psychiatric care for the population. In many cases, "care" means quite simply the prescription of mood-altering drugs, frequently prescribed as early as three years of age. The echoes of a eugenic solution are resounding.

The final question we must pose in this chapter is: How much trust can we actually put in a "science" that has committed more than its share of criminal acts, especially against children "in the name of research" and in the name of "keeping the nation pure?" And why today, when its "therapies" look so similar to those of 1940, is the name euthanasia not resuscitated? At least it would be more honest.

Listed as honorary members of the German Society for Child and Youth Psychiatry are, among others:

> Hans Bürger-Prinz
> Hermann Stutte

Also as members are:

> Helmuth E. Ehrhardt
> Hans Heinze
> Anna Leiter
> Friedrich Stumpfl

The lesson to be learned from this chapter in German postwar psychiatry is that there was virtually no intellectual deviation after the Second World War from the horrific theories of prewar child and adolescent psychiatry. The Nazi psychiatrists' legacy is carried forward by their students and protégés, and when anything changes at all, it is usually nomenclature. Primarily through the use of mood-altering drugs on children, methods were refined considerably, but the core beliefs stand immutable, as if they were etched in stone: that mental illnesses are, in numerous cases, hereditary (which is extremely controversial and not generally accepted) and are to be treated with more or less drastic measures including pharmacology and, perhaps, in the near future, surgery.

To this point, the focus has been almost exclusively on the teachers and their students who have kept the Nazi-style psychiatric theories and methods alive and in practice. Now the focus shifts toward psychiatric research. How did all the "scientific realizations" (before, during and after the war) which psychiatry would use as a reference point come into existence? There is yet another institution which played a crucial role in this analysis, with some frightening consequences.

CHAPTER 4

*"I had heard they were going to do it, so I went there and said
to them, 'Look here, boys, if you kill these people anyway, then at
least remove their brains so that the material can be used....'"*[1]
> Dr. Julius Hallervorden,
> German psychiatrist at the
> Kaiser Wilhelm Institute for
> Brain Research

RESEARCH AND GENETICS
AN OLD PRODUCT IN A NEW PACKAGE

In 1900, German industrial magnate Friedrich Krupp offered a prize of
over 30,000 marks to the scientist who could most convincingly demonstrate the significance of biological and racial lineage to domestic political development. Whatever his ulterior motives may have been, they are
lost behind history's shroud. However, we do know that among those who
joined the quest for the prize was the notorious racial hygienist Alfred
Ploetz, about whom we wrote in the first part of this book. He and his colleagues spent quite a bit of time together devoting themselves to the pursuit of Krupp's prize.

Ultimately, Ploetz and his cohorts extrapolated from the population
dogmas of Malthus and Gobineau and created a new kind of racial
hygiene theory which posited that society would be guided by the "genetically superior" human, while "inferior" humans—who by nature would be
"unworthy of living"—would form the "sediment."[2] The result was the
first eugenical efforts aimed at promoting the procreation of a genetically
healthy population on the one hand, and the prevention of those "unqual-
ified" to bear children on the other.

By 1911, Ernst Rüdin and Max von Gruber, who was the chairman of

REPRODUCTION INHERITANCE RACE HYGIENE

Catalogue of the Group Race Hygiene at the International
Hygiene-Exhibition   1911 in Dresden

Published by Prof. Dr. Max von Grüber
Director of the Hygiene Institute in Munich

and

University lecturer Dr. Ernst Rüdin
Chief Physician at the Psychiatric Clinic in Munich

Explaining Text with 230 Pictures
by M. v. Grüber

With a Bibliography by Dr. Rudolf Allers

J.F. LEHMANNS PUBLISHERS   MUNICH

the Hygienical Institute in Munich, published a detailed treatise on racial hygiene, stating:

"Hopefully the time is near when legislators understand that certain individuals should be compensated for propagating a qualified new generation, just as for other things; while those who deny their own personal comfort by denying their service in this regard, should be required to carry the costs of the matrimonial fruitfulness of those racial elements whose strong increase is imperative for the welfare of the nation. Only in such a manner can the destructive evil of the so-called 'woman's emancipation' movement be controlled.

"...Rational thinking should also rule the sexual sphere; one can count on uncontrolled childmaking only among the intellectually and morally inferior who have to be stopped from doing just that. For the others, an opportunity for the rational care and rearing of children has to be created. A moderate prosperity that still needs a certain amount of strength in order to keep it going is not harmful for procreation; what is harmful is wealth and the striving to pass it on to one's children. A wise inheritance tax would have to play a very relevant part in future racial hygiene legislation."[3]

Make no mistake. As early as 1911, psychiatrists led by Ernst Rüdin among others were openly and unequivocally demanding racial hygienic legislation.

On January 11, 1911, the Kaiser Wilhelm Gesellschaft (the Kaiser Wilhelm Society) was founded with the stated purpose of promoting the sciences. At the time, psychiatry was not yet included because it was not yet regarded as scientifically sound enough for inclusion. Natural sciences and humanities, however, were recognized under the same standard.

"At that time, approximately 200 respected German men and women entered the Society under the protectorate of the German emperor and the King of Prussia. The association's purpose was 'to support the sciences, particularly through the establishment and maintenance of scientific research institutes.' In a few days, fifteen million marks were collected by its founders as assets of the Society, and way over 100,000 marks in yearly membership fees were also guaranteed."[4]

Creation of the Kaiser Wilhelm Society represented a small revolution in the development of the sciences in Germany. The Society—*Der Stern* reverently referred to it as the world's crucible for Nobel prize winners—

has produced more than two dozen Nobel laureates.

How did this prestigious society get tangled up with Nazi psychiatry?

In 1912, the German Association for Psychiatry—the forerunner of today's GSPN—engaged psychiatrist Emil Kraepelin to prepare a study to stimulate the development of a research institute for psychiatry. The association's executives hoped to attract a subsidy from the Kaiser Wilhelm Society, but their efforts were unsuccessful. When a second attempt also failed a year later, Dr. Kraepelin embarked upon a search for sponsors expressly to endow a dedicated psychiatric research institute.

At that point, Krupp again emerges. Based on his early contest, it should come as no surprise that Krupp was attracted to a racial hygenicist like Kraepelin, and he committed funds to the proposed institute. Then in 1916, Kraepelin treated a rich American patient named James Loeb. In Loeb, Kraepelin found a second sponsor for his genetic-psychiatric research center. With the support of two such wealthy benefactors, Kraepelin's dream of a separate, dedicated institute for psychiatric research became a reality in 1917. Thanks to Loeb's generosity and Krupp's wealth and influence, Kraepelin had managed to accumulate a total of 1.7 million marks from private and corporate sources, among them the Verband der Deutschen Chemischen Industrie (Association of the German Chemical Industry). Thus endowed, and with the blessings of Bavarian King Ludwig III, Kraepelin established the "Öffentliche Stiftung Deutsche Forschungsanstalt für Psychiatrie (Publicly Funded German Research Institute for Psychiatry) in Munich. It would have far-reaching consequences.

Naturally enough, Kraepelin—who was also a professor at the University of Munich—was named the director of the Institute, and he immediately inaugurated research with a racial hygiene orientation. According to the annals of the German Research Institute of Psychiatry:

"Kraepelin proved to be typical of psychiatry after the turn of the century; on the one hand he turned the scientific orientation of his field toward research while on the other dealing in common ideas about degeneration and the increase of the mentally ill. We should briefly note here the connection of this sphere of ideas with Kraepelin's political views which were marked by a conservative nationalism."[5]

Cutting through the scholarly rhetoric, Kraepelin was certainly a conservative nationalist. But he also was a pioneer of psychiatric atrocities such as racial hygiene and sterilization, who, except perhaps for Rüdin, had no equal in his advocacy for a legal foundation for the policies of Nazi extermination.

Even before the establishment of his research institute, Kraepelin had devised a discipline he called "genetic psychiatric family research." Simply stated, this was precisely the kind of genealogical research into kinship that would later serve the Nazis as a theoretical foundation for the selection of their victims. Armed with his Institute's ample endowment, Kraepelin could for the first time conduct his quasi-scientific kinship research on a grand scale. For Kraepelin—who was essentially a student of the brain—his research consisted not just in probing possible hereditary transmission of mental illness but also the structure and nature of the brain itself. The brain, Kraepelin theorized, was the sole seat of all mental illnesses. Accordingly, it was vital for him to accelerate his brain research by studying brain anatomy. The methodology? dissection of the brains of dead rats, cats, people, whatever was available.

Kraepelin's German Research Institute of Psychiatry was subdivided into five main departments: Brain Research, Psychiatric Genetics, Experimental Psychology, Chemistry and Serology. However, he soon abandoned psychology and chemistry research due to a combination of competing demands for funds and space and the possibility that the Institute could devote itself exclusively to its primary endeavors—research into hereditary transmission and research into the structure of the brain.

Kraepelin's streamlining of the Institute's functions was also indicative of his spendthrift ways. Indeed, if Loeb hadn't bestowed an extra allowance in 1922 and directed his foundation to pump in another $50,000 in 1923, the Institute would have been bankrupt by 1924. But the Institute survived long enough to achieve the status and support Kraepelin craved. Limping toward financial ruin even after the generosity of its wealthy benefactors, however, the Institute would face a crossroads of either having to fold or be integrated into the ranks of those that had to be publicly sponsored through the Kaiser Wilhelm Institute. On March 18, 1924, based on the directive of the German senate, Kraepelin's German Research Institute for Psychiatry was incorporated into the Kaiser Wilhelm Institute.

Around that time, Dr. Rüdin met with representatives of the Institute for the first time and asked them to establish a "genealogical-demograph-ical" department. Irrespective of what it was called, Rüdin's idea was noth-ing more than still another department for conducting additional genetic and sociological research under Rüdin's direction. Hans Luxenburger, later a co-sponsor of the Sterilization Act, was one of Rüdin's colleagues in this department. Dr. Luxenburger devoted himself intensively to the research of twins, hoping for precise indications about mental dysfunctions and the probability of its hereditary transmission. Dr. Rüdin himself left for the University of Basel in 1925, and could only continue his research there on a limited scale.

In the spring of 1925, Dr. Kraepelin and a colleague traveled to the United States to ask the Rockefeller Foundation for more money for the Institute. The trip was successful. In 1926, he returned to Germany with a $325,000 donation. However, Kraepelin died the following October and never saw the re-opening of the German Research Institute on June 13, 1928 on the newly-renamed Kraepelinstrasse in Munich-Schwabing.

After a few years of personnel upheaval, Dr. Rüdin finally returned in 1931 to become the director of the Institute. It was from the Institute that Rüdin entered into an irrevocable collaboration with the Nazis who would come to power in 1933. Rüdin placed great emphasis both on twin research and on the transmissibility of mental illness. Under his director-ship, more than 9,000 twins were registered, catalogued, experimented upon and evaluated. Dr. Luxenburger, the co-author of several books on genetics and a specialist in twin research, provided extensive assistance.

Ultimately, six independent departments existed within the Institute:

a clinical department

a histopathology department (histopathological being identified here with brain pathology)

a department of serology and experimental therapy

a department of genealogy and demography, under Rüdin himself, who called it an "institute for the research of transmission of psychological dis-turbances"[6]

a chemistry department

a department for spirochtaleta research (spirochtaleta are a type of long, spiral bacteria).

The financial donations being received were increasingly earmarked for research into the genetic causes of mental illness. James Loeb, the Institute's main sponsor, died in 1933, but by that time support flowed richly from the public coffers and the Nazi state budget. The Institute was the beneficiary of the high regard the Nazis' had for Rüdin himself. After all, it was Rüdin who had provided the scientific foundation and justifications for the Law for the Prevention of Genetically Diseased Children. His support and scholarship had only been possible because of the resources and facilities of the Institute. The sterilizations that were to follow were the immediate end result of research done over many years within the Institute, which was the crucible for Nazi psychiatric and political crimes against humanity.

During the period of euthanasia (which began in 1939), the German Research Institute for Psychiatry worked with the killing department in Munich-Haar (whose director was Dr. Hermann Pfannmüller) as well as with the Ansbach and Kaufbeuren institutes, where many murders were committed. Götz Aly, a prominent writer and historian, investigated these matters and found corroboration in the form of hundreds of testimonials in the archives of the Max Planck Institute for Psychiatry in Munich,[7] about which he has written extensively.[8]

Today's Max Planck Institute for Psychiatry—the new name of the old Institute that Kraepelin founded and Rüdin led—has attempted to skirt the issue by offering a "reasonable explanation."

"When the Nazis tried to gain influence on the scientific orientation of genetic work through (financial donations)...they found in Rüdin an unwilling tool. Even donations from the SS foundation 'Ahnenerbe' ('Legacy From Ancestors' or 'Genetic Inheritance') proved to be a double-edged sword. Therefore, Rüdin had to accept a certain amount of infiltration of his department with ideological employees...racial research in accordance with Nazi ideology was never, however, performed in the genealogical departments."[9]

This claim might cause us to question, then, what might have been going through Rüdin's mind when he assembled his 1934 defense of the Law for the Prevention of Genetically Diseased Children and included the following quote from Adolf Hitler: "A person who is not healthy of body and mind is not allowed to perpetuate his suffering through the body of his child!"[10] And what else could Rüdin have possibly meant when he wrote in the same paper:

"The act is therefore to be understood as a bulldozing into the debris and small-mindedness of a bygone philosophy and an overblown and suicidal charity of past centuries."[11]

The Führer apparently didn't view Dr. Rüdin's work as brinkmanship. He responded by bestowing upon Rüdin the highest of honors: the Goethe Medal, plus the Shield of the Eagle of the Third Reich.

All this to a man who wrote:

"The Law for the Prevention of Genetically Diseased Children should itself be seen as the beginning of a new era in the public health system and in medicine in general."[12]

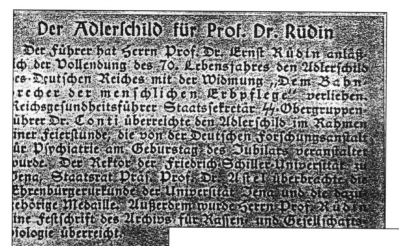

THE SHIELD OF THE EAGLE FOR PROF. DR. RÜDIN

The Führer awards to Prof. Dr. Rüdin on the occasion of the completion of the 70th year of his life the Shield of the Eagle with the dedication: "To The Pioneer of Human Genetics." The Reich's Health Minister, State Secretary and SS Obergruppenfuhrer Dr. Leonardo Conti presented the Shield of the Eagle during a ceremony organized by the German Research Institute for Psychiatry for his birthday. The Rector of the Friedrich Schiller University of Jena, Council of State, President Prof. Astel presented the certificate of honorary citizen as well as the medal that goes with it. Dr. Rüdin was also honored with a commemorative edition of the Archive for Racial and Social Biology.

On July 13, 1944, the Institute was almost completely demolished in a bombing raid. Rüdin was removed from his directorship in November of 1945 by the American military government, but he was never brought to trial. He claimed to be "only a nominal member" and with that managed to be completely exonerated. The fact was, however, that he was one of the men behind Hitler who never had to bloody his own hands. He had plenty of others all too willing to do his dirty work for him. And the major role the German Research Institute for Psychiatry—now, the Max Planck Institute for Psychiatry—really played in the Nazis' atrocities is undeniable. In fact, it is impossible to quantify the magnitude of the horrors which can be traced directly to the Institute.

But there's even more to this horrific past. For context, however, some additional history requires review.

One of the employees of the German Research Institute for Psychiatry in Munich, Dr. Hugo Spatz (1888-1969), transferred to Berlin in 1936, and became the director of the Kaiser Wilhelm Institute for Brain Research in Berlin-Buch in 1937. That facility, which had been founded in 1915 also with donations from the Krupp family, was located in a modern building, built in 1931, constructed with grants from the German Republic, the Prussian provincial government and the Rockefeller Foundation. This brain research branch of the institute devoted itself exclusively to the research of anatomical abnormalities in the brains of the mentally ill. Genetic research was also performed, as there was also an independent genetics department.

In 1937, the Institute's brain research was divided into two endeavors: an anatomy department under the direction of Dr. Spatz, the Institute's director, and a histopathological department under the leadership of Dr. Julius Hallervorden. Under the regime of Spatz and Hallervorden, the brain research Institute established a collaborative relationship with the infamous asylum (later killing institute) at Brandenburg-Görden.

That relationship was well established when, in 1939, the Brandenburg-Görden asylum became the "Reich's training institute" for child euthanasia. Not only were hundreds of children killed there under the supervision of Dr. Heinze, but dozens of physicians were also trained in child euthanasia. In 1939, Heinze himself received a seat on the board of directors of the Institute. By then, the pathological-anatomical department of the

Brandenburg asylum was managed as a branch of the Kaiser Wilhelm Institute for Brain Research. As Aly and others have thoroughly documented, the killing was now being done purely for research purposes.[13]

The ramifications of the interrelationship between the brain research Institute and the killing institute at Brandenburg-Görden are shocking in their implications: Individuals considered "interesting" cases of mental disturbances were taken to the gas chambers so that their brains could be used for psychiatric research instead.

These accusations are based on investigations conducted by many prominent scholars and authors. Federal and military archives and numerous transcripts of witness interrogations have been meticulously scrutinized.

Heinze, Catel, Schneider and Hallervorden had worked out the awarding of doctorates from this research, which were still being handed in and completed at German universities after the war and after the suicide of several doctoral recipients.[14]

Even more shocking is the recent discovery that the brains of euthanized children were stored until 1990 in the basement of the Max Planck Institute for Brain Research in Frankfurt. They came from Dillenburg, Dr. Hallervorden's home town, where he had brought his valuable inventory out of harm's way in 1944 on Hitler's instructions. Hallervorden showed them to an American medical officer named Leo Alexander, and during the ensuing interrogations Hallervorden stated:

"I had found out they would do it, so I went over and said to them, 'Look here, boys, if you want to kill all these people, then at least remove their brains so that the material can be used.' They asked me how many I could examine and I told them, 'An unlimited amount, the more the merrier'…There was wonderful material among these brains, great mental illnesses, deformities and early childhood illnesses. Of course, I accepted the brains. Where they came from and how they got there was of no real interest to me."[15]

Among the brains that found their way to the Max Planck were those of children who had been euthanized at Brandenburg-Görden. In one documented case, for example, on October 28, 1940, a group of 33 prisoners between the ages of seven and eighteen arrived at Brandenburg-Görden. After they were killed, their brains were immediately removed and dissected, many on the same day.

Hallervorden later denied having said what he said to Alexander, but ample documentation renders his denials unworthy of belief. For example, the 1940 yearbook of the Kaiser Wilhelm Society acknowledged that:

"The histopathological department (Prof. Hallervorden) continued the work on the anatomical fundamentals of congenital imbecility; data on brain injuries were newly recorded."[16]

Hallervorden and his boss, Hugo Spatz, fled to Giessen after the war but later returned to run the Max Planck Institute for Brain Research until 1957. Dr. Spatz was given an honorary doctorate by the University of Granada; it is hardly likely that anyone there knew about his former involvement in the scientific research on the brains of euthanized children. The fate of the "Hallervorden Collection" was not sealed until 1990. The Max Planck Institute for Brain Research in Frankfurt finally admitted that the "historical material" stored in its basements was the harvest of Nazi euthanasia. The "material" was eventually given a burial at a Munich cemetery.

Symbolically, that internment 45 years after war's end reflects much of the saga of postwar German psychiatry's reaction to its Nazi antecedents and its history of inhumanity. Bury it. Conceal it. Hide it. Disguise it with careful language.

For example, this is what was written about the Third Reich and psychiatric brain research in the commemorative volume called "75 Years of the Max Planck Institute for Psychiatry," which was published in 1992:

"An exclusively active or passive role cannot be attributed to either psychiatric science or the state; both acted as the beginning and the end of certain historical and ideological processes."

While we have examined the Kaiser Wilhelm Institute for Psychiatry in Munich, where Kraepelin and Rüdin both reigned, the Kaiser Wilhelm Institute for Brain Research in Berlin-Buch, the territory of Spatz and Hallervorden, yet another, equally or even more horrifying chapter of psychiatric research history unfolds when we examine the so-called Kaiser Wilhelm Institute for Anthropology.

Officially called the Kaiser Wilhelm Institute for Anthropology, Human Genetics and Eugenics, it opened its doors on September 15, 1927 in Berlin-Dahlem. Directing this institute were names familiar to students of psychiatric abuses: Eugen Fischer, Erwin Baur and Fritz Lenz.

MAX-PLANCK-INSTITUT
FÜR HIRNFORSCHUNG
NEUROPHYSIOLOGISCHE ABTEILUNG
DIREKTOR: PROF. DR. MED. W. SINGER

Telefax: (069) 67 04-433

6000 Frankfurt a. M. 71 (Niederrad)
Deutschordenstraße 46
Postfach 71 06 62   218
Telefon (069) 67 04 (1)

27-Mai-92
Si/ip

Herrn ▮▮▮▮▮▮▮

Sehr geehrter Herr ▮▮▮▮

haben Sie besten Dank für Ihr Schrei▮
Verbleib der Sammlung Hallervorden erkun▮

Als Herr Professor Wässle und ich ▮
Frankfurt übernahmen, fanden wir hie▮
histologischer Schnitte vor. Da diese ▮
war, haben wir sie dem Edinger Insti▮
Universität Frankfurt, übereignet. Da ▮
untergebracht ist, verblieben diese a▮
Haus. Es wurde mit ihnen jedoch, da es ▮
wissenschaftlich gearbeitet. Einige Ja▮
von Nachforschungen, die sowohl v▮
Medizinhistorikern hier an der Univers▮
sich in diesen Sammlungen auch die S▮
möglicherweise Präparate von Euthana▮
daraufhin von seiten des Max-Planck-In▮
umgehend unter Verschluß genommen wurd▮
für wissenschaftliche Arbeiten hinfort▮
und nur noch für historische Nachfo▮
sollte.   Der Datenschutzbeauftragte ▮
Professor Simitis, wurde damals umgehe▮
wie auch alle anderen offiziellen Stell▮
kontrovers geführten Diskussion haben ▮
durchsetzen können und diese Sammlung w▮
Max-Planck-Gesellschaft   zurückgefü▮
herausstellte, von den vielen tausend ▮
im Rahmen neuropathologischer Routineun▮
Berlin-Buch angefertigt wurden, jene h▮
Euthanasieopfern sein könnten, haben ▮
histologische Material, das zwischen 19▮
mit anderen möglicherweise belasteten ▮
Hirnforschungsinstitutes Berlin-Buch b▮
im Frühjahr 1990 am Waldfriedhof in ▮
Gedenkfeier gehaltenen Reden und die ▮
können Sie über die Presseabteilung d▮
erhalten.

Ich hoffe, Ihnen mit dieser Auskunft ge▮

Mit bestem Gruß
Ihr

Prof. Wolf Singer

Dear Sir:

Thank you for your letter inquiring into the whereabouts of the Hallervorden Collection.

When Professor Wassle and I took over the Brain Research Institute in Frankfurt in 1982, we found a voluminous collection of histological sections. Since they were of no importance for our sphere of activity, we gave them to the Edinger Institute in the department of neuropathy at the University of Frankfurt. Since the Edinger Institute is housed under our roof, the anatomical collection has remained here in the building. However, no scientific work was done with it, since it is old material. Because of certain investigations conducted by Mr. Götz-Aly as well as by medical historians here at the University, we became suspicious a few years later that in these collections as well as the Hallervorden Collection there could possibly be among them specimens from the victims of euthanasia. We then arranged through the Max Planck Institute to have this collection immediately sealed off. Thus it was assured that from then on they would not be available for scientific work and would only be accessible for historical investigations. The custodian of official data from the Hessian ministry was immediately informed about the circumstances, like all other official authorities. After a lengthy and sometimes heated discussion, we were finally able to convince him to have this collection returned to the responsibility of the Max Planck Society. It proved to be impossible to find among the thousands of specimens those that came from the euthanasia victims who had been prepared for routine neuropathological investigation in the brain research institute of Berlin-Buch between 1933 and 1945. We therefore decided to bury all of the histological material that had been collected between 1933 and 1945, together with any other possibly contaminated specimens from successor institutes of Berlin-Buch. This burial took place at the Waldfriedhof cemetery in Munich. You may request copies of the texts of speeches held at this commemoration and the inscription on the memorial from the press department of the Max Planck Society in Munich.

I hope I have been of assistance to you with this information.

With best wishes

Yours,

Prof. Wolf Singer

Lenz was the "human geneticist" who worked from 1919 until 1933 for the "Archiv für Rassen- und Gesellschaftbiologie" ("Archive for Racial and Social Biology"), a leader on the front lines of the racial hygiene movement. Collaborating with his Kaiser Wilhelm colleagues Baur and Fischer, Lenz wrote the book *Menschliche Erblehre und Rassenhygiene* (*Human Genetics and Racial Hygiene*), which was published in 1921 in Munich. Lenz's own words leave little doubt that he was one of the philosophical pioneers of Hitler's heritage:

"From actual racial hygienical books I hear that Hitler had read the second edition of Fischer-Baur-Lenz during his incarceration in Landsberg. Some parts of it are mirrored in Hitler's phrases. In any case, with great mental energy he made the essential ideas of racial hygiene and their importance his own, while most academic authorities still look upon these questions rather unappreciatively."[17]

The highly renowned Kaiser Wilhelm Society—the cradle of Nobel laureates—had admitted into its ranks and delivered prestige and power to the purveyors of the philosophical excuses upon which Hitler would be ideologically dependent for mass extermination and euthanasia—Rüdin and Kraepelin at the Kaiser Wilhelm Institute of Munich and Baur, Fischer and Lenz in Berlin. The leaders of the eugenics movement were also the leaders at the psychiatric institutes of the Kaiser Wilhelm Society. And this was long before the Third Reich, and well before they could have hoped to give tangible form to their heinous theories and treatments. They were in place awaiting political power and ideology compatible with their own. The architects of the Holocaust had gathered in the psychiatric societies, insinuated themselves directly into the domain of research, and ultimately found a forum for the expression of their own violence and madness.

The catastrophic proportions this situation would assume was enlarged even more by another pioneer of modern psychiatric research employed at the Kaiser Wilhelm Institute for Anthropology in Berlin—Dr. Otmar Freiherr von Verschuer, a human geneticist and close ally of many prominent psychiatrists. Verschuer made twin research popular, and it was he who supplied Dr. Josef Mengele with the necessary tools to commit his unimaginable crimes in the Auschwitz concentration camp.

A professor of Human Genetics and Racial Hygiene at the University of Berlin, and a department head at the Kaiser Wilhelm Institute for

Anthropology, Genetics and Eugenics, Dr. Verschuer wrote a book enti-tled *Erblehre des Menschen* (*Genetics of Humans*), in which he gave a vivid portrait of the horror to come through the application of genetic theory. Published in 1934, Verschuer presented the scientific foundation for the barbarism that was to follow, and it was plainly intended to inspire his impressionable students:

"It is necessary that new laws about life are enacted in our legislature, in our social order, and above all in the action and thinking of everyone!

"When man lived in his natural state as a hunter and gatherer, and later as a farmer, to a large degree sickly genetic traits were eradicated. Today, they remain intact. In our natural state, short-sightedness, bad teeth, weakness of the body, dysfunctional organs and inabilities to bear and breast-feed children had been pathological disturbances that were incon-sistent with the preservation of life."[18]

It hardly needs mentioning, given such sentiments, that Verschuer was an ardent advocate of the Sterilization Act.

Through his publications of various periodical medical journals, Verschuer was instrumental in propagandizing Nazi ideology within the German medical profession.[19] In 1935, Verschuer was called to Frankfurt to join the newly-formed Institute for Genetics and Racial Hygiene that shared, with the Research Institute in Munich, the leading role in the application of genetics techniques in the Third Reich. One of his close collaborators in Frankfurt was Dr. Josef Mengele, an enthusiastic apostle of twin research and later the notorious murderer of Auschwitz. Dr. Verschuer's institute, which operated under the official name of "Rassenbiologische Fachgutachterstelle für die Reichstelle für Sippen-forschung" ("Racial-Biological Special Advisory Authority for the Reich's Kinship Research") provided "expert advice" on the science of state-spon-sored mass-murder.

In 1942, Verschuer returned to Berlin and became the director of the Kaiser Wilhelm Institute for Anthropology, where Mengele—who, in the meantime, had served in the Armed SS but was drummed out for being unfit—reunited with his mentor.

On May 30, 1943, Mengele was transferred to the post of camp physi-cian at Auschwitz. It was his duty to assess prisoners and decide which ones would be sent to the gas chambers and which ones would work in the

Slave laborers in the Buchenwald Concentration Camp near Jena.

camps. It is beyond the scope of this book to plumb the depths of Mengele's well-documented cruelties at Auschwitz. However, one thing must be emphasized: With Auschwitz under his command, this ardent twin researcher and disciple of Verschuer had a research opportunity unique in psychiatric history—the anatomical dissections of twins immediately after their deaths.

Up until then, it had not been possible to test psychiatric twin theories by comparing the side-by-side autopsies of twins immediately after death, since contrary to all genetic postulations, twins almost never die at the same place and at the same time. Even in rare instances when they did, they were seldom available for immediate research.

For that reason, Mengele meticulously segregated twins who, as long as they lived and were not subjected to his brutal experiments, lived relatively well under his care. Because they had to stay healthy for his research, they were kept isolated from the usual camp diseases.

Mengele's experiments were worse than most people can imagine in their most profoundly disturbed nightmares. He injected bacterial cultures, viruses and pus into his victims and castrated some of them with X-rays and he prepared especially interesting "examples" for the German Anthropology Museum.

Besides genetic twin research, Mengele also attempted to prove the inferiority of the Jewish race. A former physician at the concentration camp who was himself an inmate reported a horrible example of this. He had belonged to the so-called "special commandos," inmates who were assigned to do whatever dirty work Mengele wanted them to do and were later shot:

"A Jewish man and his son were not immediately gassed and cremated as was usual because of some shared physical deformity, but were ordered to be carefully examined and then shot afterwards. Mengele then ordered his men not to incinerate their bodies, but to send their skeletons to the anthropological museum in Berlin. The doctor (also a Jewish inmate) was asked by Mengele for the fastest method to prepare them for shipment. Mengele ordered that the two corpses be put into boiling water until the meat could be easily removed from their bones. When the SS left the "soup pot" unwatched, the Polish inmates jumped right in, under the assumption that they had found the officers' meal unattended. After the Poles found out what they were eating, they fell into pure terror. After about five hours, the skeletons were brought back into the examination room and prepared for shipment to Berlin, but not before Mengele and some of his officers had examined them thoroughly once more."[20]

Probably the most brutal of all the Nazi butchers, Mengele was a student and co-worker of Verschuer even during his time at Auschwitz. At Mengele's request, Verschuer applied to a German research association for funding for two projects. Mengele returned the favor later by sending "scientifically especially interesting" organs and skeletons to Verschuer.[21]

In fact, Mengele and Verschuer apparently researched in close association with each other as late as 1945, but not much of it has been recovered intact. How close their connection really was or wasn't cannot fully be reconstructed. Either because their fingerprints are blurred or they did not survive to speak—or both—a cloak of silence covers the truth.

While Mengele was forced to flee to South America in 1945, Verschuer had nothing to worry about. While his theories had blazed the trail for the horrendous deeds of those who were inspired by him, it was not his hands that had killed. Although the Hessian government stripped him of the right to teach and to conduct research after the war, Verschuer still had sufficient political leverage to become a member of the Akademie der Wissenschaften (Academy of the Sciences) in 1949. By 1951, he gained an appointment as a Professor of Genetics in Münster.

The Max Planck Institute for Psychiatry in Munich

Here the unrepentant racial hygienist ordered the establishment of a genetic register into which over two million people's names were to be recorded. In 1956, he was elected to the chairmanship of the German Society for Anthropology. Finally, in 1965 he went into retirement where in 1969 he died peacefully, apparently unperturbed by his shady past or the crimes he allowed in the name of science.

Verschuer and his disciple Mengele provide excellent examples of how the antisocial doctrines of psychiatry had a polluting influence on other scientific disciplines such as anthropology and general medicine. In a time like the Third Reich, there were many guilty parties, but psychiatry was the inspiration and partner in crime of all of them.

After the war in 1948, the Max Planck Society was created as the successor to the Kaiser Wilhelm Society. All of the various Kaiser Wilhelm Institute branches that still existed were renamed as departments of the Max Planck Institute.

The German Research Institute for Psychiatry in Munich, linked to the Max Planck Society by their mutual activities, did not change, operating as it had before the war and remaining true to its old traditions.[22] Genetic and twin research were continued by, among others, Ernst Rüdin's daughter, Edith. Detlev Ploog—who would later become the director of the Institute—was a student of T4 psychiatrist Villinger. In 1964, another branch, the Max Planck Institute for Comparative Genetics and Hereditary Pathology, was renamed the "Max Planck Institute for

Molecular Genetics."

Old product, new package.

Today's focal points of research in the Max Planck Institutes for Genetics are in the field of molecular biology and genetic research. Very impressive-sounding subjects to be sure, but the theory underlying these fields is over a hundred years old, a fact that even name changes and the most clever public relations cannot change. The theories and objectives of the Nazi geneticists, in large part, remain intact. The current director of the Max Planck Institute for Psychiatry-Theoretical Institute, Dr. Florian Holsboer, is an avid proponent of the theory that all psychiatric illnesses are genetically-based.[23]

The German tradition of racial and mental hygiene has permeated psychiatry for the entirity of this century. It never went away.

"Why is it better to weigh your words like gold? So that they're not confused with tin."

> *Markus M. Ronner,*
> *German journalist and satirist*

"MENTAL HYGIENE"
WHAT DOES IT REALLY MEAN?

It is certainly not an overstatement to point out that psychiatry suffers from the same sorts of disorders that it is fond of diagnosing in others. There is, for example, psychiatry's own hereditary burden. Psychiatry has never attempted to accomplish a proper eradication of its traditional racial hygiene theories. The changes that have found their way into psychiatric thought have either been limited to nomenclature or purely cosmetic. Through redefinition, and through manipulation of nuances and connotation, psychiatry has managed to disguise its true, static, unchanging nature. Beyond that, it is essentially a matter of selective amnesia that psychiatry does not seem to recognize its continuing adherence to its racist and totalitarian roots.

Psychiatry also seems to suffer from a "schizophrenia" of convenience. It assumes whatever personality the necessity of self-preservation dictates at any particular moment. Place this so-called "science" under a microscope and ponder its history, one cloaked in arrogance and sanctimony.

Psychiatry's tragic and inhumane past is even more dramatic because the subject of mental health deals directly with people's well-being. But, as catalogued throughout this book, psychiatry has been the source of and justification for politics, ideas, theories and practices that cost people's lives. It is inconceivable that any motive but consummate evil would prompt anyone to cling to such a brutal tradition and to continue to pursue its anti-social aims. Yet psychiatry continues to embrace its historical agendas in a barely camouflaged form.

One of psychiatry's most common devices to convey the misperception of authoritative and benevolent science is to conceal itself behind a wall of pseudoscientific, hypertechnological jargon. "Psychobabble" works. Just choose anyone you know, preferably someone with an average education, and have him or her read a passage from any psychiatric text. It is virtually guaranteed that he or she will be hopelessly confused. Your subject will feel distracted and incapable of understanding it and very much inclined to surrender the field to the apparent "expertise" of the psychiatrist.

However, stripped of the facade of multisyllabic Greek and Latin—and sometimes even German—terminology, what is revealed is often as hollow as the inside of a drum. Worse still, behind that facade also lurks a sizable body of fantastic nonsense and a plethora of antisocial ideas and "therapies."

One such idea is "mental hygiene."

The term "mental hygiene" (in German, "psychohygiene") literally means "psychological health care" or "mental health." The word "hygiene" itself is borrowed from medical terminology. One of modern medical science's greatest discoveries was the recognition that procedures to safeguard cleanliness and freedom from dirt and germs, greatly diminished the chance of infection in childbirth, surgery and everywhere else. Psychiatry tried to adapt the word for its activities. Yet psychiatry has never succeeded to any significant extent in identifying or recognizing the causes of insanity, and therefore placed enormous emphasis on what it terms "prevention."

Thus to promote the idea of preventive psychiatry, the impressive-sounding phrase "mental hygiene" was coined. In Germany, the term "psychohygiene" and its attendant concepts were introduced in 1901 in a paper prepared by psychiatrist Robert Sommer. But Sommer had merely appropriated "mental hygiene," as the term had been originally coined by German-born American psychiatrist Adolf Meyer.[1]

Mental hygiene was primarily designed to characterize the goal of a preventative campaign against "all difficulties caused by psychological irregularities during an adjustment to the demands of life."[2] Within those parameters—wide and virtually limitless though they may be—Sommer hoped to achieve two things, one obvious, one more obscure. On the one hand, he plainly did hope to develop techniques to help people adjust to life. On the other hand, he also sought to justify a psychiatric philosophy and actions directed toward social problems. To Sommer, "mental hygiene" meant, among other things, a revival of insane asylums to house those who were not adequately adjusted to life. Ultimately, "psychohygiene," as Sommer and the generations of German psychiatrists who would follow him intended it, meant that psychiatry acting in the name of "prevention," would gain influence in the German health and educational systems, in welfare and legal services, the economy and in religion and ethics.

Understanding the full implications of "mental hygiene," however, is tricky because a simple definition is elusive. Some guidance is gleaned from the political and economic climate in which the concept originated. It is not a coincidence that an American psychiatrist named G. M. Beard founded the American National Committee for Mental Hygiene in 1909, with the following stated purpose:

"...to help all those who cannot adjust socially because of psychological peculiarities and to remove the deplorable state of affairs which can be traced back to public service, like the education of youth and the fight against crime and psychological peculiarities...to inform the population accordingly to assist with relevant legislative measures and to work together with the rest of the mental hygiene field as well as other private and public bodies of common interest."[3]

Thus, from its inception, mental hygiene was concerned with adjusting the person to society, not with addressing the individual needs or requirements of the person. This concept of adapting people to society is congruent with the economic and political climate in which it arose. When the mental hygiene movement was conceptualized, industrialization was in a period of rapid expansion and, more than ever before, there was a demand for what might be called a workplace-suited person. Mental hygiene, as conceived at that time, perfectly filled an important niche, as mental hygienists claimed expertise in that enigmatic subject and focused their examinations on their patients' "adjustment difficulties." Quickly, the mental hygienists found suitably impressive-sounding terms, such as "nervous exhaustion" or "hysterical reaction" to characterize maladies they encountered and to imbue them with foreboding overtones. What they were describing was not anything approaching an exotic or unusual condition.

Those obtuse labels were affixed to everyday irritations and reactions that arise at work and at home. Today we simply call it stress.

In essence, the demands of an increasingly industrialized society for a particular sort of work force created the vacuum that psychiatry first occupied, then influenced, then sought to expand from—all in the name of mental hygiene. Mental hygiene was created expressly to adjust people so they could conform to their environment. Psychiatrists oriented themselves to this need to create "human material" suitable for the workplace. Later, during World War I, they would do so for the military. Still later, all of society became their target and racism the ideology which demanded conformity.

Operating under presumptions of convenience and the dictates of need, mental hygiene's formative years watched the discipline blossom. The person who was poorly adjusted to the workplace was described as "abnormal" or "sick." With their sweeping definitions of labels such as that, psychiatry was able to diagnose entire groups of people as "in need of treatment." With the notions of precaution and prevention as integral parts of the process, the mental hygienist was expected to and did embrace within their definition of those needing their attention, people who were perfectly healthy and well-adjusted.

The implications of this notion of prevention on those who are normal and healthy is self-evident, but the dire implications expand when the precepts of mental hygiene are coupled with the psychiatric perceptions of genetics and heredity. By 1936, for example, it was not enough for Ernst Rüdin to order only the proven genetically sick to be sterilized. He would also demand sterilization for all healthy people who had a case of mental or emotional disturbance anywhere in their family. Luckily, Dr. Rüdin's call was not heeded. It was even too extreme for the Nazi party.

The expansion of psychiatry's invented and self-serving definition of illness across increasingly larger segments of the population—ultimately to embrace healthy people in the name of prevention and by virtue of a presumed hereditary burden—is the legacy of the mental hygiene movement. Along the way, psychiatry lost sight of treating patients and, like mental hygiene, concerned itself not with health care but with social or economic conformity. This is demonstrated dramatically in the application of "eugenics" and "racial hygiene" by the Third Reich.

In 1924, the German Association of Psychological Hygiene was founded by Robert Sommer. Its stated purpose sounded noble: the prevention of "mental disturbances" and preventative health protection.[4] But by 1928, its goals had been expanded to include "hereditary prophylaxis"—a synonym for eugenics. Then came the idea of organizing the care of the mentally ill both within insane asylums and outside them. We have already addressed in detail how the Nazis and their psychiatrists dealt with such social burdens once they were so nicely organized.

Mental hygiene, however, was truly an international movement. A Swiss psychiatrist named August Forel dealt with "nerval hygiene" and "mental hygiene" in his investigations of human sexuality. In Russia in 1887, Dr. J. A. Sikorsky, speaking at the first Russian psychiatrists' congress, demanded the protection of the individual and society through the means of "neuropsychological hygiene and prophylaxis (prevention)" with the idea of strengthening the "psychological powers" and "raising the psychological level" of the population.

In the Soviet Union in 1922, a Special Commission for the Protection of Neuropsychological Health was installed within the People's Commissariat for Health. In 1923, the Special Commission convened an all-Russian Congress for Mental Hygiene and Psychoprophylaxis in Moscow and demanded, among other things, the psychological hygiene of the army, especially as it pertained to the selection of new recruits.

The concept of psychological hygiene gained an expanded relationship-oriented slant through a significant propaganda machine in the United States. "Mental hygiene" became a slogan for a psycho-social-hygienical movement dedicated to the "common good" that, emanating from the United States, grew to worldwide proportions.

It is clear, therefore, that as early as the 1920s, the mental hygiene movement had established itself as a strong influence over the health policies in quite a number of countries. With its vision of "positive eugenics"— favorable genetic selection, perhaps the ultimate demand of mental hygiene—it purported to try to improve the "eugenic value" of the population and thus achieve a "healthy growth" of the population. In that regard, the improvement of the health of mother and child was declared to be mental hygiene's highest purpose. It sounded very noble, but eugenics' ugly poison rapidly polluted all semblance of nobility.

There was some resistance from the so-called scientifically-oriented school of medicine, which opposed this kind of "hygiene." Only in the 1930s did "psychological hygiene" again start to take shape—this time in Germany, and by then it was imprinted not only with the core beliefs of eugenics and racial hygiene, but also with the Third Reich.

In Germany, the whole process was neatly mapped out. By 1928, the mental hygienists' objectives had been clearly outlined in "Zeitschrift für Psychische Hygiene" (Periodical for Psychological Hygiene):

"The activity of the German Association…encompasses the application of the principles of psychological hygiene to the individual, the family, professional education, social insurance and public life. Moreover, also included in this are the prevention of psychological peculiarities and distress and susceptibility to crime caused by it, using eugenics in particular, the battle against alcoholism and other addictions to street drugs and syphilis, as well as a preventive fight against crime.…"[5]

Therefore the foundation had been laid for the extermination of certain unwanted groups. Although it could be assumed that at the time nobody had conceived of the kind of solution that would later be practiced by the Nazi regime, the German Association for Psychological Hygiene did not protest when the Nazi "solution" was imposed. No wonder that:

"The German Association for Psychological Hygiene was the organized expression of the intention to get control at last over all societal problems of abnormal behavior."[6]

It was also no coincidence that the elite of German psychiatry congregated and socialized under the aegis of the Association for Psychological Hygiene. In 1931, this association's membership included the same psychiatrists who were influential in the societies and institutes addressed throughout this book: Luxenburger (co-author of *Psychiatric Genetics and Genetic Care)*, Meltzer (who, in the 1920s, was already interviewing parents of handicapped children about euthanasia), Villinger, Kretschmer, Nitsche, and Faltlhauser (director of the Kaufbeuren institute and responsible for killing children and adults through lethal injections and starvation between 1941 and 1945).

In 1934, the association was renamed the Deutscher Verband für Psychische Hygiene und Rassenhygiene (German Association for Psychological and Racial Hygiene) and, at the request of Robert Sommer, none other than Ernst Rüdin assumed the presidency. Those who might have clung to the thought that Sommer was pursuing noble purposes through the mental hygiene movement he helped create will be disabused of that fantasy upon reading a 1934 telegram he wrote to Rüdin congratulating him on his sixtieth birthday and the publication of his textbook *Psychiatrische Erbpflege und Rassenhygiene im völkischem Staat (Psychiatric Genetics and Racial Hygiene in the Ethnic State)*. In it, Sommer delivers extremely cordial greetings in the name of the association.

A very detailed account by Hans Roemer from 1943 documents, articulated the objectives and methods of the mental hygiene movement. It is worthwhile to quote some passages:

"From about the 400,000 genetically sick...approximately 300,000 are...psychiatric cases.... An understanding of the urgent necessity for psychiatric genetic health care has spread more and more lately throughout professional medical organizations, general practitioners, lawyers and economists. This increasing understanding has led to the design of a Sterilization Act....Through this political sea change the situation has shifted in one fell swoop...the performance of a legally regulated duty has now replaced the voluntary work where the legal basis for proceeding more actively was missing...."[7]

As noted earlier, the law for compulsory sterilization did not go far enough for Rüdin. He also demanded the extermination of anyone with a mental or serious physical abnormality occurring anywhere within their immediate family.

It is important to remember that Rüdin and his followers were never interrogated after the war. Such investigations were reserved for the Nazis who supposedly "misused" psychiatry for their own twisted purposes. Nor did German psychiatry face any significant criticism to distract them after the war, certainly not from within their own ranks. Rüdin, for example, was never even questioned by the German psychiatric hierarchy. In fact, years later when Rüdin's daughter, Edith Zerbin-Rüdin, also a professor of psychiatry, was asked in an interview about her father's involvement in the highest eugenical courts of Nazi psychiatry, she defended him, pointing out that, at that time, there had been an "international eugenical movement"[8] to which her father belonged.

That is an especially troubling answer for it is both an excuse for his behavior and an insinuation of something more. If we dig deeper, we discover that this is precisely where the solution to the postwar puzzle is buried. It is where we find the answer to how and why German psychiatry escaped justice after the fall of the Third Reich.

The worldwide interconnections of the mental hygiene movement—an "international eugenical movement"—was not merely a metaphor from Rüdin's daughter, but a network that actually existed. It is fair to suggest that many of the Third Reich's most culpable psychiatrists had no fear of punishment or retribution due to their role in the Nazi atrocities, because the theories they espoused and the philosophies they pursued and even the practices they devised were also being advocated internationally by a variety of eugenical congresses and societies. They were essentially just like their colleagues, and the victorious allies would rely on their colleagues to judge them.

When Rüdin's daughter referred to an "international eugenical movement," she was actually characterizing a multitude of national societies that maintained contacts and held joint congresses from one end of the international eugenics landscape to the other. As this loose, single-minded confederacy, they formed what amounted to at least a philosophical movement that was both uniform and international.

Various parallel trends developed in practically all national mental hygiene movements. In some countries, psychiatry was dominated by extremist, racially-oriented eugenicists whose "final solution" was to be applied through "negative eugenics"—the eradication of all unwanted genetic "burdens." In other countries, more moderate practitioners sought to attain their ends through preventative measures—which they called "positive eugenics." The result is what we might call "psychiatric schizophrenia."

Each school of thought then engaged in the active dissemination of propaganda designed to make their goals seem so laudable that they could hardly be criticized, let alone opposed. For example, the demand for better care for the mentally ill outside of asylums. There had been definite advances made in this area since the birth of the mental hygiene movement. On the other hand, it was exactly these presumed "advances" that caused the radical racial hygienical elements in psychiatry to demand stronger "preventative" measures. How far these elements were willing to go (and maybe still are) were best illustrated in 1946 by Brock Chisholm, a Canadian psychiatrist and later president of the World Federation for Mental Health.

"....it would certainly be of greater advantage to the world if psychiatrists would attend to the preventative domain where the great work has to be done...The reinterpretation and eventually eradication of the concept of right and wrong...and [their] replacement through intelligent and rational thinking...are the objectives of practically all effective psychotherapy....Fact is that most psychiatrists and psychologists and many other respectable people have freed themselves of these moral chains and are able to observe and think freely...If the race is to be freed from its crippling burden of good and evil, it must be psychiatrists who take the original responsibility...."[9]

Consider the simple meaning of these words that were written, barely one year after the most devastating organized slaughter in recorded history was ended by the military vanquishing of an empire. Still, it has been well documented that many psychiatrists had freed themselves from the constricting corset of "right" and "wrong" and from any other moral feelings they may have had.

However, in 1948, the international mental hygiene movement repackaged itself in the form of an umbrella organization known as the World Federation for Mental Health, the brainchild of English eugenicist J. R. Rees. Among the WFMH's elite from Germany was Friedrich Mauz, the military district psychiatrist and T4 consultant discussed earlier. As the successor organization to the International Committee for Mental Hygiene which could not be controlled by any local government, the WFMH's stated objective was to achieve the "highest possible condition of mental health in all its encompassing biological, medical, educational and social aspects."[10] Lurking under the guise of "helping," however, was nothing more than the relentless pursuit of social control and forcing human beings to adjust to it.

Shortly after the World War II, the "Deutsche Arbeitsgemeinschaft für psychische Hygiene" ("German Work Association for Psychological Hygiene") was created under the leadership of psychiatrist Hans Merguet. In 1951, the association was absorbed into the WFMH. In the rest of Europe, an umbrella organization called the "European League for Mental Hygiene" was also founded. Werner Villinger, Hans Bürger-Prinz and Heinrich Schulte, all of whom continued to promote mental hygiene in postwar Germany, participated in the first postwar conference in 1951. By

THE MENTAL HYGIENE MOVEMENT AS A SOCIAL MOVEMENT

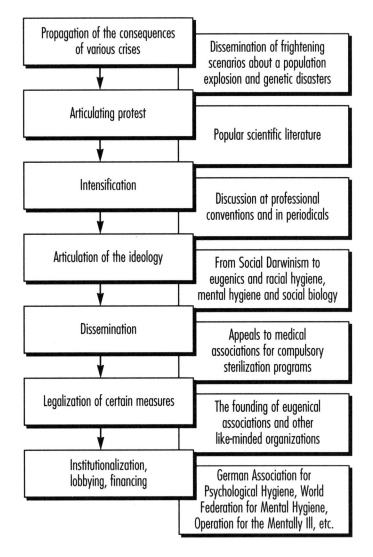

Propagation of the consequences of various crises	Dissemination of frightening scenarios about a population explosion and genetic disasters
Articulating protest	Popular scientific literature
Intensification	Discussion at professional conventions and in periodicals
Articulation of the ideology	From Social Darwinism to eugenics and racial hygiene, mental hygiene and social biology
Dissemination	Appeals to medical associations for compulsory sterilization programs
Legalization of certain measures	The founding of eugenical associations and other like-minded organizations
Institutionalization, lobbying, financing	German Association for Psychological Hygiene, World Federation for Mental Hygiene, Operation for the Mentally Ill, etc.

THE GERMAN MENTAL HYGIENE MOVEMENT

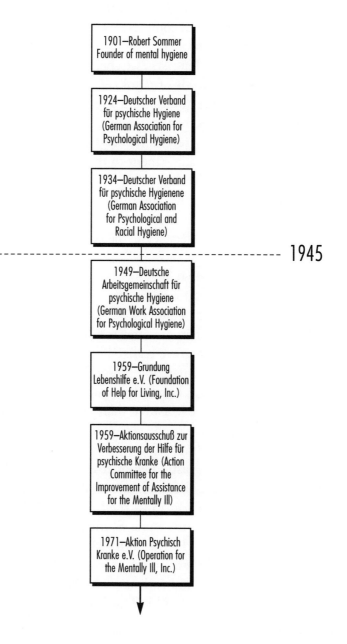

1901—Robert Sommer
Founder of mental hygiene

1924—Deutscher Verband
für psychische Hygiene
(German Association for
Psychological Hygiene)

1934—Deutscher Verband
für psychische Hygienene
(German Association
for Psychological and
Racial Hygiene)

- 1945

1949—Deutsche
Arbeitsgemeinschaft für
psychische Hygiene
(German Work Association
for Psychological Hygiene)

1959—Grundung
Lebenshilfe e.V. (Foundation
of Help for Living, Inc.)

1959—Aktionsausschuß zur
Verbesserung der Hilfe für
psychische Kranke (Action
Committee for the
Improvement of Assistance
for the Mentally Ill)

1971—Aktion Psychisch
Kranke e.V. (Operation for
the Mentally Ill, Inc.)

1973, The European League's president was Dr. Helmut Ehrhardt, a student of both Villinger and de Crinis.

In 1958, Ehrhardt, Detlev Ploog (a student of Kretschmer and Villinger) and Stutte published the book *Psychiatrie und Gesellschaft* (*Psychiatry and Society*). The book presents essays on mental hygiene, among them Heinrich Schulte's comprehensive "Geschichte und Aufgabe der Psychohygiene in Deutschland" ("History and Duty of Mental Hygiene in Germany"). Psychiatrists Nitsche, Rüdin, Mauz and Villinger are all acknowledged with words of thanks.

Here are some memorable quotes from *Psychiatry and Society*:

"The mental hygiene movement has now advanced from reforming the insane asylum system to the preventative battle against all difficulties the individual experiences in the adjustment to the demands of life caused by psychological abnormalities. Today it strives for the maintenance and support of the mental health and welfare of the individual and society.... It goes without saying that...influence will be exerted upon the health and education system, welfare and legal care, the economy and the field of religion and ethics."[11]

"Luxenburger's statement that 'heredity is not fate but the threat of fate' is in the best interest of mental hygiene."[12]

"We all know that some hereditary diseases manifest themselves completely only when certain environmental conditions are present. We can see how important this is when we realize how much the hereditary burden represents a constant traumatizing poison."[13]

"In addition, because of our bitter experiences, the population here [in Germany] to this day is more sensitive than other countries against slogans of any kind which appeal to the emotions behind which anonymous claims to power could be hiding...."[14]

In 1959, Lebenshilfe für geistig behinderte Kinder e.V. (Help in Life for Mentally Handicapped Children, Inc.) was established by Dr. Stutte in Marburg. It is noteworthy that in 1984, the Lebenshilfe dedicated its new convention center to Stutte—the same Stutte who had been awarded a doctorate under the Nazi psychiatrist Fritz Hoffmann in 1935, and who was still reminiscing fondly about his teachers Hoffmann, Mauz and Gaupp as late as 1977. Stutte didn't distance himself much from the anti-social science and methodology of his Third Reich mentors.

Since about 1972, the Lebenshilfe has recommended its members to have a consultation with a "human-geneticist":[15]

"Research and Human Genetics throw themselves into a boom of genetics where the outlines are becoming noticeably more indistinguishable. Today already geneticists talk about 3,000 symptoms with a 'clear deviation from the average.' The borders between 'sick' and 'healthy' fluctuate: Since alcoholism, psychological disturbances, susceptibility to cancer, homosexuality and lactose intolerance are genetic oddities, it is foreseeable that the fear of being handicapped will be an entrance point and more 'undesirable' symptoms will follow."[16]

This is mental hygiene—and racial hygiene—in yet another new disguise: Human Genetics. In reality, to the trained observer, Genetics, Human Genetics and Racial Hygiene are virtually interchangeable concepts. A new term has been coined but the objectives are as old as they are despicable.

It is certainly interesting that "Human Genetic Consultation" originated in Marburg, the hometown of both Villinger and Stutte. And as improbable as it might seem, it is true that an economist named Hans von Stackelberg detailed the economic aspects of genetic consultation as late as 1981:

"Using documents from the Marburg Genetic Consultation Office, he adds up the expenses of the care of the handicapped, from the hospital subsidies to special child care, from medication to placement in a nursing home, from the increase in national income through the birth of more healthy children and the freeing up of nursing manpower or the savings from needless social services. This sum he compares to the costs for comprehensive genetic consultations of future parents, and he comes to the conclusion that genetic consultation increases the 'vital property' of the family and the society."[17]

Aren't the echoes of extermination deafening?

Clearly, no one criticizes honest and welcome efforts to improve care for the sick and the disabled. But there is a danger in leaving control over this seemingly noble pursuit to a discipline which is linked with the darkest episodes of Nazi madness. Psychiatry has proven incapable of self-criticism, self-condemnation and self-policing, and even today remains nothing more than the modern incarnation of its Third Reich progenitors.

CHAPTER 6

"On this planet, might makes right."
Adelbert von Chamisso,
Die Giftmischerin

"OPERATION MENTALLY ILL"
THE NEW STRATEGIES OF THE MENTAL HYGIENE MOVEMENT

As already noted, from the beginning of the 1920s until the end of World War II, psychiatric research was funded in large measure by wealthy patrons and private financiers. Without this money, psychiatry, in all likelihood, would have remained essentially powerless. At the mercy of poverty or the caprice of government funding, it may have been just another trend that barely outlived its own birth. The financial infusions that rescued and sustained it came from many sources: Krupp, Loeb, the German Association of Chemical Industries, the Rockefeller Foundation and, between 1933 and 1945, the Nazi treasury.

The real mystery is how money continued to flow to psychiatric research after the war.

Oddly, one of psychiatry's major postwar funding sources continued to be the government. Beyond that, just as psychiatry's theories and methods survived the war virtually unscathed, so did psychiatric research's financial strategy. It consisted of four basic steps:

Step 1: Creating arbitrary and remarkably flexible definitions of "normal" and "abnormal," "healthy" and "sick."

Step 2: The enactment of laws or governmental decrees to enforce psychiatric treatment and therapeutic measures.

Step 3: The assumption of the role of agents of governmental mandates.

Step 4: An expansion of the definition of "mental illness" to cut further across social strata, leading to an enlargement of the psychiatric sphere of influence, with the cooperation of the government.

The history of psychiatry is one of the best camouflaged pieces of social and political manipulation ever staged by a "science." Certainly no other branch of the sciences or the humanities has had the arrogance to embark on a systematic campaign to gain a pervasive, but hidden, influence on the fate of a society and how it behaves.

To illustrate psychiatry's fund raising strategy, here is a brief summary of how the four steps outlined above were put into action before 1945:

STEP 1: ARBITRARY AND FLEXIBLE DEFINITIONS OF TERMS

The creation and use of arbitrary and exceptionally elastic definitions to expand psychiatry's orbit of influence began with the earliest advocates of compulsory sterilization and euthanasia—Binding and Hoche, Rüdin, Kraepelin and Aschaffenburg. Their early definitions of what is abnormal included "women," "Frenchmen" and "democrats." They never really struck gold with any of this until they hit upon the definition of "hereditarily sick," which was so far-reaching that even a grouchy person could be classified as having "camouflaged schizophrenia," an illness that was not visible but could break out at any time.

The psychiatrists' skill with semantics was truly remarkable. They used their ability to coin impressive sounding names for "illnesses" to deceive everyone—especially well-to-do benefactors and political leaders.

STEP 2: THE ENACTMENT OF LAWS OR GOVERNMENTAL DECREES TO ENFORCE PSYCHIATRIC TREATMENT OR "THERAPEUTIC" MEASURES

In 1932, a bill to authorize compulsory sterilization failed to garner enough votes to become law in what was still a democratic German parliament. It wasn't until the following year, after the Nazis came to power, that the German parliament flip-flopped and the sterilization laws were passed. They went into effect on January 1, 1934.

The significance of that statutory go-ahead cannot be overstated. In particular, the sterilization laws were applauded by the racial hygienists as a new dawn. Psychiatry was no longer a self-proclaimed voice in the wilderness clamoring for the preservation of the Aryan genotype. In their own estimation and in no small measure through their own efforts, psychiatrists now stood as the Nazi regime's right-hand men.

From 1920 on, psychiatrists had also worked hard to create both a demand and a legal basis for euthanasia programs. During the Third Reich, under the supervision of Hans Heinze, Hitler's psychiatric committee planned and developed what became the child euthanasia program. Thereafter, they did the same for an adult version of the state-sponsored mass murder. The organization of these activities grew more streamlined and sophisticated, until it assumed the devastating efficiency of T4 and eventually resulted in the Nazis' near-obliteration of the Jews and other ethnic groups.

STEP 3: THE ASSUMPTION OF THE ROLE OF AGENTS OF GOVERNMENT MANDATES

The philosophical affair had long thrived before the Law for the Prevention of Genetically Diseased Children took effect. According to a much quoted book called *Erblehre und Rassenhygiene im völkischen Staat* (*Genetics and Racial Hygiene in the Ethnic Nation*):

"...the performance of a legally regulated duty, namely the execution of the Law for the Prevention of Genetically Diseased Children now replaces the heretofore voluntary work performed when a legal basis for a more active proceeding was missing.

"The sole duty of the director of an institute is the appropriate execution of the law...."[1]

With this direct and uncompromising statement, it became apparent that psychiatry had succeeded to the point that major legislation was passed at psychiatry's urging which could affect or even end human life. It essentially gave them the status of agent of the federal law. Yet the state alone, not psychiatry, ultimately was held responsible. Psychiatry, it seems, had found a perfect camouflage.

Today, however, we know exactly whom to blame for this law:

"The farsightedness of our Führer, Adolf Hitler, has replaced a lazy acceptance (of our problems) with an extremely bold program and has begun to implement it with the utmost energy."[2]

"Only one person in 1923 and 1924 has put down these intellectual

181

explorations in writing and has made the question of race the basis of all his political thinking and ambitions, our Führer, Adolf Hitler."[3]

In other words, it was Hitler who was portrayed as the source of the inhuman psychiatric philosophies. Psychiatry, the real originator of these laws, had found the ultimate disguise. The very limited authorization of euthanasia by the Führer gave psychiatry a legal basis sufficient for the subsequent killings, even though all their previous attempts to have Hitler legitimize euthanasia failed. The public relations line was that psychiatry had acted on orders from the Führer—a fact that, after the war, would play a large role in downplaying the legal consequences to psychiatry for its own atrocities.[4]

STEP 4: AN EXPANSION OF THE DEFINITION OF "MENTAL ILLNESS" TO ENLARGE PSYCHIATRY'S SPHERE OF INFLUENCE

As early as 1934, we can see a concerted effort to expand the definition of "illness." As Dr. Rüdin said of the sterilization law:

"With this law, it is not possible to eliminate all individuals who pass on diseased germ cells….Despite this, the lawmakers did not deem it necessary…to include those who are outwardly healthy with no sickly genetic code…to the terms of the law, since the majority of the German population would not understand this…the expansion of the definitions for these people will have to wait until later."[5]

Recalling what was noted earlier—that Rüdin wanted to sterilize everyone in a family where mental or hereditary illness could be found—consider more of Rüdin's views:

"Since the law does not allow for the sterilization of these people, a wide field of research and development will be dedicated here for the public health care system to enlighten wide spheres of society."[6]

What Rüdin was talking about was the beginning of the Holocaust, performed in German institutions, contrived as a camouflaged operation "for the welfare of the nation," and culminating with the deaths of millions of people.

That is also what German psychiatry generally was talking about after 1945. Amazing parallels exist.

By 1943, Nazi mass murder was a daily occurrence. It was in that climate that several leading psychiatrists got together and drew up a memorandum on the future of psychiatry in Germany which, to this day, has served as the foundation for a variety of psychiatric programs and activities with impact at virtually every social and political level. More than tradition went forward after World War II. The leaders of the psychiatric community during the war—the ones who were responsible for the mass executions in the psychiatric institutions—not only ran psychiatry's societies after the war, they also articulated psychiatry's objectives and described its future goals. They defined the very goals and objectives which, to this day, have barely been revised or modified since their Nazi origins.

On June 26, 1943, the head of T4, Paul Nitsche, sent the General Commissioner of the Führer for the Medical and Health System, Professor Karl R. Brandt, "a brief memorandum about the future development of psychiatry with a request to please take note."[7] The genesis of Nitsche's memorandum was an "agreement between Professor Rüdin of Munich, Professor de Crinis of Berlin, Professor C. Schneider of Heidelberg, Professor Heinze of Gorden and Professor Nitsche of Berlin." In other words, the elite of lethal psychiatry.

In the memorandum's first two paragraphs, the psychiatrists' perceptions of the "advances" of modern psychiatry are detailed. Moving away from the "departments of rage" in the prewar psychiatric hospitals, the psychiatrists praise "new treatment methods" with insulin, electro-convulsion, hormones and dietetic therapies, but neglect to mention either the euthanasia program or the 100,000 or so persons whom the killing institutes had already murdered at the time of the memo. Notwithstanding such unprecedented mass murder, the memorandum characterizes psychiatry as basically a "medical healing discipline." The memorandum also proclaimed that "duties of fundamental importance arise for the psychiatrist in the Nazi state in the performance of the systematic registration and examination of the hereditary health condition of the German people as well as the prevention of hereditary diseases.

"...Psychiatry has to assist in this matter...it is also its duty to educate the medical profession as a whole."

Then comes the most remarkable statement of all:

"[Professor Rüdin] elaborated on the most unfortunate fact that frequently the reputation of the psychiatrist is undermined and that the psychiatrist is portrayed as standing on lost ground and useless. His work is invalidated and discredited. This is due to the completely wrong demands of the hereditarily sick with whom the psychiatrist has to deal to a large degree."

Those words offer a virtual clinic on arrogance. Rüdin was complaining that psychiatry was getting a bad name, that its practitioner's work was viewed as useless, and that its reputation had been severely undermined. Remember that the practices which Rüdin believed should not result in psychiatry's loss of esteem included sterilization, euthanasia, and racist extermination, all of which were designed and executed by psychiatrists. Poor psychiatry, thought Rüdin, lamenting the bad name that his line of business has acquired despite such noble endeavors.

Naturally enough, when the fall of the Third Reich led to the collapse of the killing centers and its research institutes, psychiatry feared for its continued existence as a medical profession. In the notorious 1943 memorandum, a department head was quoted as saying that "physicians will probably not be needed for the mentally ill at all after the war...Everything has to be done now to counteract the customary discrediting of the psychiatric profession. The importance and the scientific as well as practical value of psychiatric work must be emphatically pointed out....

"...The measures of euthanasia will, however, find a higher general understanding and acceptance to the degree that it is demonstrated that all avenues were exhausted in every case of mental illness to heal or at least improve the sick to a point where they can be given an economically viable activity, be it in their profession or in some other area."

The memorandum's bluntness is chilling. It is this and nothing else that psychiatry was concerned about: only the "economically valuable" person had the right to live. The disturbed, abnormal or mentally ill person—anyone whom the psychiatrists considered a "burden" to others—was to be removed to "protect" the rest of the country from the impositions that such "burdens" represented.

An examination of the 1943 memorandum is an education in terror. It is essentially a checklist for the future conceived by Nazi psychiatrists for the continued Nazi-like practice of psychiatry on a grander, more sophisticated scale. It is also psychiatry's essential postwar agenda, as if the Nazi era had never occurred. Indeed, there are objectives stated in the 1943 memorandum which have become cornerstones of psychiatry's postwar agenda in Germany:

"1. The uniform orientation of the German mental health system.

"2. A basic guarantee of psychiatric management (or at least psychiatric supervision) of all institutes for the mentally abnormal.

"3. The elimination of all access to private institutions for mentally abnormal persons.

"4. The utilization of all institutes for the mentally abnormal for research, with direct links to the German Research Institute for Psychiatry, university clinics and other research institutes.

. . .

"8. The establishment of outpatient departments in the institutes for the continued treatment of released patients in order to safeguard the success of the treatment and the use of their labor.

"9. Wherever possible, the establishment of psychiatric clinics and institutes to be connected peripherally with hospitals for the physically ill, since psychiatry today has to maintain close connections to somatic medicine, especially to the field of internal medicine.

"10. The integration of institutional psychiatrists into the policies regarding national youth welfare, criminal-biological oversight of certain districts and similar operations."

There it is. The vision of T4 became the mission of postwar psychiatry.

In 1959, the Aktionsasschuß zur Verbesserung der Hilfe für psychisch Kranke (Action Committee for the Improvement of Assistance for the Psychologically Ill) was incorporated into the Deutscher Verein für offentliche und private Fürsoge (German Association for Public and Private Care). Many prominent mental hygienists were among its members and employees: Helmuth Ehrhardt (a T4 disciple and military district psychiatrist); Friedrich Panse (a former T4 and military district psychiatrist); and students of former Nazi psychiatrists such as Walter Ritter von Baeyer, Rüdin's student at the German Research Institute for Psychiatry, and Ludwig Manger-König (a student of Villinger and later Secretary of State for the Federal Ministry of Youth, Family and Health).[8] Professor Hans-Werner Müller, also a member of the committee, was a student of Max de Crinis. In 1942, he was awarded a doctorate for a thesis entitled "On the Deformities of the Inner Organs of the Mentally Ill."

At first glance, and a superficial glance at that, the connection between the Action Committee of 1959 and the stated objectives of the 1943 memorandum are elusive. But superficial impressions can be false, and guilt can be disguised as innocence by clever semantics and the manipulations of public relations. Under closer scrutiny, the objectives of the postwar group reveal almost exact parallels to the points in the Nazi-era memo and brazenly display their direct connection.

"In cities and population centers, psychiatric/neurological hospitals of an appropriate size are to be built. It would be advantageous here to establish these installations not just for psychiatric patients and especially not for the exclusive treatment of psychosis. This is because of the theoretical and practical connection of psychiatry with the fields of neurology and internal medicine. As it is especially urgent for the practical care of the population, the combining of psychiatry and neurology within the same institution had already been demanded by the German Association for Psychiatry in 1933."[9]

The 1943 memorandum states:

"Wherever possible, the establishment of psychiatric clinics and institutes to be connected peripherally to hospitals for the mentally ill…"[10]

Remember that in 1959 an Action Committee was formed to initiate "psychiatric reform." Among its members were psychiatrists from the Nazi era and their students. The recommendation of the Action Committee was to ensure that psychiatry, neurology and internal medicine remained in close proximity. The care of the entire population through psychiatric institutions was a central theme of these recommendations.

On March 5, 1970, the time was ripe for the next step. Various representatives filed a petition in parliament for a "comprehensive study on psychiatric mental hygiene care for the population."[11]

It was "to be established, in addition to an analysis of the current situation, what measures would be necessary for the psychiatric mental hygienical care for the population, given today's valid scientific discoveries in the field."[12]

This at first appears rather harmless, rather benign. After all, nobody can express serious reservations about a satisfactory resolution of the problems of people who are profoundly mentally disturbed or a concern that a nation have good, sound mental health among its people. But examine the basic reasoning behind the petition:

"Mental illnesses are the most frequent form of disease in our society....In view of the fact that in any modern society 10 percent to 12 percent of the population is in need of psychiatric care, it is imperative that the parliament and the federal government concern themselves seriously with the problems of mental illnesses."[13]

And with that we have come full circle, to the definition of what is "normal" and "abnormal," "sick" and "healthy." The only real difference is the startling claim that as much as ten to twelve percent of the German population at that time were defined to be in need of psychiatric help. That translated into more than six million people. The definition of "who is in need of treatment and who is not" (or more strictly speaking, who is "normal" and who is "deviating") that was previously assumed to be obvious was now taken as a basis of a large-scale study. This, in accordance with the psychiatric methodology, served as the basis for new legal edicts and decrees.

The development of mental hygiene was carried forward to a new generation. On January 18, 1971, "Aktion Psychisch Kranke" ("Operation Mentally Ill") was founded. This association was devoted to paving the way for the enactment of certain laws which would secure and expand psychiatric influence in German society.

In the group's inaugural minutes, rules and regulations its objectives are revealed:

"Carry out reform efforts with psychiatry as far as the required political decisions are concerned."[14]

And:

"The association wants to promote the reform of psychiatric care for the population according to modern medical and social discoveries and possibilities."[15]

Those same minutes stipulated that the group's financial base capital should be guaranteed by a "subsidy of 150,000 Deutschmarks, which is incorporated into the budget of the Federal Ministry of Youth, Family and Health."

This subsidy was actually an endowment of the mental hygiene movement. For proof, just look at the people who made up the Executive Committee of the newly established "Operation Mentally Ill":

President: Walter Picard, member of parliament and inquiry petitioner[16]

Vice-President: Prof. Caspar Kulenkampff, a psychiatrist[17]

Treasurer: Prof. Albert Huhn, a psychiatrist[18]

Some of its members included:

Prof. Heinz Hafner, a psychiatrist and a student of Kretschmer[19]

Prof. Joachim-Ernst Meyer, a psychiatrist and a student of de Crinis[20]

Prof. Walter Theodor Winkler, a psychiatrist and a student of Kretschmer[21]

This lobby group boasted a high caliber team indeed, one that was well-designed to represent both the legacy and the agenda of their mentors.

The next step, naturally, was the enactment of legislative measures. To this end, an expert panel was formed, called the Psychiatrie-Enquete (Psychiatry Inquiry). Its first job was to investigate psychiatry's standing in Germany and to propose concrete steps for its improvement. On August 31, 1971, the Inquiry convened, under the chairmanship of Ludwig Manger-König, a psychiatrist and vice president of the European League for Mental Hygiene, who had been a student of Villinger and later the Secretary of State for the Federal Ministry of Youth, Family and Health. It did so through an expert panel.

The president of the panel was Prof. Kulenkampff (the vice president of "Operation Mentally Ill") and its vice president was Prof. Häfner (Kretschmer's protégé and member of the Executive Committee). Also represented on the panel were psychiatrists Huhn, Meyer and Winkler and—not coincidentally—the entire Executive Committee of Operation Mentally Ill.

Psychiatry's upper echelons, operating through its lobby group, had executed a remarkable ploy. Their own people, operating out of the Health Ministry, had convened an "independent expert panel" under the aegis of the German parliament which consisted largely of the leadership of the lobby group which also was the panel's primary subcontractor. What was made to look like governmental action was nothing more than the psychiatric leadership cloaking itself in the guise of government serving its private agenda in the guise of public service.

In a published interim report, the expert panel made a variety of recommendations. Here are some excerpts:

"The expert commission takes the strong view that psychiatric patient care is a basic part of general medicine. Accordingly, the psychiatric care

system must be integrated into the existing common preventive and public health service system."[22]

And:

"Wherever possible, the establishment of psychiatric clinics and institutes to be connected peripherally with hospitals for the physically ill, since
psychiatry today has to maintain close connections to somatic medicine,
especially to the field of internal medicine."[23]

More, even partially literal parallels between the 1971 panel's interim
report and the 1943 memorandum could be quoted here, such as the
demand for expert supervision ("A guarantee of psychiatric management
of…supervision"), or psychiatric outpatient clinics ("…outpatient clinics
are to be established within the institutes") or for additional progressive
education ("…its duty is to educate the medical profession as a whole").

In retrospect, the parallels are as obvious as they are chilling. The 1943
agenda was essentially photocopied by the 1971 panel.

"A Report about the Situation of Psychiatry in the Federal Republic of
Germany"—the panel's final conclusions—is dated November 25, 1975:

It is especially shocking that about one-third of the population is strick-
en at one time or another with a mental illness—chronically, repeatedly, or
at least once, and that approximately one million people a year become
"urgently in need of psychiatric and psychotherapeutic treatment."

Psychiatry had succeeded in its aims. They had established themselves
as the "experts" on the classification of "sick" and "healthy," and who was
in need of treatment. During the Third Reich, they had exercised the same
power over the "flow of the genetically sick."

The report goes one step even further:

"Not counting the mental consequences for the affected, these compulsory measures, made possible through a misuse of research results, brought
discredit to genetic research in our country for decades after the war. The
current views about the application of voluntary sterilization are also burdened by the Nazi past."

In other words, it is necessary to escape the burdens of the Nazi past so
that the ideas and plans of the architects of that past can be pursued unimpeded.

Some members of the investigatory committee published an article in the
periodical *Neue Anthropologie* in February 1974 on the same topic, entitled

AKTION PSYCHISCH KRANKE
Vereinigung zur Reform der Versorgung
psychisch Kranker e. V.

Aktion Psychisch Kranke   Graurheindorfer Str. 15   5300 Bonn 1

An ▮▮▮▮▮▮▮▮▮▮▮▮▮▮▮▮▮▮▮▮▮▮▮
▮▮▮▮▮▮▮▮▮▮▮▮▮▮▮▮▮▮▮▮
▮▮▮▮▮▮▮▮▮

Graurheindorfer Straße 15
5300 Bonn 1
Telefon (0228) 631545

Przy./Marzi.   Bonn, den 14.03.91

Sehr geehrter Damen und Herren,

auch die Aktion Psychisch Kranke e.V. **arbeitet nicht direkt mit psychisch kranken Menschen.**
Wie Sie der beigegügten Selbstdarstellung entnehmen können,sind wir
eine Art "Lobby-Organisation", die durch vielfältige Maßnahmen auf
das System der psychiatrischen Versorgung in der Bundesrepublik Ein-
fluß genommen hat.

Wir arbeiten ferner nicht als Träger von Einrichtungen für psychisch
kranke Menschen **und führen weder** Beratung noch Behandlung **durch** und
können Ihnen von daher leider nicht behilflich sein.

Mit freundlichen Grüßen

Chr. Przytulla
Geschäftsführerin

Vorstand: W. Picard, Vorsitzender, Bonn
Prof. Dr. C. Kulenkampff, stellv. Vorsitzender, Lübe...
Prof. Dr. A. Huhn, Schatzmeister, Bonn
Bankverbindung: Sparkasse B...

Honored ladies and gentlemen,

Operation Mentally Ill does not work directly with mentally ill people.
As you can deduce from the attached handbook, we are a type of lobby
organization that has, through many and varied measures, exerted influence on the psychiatric care system in the Federal Republic.

We do not operate as representatives of institutions for mentally ill people. We perform neither consultation nor treatment and therefore we are,
regrettably, unable to help you.

Cordially,

Chr. Przytulla
Manager

"Die Rolle der Vererbung im menschlichen Verhalten" ("The Role of Hereditary Transmission in Human Behavior"). Here are some excerpts:

"We have examined a large body of evidence about the possible role of hereditary transmission in the development of human abilities and behavioral mannerisms and we are of the opinion that these hereditary influences are very strong."[24]

Read that in the context of the expert panel's observation that "some of the improvements suggested in this report will fulfill another obligation beyond their common humanitarian

Professor Ludwig Manger-Koenig (1972)—Racial hygienist and a student of Werner Villinger

task,"[25] and both the nature and character of the "other obligation beyond" humanitarianism becomes all too clear.

After the panel had completed its work, the next step of the psychiatric program was the assumption of the role of agent of the government's "mandates" regarding the mental health of its citizens. "Operation Mentally Ill" had changed its stated objective to the "reform of care for the mentally ill and handicapped by taking into account the suggestions of the report regarding the situation of psychiatry" and the effort to realize those suggestions.

Here is what their original rules and regulations stated:

"The association wants to promote the reform of psychiatric care of the population according to modern medical and social discoveries and possibilities."

After the insinuation of "Operation Mentally Ill" into every aspect of governmental stewardship of the mentally ill, this became the revised purpose of the association:

"Bringing influence to bear upon the parliaments of the Länder and the

German Bundestag."

At the same time, one tenth of the population had been classified as "psychiatrically ill," and the taxpayers bore the tab for psychiatry's self-promotion and entrenchment. Mental hygiene had once again managed to smuggle itself into society in the form envisioned by its progenitors of T4 and the KZs. It had cleverly infiltrated politics and conquered it. It had cleverly proposed legal ways and means to achieve its aims and obtained their enactment. It had cleverly plotted out what was to become a reality, all under the banner of human genetics, and made it reality all over again.

CHAPTER 7

"Psychiatry can nowadays look at the whole world as a suitable sphere for its activity and need in no way be frightened by the magnitude of this task." [1]

*Howard P. Rome
former president of the
American Psychiatric
Association*

FROM SOCIAL DARWINISM TO HUMAN GENETICS
RESEARCH IN THE NAZI TRADITION

Reconstructing the way in which psychiatry's traditional doctrines shed their Nazi skins and have been disguised, revived and implemented is only part of our endeavor. Not every part of that process was accomplished directly within the confines of psychiatry. There was an array of similar disciplines which psychiatry either joined or exploited to advance traditional psychiatric objectives. One such discipline is genetic research.

In 1962, leading genetic researchers from all over the world were invited to a symposium in London organized by the Ciba Foundation. The public had no idea about what was going on behind the firmly closed doors of the symposium, during which a new course was to be charted for new genetic research—or, more accurately, old genetics research in new packaging.

The revolutionary new term for genetic research was "gene research."

Genes are, as most know, the information carriers of the genotype. They are located in the chromosomes, the threadlike structures visible under the microscope that carry the cell's blueprint. These genes can, in turn, be reduced to even smaller units at a molecular level. Here we find the DNA, that mysterious substance which contains all of an organism's cellular information, both "good" and "bad." Like the racial hygienists who tried to formulate certain scientific laws to predict who would fit their definition of genetically damaged or inferior, the "gene hunters" (as the participants of this historic conference were called) decided from the beginning to define the "ideal" human being.

If the London symposium had been intellectually honest, it would have candidly announced at the outset that gene technology and molecular biology are actually hollow concepts which bear frightening parallels to Nazi-era genetic and racial hygiene ideology. Once again we encounter a science in which it is clear, after only the beginning of the analysis, that the modern nomenclature is merely a masquerade. What is called "human genetics" today was called simply "genetics" in the 1930s—the words and concepts are essentially interchangeable. In the past thirty years, researchers' interests have for all intents and purposes turned to the gene and its hereditary molecule, DNA. It is now at that level that the search continues for the perfect human being.

In the 1962 London symposium, there was a highly enlightening series of observations by Francis Crick, a Nobel laureate and co-discoverer of DNA, Norman Pirie, a biochemist, Sir Julian Huxley, the former general secretary of UNESCO, Hermann Muller, a geneticist and Nobel laureate, Joshua Lederberg, also a geneticist and Nobel laureate, biologist J. B. S. Holdane and others.

Francis Crick:

"I'd like to concentrate on a certain issue. Do people even have the right to have children? As we have heard, it would not be difficult for governments to add something to the food supply which would prevent procreation. In addition, and this is hypothetical, the government could keep another substance at hand which would counteract the effect of the first one, and only people whose procreation is desired could receive it. This is definitely not out of the question."

Norman Pirie:

"Looking back at Crick's argument, if anybody has the right to have children in a society where the community is responsible for the common welfare, for health, hospitals, unemployment insurance and so on, I would answer 'No.'"

Sir Julian Huxley:

"At this point in time, mankind will certainly not submit to compulsory sterilization measures. But if you begin with a few, of course, voluntary experiments and show that they work, you could within one generation achieve results on the whole population. Because moral values grow and mature just as everything else."

Francis Crick:

"If you could convince people that their children are not a private matter, that would be a tremendous step forward. I suspect that through the results of science, we will in time become less and less Christian."

Hermann Muller:

"Probably close to 20 percent of the population, if not more, have inherited a genetic defect. If that is right, in order for us to avoid genetic degeneration, then that 20 percent of the population should not be allowed to reach sexual maturity or, if they live, they would not be allowed to procreate. Finally, there are certainly great opportunities available for improvement in our transformation of the genetic makeup itself. To investigate these problems, we have to free ourselves from our prejudices and open our minds to the new possibilities that science and technology are offering us. Artificial insemination has opened the door to these possibilities for the first time. There are people who are prouder for what they create with their hands and minds than for what they produce in their loins on a more or less stimulus-response basis, and who consider their contribution to the welfare of their children and mankind more important than the increase of their own genetic peculiarities."

Joshua Lederberg:

"The situation regarding human procreation is dark. Wouldn't we be sinfully wasting a treasure of knowledge if we neglected the creative possibilities of genetic improvement? Shouldn't the same culture that has produced the unique possibility of global destruction also create a maximum amount of intellectual and social insight to ensure its own survival? The more recent advances in molecular biology offer us better eugenic ways to reach this objective. The last step of the application of molecular biology would be the direct control of nucleic acids. I can foresee, for example, having the fundamentals very soon to develop a technique to enlarge the human brain through prenatal or early postnatal interventions."

J.B.S. Holdane:

"It might be possible to synthesize new genes and to insert them into human chromosomes. With the help of such grafting procedures in the nucleus, our descendants could acquire many valuable properties of other species without losing their specific human qualities...Under such circumstances it might be good to have four legs, or, at least, very short legs...[From this] I might conclude that many parents would be ready to risk the life of their small child if there was a chance it would develop extraordinary strength. I have designed my own utopia, or as others might suppose, my own private hell. I justify myself with the fact that utopian designs have influenced the course of history."[2]

To be fair, we have reprinted only excerpts of the text and that in condensed form, and we have presented a compressed summary of some of the ideas discussed by the researchers in 1962. Nevertheless, these excerpts are profoundly alarming.

At first glance, this subject seems to go beyond the scope of a book called *Psychiatrists—the Men Behind Hitler*. After all, the participants at the London symposium were not Nazis and certainly were not part of Hitler's Third Reich. There was also no talk about psychiatry. An unsuspecting observer might think that some imaginative researchers, among them some eminent Nobel laureates, came together and simply let their creative visions run wild out loud.

Unfortunately, the reality is a lot more frightening. This symposium was neither a coincidental nor a casual meeting of prominent scientists, as can be surmised by the fact that its sponsor is the foundation of one of the biggest pharmaceutical corporations in the world (which, by the way, is a producer of the psychiatric drug Ritalin). Moreover, the assembled scientists shared reflections that are strikingly similar to the thoughts expressed by highly influential men known now as Nazis, geneticists and racial hygienists.

The talk at the London symposium centered around concepts of molecular biology, the employment of which would enable eugenic objectives to be achieved. Molecular biology is, however, a science which is devoted to some degree to exerting influence over hereditary material. Gregor Mendel, who codified hereditary laws late in the nineteenth century, was an inspiration not only to the racial hygienists of the 1930s, but also to the molecular biologists of 1962.

Geneticists occupy the same philosophical tradition as the hereditary transmission mythologists who eventually were responsible for the exterminations at Auschwitz. While the horror of the KZs was ended fifty years ago, the underlying theories and opinions about hereditary transmission and its relationship to race are theoretical components of the philosophical underpinnings of modern genetics and molecular biology. After all, both subjects ponder and experiment with shaping and managing the individual. It is a very short step from that level of theory and practice to notions of selection, extermination and breeding of people.

There is a fear, therefore, that is amply justified—that we could be heading for a new and molecular Auschwitz. As before, certain beliefs and behaviors have crept into society disguised as help which, if politically used, could impose upon mankind a new brand of space-age eugenics.

"In the name of help, another philosophy will be stealthily introduced that first defines certain people as in need of people. Then, when society cannot, for example, raise the needed funds, they are eliminated. Thus we could be headed for a state of affairs where it would not be possible for people like Dostojevsky, van Gogh, Kant, Beethoven or Virginia Woolf to be born, because they would have been found to have had genetic defects. These people in particular have shown us how tremendously important it is to have people around with abnormal behavior, who can hold a mirror up to our society."[3]

So far we know this. Racial and genetic research was undertaken in the 1930s in the German Research Institute (then the Kaiser Wilhelm Institute) for Psychiatry in Munich. In 1964, the Max Planck Institute for Comparative Genetics and Hereditary Pathology (the successor of both of those organizations) was renamed the Max Planck Institute for Molecular Genetics.

After the end of the war, genetic research accelerated at the Max Planck Institute for Psychiatry. Edith Zerbin-Rüdin, Ernst Rüdin's daughter, was a major force in that research, and, as we have seen, she also devoted her efforts to minimize the perceptions of her father's role in the Third Reich.

The promises of today's advances in human genetics and molecular biology are bewitching. New discoveries hold great hope for mankind in disease prediction, prevention and eradication. Their potential for good is seductive. Therein lies the parallel and therein lies the threat.

Psychiatrists could easily resurrect an old-fashioned code phrase like "genetically sick" and a dangerous time bomb could be armed and set. The return to Social Darwinism through "modern" human genetics, anthropology or psychiatry has to be vigilantly guarded against. After all, it is how the Nazi movement got started.

How far could all of this go? Here are some frightening examples.

Modern technology gives genetic researchers extremely tempting ways of manipulating DNA and facilitating a prenatal selection of traits or characteristics. Thus we see that an American biotechnological company, Integrated Genetics, has developed the so-called FISH method, where nearly 90 percent of all genetic defects can be easily detected through the removal and examination of embryonic cells.[4]

As important and advantageous as these examination methods may be in many respects, they are nevertheless potentially dangerous. Hereditary illness could be identified and anticipated. Then what? Abortion? And if so, which fetuses should be killed? Is a minor genetic defect a good enough reason? And what is minor and what is not? Will the "potential" criminal be screened out—or will the grouch or the genius? Or have we merely returned to 1941, when at the founding congress of German child psychiatry, attendees were urged that "[c]onsideration toward parents, kindness, mercy or good-naturedness are not appropriate here?"[5] Is only the completely healthy child—by someone's definition—desired? Or are even more reaching desires to be engineered, like a certain type of beauty, special intelligence, sporty legs, sexy breasts or a huge brain? Where will this medicine end and where does the breeding of humans begin? Who decides? Who monitors those who decide?

These are questions that have no good answers, only frightening ones. Meanwhile, supposedly responsible and apparently thoughtful and caring physicians actually espouse the notion that defeating a handicap can be accomplished either by getting rid of the handicapped or preventing the handicapped from coming to be. At this point, the echo of the Third Reich is loud and clear, for this is prenatal euthanasia, no matter what other softer label is suggested or applied.

Psychiatry rejoices in its connection to genetics, because in genetics, psychiatry sees an ally. Therefore, it should come as no surprise that there have been renewed attempts to disseminate the cold precepts of Social Darwinism and its attendant propaganda, albeit dressed up and repackaged as something called "social biology."

This sort of advocacy occurs mostly within sociopolitical channels—through political organizations and social scientists. Their targets, though, are vital and vulnerable, because social biology focuses on education, work and health. In the United Kingdom, for example, an age limit has been introduced for the patient care after which patients may not be given a health insurance allowance for procedures such as hip replacement or pacemaker installation, procedures far more prevalent among the elderly and often necessary for survival. In Germany, the rising cost of health care is starting to threaten the availability of high-quality medical and physical therapy to certain patients. Economics governing medical choices should sound familiar. It is the precise justification of the Nazi party, its psychiatrists, and its eugenicists for what they did.

In the workplace in some countries, a screening process is already in use which is designed to determine, or at least predict, potential employees' genetic predisposition—*i.e.*, their genotype. Such screening processes are nothing more than search tests and mass genetic examinations. These procedures could be performed before birth in a human genetic consultation, to find out, for instance, if there is a risk of a genetically caused illness or deformity. Or there could be a newborn screening in which all newborn babies are examined for certain genetic characteristics immediately after birth.

Obviously, these screening processes are vulnerable to political abuse, such as a centrally controlled policy on "population control." They are also vulnerable to a doctor or technician with a particular bigotry. Certainly procedures such as this can contribute to the avoidance of disease. Above all, however, they serve as potentially dangerous litmus tests—on "qualifying" and "not qualifying" or being "adjusted" and being "maladjusted."

Forget rhetoric, semantics and scientific jargon—these are the old objectives of eugenics, mental hygiene and human genetics. These are reprises of the choruses of the Nazi psychiatrists, a new and modern form of human selection. Nobody is perfect, and it is hard to imagine public support for a "science" whose answer for imperfection is to kill the imperfect or to kick them out of society. Picture a society where, through centralized gene files, the population is subject to total control. Until recently, an individual health card formatted to look like a credit card had not existed. It does now. It would be simple to store all of a person's genetic technological information on it, along with any other easily accessible data base, without even the knowledge of the cardholder.

Who will stop or even monitor the psychiatrists who, through the use of such methods, could brand certain groups as undesirable whenever they choose to target someone under their remarkably flexible definitions— adolescents, foreigners, Moslems, blacks, children of criminals, Jews, opponents of psychiatry, Frenchmen, women, sectarians, socialists, left-handed people, hazel-eyed people, short people. The list is as expansive as a bigot's hate, and it is just as real. Psychiatrists could create a category of "genetically handicapped" people who, though actually healthy, are social-ly discriminated against due to "camouflaged genetic weakness" or the fact that they are not "adjusted." This would signal a transition from a democ-racy to a "geneocracy"[6]—and an utterly arbitrary one at that. It would also be the triumph of the Nazi legacy resurrected from the ashes of the Reich.

These are difficult and disturbing concepts to ponder, but their threat is real and tangible. Remember that the psychiatric vision of an individual gene card is definitely on the horizon. In fact, it's a quite simple process:

"Every new-born receives information about his or her inborn traits, defects, illnesses and weaknesses. Only those who adjust their lives to their personal genetic credit card will be allowed to be supported by the state."[7]

It is revealing that the directions of modern human genetics correspond precisely with what T4 psychiatrist Max de Crinis formulated in 1945 as integral components of psychiatry. De Crinis maintained that spiritual processes purely and simply do not exist without physical evidence. Today, we can observe a similar phenomenon. The countless failed dissertations on schizophrenia in search of a biological basis for mental illness are now bol-stered by genetic research. There is a clear threat that through gene manip-ulation, a new eugenics will once again emerge, like the one of the early Social Darwinists like Alfred Ploetz. In the next few pages, we'll see an even clearer appeal along a similar line in the early 1970s—signed by the very people we have already identified by their Nazi roots and heritage.

Social Darwinists differentiated between "positive" and "negative" eugenics. "Positive eugenics" promoted the welfare and procreation of the "qualified" and "valuable" elements of society through facilitating marriage, tax breaks, subsidies, and other advantages. "Negative eugenics" was the prevention of the "unwanted" through limited procreation, marriage restrictions, sterilizations, or, the direct eradication of the carriers of the genotype deemed to be inferior through isolation, incarceration and, ultimately, murder.

With "genetic engineering," we have a technology with a purpose and even the desire to clone characteristics perceived as "desirable." Propaganda aside, this is nothing more than state-of-the-art positive eugenics. The corresponding version "negative eugenics" is the removal of unwanted physical and genetic characteristics from a person, or preventing their occurrence.

"Most researchers believe that advances in the elimination of physical defects will come first with negative eugenics. By doing this, negative mental characteristics will be eradicated. Only then will positive eugenics be possible."[8] While the slow elimination of genetically caused diseases appears to be a possibility, much more likely would be the abolition of genetically caused diseases through what would amount to a prenatal euthanasia.

"With increasing frequency, an amniocentesis is performed in order to abort the fetus should there be a suspicion of a genetically caused disease...,"[9] wrote Allen R. Utke, a professor of chemistry at the University of Wisconsin at Oshkosh. He goes on quite rightly to ask if this technology could possibly be a precursor of other standards of selection and if, in following this path, the end result would be the loss of respect for life.

Indeed, Professor Utke's objection is justified. What are the values of a society which routinely destroys life in its early stages? Would the next step be this same type of "help" for the elderly, the sickly and the mentally retarded? Could the same ethical justifications that permit the elimination of a fetus do the same for other times and conditions of life? Here is the eugenicists' train of thought: Whoever is handicapped according to their gene card could be selected, put aside, treated and removed because he or she is a burden. Or because he or she costs money. Or maybe because he or she is just a thorn in somebody's side. Or maybe because he or she is the wrong race or religion.

The resurgence of a revitalized, high-tech eugenics threatens us all, especially since today's version is not saddled with the obvious cruelty of a racial hygiene program. It is disguised as a health service. The camouflage techniques of modern-day geneticists is just as well thought out as the justifications during the Nazi era of the necessity of the Law for the Prevention of Genetically Diseased Children.

The handicapped person, the sick person and the person seeking help require more attention than others. It would be self-destructive to surrender to the Social Darwinist's vision of a fight for survival, of the survival of the strongest or of the biologically superior. It would also be self-destructive to label our handicapped as more or less "unfit to live." It would be self-destructive if we permitted psychiatry to define the social norm (whatever that may be) as the binding standard of comparison or any sort of orientation point. In this way, individually different behavior would be killed off and culture would be reduced to cookie-cutter personalities. It would be self-destructive if we subjected ourselves solely to the industrial pressure to perform, for doing so would cost us our humanity. It would also be the final victory of conforming people to society and the triumph of what became the Third Reich's ideology.

We should therefore learn to live with and overcome illness, not eradicate it for the sake of social or political systems. It is irresponsible, for example, to suggest as Professor Rainer Tolle of Munich did, that a patient suffering from melancholy should be treated with such barbarous methods as sleep deprivation, electroshocks and antidepressant medication that have dangerous side effects.

In a 1984 book on the Nazi killing of the "mentally ill," it said"When I think nowadays about the history of the effect genetics has had on anthropology and psychiatry, I see a wasteland of destruction. The blood spilled by millions has been energetically forgotten. The most recent history of this gene-obsessed human science is confusing and full of nightmarish crimes. Many geneticists, anthropologists and psychiatrists have slipped out of this nightmare and into the deep sleep of amnesia."[10]

CHAPTER 8

*"The degree of knowledge in psychiatry is still so unsatisfactory
that a great deal of guesswork cannot be avoided."*
> Dr. Fritz Reimer
> Director of the psychiatric
> state hospital of Weinsberg

PSYCHIATRIC TREATMENT TODAY

We turn now to the so-called "therapies" of modern psychiatry. Now that it is no secret that the Nazi legacy survives and that students of the Third Reich's criminals are still active in many psychiatric institutes, it should come as no surprise that their methods are as static as their theories and philosophies.

Psychiatric treatment methods can be divided into three basic categories:

1. Treatment using "shock" (electroshock, insulin shock, etc.);
2. Treatment using surgery (lobotomies, etc.); and
3. Treatment using drugs.

Conceivably, there is another miscellaneous category under which any other psychiatric treatment would fall. Occupational therapies, psychotherapies (which have finally been recognized after years of heavy resistance by the psychiatric community) and various other so-called "therapies" belong in this category. However categorized, what can be seen in psychiatric treatments throughout their historical use, is that they violate human rights and dignity and, indeed, life itself.

A SHORT HISTORY OF PSYCHIATRIC TREATMENT

This examination starts in what is psychiatry's Middle Ages, which lasted until approximately the end of the nineteenth century. The treatments then in vogue included:

"Constraining cabinets…coffin-like lockers,…coffins…leg enclosures, leg locks, restraining chairs, enshacklement to walls, metal tracks, steel balls, park benches…solitary confinement lasting for weeks…spinning motions on the 'Darwinian Chair' (as it was named by its inventor) in which patients were spun around until blood flowed out of their mouth, nose and ears,…sudden explosions with gunpowder, the thunder of cannons…and the 'cat's piano.'"[1] The "cat's piano" was a particularly ingenious invention of psychiatrist Johann Christian Reil (1759—1813), which worked this way:

"The animals selected were placed with the tails turned backwards, onto which fell a keyboard equipped with sharp nails. That cat that was hit gave its sound. The noise created by this instrument, especially if the patient is placed in such a way that he does not miss the physiognomy and the gesticulations of these animals, would have brought even Lot's wife out of her catalepsy and back to level-headedness."[2]

Other methods of physical "therapy" were:

"Steam and gas heating equipment,…strapping the patient to the warmth of a horse…drops of burning sealing wax onto the hands and burning the vertebrae of the neck or head with a red hot iron…the dripping of cold water onto the head for hours or even days,…injections of ice-cold water into the vagina,…direct stimulation of…nipples and genitals…"[3]

The forgoing is only a small portion of the rich therapeutic repertory of a science that started at the end of its own Middle Ages by characterizing such methods as medicine. Here are a few more elements of psychiatry's primitive chemical and biological repertoire of therapies:

"…caustic substances…ammonia…carbon dioxide…iron filings…."[4]

Also from the psychiatric medicine chest come such antiquated tortures as what Peter Lehmann described:

"…to tell the patient in advance that they will be burned if they don't confess their sins…the spreading of fear and terror by, for example, putting them into a sawdust box, into a barrel of live eels (in the dark, of course, the person would believe that they were snakes)…hypnotic suggestions…shooting water against genitals or into the face…pulling patients up with ropes or pulleys and letting them hang there for hours…a full and vigorous treatment of terror, fright or torture…alternatingly rewarding and beating the patient across the hands with a stick,…"[5]

To round out the psychiatric protocols, here is more from their spectrum of "therapies:"

"…castration…the removal of the clitoris…the injection of scabies, cutting the nerves of the penis…the injecting of the smallpox virus…x-ray treatment… sterilization…the injection of typhoid bacteria.…"[6]

Several of psychiatry's most heinous treatments merit special, in-depth examination.

SHOCKING THE BRAIN

As the nineteenth gave way to the twentieth century, psychiatry experimented with new methods and dabbled in new theories. Among the new developments of the era was the idea that electrical current might be therapeutic. Originally, the idea was to make World War I era German soldiers ready for combat again. "Kaufmann Therapy" was the prevalent method to accomplish that end and was used widely.

Kaufman Therapy was never scientifically tested. At a neurology conference in Baden-Baden, even some of the psychiatrists in attendance warned against the use of electrical current on neurotics. At the time they noted that Kaufmann did not have an iota of evidence that the "treatment" produced any positive results. Indeed, Kaufmann Therapy was pursued on nothing other than Kaufmann's nonsensical idea that one shock—war—is best treated with another shock—electrical current.

Patients were singularly unenthusiastic about Kaufmann Therapy, which bore more of a resemblance to torture than it did to therapy. It amounted to little more than strong shots of both direct and alternating currents. The well-known psychiatrist Ernst Kretschmer described Kaufmann Therapy with remarkable detachment:

"In the semi-darkness surrounded by all kinds of fantastic instruments lies a hysterical old person on the treatment table in my therapy room.… I take the…electrode into my hand. Just a moment before he had been relaxed and friendly as he talked to me. Then something incomprehensible occurred: in front of my eyes he changed suddenly into another person, like when one throws a lever of a smoothly running machine and unexpectedly a roaring set of wheels cuts in. Staring eyes, a contorted face, muscles tight as a drum, pressing this way and that way and crunching together as if over something invisible so much that you want to tear yourself away from him....Together with this is a second action which goes into gear: a trembling, heaving and twitching. Teeth rattle, hairs stand up, sweat beads turn up on his pale face. Adding to this commotion are brief sharp yells, clutching grasps and quick strong pain. Under these electrical stimulations and with a sudden jerk, another transformation takes place. There is almost a physical sensation from this, as if a dislocated joint pops back in. Suddenly the will is smooth and straight and the muscles calmly and willingly follow its motor functions."[7]

Electrical torture did not stop with the end of World War I. On the contrary, it got even crueler and more alarming. Electroshock therapy, later renamed "electroseizure therapy" or "electroconvulsive therapy"—the euphemism "convulsion" is much nicer to hear than the word "shock," but it does nothing to change the nature of the action—was developed. The newest name for this inhuman torture in professional circles is "neuroelectric therapy" or "NET" for short. The attempt to mask the brutality of "treatment" with a strong electric current of several hundred volts through cosmetic word changes will probably last until this therapy is finally outlawed.

A 1938 discovery by an Italian psychiatrist led to a small revolution in the study of the brain. Dr. Ugo Cerletti visited a slaughterhouse in Rome hoping to find an inspiration for another psychiatric project.[8] Cerletti himself describes the discovery and development of this contemporary "therapeutic" process as follows:

"I went to the slaughterhouse in order to have a look at the so-called electrical slaughtering, and I observed then that large metal tongs were attached to the temples of pigs and hooked up to an electrical circuit. Immediately thereafter the pigs fell over unconsciously, stiffened and shaken by seizures, just like dogs in our experiments. While they were unconscious, the butcher could slaughter them without difficulty and let them bleed dry.

"At that moment I had the feeling that we could also do the same experiment on a human being. I instructed my assistant to be on the lookout for a suitable test subject."[9]

It is said that Cerletti experimented on a disoriented vagrant. Two large electrodes were attached to each side of the man's temples. Once he was wired, Cerletti began carefully, with 80 volts for a period of 0.2 seconds. The description of the experiment reads like a script of a horror movie:

"Immediately after the rush of current, the patient reacted by twitching and his muscles became stiff. Without losing consciousness, he then fell into bed. Suddenly, he started to sing at the top of his lungs with a strange high voice. Shortly thereafter he calmed down. Those of us who had performed the experiment were understandably under a lot of emotional stress. We knew that we had already taken a considerable risk. However, it was obvious to us all that the voltage that had been applied was too low. Somebody suggested that we allow the patient to rest and repeat the experiment on the next day. That's when the patient, who had obviously heard us, said: 'Not another one. This is deadly.' My determination to continue the experiment almost began to waver after this almost command-like accusation. But for fear I would give in to my emotions, I decided to continue. The electrodes were once again attached, this time with a voltage of 110 for 0.2 seconds."[10]

And so the psychiatric experiments and the various permutations of ECT continued. The next significant attempt to find a useful treatment using electrical current was undertaken completely for the interest of the state. Friedrich Panse, who would later become the president of the German Society for Psychiatry and Neurology, re-addressed himself to Kaufmann Therapy after World War I and refined it supposedly to render soldiers who were psychologically unfit for the front combat-ready again. During "Pansen," direct current was applied instead of the alternating current of Kaufmann Therapy during World War I. This type of "therapy" created an "extremely impressive experience, which stirs up the whole body."[11]

A mechanical device was devised for the express purpose of providing electrical treatment near the front. The device, developed by an engineer named Stark of the German company called Siemens was known as the "Aktionsstromgerät" ("Electrical action device"). Although originally intended to be used after the war, it was discarded in 1945.

Cases of soldiers killed by psychiatrists with electroshocks were not uncommon. Dr. Emil Gelny, a psychiatrist who began his questionable career in the Austrian Institute of Gugging on October 1, 1943, had been a member of the Nazi party since 1933 and had achieved the rank of Sturmbandführer of the Sturmabteilung (Army Lieutenant of the Stormtrooper Division). He "added much to the ways of killing through euthanasia with a new variation." His "new variation" was using electroshock "according to the same principle as the electric chair to execute those sentenced to death." Every day he "managed" between seven and ten patients also using medications and air injections. The process of "electro-executions" has been described as follows:

"Once the patient went unconscious from the effects of the electricity, the caretakers then had to attach four other electrodes to the hands and feet of the patient. Dr. Gelny ran high voltage through them and after ten minutes at the most the death of the patient would set in."[12]

The number of soldiers killed in institutions may never be precisely reconstructed. We know for certain that murders of soldiers deemed unfit for military service had been carried out in Hadamar as well as in Meseritz and in killing institutes such as Lindenburg.[13]

Besides the highly questionable results, the side effects of electroconvulsive therapy (ECT) are horrible. Since the beginning of the wide application of this method, there are documented cases that graphically illustrate this hard truth. One documented side effect of ECT is amnesia. In fact, amnesia, is a certain symptom of what is known as "brain scorching," where millions of brain cells are destroyed. How much the brain itself is affected can be deduced from experiments with animals:

"When doing experiments with cats it was found that an electrical conduit for the current could be established through tissue sections."[14]

The animal experiments in question were performed in the 1960s by German scientists Jochin Quandt and Helma Sommer in the district hospital of Bernburg an der Saale. Their studies established that after four electric treatments the death rate of the brain cells becomes incalculable. There can be no doubt that irreversible brain damage occurs through the direct impact of the electrical current upon the brain.[15] Even psychiatrist Hanfied Helmchen agreed in the 1973 edition of the *Lexikon der Psychiatrie* (*Encyclopedia of Psychiatry*)—which was, ironically, generally ignored by the professional world.[16] He agreed that what applies to cats does not necessarily apply to people, but the results of the investigations by Quandt and Sommer cannot be invalidated even to this day. The appalling conclusions of Helma Sommer must be seen as valid: "irreversible, intracellular dysfunction is unavoidable."[17] Other researchers also obtained similar results through experiments with cats, such as Jules H. Masserman and Mary Grier Jacques in the United States. They succeeded in proving that serious side effects occurred as a result of ECT in experiments with animals.[18] It has essentially been undisputed since the 1950s that ECT destroys brains cells and certain brain functions.[19]

Other debilitating side effects included lapses and disturbances of memory—called "erasure effect"—headaches and dizziness, lack of ambition, apathy, learning difficulties, loss of bowel and bladder control, loss of appetite, delirium, disorientation, delusions, hallucinations, motor imbalances, debilitating fear and more.[20] The brain is not the only site of damage. Much of the rest of the body suffers damage, in particular the spine, clavicle and femur.[21]

It is hard to imagine something with more contraindications, yet this form of treatment boomed in the 1950s. "There was hardly any syndrome to which electroshock was not applied."[22] As late as 1977, the *Deutsche Zeitung* proclaimed that more than two-thirds of all psychiatric hospitals continued to use ECT during treatment,[23] despite the recent and scientifically reinforced discovery that electric shocks kill entire pathways of brain cells throughout the brain and lead to massive memory disturbances. Even today, patients are tortured with electroshock, contrary to all assurances by psychiatry, "especially in cases of endogenetic depression, certain forms of schizophrenia…and for pharmacologically and therapeutically 'finished' patients."[24]

More than just terminology has changed. "Contrary to earlier days, the patient does not twitch anymore. The patient is being anaesthetized, and the medication suppresses the convulsion. Lawyers have enforced this so-called 'humanization' of electroshock through lawsuits based on numerous complaints by patients. But an electric shock of 100 to 200 volts still races through the brain, just as before."[25]

The current euphemism for firing electric current through a human brain is "neuroelectric therapy," a term that was probably coined immediately after it became widely known that "therapeutic convulsion" was the same as electroshock. Rather than being a brutal memory, ECT is still very much in use.

For electroshock treatment, 1992 was a banner year. At the E-Schock Kongress (Electroshock Convention) in Graz, for example, leading international electroshock specialists and technicians came together at an event one critic dubbed "torturers amongst themselves." It was no coincidence, however, that the leading electroshock practitioners from the United States were the most requested speakers, since the therapy is viewed much less skeptically in America than it is even in Germany. Two remarkable lectures delivered at this conference are of special interest.[26]

A Viennese psychiatrist named Norbert Loimer attempted to rewrite history by claiming that, while deaths from electroshock undoubtedly occurred during the Nazi era, no direct evidence exists to link psychiatrists to such executions. Loimer made that claim despite the fact that Klee had already documented exactly the opposite, based on eyewitness accounts addressed in our chapter on T4. It is difficult to imagine anyone taking Loimer's argument seriously. Who else but psychiatrists could have killed patients in psychiatric clinics with electroshock paraphernalia?

A lecture by Stella Reiter-Theill of the Göttingen Academy for Ethics in Medicine is particularly noteworthy for its position on the issue of the patient's consent to electroshock therapy. The gist of Reiter-Theill's argument is that, in all cases, the patient must be informed about the therapy and its possible consequences and must give his or her consent.

But there is a catch. While psychiatrists should respect a rejection of the procedure by an informed, sane and competent patient, "irrational" rejections, however, by a patient whose ability to reason is limited by "disorderly cognitive functions" should be ignored.

This sort of illusory and frightening discretion is not consent, but it is alarming in the extreme. It is nothing more or less than carte blanche for the psychiatrist to shock whomever he or she wants. The psychiatrist can always later attest that the patient had limited discernment. This is yet another example of the psychiatric community's arrogance, its repeated insistence that it should be free to interpret the facts and the law however it wants.

Another event, an "ECT Workshop," took place on October 14 and 15, 1992, under the direction of Professor Hans Lauter, the director of the Psychiatrischen Klinik und Poliklinik (Psychiatric Clinic and Outpatient Department) of the Technical University of Munich, was presented solely for the purpose of making electroconvulsive therapy more socially palatable.

An interesting side note is that one of the leading advocates of electroshock—and a student of Emil Kraepelin, Ugo Cerletti, Wagner von Jauregg and Max Nonnes—is psychiatrist Lothar B. Kalinowsky. An honorary member of the German Society for Psychiatry and Neurology, and a recipient of the Griesinger Medal, Dr. Kalinowsky is known as the "exporter" of electroshock treatment into the United States. Dr. Kalinowsky moved to Rome in 1933, where under Dr. Cerletti he attended the first electroshock treatment in 1938. In 1939, Kalinowsky emigrated to the Untied States. In the March 1970 issue of *Der Nervenarzt*, Hanns Hippius wrote:

"Against great opposition by antisomatic psychiatry, which had been established by Adolf Meyer and the psychoanalysts, Lothar Kalinowsky had introduced electroshock treatment to the U.S.A."[27]

At the 1992 Electroshock Workshop in Munich, Kalinowsky was specially honored by Hippius and other speakers. So, naturally enough, was ECT:

"Of course, it has become increasingly obvious in the last few years that some patients simply do not respond well to these medicinal procedures. It is also known that there can be troublesome and unpleasant damages with medicinal procedures....

"There exist good hypotheses about what exactly the actual effect of the treatment is, but absolutely no certain understanding."[28]

Could there ever be a better formal confession of quackery by a pseudoscience?

There are many prominent and tragic examples of the devastating effect of electroshock. Ernest Hemingway, one of the most brilliant writers of the twentieth century, received two series of electroshocks in 1961. Afterwards, Hemingway complained bitterly about them, and demanded that the treating physicians stop because he was convinced that they would destroy his memory and thus ruin him as a writer.[29] He complained to a friend that he feared that he had had his memory taken from him and his ability to write destroyed.[30] Within thirty days after ECT, Hemingway committed suicide.

For every public and prominent Hemingway, however, there are thousands of private, unknown victims whose destruction went unnoticed, unlamented, and unvindicated. The cries of most patients remain disregarded.

With ECT being so controversial, we must ask ourselves why something so brutal, something so lethal has proponents. The answer is plain, but subtle. Reports that laud ECT and argue that it has actually been helpful must be received with caution and skepticism. They are self-serv-ing reports by ECT proponents trying to justify their actions. ECT defi-nitely will temporarily change things—a shift of symptoms causing mem-ory loss so that the person may "forget" the problem they're facing. But ECT is psychiatry's equivalent of throwing out the baby with the bath water. It will certainly not solve the problem. It cures nothing.[31] ECT must be unequivocally denounced as inhuman and banned.

Even without the implications and consequences of the Nazi move-ment's influence on the history of psychiatry, it is time to outlaw ECT. The destruction of brain cells through electroshock therapy is simply mental murder. There have been positive developments in this regard. The Dutch government has enacted a resolution barring shock treatments and per-sonality-changing brain operations on patients of psychiatric institutions. With luck and justice, the Dutch example will be emulated elsewhere.

The level of inventiveness shown by psychiatrists has no bounds. What follows are some more examples which, though they are not immediately connected to the Nazi era, share a recognizable tradition of barbarism and the psychiatric philosophy of the Third Reich.

CUTTING THE BRAIN

In 1935—three years before electroshock treatment was developed—psychosurgeons began using their scalpels on the brain. It was a Portuguese physician who first performed psychosurgery:

"The surgeon drilled two or more holes into the skull of the locally anaesthetized patient, thrust wildly with an instrument that resembled a butter knife into her brain and sliced or mashed the nerves in the frontal lobe area with rotating movements, as if removing the core of an apple."[32]

The results were immediate: The patient fell into a state of utter indif-ference to life. Moniz saw this as proof of the treatment's success and cut through the frontal lobes of another hundred patients. One of his patients finally fired five bullets into the brain butcher's back and paralyzed him. As a reward for his great discovery, however, Dr. Moniz was awarded the 1949 Nobel Prize for medicine.

In the decades to come, between 50,000 to 100,000 people were sub-jected to this exercise in unadulterated torture, which, though hard to imagine, is more brutal even than electroshock.

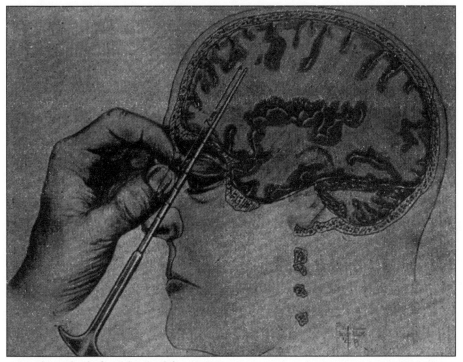

An early method of conducting lobotomies

A later form of psychosurgery involved a thin knife inserted directly above the eye and into the frontal lobe of the brain. One of the most devoted students of Moniz, Walter Jack Freeman (also called "Jack the Brain Slicer") developed this technique. He first gave his patients an electroshock and then mutilated their brains by driving his knife above the eye seven centimeters into the cranium with spinning motions, supposedly to "cure" their "mental illness."

"Those treated ranged from sex offenders to obsessive neurotics to aggressive children. The mutilation of the brain was even recommended for adultery, kleptomania, obesity and irregular bowel movements!"[33] More than 4,000 people were subjected to this by Freeman.

If the patient treated in this way does not die immediately, he or she could certainly expect to die a slow, painful death. Suicide after psychosurgery was common as the person was brain-damaged into an apathetic state.

By the end of the 1940s, psychosurgery was refined to a point where brain tissue was destroyed by being burned by a fine probe. An elegant

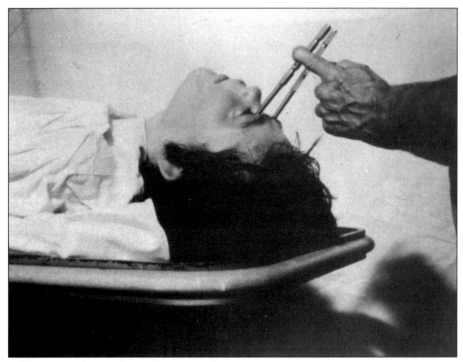

A lobotomy technique being demonstrated

expression was chosen for cauterizing live brain tissue—"stereotactic operation." The result, however, was hardly convincing, even for many psychiatrists. What little was left of the patient did not include his or her dignity.

In his 1957 study "Psychopathologie des Stirnhirns 1939-1955" ("Psychopathology of the Frontal Brain from 1939 to 1955"), psychiatrist Heinz Häfner recommended that this slaughterhouse surgery ought to be abandoned:

"Already more than 50,000 patients today have been subjected to one of the many various psychosurgical operations on the frontal lobes. Observation material was obtained through mass experiments that are unique and unparalleled in its scope....This incomparable evidence not only contradicts the notion of the localization of neurological functions in the prefrontal region, but has decisively changed our theories about the Psychological Forehead Brain Syndrome. Above all, all attempts of connecting unique psychological dysfunctions with certain frontal cortex areas ...have to be considered as having failed."[34]

In other words, more than 50,000 defenseless patients were subjected to the surgical mutilation of their frontal lobes, just so some psychiatrist could later come to the conclusion that there is no connection whatsoever between mental travail and the frontal region of the brain. Dr. Häfner was not shocked by this; on the contrary, he applauded the evidence. It is impossible to regard this arrogant "nothing to do with me" attitude as anything but antisocial. "Lobotomy"—the surgical incision into the brain lobe—cost upwards of 50,000 patients their personalities before someone realized that it didn't work. Worse, the following documents illustrate that the impact of these realizations were short-lived.

A research report from the University of the Saarland in 1977 revealed that psychiatrists destroy the hypothalmus to treat "addiction delinquency" and sexual behavior.

"It has been supported several times by animal experiments that stereotactic elimination of the so-called "sexual behavioral center" in the frontal hypothalamus leads to a reduction of the sex drive. This leads us to believe that homosexual behavior can be controlled and adjusted to the requirements of society. Secondly, we found that excessive yielding to hypersexuality and sexual aggressiveness could be removed through a one-sided stereotactic operation of this type." [35]

G. Hugo Dieckmann of the University of Homburg/Saar also reported on stereotactic operations on children. From 1964 to the end of 1975, 57 children were subjected to psychosurgery. [36] Dieckmann was awarded his doctorate in 1954 under Richard Jung, a professor of neuropsychology and psychiatry who worked busily in the field of "genetic psychoses" and "schizophrenia" research during World War II.

DRUGGING THE BRAIN

Psychiatric drugs have experienced a remarkable rise in popularity since about 1952, despite the fact that many of these medications have horrifying side effects and can be addicting. [44] According to one study, 9,000 people die annually from the side effects of psychiatric medications. [45] Perhaps more significantly, the parallels to the practices of psychiatry during the Third Reich are definitely not to be dismissed.

The Nazi regime encouraged broad production and marketing of pharmaceutical products. Frequently the tests that resulted in pharmaceutical advances were paid for with the lives and health not only of the inmates of concentration camps, but also of hospitalized soldiers. Nevertheless, the administration of psychiatric drugs was nothing compared to today.

It is a tragic fact that many people who begin psychiatric treatment will receive one or more psychiatric medications, whether the patient really wants it or not. These medications, however, have very controversial and frequently unpredictable side effects, for not every person reacts the same way. "Neuroleptics" are the strongest of these substances, having an immediate influence on the psyche and are used in most cases of schizophrenia or psychosis, which are among the most violent of mental disturbances. They "do not heal but only change the course of the psychosis."[46] "Neuroleptics" are on the market under different trade names.[47] They are common and familiar, but their side effects are, in the opinion of many critics, so complex that they can barely be tracked.

In many cases, the effects of these neuroleptics are amazingly similar to those of psychosurgery, especially lobotomy—whether drug-induced or the result of the surgical destruction of nerve channels in the brain, the zombie-like condition that results is interpreted by psychiatry as a healing effect. Indeed, the lobotomy-like effects of neuroleptics were the result of public relations stigma that enveloped its surgical ancestor. Decades ago, brain surgery became so unpopular that psychiatrists searched for a suitable substitute that would create the same effect—a patient who would remain quiet, apathetic and motionless and cause, few if any, commotions in her environment—without the public relations fallout. There are reports of patients who received Haldol, for example, who could neither control their thoughts nor speak while under the drug's influence.

No wonder there is talk of a "chemical lobotomy" in professional papers.[48] Those who know have labelled psychopharmaceutical treatment as a "lobotomy without a scalpel." It is certainly possible to obtain lobotomy-like results without bloodying one's hands or sullying one's reputation. Just do what doctors do all the time—prescribe a pill.

Especially with the elderly, it is convenient to put patients under psychiatric drugs in order to rid oneself as discreetly as possible of the burden of a person who is sick and demanding. This is not euthanasia so much as a way to turn a human being into an apathetic and compliant creature. It makes people quiet.

Another side effect of most of the neuroleptics is a dramatic dampening of libido—sex drive—and sexual potency.[49] In psychiatric circles it has long been deemed undesirable for mentally handicapped and sick people to procreate. Loss of sexual urges and potency may be a side effect of psychopharmacology that the doctors actually desire—after all, the ability to procreate is strongly hindered. No one advocates an absence of judgment or encouraging promiscuity. But the neuroleptic's form of clandestine sterilization is not even good eugenics practice, let alone acceptable medicine.

A particularly significant aspect of this controversial subject is the use of psychiatric drugs on children. One of many psychotropic (mind-altering) drugs is Ritalin. Among its side effects are hallucinations and delusions.[50] One American study documents four shocking cases:

A thirteen-year-old boy hanged himself in the front yard of his parents' house only a few days after he had been taken off Ritalin.

A ten-year-old boy hanged himself in the garage of his family home two days after Ritalin was discontinued.

A sixteen-year-old hanged himself in his parents' garage a few days after his Ritalin dosage was reduced.

An eighteen-year-old killed himself with automobile exhaust fumes four days after being taken off Ritalin.

Regrettably, Ritalin is prescribed not only by psychiatrists but by pediatricians as well, and it is currently the medication of choice for what is called "hyperactivity" or "hyperkinesis." Psychiatrists devised a ten-point scale to assess hyperactivity:

1. Restless and overactive
2. Excitable and impulsive
3. Disturbs other children
4. Starts something and does not finish it, has a short attention span
5. Fidgets constantly
6. Easily distracted
7. Wishes must be fulfilled immediately; easily frustrated
8. Cries often
9. Swift and extreme mood shifts
10. Tendencies toward fits of anger

This is yet another dramatic example of how psychiatry has been successful in defining a mental disturbance—in this case, hyperactivity—to justify one of its dubious "therapies." It, therefore, should not be surprising that the number of children classified as in urgent need of psychiatric treatment has been estimated by psychiatry at about 800,000 and growing—in Germany alone. This estimate is used constantly as an argument for the expansion of psychiatric caretaking facilities. The target of such psychiatric propaganda is the government, and the objective is funding—a dangerous tendency, similar to what happened prior to 1933.

Even those drugs classified as less strong (like sedatives, antidepressants and sleeping pills) should be closely and critically examined. Sedatives like Valium (whose generic name is the widely distributed Diazepam) and related substances (like Librium and many more) are potentially hazardous and accompanied by potentially debilitating side effects. As early as 1970, a textbook pointed out many concerns over the side effects of psychiatric drugs, among which was that their active ingredients could lead to violent acts and even murder and suicide.[51]

A 1975 Canadian study reinforced the suspicion that the rapid increase in the consumption of Valium and other sedatives could be correlated to the increase in aggression in society.[52]

And the manufacturer of a widely prescribed sleeping pill, Halcion, had this to say of it:

"...by taking the substance, states of fear, aggressiveness, depression and loss of memory can occur twice as often and stronger than previously indicated.... The FDA lists Halcion no less than number one on its list of substances that are linked with violent acts."[53]

According to some critics, antidepressants—which are sometimes given to children simply because they wet their bed—are also potential disasters. Aggression, hostility, irritability, excitability and violent, suicidal behavior are linked with this group of drugs.

The most damning understatement actually comes from a psychiatrist:

"The level of knowledge in psychiatry is still so unsatisfactory that a great deal of guesswork cannot be avoided."[54]

The conclusion we must draw is that no therapeutic advances worth mentioning have been achieved since the Nazi era through the use of psychotropic drugs. If anything, the development of pharmaceutical treatment of mental illnesses after the war has taken on almost a sinister color and done more harm than good.

As can be seen, psychiatric "treatment" has travelled no great distance since the Middle Ages. While the actions may be cloaked under the false mantle of science, they are nonetheless merely the same brutality embellished by modern technology and medical terminology.

PART THREE

"THE MEN BEHIND HITLER" IN AMERICA?

CHAPTER 1

*"The destiny of mankind is not decided by material computa-
tion. When great causes are on the move in the world...we learn
that we are spirits, not animals...."*
> Winston Churchill
> Radio broadcast to America
> June 16, 1941

THE BEGINNINGS OF PSYCHIATRIC INFLUENCE IN THE UNITED STATES

U nfortunately, the legacy of the men behind Hitler is not confined to Germany. Similarly inspired movements have since sprung up and taken root all over the world. Perhaps the most powerful of these enclaves is in the United States, where psychiatry influences many of the institutions that are simply taken for granted: politics, education, health and the court system. The result of this unfortunate influence can be found by a quick glance around our nation's cities and towns: dramatic increases in illiteracy, drug abuse, crime, teenage pregnancy, poverty and insanity. All concurrent with the presence and expansion of this psychiatric influence.

Statistically speaking, the psychiatric "reforms," so loudly trumpeted as essential to the welfare of modern society, have not brought us an improved and enlightened culture, but quite the reverse—a society besieged and increasingly dependent upon government for protection; where children bring guns to drug-infested high schools that eventually give them diplomas despite their inability to read or write; where the inner city murder rate is so high that many share the doubt that they will reach the age of twenty-five; and where a welfare state demoralizes and degrades its beneficiaries and burdens the tax-paying public.

To understand how this came to be, however, we must retrace our steps to the very beginning, to a man whose name is obscure except to students of his field, but who is nevertheless almost single-handedly responsible for the "philosophy" known as "experimental psychology."

WILHELM WUNDT

When Wilhelm Maximilian Wundt first became interested in psychology at the University of Heidelberg in 1856, the subject itself was quite different from what we know it as today. Early "psychology" was nothing more than the study (-ology) of the soul (psyche-), or mind.

As Professor of Philosophy at the University of Leipzig (which included teaching psychology), Wundt became so enthralled with the study of psychology as a separate subject that in 1879, he established his own psychological laboratory where he had the freedom to conduct experiments and demonstrations.

Wilhelm Wundt—Established the first experimental psychology laboratory at the University of Leipzig in Germany

Psychiatrist E. G. Boring paid Wundt this tribute:

"Wundt is the senior psychologist in the history of psychology. He is the first man who without reservation is properly called a psychologist. Before him there had been psychology enough, but no psychologist. …Wundt held a chair of philosophy, as the German psychologists did, and wrote voluminously on philosophy; but in his own eyes and in the eyes of the world he was, first and foremost a psychologist. When we call him the 'founder' of experimental psychology, we mean both that he promoted the idea of psychology as an independent science and that he is the senior among 'psychologists.'"[1]

With a degree in philosophy, Wundt was never a medical doctor. In his day, however, Germany was known worldwide as a center of scientific advancement. Especially impressive was the Germans' ability to apply scientific techniques to areas of study previously thought of as non-scientific. In Berlin, for example, G.W.F. Hegel attempted to turn history into a scientific field. Karl Marx combined and codified principles of economics and political philosophy.

Wundt, also a product of this urge to reduce the ethereal to the scientific, felt no different about his field of interest.

To him, it was not possible to study anything if it could not be sensed, measured and experienced in the physical universe. Scientific demonstration demanded observable and quantifiable results. Seeing no hope of being able to do this with the human soul, Wundt changed the subject of psychology around to suit the needs of his view of science. From Wundt forward, psychology would not concern itself so much with the study of the soul, but with the study of observable phenomena related to human behavior:

"…it truly appears to be a useless waste of energy to keep returning to such aimless discussion about the nature of the psyche, which were in vogue for a while, and practically still are, instead, rather, of applying one's energies where they will produce real results."[2]

The laboratory that Wundt was given, though initially small, expanded quickly to eleven rooms. In the following years, Wundt and his many students produced a wealth of studies which would define the field of psychology through the turn of the twentieth century. During this period, Leipzig was the place to come to for any student who wanted to study the cutting-edge developments of a new, dynamic discipline.

Wundt's data-gathering techniques centered around the scientific measurement of physiological reactions to given stimuli. This, he claimed, would result in an understanding of how people experience sensation. According to Wundt, all thought was derived from a four-step chemical reaction in the brain:

1) Perception, where the person receives the stimulus;

2) "Apperception," where the body (notice that the idea of a human "soul" is no longer mentioned) recognizes the stimulus;

3) A decision to act (not an independent decision, but a reflexive reaction to the given stimulus), and;

4) The reaction to the stimulus.

In Wundt's own words:

"Observation of the fact of consciousness is of no avail until these are derived from chemical and physical processes. Thought is simply a result of brain activity. Since this activity ceases when circulation is arrested and life departs, thought is nothing more than a function of the substances of which the brain is composed....The most clearly marked and most permanent of these [mental] disturbances are the various kinds of insanity. The particular forms of insanity, as you know, are so many and so different that pathological psychology has as good a claim to rank an independent discipline, beside normal psychology, as has pathology of the body..."[3]

In other words, in believing that all thought is derived from chemical reactions in the brain, Wundt completely denied the existence of a soul. Man, according to Wundt, was a stimulus-response animal, nothing more than a pattern of responses based upon past experience as translated through chemical processes. This philosophy can be seen in the work of some of his more famous philosophical descendants such as Ivan Pavlov, who studied in Leipzig in 1884, and whose quaint experiments involving salivating dogs were actually conducted to determine whether humans can be so influenced.

Wundt's students were encouraged to examine every action and reaction of their subjects closely and attempt to measure them, and then to determine the reason for the individual differences from person to person. The focus of "physiological psychology" (later to be called "experimental psychology") gradually turned into the physical study of the brain and central nervous system and how they respond to external stimuli. At the core of Wundt's philosophy, therefore, was the conviction that man had no self-determinism— he could only respond to whatever the world chose to throw at him:

"If one assumes that there is nothing there to begin with but a body, a brain and a nervous system, then one must try to educate by inducing sensations in that nervous system. Through these experiences, the individual will learn to respond to any given stimulus with the 'correct' response. The child is not, for example, thought capable of volitional control over his actions, or of deciding whether he will act or not act in a certain way: his actions are thought to be preconditioned and beyond his control, because he is a stimulus-response mechanism. According to this thinking, he is his reactions."[4]

Had Wundt been a medical doctor, he would have discovered, as many competent doctors of his time did, that mental disturbances or insanity were not "brain diseases" at all, but actual symptoms of underlying physical illness, which, if cured, would also result in the disappearance of the psychological problem.

If the value of a philosophy is determined by its workability, then we can judge Wundt's by its legacy. His work in psychological conditioning (later championed by Pavlov) ushered in the work of the American behaviorists John B. Watson and B.F. Skinner, inspired the idea that man should adapt to his environment (as opposed to creating his environment in a constructive way to serve his needs), and would later provide the scientific justification for psychiatric atrocities such as electroshock, brain surgery and drug therapy. After all, if man is merely a stimulus-response animal at the mercy of external environmental stimuli, it would be senseless to concentrate upon his intellectual improvement. Instead, Wundt believed that he should be "conditioned" to get along with others and not to strike out on his own. What ultimately emerges is a society like the one we have today, increasingly obsessed with immediate gratification and materialism and less concerned with individual responsibility, ethics and personal achievement.

Even among fellow psychologists, Wundt's extremely debatable ideas had their prominent critics. In a letter, psychologist William James said of Wundt:

"He aims at being a sort of Napoleon of the intellectual world. Unfortunately, he will never have a Waterloo, for he is a Napoleon without genius and with no central idea which, if defeated, brings down the whole fabric in ruin...[W]hilst (his confreres) make mincemeat of some one of his views by their criticism, he is meanwhile writing a book on an entirely different subject. Cut him up like a worm, and each fragment crawls; there is no 'noeud vital' in his mental medulla oblong so that you can't kill him all at once."[5]

If Wundt had stayed ensconced in his laboratory, no one would have heard of him today. But he was the only professor of psychology of his kind in a country whose technical achievements were then the envy of the civilized world, with a laboratory that attracted students from all over the world fascinated by his novel approach. During his time in Leipzig, Wundt's teachings spawned the first generation of professors, practitioners, researchers and supporters of experimental psychology, many of whom returned to their native countries in Europe and North America to disseminate this new subject:

"Through these students, the Leipzig Laboratory exercised an immense influence on the development of psychology. It served as the model for the many new laboratories that were developed in the latter part of the nineteenth century. The many students who flocked to Leipzig, united as they were in point of view and common purpose, constituted a school of thought in psychology."[6]

In very short order, Wundt acquired so many disciples that a student could attend almost any major university in Europe and America and study with someone who had learned the new "experimental psychology" directly from the master:

"Naturally Leipzig became the Mecca of students who wished to study the 'new' psychology—a psychology that was no longer a branch of speculative philosophy, no longer a fragment of the science of physiology, but a novel and daring and exciting attempt to study mental processes by the experimental and quantitative methods common to all science. For the psychology of Leipzig was, in the eighties and nineties, the newest thing under the sun. It was the psychology for bold young radicals who believed that the ways of the mind could be measured and treated experimentally—and who possibly thought of themselves, in their private reflections, as pioneers on the newest frontier of science, pushing its method into reaches of experience that it had never before invaded. At any rate, they threw themselves into their tasks with industry and zest."[7]

Many of Wundt's American students returned to start departments of psychology in major American universities. This was not difficult, since the distinction of having studied under Wundt in Germany carried with it a prestige that made them much sought-after. Wundt's disciples taught hundreds of students of their own, establishing Ph.D. programs that were, in turn, replicated all over the United States.

The "Who's Who" of early American psychology flows directly from Wundt.

G. STANLEY HALL

G. Stanley Hall was Wundt's first American student. After returning from Leipzig in 1883, he went to Baltimore to join the faculty of Johns

Hopkins University. This was not accidental, for Johns Hopkins had just recently opened, and was modeled after the great German universities of the time. Within four years, Hall had established a psychological laboratory there, and began to publish *The American Journal of Psychology*, a periodical which provided for the "adherents of the new psychology not only a storehouse for contributions both experimental and theoretical, but a sense of solidarity and independence."[8]

In 1889, Hall accepted an offer to become the first president of Clark University in Worcester, Massachusetts, with the intention of making Clark the preeminent center of psychological research in the United States. One of the founders of the American Psychological Association in 1892, Hall concentrated heavily on child development, publishing a two-volume study, his life's work, called *Adolescence: Its Psychology and Its Relations to Physiology, Anthropology, Sociology, Sex, Crime, Religion and Education*. His teachings as passed on by his students would later have a major impact on the American educational system, especially during the reforms of the late 1950s and early 1960s.

One of Hall's most famous students was John Dewey, who was responsible for the implementation of the Wundtian view of education into the American school system by:

"... feeding experiential data to a young brain and nervous system, rather than the teaching of mental skills, [which] led to the abdication of the traditional role of the teacher as educator. Its place was taken by the concept of the teacher as a guide in the socialization of the child, leading each youngster to adapt to the specific behavior required of him in order for him to get along in his group."[9]

To Dewey, education was a social process, and the school was above all a breeding ground, where children could be trained to become a valuable part of the community at large, adapting themselves to its demands as needed.

Perhaps Dewey's real socialist intentions become most clear when he demands of public schools that they "take an active part in determining the social order of the future...according as the teachers align themselves with the newer forces making for social control of economic forces."[10]

It is a sad commentary on the "Father of American Education" that his training derives from the scientists who excluded the soul from man's component parts and his theories have culminated in the sorry state of affairs in which we find our modern educational system today.

SIR FRANCIS GALTON

Sir Francis Galton (1822—1911), was Charles Darwin's cousin and another of Wundt's students—the one who first coined the term "eugenics" in 1883. Inspired by his German master, Galton wanted to see if psychological testing could be applied to the identification and elimination of unwanted mental traits by selective breeding.

His basic theory was that "a man's natural abilities are derived by inheritance, under exactly the same limitations as are the form and physical features of the whole organic world."[11]

These theories were widely exported by Galton himself, who traveled extensively, spreading his gospel throughout Europe and America. His theories were very attractive to German, English and American psychologists, as a hereditary cause of mental illness fit neatly into the theories then in vogue which they were attempting to prove.

However Galton believed "that if [eugenical] decisions were to be made as to which human beings were to survive and reproduce, it would be necessary to have some criteria for survival. So he formed his anthropometric laboratory for the measurement of man, with the hope that by means of tests he could determine those individuals who should survive. Note that he was not deciding who should be selected for jobs in a given industry, but who should survive to reproduce."[12]

Underneath this "scientific inquiry" lay the fact that Galton was a racist who used his theories to confirm his own prejudices. He wrote:

"The Jews are specialized for a parasitical existence upon other nations, and that there is need of evidence that they are capable of fulfilling the varied duties of a civilized nation by themselves."[13]

Galton also felt a special contempt for black people:

"...the average intellectual standard of the Negro race is some two grades below our own."[14]

After spending two years in South Africa studying the native tribes, Galton wrote of one of them, the Damaras: "These savages court slavery. You engage one of them as a servant, and you find that he considers himself as your property, and that you are, in fact, become [sic] the owner of a slave. They have no independence about them, generally speaking, but to follow a master as a spaniel would."[15]

Not even the Irish were spared Galton's prejudice:

"Visitors to Ireland after the potato famine generally remarked that the Irish type of face seemed to have become more prognathous, that is, more like the negro in the protrusion of the lower jaw; the interpretation of which was that the men who survived the starvation and other deadly accidents of that horrible time were more generally of a low or coarse organization."[16]

Galton was not alone among the Wundtians in his unconcealed hatred for other races. Even G. Stanley Hall asserted that Africans, Indians and Chinese were "adolescent races" at a stage of "incomplete growth."[17]

Let's not mince words here. From the very beginning, the idea of "eugenics," coined by one of Wundt's own students, was racist. Period. This was never a philosophy that was at any time intended to help anyone. Rather, it was invented as a justification for the repression of certain ethnic groups or political opponents on the basis of their being "inferior."

Of course, it was for this very reason that eugenics became so popular among the powerful and the social and political elite in England, the United States and especially Germany.

JAMES M. CATTELL (1860-1944)

American psychologist James M. Cattell was Wundt's first assistant in Leipzig, working with him for three years.

Passionately interested in mental testing to find the reasons behind individual differences in ability, Cattell discovered during an experiment that literate adults could recognize the words they read without having to sound them out. They saw them as "word pictures." He expanded upon this idea by suggesting that children be taught to view words as units in and of themselves, rather than a collection of individual letters. This led to the "sight-reading" method, a precursor of today's "Whole Language" technique that pervades many of today's American school systems.

The use of "sight-reading" (also known as "look-say") and its descendants led to the needless discarding of the phonics method, the efficacy of which was proven in the 1955 classic entitled *Why Johnny Can't Read*, by Rudolf Flesch. In his book, Flesch discusses his research at Columbia

University's Teacher's College, where in eleven cases where children were taught with and without phonics, the use of phonics got better results in every instance.

In 1887, Cattell went to England, where he lectured at Cambridge and met Sir Francis Galton, with whose theories he was deeply struck. He quickly absorbed Galton's approach to eugenics, selective breeding and the measurement of intelligence, and furthered Galton's work by devising what he called "mental tests,"[18] which attempted to measure an individual's educational and psychological abilities. Some of these tests involved such activities as "the greatest possible squeeze of the hand,"[19] and the patient's height, weight and ability to remember.

Upon his return to the United States, Cattell joined the staff of the University of Pennsylvania, and made history by becoming the world's first Professor of Psychology. Even Wundt had not accomplished that feat, having remained a Professor of Philosophy for his entire career. Cattell then established one of the first psychological laboratories in the United States, modeling it after the one in which he had worked with Wundt for three years in Leipzig.

Leaving Penn for Columbia University in 1891, Cattell became head of Columbia's newly-formed psychology department, and helped Columbia's Teachers College—which was already deeply stamped with Wundtian philosophy—become one of the most influential teaching institutions in the world. The seeds also had been planted for the domination of American education by experimental psychology.

During his twenty-five year tenure at Columbia, Cattell promoted his new "science" by publishing magazines intended to disseminate and promote his views and provide the latest discoveries in the field. The first such publication was *The Psychological Review* which debuted in 1894. After that came *Science*, a weekly, which he bought from Alexander Graham Bell and converted into the official organ of the American Association for the Advancement of Science. In 1900, he started *Popular Science Monthly* (later the *Scientific Monthly*), and *School and Society*. With such reference books as *American Men of Science*, *Leaders in Education*, and *The Directory of American Scholars*, Cattell legitimized the new field of experimental psychology and placed it alongside the accepted scientific fields of the day.

Having assumed a significant amount of power and influence in teacher's colleges and the American educational system, the experimental psychologists could now control the direction of public policy regarding how we teach our children. In *Why Johnny Can't Read*, Rudolf Flesch underscores the dangers inherent in allowing such totalitarian control:

"It's a foolproof system all right. Every grade school teacher in the country has to go to a teacher's college or school in education; every teacher's college gives at least one course on how to teach reading; every course on how to teach reading is based on a textbook; every one of these textbooks is written by one of the high priests of the word method. In the old days, it was impossible to keep a good teacher from following her own common sense and practical knowledge; today the phonetic system of teaching reading is kept out of our schools as effectively as if we had a dictatorship with an all-powerful Ministry of Education."[20]

Of course, this "dictatorship" resided in the hands of American Wundtian psychologists.

In 1904, Cattell invited John Dewey to join the staff of the Teachers College at Columbia, which Dewey did. As we have mentioned earlier, Dewey believed that the primary purpose of the American educational system was not to teach children and enhance their native abilities as much as it was to make them better citizens by guiding their social development. In other words, schools were not meant to teach children to lead, but rather to conform to society. That this view would have disastrous consequences that plague us today has seemingly not lessened the esteem in which Dewey is held by the academic community, most notably the National Education Association.

Cattell's influence upon American education cannot be underestimated. During his tenure at Columbia, he turned out 344 successful doctoral candidates in psychology, many of whom later trained their own students to spread the word. He was elected president of the American Psychological Association in 1895 and in 1900 became the first psychologist to be voted in as a member of the National Academy of Sciences. His contributions to the field of experimental psychology were less in the area of research as in promotion. Through his efforts, publications were begun and sustained, teaching institutions were created and his students and colleagues' appointments to major positions in universities across the country were effected.

The damage that he caused was likewise incalculable.

EMIL KRAEPELIN (1856-1926)

Another very important student of Wundt's was a fellow German, Emil Kraepelin, of whom we have already spoken at length.

Kraepelin was fascinated by Wundt's research with mind-altering drugs. His teacher's observations on their effects on the human brain so impressed Kraepelin that he decided to devote his life to the study of psychology. From 1883 to 1893, he studied in Leipzig, gaining what his star pupil Adolf Meyer (whom we will discuss at length a little later) called "a steadfast Wundtian attitude." [21]

We already know of many of Kraepelin's other students and the devastating effect they had upon Germany before, during and after the Third Reich. They included psychiatrists such as Aschaffenburg, Gaupp and the notorious Ernst Rüdin.

After his time with Wundt, Kraepelin went to Munich, where he took on the practice and teaching of clinical psychiatry in the Kaiser Wilhelm Institute of Psychiatry in Munich, continuing his research into "organic" (i.e. hereditary) reasons for mental illness. His main preoccupation was schizophrenia, a word then newly coined by a Swiss colleague, Eugene Bleuler. Kraepelin's schizophrenia research remains a primary basis of today's continuing investigations. In fact, both Kraepelin and Bleuler's studies are still referenced in the Diagnostic and Statistic Manual (DSM), psychiatry's "bible," as sources of the diagnostic criteria for schizophrenia.

ERNST RÜDIN (1874-1952)

One of Kraepelin's most famous and accomplished students was Ernst Rüdin, the psychiatrist who outlined the racial purity theories that were employed by the Nazis to create their racial hygiene and eugenics policies. Rüdin was the director of the Kaiser Wilhelm Research Institute until the end of the Second World War, when he fled the approaching Allied armies.

At the time of Rüdin's discovery and house arrest in 1945, Victor H. Bernstein of the newspaper *P.M. Daily* described him as "a gentle-mannered old man of 74, with a shock of white hair, china-blue eyes and tender pink cheeks.... I am sure that Prof. Rüdin never so much as killed a fly in his 74 years. I am also sure that he is one of the most evil men in Germany." [22]

Despite all the protestations he made of his innocence, Rüdin was clearly a major contributor to the insanity of the Holocaust. In June 1933, this "innocent scientist" received a letter from Hitler's Ministry of the Interior Wilhelm Frick, which said in part:

"I hereby tender you the assignment as my honorary representative at the Society for Race Hygiene and the German League for Hereditary Science and Racial Improvement.

"The theory of inheritance and race hygiene are of the utmost importance for the structure of the Reich and for improvement of the race of the German people, therefore, I would like you to carry through the reconstruction work in closest collaboration with my ministry."[23]

The honors he would later win from the Nazi government testify to the fact that Rüdin did more than the bare minimum required of a state's subject. There is incontrovertible evidence that he plunged into his murderous work eagerly. His devotion to the central themes of eugenics is evident from lecture notes compiled by Dr. Gretz Nikola, a former student of Rüdin's at Munich University Medical School:

"Many things act for selective elimination of the weak among humankind—infectious diseases and infant mortality, for instance. But this normal elimination is extensively disturbed by medical science which tends to perpetuate the inferiorities which nature, if left alone, would have eliminated."[24]

Rüdin's eugenical beliefs and the power he received from the Nazi government would prove deadly when combined with his racist attitudes. Here are two racial analyses Rüdin made, as recorded in Dr. Nikola's lecture notes:

"Nordics—tall, slim, narrow and long-headed. Blue-eyed, creative, brave, heroic spirit, self-restrained, cautious, self-respecting, honest.

"Jews—racial mixture, predominantly Near Eastern, oriental and negroid. Characterized by persuasiveness and importunacy; early maturity, quickness of understanding but not creative; thiebhaft (tendency to follow baser instinct with emphasis on sexual crimes); dishonest (tendency to swindle); tendency to agitate (Karl Marx, Kurt Eisner)."[25]

In 1943, he would write in the periodical *Rassen- und Gesellschafts Biologie* (*Racial and Social Biology*):

"It is the unfailing historical merit of Adolf Hitler and his true followers that they dared to take the first decisive step past the purely scientific discoveries to open the way for the ingenious racial hygienic work in and on the German people. It was important to him to…keep pure the German race, to fight the parasitic races of foreign blood such as the Jews and the gypsies, and to further increase the population according to quantity and quality and prevent the propagation of the hereditarily ill and inferior.…

"…the Nuremberger Law, the State Citizen Law and the Law of the Protection of the Blood made because of a build-up of Jewish influence, particularly prevented the further infiltration of Jewish blood into the German gene pool."[26]

Thirteen years earlier, Rüdin had been invited to speak at the First International Congress on Mental Hygiene, which was held in Washington, D.C. Representatives from 53 countries attended this convention, where the International Committee for Mental Hygiene (now called the World Federation for Mental Health, for obvious reasons) was formed. The purpose of this gathering was to bring together the world's leading psychiatrists to consolidate and advance the dissemination of preventive psychiatry throughout the world.

Other prominent attendees were Adolf Meyer, Franz Alexander, Edward Strecker, Evelyn Fox, Charles Davenport, Harry Laughlin and Eugen Kahn. Dr. William White of St. Elizabeth's Hospital in Washington—one of the leading psychiatric hospitals in the United States—served as the President of the Congress. The Secretary was Clifford Beers, the founder of the mental hygiene movement in the United States. The Honorary President of the Congress was none other than the President of the United States, Herbert Hoover.

Rüdin lectured on "The Significance of Eugenics and Genetics for Mental Hygiene," which dealt almost entirely with Nazi psychiatry's ideology regarding the elimination of unwanted hereditary traits either by voluntary sterilization or, if that didn't work, by compulsory means.

He went on to state that even if a person should be cured of his insanity by medical means, he would still be capable of passing on his hereditary defects through his genetic make-up:

"We know the abuses occasioned by the enormous number of the hereditarily diseased, inside and outside of insane asylums, by the feebleminded, the paupers, the neglected, those criminally inclined through heredity, the chronic drunkards, the psychopaths, whose disorder is caused by hereditary physical disease or defect. And mental hygiene is right to seek to combat these abuses in every possible way. However, these are not merely consequences of a hitherto deficient individual prevention, precautionary education and therapy, but to a large extent results of pathological heredity and so of a lack of eugenics."[27]

ADOLF MEYER (1866-1950):

Adolf Meyer was another student of Kraepelin's who attended the groundbreaking 1930 congress held in Washington and without a doubt, it is Meyer who did more to solidify Wundtian experimental psychology as the dominant school of thought in America than anyone, before or since. By pushing out all other philosophies and approaches to the fields of mental health and education, Meyer in effect cornered the market and established an impregnable beachhead for psychiatry in America which would continue its essentially unproven and unworkable practices right up to the present day.

Adolf Meyer—German-trained psychiatrist who came to the U.S. in 1892 and became known as the "Father of Modern American Psychiatry"

Adolf Meyer studied under Kraepelin in Munich, where he received his doctorate with a thesis on the reptilian forebrain. During this time he is said to have made many important contacts with prominent psychiatrists and neurologists from all over Europe.

In 1892, at the age of 26, Meyer—who would later eulogize Kraepelin's "staunch devotion to the cause [as] an ever impressive example to the many workers he stimulated,"[28] emigrated to America. Eventually he became a lecturer in psychiatry under G. Stanley Hall at the newly formed Clark University, which was rapidly becoming the most active educational center for psychiatry in America. Meyer brought with him the Wundtian principle that man is a stimulus-response animal. As he wrote in an 1897 article:

"Owing to the marvelous change of thought in this century we have learned that man is not so different from the rest of creation as was formerly thought. We are subject to the same laws of the universe with all other creatures....The infant goes on growing, and with the development of the brain gives evidence of what we call sentient or conscious life, a feature common to all higher animals at least....Thus we have three fields of observation in the higher animals—anatomy, physiology and psychology." [29]

Combined with his interest in the studies of Carl Jung (a student both of Wundt and Freud), which was less empirical, more psychoanalytical and emphasized certain investigations into mental processes using free association, dream interpretation and the like, Meyer created the field of "psychopathology," which examined the causes of the symptoms of diseases. Psychopathology created feverish interest among American psychiatric academicians.

In 1902, Meyer moved to New York City, where he worked for the New York state hospital service, transforming their Pathological Institute into a Psychiatric Institute. While in New York, Meyer established a training program for clinical psychiatrists at the Manhattan State Hospital on Ward's Island, where he taught what would become the accepted model for the study of case records of psychiatric patients.

After five years as a Professor of Psychiatry at Cornell University Medical College (1904-1909), Meyer accepted an appointment as Professor of Psychiatry at Johns Hopkins University in Baltimore, a move which would forever alter the landscape of the study of mental health in America.

His first year in Baltimore was eventful. In 1910, he and his former mentor G. Stanley Hall formed the American Psychopathological Association (APPA), which was designed to bring together the leading psychopathologists across the United States to form a powerful coalition. This group's members, all prominent and influential leaders in psychiatry, neurology and pathology, would soon become the nerve center for the advancement of the cause of psychiatry through research, government funding and legislation, military intelligence and mind control programs, social policy and community health programs. That overwhelming influence persists right up to the present day.

In 1913, Meyer's fondest wish came true when the university built a psychiatric clinic and appointed him director. Modeled after the great German universities of the time, this Johns Hopkins clinic would become Meyer's workshop for the rest of his active years as a psychiatrist and attract leading scholars in psychiatry and neurology from all over the world. A residency in this clinic became a highly sought-after prize for any English-speaking psychiatrist, many of whom used Meyer's clinic as the model for their own clinics elsewhere in this country and abroad.

Perhaps Meyer's most important innovation was the four-year course curriculum. It was an innovation, since all other medical schools required only one year (or sometimes two) of psychiatric study. His development of required courses in psychiatry and psychobiology in all four years is now the norm widely practiced by American medical schools.

THE ROCKEFELLER CONNECTION

In the late 1800s and early 1900s, certain events combined to advance and greatly secure psychiatry's future, both financially and as a social force. Psychiatry allied itself with the Rockefellers, then the wealthiest family in the world.

John D. Rockefeller, Sr.'s daughter Bessie was married to Dr. Charles Strong, with whom Rockefeller was said to have had a close personal friendship. Strong had studied psychology in Germany, returning to the United States to become a Professor of Psychology, first at Clark University in 1890 under G. Stanley Hall. From 1896 to 1913, he was on the staff of Columbia University`s Teachers College in New York City under James M. Cattell.

Meanwhile, in 1901, Rockefeller's third daughter, Edith, began ten years of psychoanalysis in Switzerland with Carl Jung, who would become co-editor of the Nazis' *Journal for Psychotherapy*. She returned to the United States "without visible improvement." [30]

During this time, John D. Rockefeller had begun endowing universities. Among his first beneficiaries—the recipient of a $500,000 gift in 1889—was the University of Chicago, which had originally been established by the leaders of the Baptist Church, of which Rockefeller was a staunch parishioner. Rockefeller began to fund medical schools in 1904, when much of

John D. Rockefeller Sr. and John D. Rockefeller Jr.—Psychiatrists convinced them to fund psychiatric curricula being placed in U.S. medical schools.

the Johns Hopkins Medical School was destroyed by fire. (Adolf Meyer, incidentally, began his tenure at Johns Hopkins in the same year.) Dr. William Welch was then the head of the university, and he was a personal friend of Rockefeller. He was also a pathologist who had trained at Leipzig University at the same time as Kraepelin. Rockefeller's largesse was instrumental in rebuilding the Johns Hopkins Medical School.

At the same time, John D. Rockefeller, Jr., anxious to make his own mark on the world and inspired by the examples of the Pasteur Institute in Paris and the Koch Institute in Berlin, set out to create a medical research center in New York City that would dwarf them in scope and ultimately in importance. Thus was born the Rockefeller Institute for Medical Research in 1902, which many years later would be renamed Rockefeller University.

Dr. Welch was initially approached to head the Rockefeller Institute, but he declined, preferring to remain at Johns Hopkins. However, he recommended a colleague of his, Simon Flexner, who had trained under Welch at Johns Hopkins and had become a Professor of Pathology there. Flexner had also studied in Germany, shuttling between various institutes of pathology in Leipzig, Heidelberg and Berlin. Rockefeller appointed Simon Flexner as the first Director of the Rockefeller Institute. However, it was Simon Flexner's brother who would more profoundly influence psychiatry in America.

ABRAHAM FLEXNER

As mentioned earlier, in the late 1800s and early 1900s, Germany had an educational system that was the envy of Europe and America. Medical training was no exception, since medical schools in Germany were typically associated with the prestigious universities. Premedical training could be conducted at the university, while practical experience could then be obtained in the affiliated medical schools. Affiliation with a well-endowed and prestigious university would not only give a medical school top-notch laboratory facilities for its students, but would attract the most eminent professors in the civilized world.

As a result, any American medical student with substantial aspirations endeavored to undertake his postgraduate work in Germany, and between 1870 and 1914, many of them did:

"Just as Edinburgh had replaced Leyden as the leading medical center of the eighteenth century and Paris had taken that position in the early nineteenth century, Germany became the medical capital of the world in the late nineteenth century."[31]

Americans returning to the United States understandably deplored the comparatively shoddy state of American medical education. American schools could not hope to compete with the well-equipped laboratories in Germany or with the erudition of their faculties.

At the turn of the century, German influence was clearly felt all over the American educational landscape. Johns Hopkins was based on the German example, and German-trained Americans returned to such universities as Harvard, Cornell and the University of Michigan to revolutionize the teaching orientation of their schools, following the example of their German mentors.

In 1908, a project was co-sponsored by the Rockefeller Foundation and the Carnegie Foundation which would forever change the face of American medical education. The Carnegie Foundation made a grant for a study of all medical schools in the United States and Canada, large and small, in order to create a uniform standard for teaching medicine.

Dr. Abraham Flexner, the brother of Dr. Simon Flexner, first director of the Rockefeller Institute, was appointed to conduct this study. Abraham Flexner suited the Carnegies and the Rockefellers very well; he had studied under Dr. Welch at Johns Hopkins as well as in Germany, mostly at

the University of Berlin. When he returned, he had decided that his calling was in the field of education, not medicine.

Abraham Flexner's job was to go on an eighteen-month tour, visiting
each of the 155 medical schools in North America. He would then prepare a report and recommend which of those schools should receive phil-
anthropic funding and which should not. The 1910 publication of his
findings, which became known as the "Flexner Report," recommended
sweeping reforms in medical education, and selected only those larger and
well-funded schools which adhered to the German model as deserving
continued funding.

Flexner proposed that of the 155 schools visited, all but 35 should be
closed down or consolidated with other schools. The schools which he recommended for closure taught what is now known as "alternative medicine"—osteopathy, homeopathy, physical medicine and chiropractic.
Flexner was especially harsh on chiropractic:

"They are unconscionable quacks, whose printed advertisements are tis-
sues of exaggeration, pretense and misrepresentation of the most unquali-
fied mercenary character. The public prosecutor and the grand jury are the
proper agencies for dealing with them."[32]

All of the medical schools that accepted women for training at the time
were shut down, as were six of the eight medical schools for African-
Americans. In defending his decision to keep two black medical schools
open, Flexner wrote:

"The medical care of the Negro race will never be wholly left to Negro
physicians. Nevertheless, if the Negro can be brought to feel a sharp
responsibility for the physical integrity of his people, the outlook for their
mental and moral improvement will be distinctly brightened. The practice
of the Negro doctor will be limited to his own race, which in turn will be
cared for better by good Negro physicians than by poor white ones."[33]

It was only because of that attitude that Howard University Medical
School in Washington, D.C. and Meharry Medical School in Nashville
were spared. The fact was, however, that a certain "medical elite" had cornered the market and managed to create their own monopoly. Wundtian
medicine was the only game in town, and its representatives and practitioners had no desire to share the health field with anyone else, particularly those who represented a different philosophy, no matter how workable

or beneficial it might be.

Flexner went even further in his reports, making the following revolutionary recommendations:

There should be uniform criteria for premedical training;

Medical schools had to conform to certain standards of education and curriculum;

Professors had to be full-time instructors in their specialty (not private practitioners who taught part-time at the medical school, as was the case earlier;

All medical schools had to be fully equipped with laboratories for chemistry and pathology;

All graduates had to pass examinations from the state licensing board in order to practice medicine;

All medical schools had to be accredited in order to accept students and receive funding.

The Flexner Report delighted the sponsoring foundations. The medical schools, however, found that without the Flexner Report's seal of approval, they had no chance of being funded by the two foundations and the many financial sources that they influenced. Further, the Rockefeller and Carnegie Foundations possessed considerable political influence, and they quickly got tough state and federal licensing requirements passed that would "accredit" only those schools that were either approved by the Flexner Report or conformed to its standards. The others were left to die out, unrecognized by the scientific and government communities, and unfunded by the major philanthropists. Any student who graduated from an "alternative school" could not be accepted for an internship anywhere, nor would he be able to acquire a state license to practice medicine. Understandably, students abandoned these schools in droves.

A monopoly thus was formed based on the German medical school model, Wundtian theory and German eugenical drug therapy theory to the exclusion of other therapeutic theories. In the *Journal of the American Medical Association* on September 16, 1911, Dr. W. A. Evans, the Commissioner of Health of Chicago, wrote:

"As I see it, the wise thing for the medical profession to do is to get right into and man every great health movement. Man health departments, tuberculosis societies, child and infant welfare societies, housing societies, etc. The future of the profession depends on keeping matters, so that when the public mind thinks of these things, it automatically thinks of physicians and not of sociologists or sanitary engineers. The profession cannot afford to have these places occupied by other than medical men."[34]

And what was the model medical school identified by Abraham Flexner's report? Not surprisingly, it was his alma mater, Johns Hopkins, a stronghold of German influence, under the leadership of fellow Wundtians Welch and Meyer.

The subsequent reforms resulted in the installation of a four-year psychiatric program in every accredited medical school in the United States, just as in Johns Hopkins. The Rockefeller Board was so pleased with Flexner that they gave him a position on their General Education Board, one of the philanthropies they had established for the express purpose of funding educational programs of their liking.

Primary medical schools funded by Rockefeller's General Education Board on the recommendation of the Flexner Report included Johns Hopkins Medical Center, the University of Chicago Medical Center, Yale University Medical Center, Washington University in St. Louis, Cornell University, Columbia University's College of Physicians and Surgeons, Harvard Medical School and the University of Iowa. Each of these universities would play a major part in the training and advancement of psychiatry in the United States, and would also serve as havens for certain Nazi psychiatrists who would flee Germany before, during and after World War II.

EARLY AMERICAN EUGENICISTS

The early psychiatric influence on the American educational system was, tinted with a pivotal social philosophy that later inspired the men behind Hitler to commit the atrocities of Nazi Germany.

That social philosophy was, eugenics.

As we have seen, it was Thomas Malthus, the first professor of political economy in Great Britain who attracted a following with his theory of overpopulation. In the sixth edition of his famous "Essay on the Principle of Population," he spelled out his philosophy very clearly:

"We are bound in justice and honor formally to disclaim the right of the poor to support. To this end, I should propose a regulation to be made, declaring that no child born from any marriage, taking place after the expiration of a year from the date of the law, and no illegitimate child born two years from the same date, should ever be entitled to parish assistance.... The infant is, comparatively speaking, of little value to society, as others will immediately supply its place."[35]

The idea of government aid to the poor and helpless plainly was abhorrent to Malthus. His attitude toward "inferiors" ominously foreshadowed what would actually occur over a century later in Nazi Germany:

"...we should facilitate, instead of foolishly and vainly endeavoring to impede the operations of nature in producing this mortality; and if we dread the too frequent visitation of the horrid form of famine, we should sedulously encourage the other forms of destruction, which we compel nature to use. Instead of recommending cleanliness to the poor, we should encourage contrary habits. In our towns we should make the streets narrower, crowd more people into the houses, and court the return of the plague. In the country, we should build our villages near stagnant pools, and particularly encourage settlements in all marshy and unwholesome situations. But above all, we should reprobate specific remedies for ravaging diseases; and those benevolent, but much mistaken men, who have thought they were doing a service to mankind by projecting schemes for the total extirpation of particular disorders."[36]

Malthus' views were very much in keeping with those of the ruling aristocracy after the Industrial Revolution in England in 1789. In his 1798 "Essay on the Principle of Population," he advanced the idea that poverty was the "necessary stimulus to industry" and that any social legislation to improve the lot of the worker would hinder his desire to work. This included welfare and medical assistance, vaccinations against disease, public schooling, sanitary and housing standards and any hope of upward mobility out of their miserable conditions.

We jump ahead to Charles Darwin and his theory of natural selection, whose central theme was paraphrased and corrupted by the English philosopher Herbert Spencer as "survival of the fittest." As we have also seen earlier, Social Darwinism, or the application of the idea of natural selection to human society, was its somewhat illogical next step, which nonetheless was not disclaimed by Darwin himself.

Darwin's cousin, Sir Francis Galton, coined the term "eugenics," and gave lectures all over Europe and North America, in which, according to Karl Pearson, Galton's protégé and apologist, "eugenics [was treated] not only as a science, not only as an art, but also as a national creed, amounting, indeed, to a religious faith."[37]

Galton's zeal inspired converts in America, who would spread his message—and find some influential ears.

CHARLES B. DAVENPORT (1866-1944)

One of the eugenics converts was Charles Benedict Davenport who went to England in 1897 and met with Galton and Pearson. He returned to America as a Professor of Biology at the University of Chicago from 1901 to 1904, eventually becoming an internationally known expert on plant, animal and human heredity.

In 1906, Davenport organized the first eugenics movement in the United States by forming a committee of the American Breeder's Association (ABA) to "investigate and report on heredity in the human race and to emphasize the value of superior blood and the menace to society of inferior blood."[38] The ABA had originally been formed in 1903 by breeding experts in government and agricultural sectors to investigate and develop Mendel's discoveries in the field of hybrid breeding techniques. In only three years, it became the host committee for eugenics research.

Davenport was summarily elected as Secretary of the ABA's Eugenics Section. Though he was not its Chairman, he was the one who actually ran it from the start. Its Chairman, David Starr-Jordan, then the president of Stanford University, depended on what he saw as Davenport's unparalleled knowledge of genetics and relied completely on his expertise for three decades.

Under Davenport's direction, the ABA Eugenics Section established ten research subcommittees, dealing with the Heredity of Feeble-mindedness; the Heredity of Insanity; the Heredity of Epilepsy; the Heredity of Criminality; the Heredity of Deafmutism; the Heredity of Eye Defects; Sterilization and Other Means of Eliminating Defective Germ-plasm; Genealogy; the Inheritance of Mental Traits; and, of course, Immigration."[39]

To many in the American scientific community, eugenics was a new and exciting idea, an innovative method for improving mankind by eliminating the hereditary diseases that affect everyone. To Davenport, any given human trait was produced by a corresponding gene. There could, therefore, be genes that gave a person intelligence, grace, beauty, poise, the ability to make money or to be moral. On the other hand, there were also genes that caused criminality, promiscuity, greed, laziness, feeble-mindedness and a predisposition to diseases like tuberculosis, measles, malaria, pneumonia, and other infectious or parasitic diseases normally associated with poverty or squalor.

The task was easy. Using Mendelian logic previously applied to create hybrids in plants, Davenport and his American eugenics movement decided to effect the selective mating of people born with "good" genes. To Davenport, "good" meant the "Nordic" or "dolichocephalic" (long-headed) race. Conversely, he determined that it would also be necessary to prevent the further progeny of "beaten men from beaten races." [40]

As we saw in the Nazi era, these ideas were irresistible to those who controlled government purse-strings. Not only would they alleviate government of any responsibility for the condition of some of its poorer constituents (by blaming nature for their situation in life), but it would lift its obligation to spend precious tax dollars on social programs like health, education and welfare, since the poor were genetically doomed by their inferior genes to be sickly, uneducable and immoral anyway.

Immediately upon the opening of the Carnegie Institution in Washington in 1902, Davenport lobbied hard for a biological laboratory, to be established in Cold Spring Harbor, New York. His persistence paid off in 1904 when he became the Director of the Carnegie Institution's Station for Experimental Evolution. This led to his founding, in 1910, of the Eugenics Record Office (ERO) after the successful solicitation of seed money from Mrs. E. H. Harriman, the widow of a railroad tycoon. Over the next eight years, Mrs. Harriman would donate over half a million dollars to the facilities and the operation of Davenport's project, until the ERO became part of the Carnegie Institution's Department of Genetics in 1918. It would be closed down in 1940, but its eugenics records would be transferred to the University of Minnesota's Dight Institute, an organization which we will cover in greater depth in a later chapter.

Davenport's Eugenics Record Office, modeled after Galton's Eugenics Record Office in London, was Davenport's dream come true. In a letter to

Galton on October 26, 1910, Davenport wrote:

"...we have a plot of ground of 80 acres near New York City, and a house with a fireproof addition for our records. We have a Superintendent (H.H. Laughlin), a stenographer and two helpers, besides six trained field workers. These are all associated with the Station for Experimental Evolution, which supplies experimental evidence of the methods of heredity. We have a satisfactory income...and have established very cordial relations with institutions for imbeciles, epileptics, insane and criminals."

Later in the letter he adds:

"...as the years go by, humanity will more and more appreciate its debt to you. In this country we have run 'charity' mad. Now a revulsion of feeling is coming about, and people are turning to your teaching."[41]

The Eugenics Record Office was certainly a very busy place. It held classes for its field workers, published reports on its various research projects and studies and engaged in the successful lobbying of influential government officials. It sponsored lectures and symposia on eugenics and selective mating, and its monthly newsletter *Eugenical News* was widely read.

Davenport also imitated Galton's reliance on genealogy and physiognomy questionnaires, which were mailed out to prominent members of society—bankers, stockbrokers, newspaper editors, political leaders and academicians—along with a letter explaining that the ERO needed the information to encourage the breeding of more people like them. Delighted, the respondents quickly returned the questionnaires, not infrequently with a contribution, sometimes hefty, to the cause of eugenics.

Davenport relied on field workers to collect information on "good" and "bad" genes in America. Modeled (again) after the scientific investigators employed by Galton and Pearson in England, Davenport's researchers were mainly young women from wealthy families, a few of whom were college graduates and almost none of whom had a postgraduate degree. Trained by psychologist Henry H. Goddard at the Vineland Training School for Feeble-minded Girls and Boys in New Jersey, the field workers were expected to be able to spot certain hereditary mental conditions— such as "criminalism," "shiftlessness" and "feeble-mindedness" at a glance —and interview friends and relatives, priests, doctors and even local gossips regarding their subjects, the end result being a supposedly "scientific" document on their genetic disposition.

It is frightening to realize that Davenport and Goddard were not the only ones who used this data for their studies. Other leading eugenicists relied on it as well. The college textbooks of the time were also largely based on these records.

H. H. LAUGHLIN (1880-1943)

One of Davenport's strongest supporters was Harry Hamilton Laughlin, the superintendent of the ERO. From 1910 to 1940, Laughlin helped Davenport formulate and promote the two main objectives of the American eugenics movement:

a) an immigration policy restricting the number of non-Nordic people entering the country; and

b) the enactment of laws enforcing compulsory sterilization of the "socially inadequate."

The idea of compulsory sterilization had been kicking around the United States since 1897, when a bill proposing it was rejected in Michigan. Two years later, Dr. Harry Sharp, a physician at the Indiana State Reformatory, impressed by Galton's "scientific discoveries," proposed vasectomies of all inmates he deemed genetically defective.

In 1905, "an act for the prevention of idiocy" was passed by the Pennsylvania legislature, declaring:

"Whereas heredity plays a most important part in the transmission of idiocy and imbecility…[it must] be compulsory for each and every institution in the state, entrusted exclusively or especially with the care of idiots and imbecile children…to examine the mental and physical condition of the inmates…[if the] procreation of the inmate is inadvisable, and there is no probability of improvement in the mental and physical condition of the inmate, it shall be lawful for the surgeon to perform such operation for the prevention of procreation as shall be decided safest and most effective."[42]

The bill was vetoed by the Governor.

In 1907, a measure called "an act to prevent procreation of confirmed criminals, idiots, imbeciles and rapists" was passed in Indiana, which imposed compulsory sterilization on those inmates of the state institutions who matched that description. Echoing the refrains of Galton, Pearson and Davenport (as well as countless college professors in universities across the nation who taught eugenics as a scientific discipline), the Indiana legislation stated that "heredity plays a most important part in the transmission of crime, idiocy and imbecility."[43]

In 1909, three other states—Washington, California and Connecticut —followed suit, passing nearly identical compulsory sterilization laws.

The Eugenics Record Office was a historical phenomenon that galvanized the eugenics movement, forming a juggernaut that was difficult to resist. Laughlin was at the head of this movement, inveighing against what he called the "socially inadequate." To assist sympathizers in getting legislation passed in various states, Laughlin drafted a Model Eugenical Sterilization Law, and distributed it to politicians, educators, clergymen and members of the press far and wide. It was to be designed for:

"All persons in the State who, because of degenerate or defective hereditary qualities are potential parents of socially inadequate offspring, regardless of whether such persons be in the population at large or inmates of custodial institutions...."[44]

In other words, Laughlin wanted to sterilize everyone with these qualities. His law was intended as an:

"Act to prevent the procreation of persons socially inadequate from defective inheritance, by authorizing and providing for eugenical sterilization of certain potential parents carrying degenerate hereditary qualities."[45]

Laughlin gives us a frightening vision of his totalitarian world view by defining "socially inadequate" in section 2 of his "model law" as "one who...fails chronically...to maintain himself or herself as a useful member of the organized social life of the state...."[46]

But Laughlin went even further, categorizing the "socially inadequate" into ten classes:

"(1) Feeble-minded; (2) Insane (including the psychopathic); (3) Criminalistic (including the delinquent and wayward); (4) Epileptic; (5) Inebriate (including drug habitues); (6) Diseased (including the tuberculous, the syphilitic, the leprous, and others with chronic, infectious and legally segregable diseases); (8) Deaf (including those with seriously impaired hearing); (9) Deformed (including the crippled); (10) Dependent (including orphans, ne'er-do-wells, the homeless, tramps and paupers)."[47]

There was some resistance. The Supreme Court of New Jersey struck down then Governor Woodrow Wilson's brutal sterilization bill as unconstitutional. In other states such as Vermont, Nebraska and Idaho, governors vetoed versions of the model act as violations of the provision in the Bill of Rights forbidding cruel and unusual punishment.

Nevertheless, due to Laughlin's persistence, 18 states had passed compulsory sterilization measures by 1912, and by 1940, no less than *30* states (and Puerto Rico) had such laws on their books. By that time, over 100,000 sterilizations had been forcibly performed on American citizens by their own government.

Only a decade after Laughlin's 1914 model law was written, its influence would be felt across the sea when a young Austrian convert to eugenics named Adolf Hitler was moved to write:

"The folkish state has to make up for what is today neglected in this field in all directions. It has to put race into the center of life in general. It has to care for its preservation in purity. In this matter the State must assert itself as the trustee of a millennial future, in the face of which the egoistic desires of the individual give way before the ruling of the State. In order to fulfill this duty in a practical manner, the State will have to avail itself of modern medical discoveries. It must proclaim as unfit for procreation all those who are afflicted with some visible hereditary disease or are carriers of it; and practical measures must be adopted to have such people rendered sterile." [48]

Less than a decade later, the Third Reich enacted a Sterilization Act. Part of this legislation—the Act for Prevention of the Genetically Sick Next Generation—was taken almost verbatim from Laughlin's Model Eugenical Sterilization Law. Those that the Nazis deemed "life unworthy of living" followed almost the exact same guidelines. By the end of the war and the fall of the Third Reich, over two million Germans had been compulsorily sterilized, an average of about 450 people a day.

Laughlin's other mission was to prevent the immigration of those he thought would dilute the American gene pool. Working with the Immigration and Naturalization Service, he achieved passage of certain restrictions against Italians, Jews, Poles, Slavs and other non-Nordic and non-Aryan refugees.

An "IQ" test, coined and developed by psychologist Alfred Binet, was tested by Goddard in Vineland and taken to Ellis Island in New York Harbor, then the largest immigration port in the country. According to its results, these tests "proved" the inferiority of certain races:

"In no time at all, the Goddard versions of the Binet tests were convincing thousands of educated Americans that 83 percent of all Jews were feeble-minded, a 'hereditary' defect the Jews shared with 80 percent of all Hungarians, 79 percent of all Italians, and 87 percent of all Russians."[49]

That these immigrants did not speak English and the tests were delivered through interpreters apparently did not figure into Goddard's calculations. Nor did the preordained prejudices of those responsible for the tests.

Ironically, Laughlin's and Davenport's life works were delivered a crushing blow when the United States declared war on Germany in 1941. Immigration doors were flung open to welcome political refugees from all corners of war-torn Europe, undoing the American eugenicists' careful plans for a master race in the United States.

"Since man began, he has tried to influence other men and women to his way of thinking. There have always been these forms of pressure to change attitudes. We discovered in the past thirty years, a technique to influence, by clinical, hospital procedures, the thinking processes of human beings...Brainwashing is formed out of a set of different elements...hunger, fatigue, tenseness, threats, violence...drugs and hypnotism."

Edward Hunter
CIA propaganda specialist

NAZI PSYCHIATRISTS ENLIST IN THE AMERICAN MILITARY

WHO LET IT HAPPEN AND WHO MADE IT HAPPEN

The opening of the Rockefeller Institute for Medical Research in New York in 1904 was surrounded by high hopes. Its sponsors intended it to equal or exceed the top research institutes and laboratories in Europe, and thus attract top scientists from all over the world.

One such scientist was the French-born Alexis Carrel, who joined the Institute in 1906 and remained there as a researcher until 1939. Although his innovative developments in organ transplantation and the art of suturing arteries and veins made him famous as a surgeon and won him the 1912 Nobel prize for medicine, Dr. Carrel was an enthusiastic eugenicist and staunch admirer of the Nazi eugenics programs of the 1930s. In his 1935 book, *Man, the Unknown,* he outlined the basic philosophy behind his research:

"The studies to be undertaken in the laboratories for medical research should include all the subjects pertaining to the physical, chemical, structural, functional, and psychological activities of man, and to the relations of those activities with the cosmic and social environment....Such an organization would be the salvation of the white races in their staggering advancement toward civilization."[1]

To Carrel, eugenics played a great part in the solution:

"Eugenics is indispensable for the perpetuation of the strong. A great race must propagate its best elements....It is the newcomers, peasants and proletarians from primitive European countries, who beget large families. But their offspring are far from having the value of those who come from the first settlers in North America."[2]

Later on in the book, Carrel professes his agreement with the Nazi psychiatrists that the insane and feeble-minded should be prevented from procreating. Criminals, he thought, "should be humanely and economically disposed of in small euthanasic institutions supplied with proper gases. A similar treatment could be advantageously applied to the insane, guilty of criminal acts."[3]

This proposal, written by one of Rockefeller's own doctors in the United States, preceded the Nazis' actual use of poison gases by a handful of years.

Another influential psychiatrist who came to the United States from Germany was Franz J. Kallmann. Dr. Kallmann had a particularly strong research interest in schizophrenia, which had led him first to the Berlin Psychoanalytic Institute to study under Franz Alexander and Sandor Rado. It was there, before the Nazi-sponsored International Congress for Population Science, that Kallmann strenuously argued for the sterilization not only of schizophrenics, but of their apparently healthy relatives as well, since he believed that schizophrenia was a genetically recessive disease.

From there, Kallmann went to the Kaiser Wilhelm Research Institute for Psychiatry in Munich under the directorship of Ernst Rüdin, who also was an ardent proponent of eugenical sterilization of schizophrenics and their otherwise healthy relatives.

Expelled from Germany in 1936 because he was half Jewish, Dr. Kallmann emigrated to the United States to work for the Rockefeller-funded New York State Psychiatric Institute. There he was able to continue his research into the heredity of schizophrenia using twins, a practice that was continued on in Germany in his absence by such luminaries as Rüdin, Hallervorden and Mengele.

His research was typified by mountains of statistical data. After studying a thousand pairs of twins, Kallmann reached the conclusion that if one twin were schizophrenic, there was an 86.2 percent chance that the other would also be. He also calculated that if two schizophrenic parents had a child, there was a 68.1 percent chance that the child, too, would be schizophrenic.

"In 1938, he [Kallmann] reached the conclusion that schizophrenics were a source of maladjusted crooks, asocial eccentrics, and the lowest type of criminal offenders. Even the faithful believer in...liberty would be much happier without those....I am reluctant to admit the necessity of different eugenic programs for democratic and fascistic communities ...there are neither biological nor sociological differences between a democratic and a totalitarian schizophrenic.'"[4]

Kallmann's obsession with the sterilization of anyone even remotely associated with a schizophrenic is readily apparent in his 1938 study. Harping on what he perceived as the recessivity of the disease, Kallmann also demanded the sterilization of the schizophrenic's children and siblings, his marriage partner and even stepchildren.

For his groundbreaking work in this field, Kallmann became the most influential psychiatric geneticist in the world. Ultimately, he would be the president of the American Society for Human Genetics.

Kallmann's 1938 study, "The Genetics of Schizophrenia," was simultaneously published in Germany and the United States. It received an enthusiastic following throughout the psychiatric community—both in America and in the Third Reich—which used the study as a scientific justification for the sterilization—and even euthanasia—of mental patients.

Kallmann's work as the principal genetic research scientist at the New York State Psychiatric Institute resulted in the popularizing of schizophrenia as the cash cow for psychiatry. In the coming years, hundreds of millions of dollars in research grants would be given to study the disorder and to finance experiments with drugs and other treatments designed to control the patients' symptoms. Controlling the symptoms was all their studies had indicated they could do. They had already been spuriously claiming that schizophrenia was an inherited disease and therefore temporary solutions would have to do until a genetic source could be located. For practically a full century, the research has been grinding on, without an answer in sight.

That no clear-cut definition for schizophrenia has ever been formulated hardly seems to bother the psychiatric community. Instead, schizophrenia has developed into something of a miscellaneous category to which any mystery ailment might be assigned.

A perfect example of this was revealed in a famous 1973 California study by David Rosenhan, where perfectly normal volunteers were sent into mental hospitals complaining of hearing voices. Many of them were immediately hospitalized. In the next step of the experiment, the pseudo-patients were to tell their doctors that the symptoms had gone away, and that they wanted to go home. These requests were ignored, as the prevailing attitude was that psychiatric patients had no right to comment upon their own state of mind. It was only after a considerable amount of time and effort that the pseudo-patients were allowed to leave. In one case, a volunteer in one of the hospitals who was writing notes was diagnosed by one of the nurses as having "compulsive writing behavior."

Kallmann was not the only German psychiatrist who would design the landscape of the modern American mental health movement in the 1920s and 1930s. Other emigres included:

Lothar B. Kalinowsky, a pioneer of electroconvulsive therapy

Franz Alexander, a leading German psychiatrist

Erich Lindemann, a military psychiatrist who experimented with truth drugs

Heinz Lehmann, a strong proponent of drug therapy

Sandor Rado, professor of psychiatry at the Berlin Psychoanalytic Institute

Zigmund Lebensohn, who would train military psychiatrists at St. Elizabeth's Hospital in Washington, D.C. under Winfred Overholser

Paul Hoch, who worked with Kallmann and Kalinowsky at the New York State Psychiatric Institute and later in CIA mind control programs

Leo Alexander, an American military psychiatrist who investigated Nazi psychiatric war crimes at Nuremberg.

LOTHAR B. KALINOWSKY

Born and educated in Berlin, Kalinowsky—who like Kallmann, was half-Jewish and was forced to flee Germany for Italy in 1933—joined the staff of Ugo Cerletti, the shock treatment pioneer. At the time, Cerletti was searching for a suitable replacement for Metrazol, a synthetic camphor-like drug which had the unfortunate drawback of having a one-minute lag between the injection and the actual convulsion, during which patients would undergo extreme and excruciating pain. He found his cure, as we have mentioned earlier, in electric shock, during a visit to a Roman slaughterhouse.

Kalinowsky was present at Cerletti's first test of electroshock on a human being, and he was obviously impressed, for soon he would become one of the most ardent and vigorous proponents of ECT in the world.

After the 1938 Axis pact between Germany and Italy, which required the return of Jewish Nationals to Germany, Kalinowsky left Italy, traveling through Allied Europe with his diagrams for the ECT machine. He is quoted as saying:

"I stopped in Paris and introduced the technique during a short stay and then the same in Holland and then in England. Then in 1940 I came to the Psychiatric Institute at Columbia and for several years I treated three days a week at the Medical Center [at Columbia] and three days a week at Pilgrim State Hospital [Long Island]."[5]

In addition to the work provided for him at Columbia and Pilgrim State Hospital, immediately upon his arrival in the United States in 1940, Kalinowsky was also offered a position of attending physician at the New York State Psychiatric Institute, which was by that time serving a significant function as a haven for escaping Wundtian psychiatrists.

For the next half century, Kalinowsky would enthusiastically promote his ECT machine. By 1941, 74 percent of private psychiatric hospitals and 94 percent of state asylums were using ECT, Metrazol or insulin shock treatments on a total of 68,888 patients. By 1969, the numbers had increased to 89 percent of private and 91 percent of public and university institutions active in ECT.

Electroconvulsive therapy is now used not only for the treatment of schizophrenia (its original use) but also for anxiety, hysteria, obsessive behavior, anorexia, and "general neuroses" such as sexual compulsions and stuttering. It is even currently being used for drug addiction, asthma, "phantom limb" pain, alcoholism and backaches.

THE TAVISTOCK CLINIC AND THE CREATION OF A "PSYCHIATRIC SOCIETY"

The Tavistock Clinic was created in 1920 as one of the first public hospitals in England to provide psychoanalytical care for out-patients who could not afford private care. By the mid-thirties it was receiving endowments from the Rockefeller Foundation's Medical Sciences Division.

Dr. J.R. Rees, who would become the driving force behind the activities of the Clinic in the years preceding, during and after the Second World War, was especially interested in putting it at the vanguard of military psychiatric research. In 1929, while still the Clinic's deputy director, he organized a conference in London for mental health professionals from all over Europe, the United States and Canada. This meeting was the first conference ever on mental health and was sponsored by a special committee called "The Joint Committee of the National Council for Mental Hygiene and the Tavistock Clinic."

The main strategy outlined by the Tavistock psychiatrists involved expanding their activities beyond the asylums as caretakers of the insane and into the public generally by establishing preventive and social work programs, much of it directed toward children. They knew that up until then their reputation and standing in the recognized scientific community—and in society at large—had been minimal. It was essential to move into these wider spheres of activity and open up new avenues to gain influence and attract funding.

"Prevention" was the theme of the conference. The first speaker read a letter from the British Minister of Health which said, "The creation of a well-informed public opinion is one of the essential conditions of progress in this field. For the keynote of such progress must surely be Prevention."[6]

Having no known cure for mental illness, and no treatment other than confinement and barbarous techniques, the psychiatrists had discovered that "prevention" was a brilliant new tool. Not only might this be an area they could do something about, but it could also serve as an alibi for their past failures to produce tangible results. Laying the blame for psychiatric illness on such scapegoats as heredity, strict upbringings, repression of sexual curiosity, religion, education, the penal system and the like (the list goes on virtually without end), psychiatry attempted to effect prevention by social change—with themselves as the exclusive and self-anointed "experts." With this strategy, psychiatry tried to move into the political arena, quite a jump for a pseudoscience whose only known accomplishments involved the destruction of human brain cells and whose advocacy promoted racial hygiene, compulsory sterilization, and euthenasia.

The 1929 conference articulated the plans for preventive measures. It would stress the importance of children's programs where teachers would be trained to look out for early signs of mental disturbance and recommend highly-trained experts to handle the child's illness.

Sex education would be promoted as part of an overall education:

"The practical problem we have to meet to-day is to translate the small amount of scientific knowledge we do possess affecting the normal development of the sex life of the individual into popular teaching...." [7]

Juvenile courts were seen as too harsh in their punishment. Instead, speakers at the conference recommended that it should be up to the "experts" to diagnose juvenile delinquency. From then on, the courts would be the place to spot signs of future criminality in children, who would then be remanded to psychiatrists for appropriate "treatment."

Echoing the words of John Dewey in America, another speaker saw children as suffering "...unnecessary torture, forcing themselves to endure what should be re-adjusted to.... Resignation is an over-rated virtue necessitating the constant exercise of will-power, and no one should continually have to exercise self control and will.... How can a child be trained to adaptability?... indeed, it *comprises all education*, but the training is very early begun...." [8]

In time, the Tavistock Clinic would staff the growing number of British "child guidance clinics" with graduates from its Children's Department and thus strongly influence the field of psychiatric social work throughout England. With this conference, its psychiatrists had defined their vision for the role that they would play in society.

Religion was one of their targets. One member of the conference was Canon T.W. Pym of the Church of England, who noted the multitude of developments in psychiatry during the previous ten years and astonishingly abdicated the role of religion in spiritual and social matters:

"I, for one, welcome the changes and look for more....The minister of Christ, in trying to help individual people in the moral and spiritual realm, is frequently groping in that shadowland where the apparently moral or spiritual difficulty is largely mental. He is competing with the results of uninformed teaching on sex, with the wrong home upbringing...with wrong education. The Church of England—for which alone I can speak with any knowledge—is slowly waking up on this matter. But its ministers are too often lacking...and too often share the opinion of the general public that psychology, as the study of mental states and processes, is concerned only with people who are already sick...a side-line suitable for cranks alone."[9]

ALLIANCES ARE MADE AND PSYCHIATRY GAINS MOMENTUM

Two other conferences occurred at about this time which must be noted, for they resulted in the formation and cultivation of key relationships between influential leaders within the psychiatric community with various important government leaders.

The first we have already touched on earlier: the First International Congress on Mental Hygiene, which convened in Washington, D.C. in May 1930 and was attended by delegates from 53 countries.

Among the speakers were:

Dr. Adolf Meyer, on "The Organization of Community Facilities for Prevention, Care and Treatment of Nervous and Mental Disease";

Dr. Ernst Rüdin, on "The Significance of Eugenics and Genetics for Mental Hygiene";

Dr. Franz Alexander, a German psychiatrist who emigrated to the United States that same year, on "Mental Hygiene and Criminology";

Dr. Edward Strecker, a military intelligence psychiatrist who worked extensively in the field of mind control, on "Psychiatric Education";

Evelyn Fox, a prominent mental hygiene advocate in the United Kingdom, on "Community Schemes for the Social Control of Mental Defectives."[10]

Government officials who comprised some of the vice presidents of the mental hygiene congress included the Chief of the United States Children's Bureau, the Surgeon General of the United States, and the Secretary of the Interior.

The second of these conferences, the Second Biennial Conference on Mental Health, convened in London in May of 1931. It was sponsored by the National Council on Mental Health, whose objectives, as stated in the inaugural address by the British Minister of Health, were "to promote and enlighten public opinion on this great question of health and mental hygiene.... This work of educating and guiding public opinion, of touching the springs of action and administration, is a blessed work."[11]

The topic of discussion was "The Human Factor" in such areas as crime, industry, social services, education, and most importantly, "International Problems." The main speaker on this was the English psychiatrist John R. Lord, a member of the Executive Council of the International Committee for Mental Hygiene who had also spoken at the Washington congress in 1930. At this conference, his vision was even more grandiose:

"In the mental hygiene movement will be found the remedy of war...I have put forward two slogans as useful in the mental hygiene peace programme: To learn to think international and the necessity to disarm the mind." [12]

Lord went on to make practical recommendations for the psychiatrists attending the conference, which would set the stage for psychiatric infiltration of the military, government, business, academia—in fact, practically all aspects of human endeavor. These recommendations included:

"1. Mental hygiene must direct its efforts in all nations to deal effectively with the emotionally unbalanced or criminally disposed section of the public.... Many of these are mental defectives, morons [sic] and the like, who should be under constant institutional care.... Improved methods of school teaching, child guidance and parental education, the encouragement of trained workers in every field of social and economic activity, are all measures of sound prophylaxis, and would rid future generations of many such dangerous elements.

"2. It is imperative, too, that instruction in mental hygiene should be compulsory in all colleges and universities, from which the ruling classes are largely drawn.

...

"...7. Nations must see to it , and provide machinery for the removal of all monarchs, rulers and governors who are mentally and morally unfit for their high duties and great responsibilities. Princes in the line of succession in monarchical countries should have psychiatrists and psychologists among their medical advisors....

"8. Equally important in democratic countries is the mental health of high officers of state, and especially those occupying executive positions; nor can such education be neglected by lesser legislators and administrators." [13]

Lord concluded his speech by saying, "The survival of the fittest will be a survival, not of the strongest in the merely physical struggle to live, indifferent to all moral considerations, but of the fittest in a natural evolution for social advancement and righteousness on earth." [14]

The plans outlined in these two key conferences had an enormous impact on the shaping of psychiatry's strategy for insinuating itself into all facets of society—by first targeting those in power in the government and the military.

This was not lost on Rees who, upon rising to the directorship of the Tavistock Clinic in 1934, would exert tremendous influence over the military in the United Kingdom. This influence was noted in the Tavistock's jubilee volume celebrating its 50th anniversary:

"Although it would be presumptuous to claim that the major contributions of the Army psychiatric service during the Second World War were all Tavistock achievements, it remains true that the groundwork for most of them originated in the thinking and planning of J.R. Rees and his two earliest principal aides, Ronald Hargreaves and A.T.M. Wilson." [15]

Just as Rees supervised the psychiatric inroads into the British military, in Canada the planning was implemented by G. Brock Chisholm, the head of psychiatry for the Royal Canadian Armed Forces and later the co-founder of the World Federation for Mental Health. In the United States, the responsibility for the program was assumed by Winfred Overholser, a leading military intelligence psychiatrist and the superintendent of St. Elizabeth's Hospital, the federal insane asylum in Washington, D.C.

Due perhaps to their prominent role in the early international psychiatric conferences, Rees and the Tavistock Clinic enjoyed strong connections to powerful psychiatric opinion leaders around the world. Besides being a highly influential member of Britain's National Council for Mental Hygiene, Rees also sat on the International Committee for Mental Hygiene, the British Medical Association, and the World Health Organization. He was also an honorary member of the American Psychiatric Association and the Psychiatric Associations of Denmark, India, Austria, Germany, Peru and Mexico as well as being a co-founder and first president of the World Federation for Mental Health.

Rees strongly believed that only psychiatry was qualified to lead a nation. In a lecture he gave in 1940 at the Annual Meeting of the National Council for Mental Hygiene, he challenged his colleagues to do more to accomplish this dream:

"Especially since the last world war we have done much to infiltrate the various social organizations throughout the country, and in their work and in their point of view one can see clearly how the principles for which this society and others stood in the past have become accepted as part of the ordinary working plan of these various bodies. That is as it should be, and while we can take heart from this we must be healthily discontented and realize that there is still more work to be done along this line." [16]

PSYCHIATRY GETS INTO THE AMERICAN MILITARY

In the first part of this book, we saw how the German military leadership had a great deal of trouble handling the war-related neuroses of its soldiers in World War I. This was also true of the United States. In 1917, the 693 licensed psychiatrists in America were confronted with a condition known colloquially as shell shock, for which they knew they had no answer. They also were avalanched with telexes from the front demanding a better selection of recruits who would not fall victim to this dreaded mental disturbance.

As a young American psychiatrist, Winfred Overholser did a tour of six months in France. In the diary he kept at the time he wrote:

"We are trying to treat psychoneurotics according to the Order of the Day. We have managed to set up a primitive sort of psychotherapy. We are using suggestion and hypnosis when it is possible. Time is on our side and some of the patients get well in spite of us." [17]

During World War I, the federal asylum at St. Elizabeth's Hospital increasingly became the destination for soldiers with serious psychological disturbances. These soldiers were considered wards of the United States Public Health Service, and thus eligible for war risk insurance. During this period, the institution was run by psychiatrist William White, a close friend of J.R. Rees.

Upon White's death in 1937, Overholser was appointed as the superintendent of St. Elizabeth's. An early advocate of psychotropic drugs, Overholser supervised its research at St. Elizabeth's, where he began experimentation with drugs and hypnosis on the hospital's veterans.

During World War II, St. Elizabeth's went from a hospital serving both soldiers and civilians to an exclusively military institution. In this period, over five thousand naval officers and enlisted men were treated. To handle the immense influx of mentally disturbed patients, Overholser instituted a training school where about 125 naval medical officers, 100 nurses and 800 hospital corpsmen were given extensive training in psychiatry. This teaching program was eventually expanded for physicians from Central and South America who would receive "short courses in modern psychiatry and are thus exposed to the American viewpoint in this field."[18] The hospital also ran a School of Nursing and trained graduate students from such diverse fields as medicine, social services, occupational therapy and even theology.

From his position as the head of the leading military psychiatric hospital — and due to the facility's location in the nation's capital—Overholser was able to form strong alliances in influential government circles. He was often asked to appear before Congressional hearings where he could—and did— promote psychiatric interests. In 1940, for example, the National Research Council set up an advisory committee to the Surgeon General on neuropsychiatry. Overholser was named its chairman, a post which he held until the end of the World War II. From that position, he was able to influence federal agencies and sit on the board of professional lobbying organizations.

Overholser was not, however, alone. The invasion of psychiatry into the military was also ensured through the efforts of his close colleagues William Menninger, Jack Ewalt and Francis Braceland, who placed psychiatrists in field hospitals all over Europe.

By now, each branch of the military had a prominent psychiatrist in its ranks whose job it was to make psychiatry an important, if not major, part of its Medical Corps. Menninger was the head of psychiatry in the Army, Braceland in the Navy, and Daniel Blain, who, after introducing psychiatry into the Merchant Marines, became the Chief Psychiatrist for the Veterans Administration after the war.

Psychiatrists in Canada followed suit. G. Brock Chisholm, a close friend of Rees and Overholser, was made head of psychiatry for the Canadian Armed Forces and given the rank of Brigadier General.

In the fall of 1940, Overholser wrote a report for the Federal Board of Hospitalization, which came to the attention of President Roosevelt. This led directly to Overholser's wartime appointment to the psychiatric advisory committee of the Selective Service, which oversaw the fitness of military recruits. His position enabled him to extend psychiatry's reach by ensuring that other psychiatrists were appointed to similar posts in regional Selective Service Boards throughout the country.

Now, for the first time in history, potential recruits were subjected to psychological testing along with regular medical and physical tests. The fact that nearly two million civilians were rejected on psychological grounds was proclaimed as proof of a growing mental illness in the United States. This statistic was later used in the 1950s and 1960s to push through legislation that would give psychiatrists federal funding to build huge facilities designed to handle the alleged epidemic sweeping the country.

Overholser also made sure that psychiatry would play a major role in military intelligence by working in concert with General William ("Wild Bill") Donovan, then the head of the Office of the Coordinator of Information (OCI). A year later, Donovan changed the name of his agency to the OSS (Office of Strategic Services) and installed his own Psychological Division, of which Overholser was a part. Later, the OSS would be abolished and much of its organization reassigned into the newly-created Central Intelligence Agency.

This incestuous relationship between psychiatry and the American intelligence and business communities is made all the more interesting when we see that not only did Donovan receive his intelligence training at the Tavistock Clinic under Rees, but so did all of his intelligence personnel at the OCI and OSS. Later, Donovan would send them to St. Elizabeth's, to be trained by Overholser's disciples. Furthermore, the British intelligence M5 branch (whose personnel were also trained at the Tavistock Clinic) ran their covert operations from an office located in Rockefeller Center in New York. Its head, William Stephenson, set up the British Security Coordination there and ran it directly under Churchill and Roosevelt.

WILLIAM MENNINGER

Born in 1899, William Menninger received his doctorate from Cornell Medical School and from 1924 to 1925 served his residency at St. Elizabeth's. Upon returning to his home state of Kansas, he worked in a number of psychiatric hospitals (including a VA hospital) before setting up the Menninger Clinic and Foundation in Topeka in the 1920s with his father Charles and brother Karl. This clinic would become world-famous as a hospital and school of psychiatry.

In 1942, Menninger became a Brigadier General in the U.S. Army and head of the Psychiatric Division of the Surgeon General's Office, a position he would hold until 1946. During this time, Menninger, dissatisfied with the old psychiatric nomenclature largely invented by Kraepelin,

devised a new system of categorizing both mental illnesses and the patients that suffered from them. The new classification system that Menninger created was so successful that it was adopted by the Army, the Navy and later by the Veterans Administration. In 1952, it was adopted by the American Psychiatric Association and published as the *Diagnostic and Statistical Manual of Mental Disorders* (*DSM*) of the APA, which is now the psychiatric community's official manual of nomenclature and categorization of mental illness.

William Menninger—Head psychiatrist for the U.S. Army Shipping Administration (now the Merchant Marines) during World War II, he was highly influential in getting legislation passed that provided government funding to place psychiatric clinics in communities around the U.S.

The other side of Menninger's reclassification of mental illness was that more civilians than ever were classified as mentally unfit to serve in the Army, more soldiers than ever were classified as

mentally ill, and more patients than ever were eligible for "treatment" in the burgeoning number of VA hospitals and clinics such as Menninger's. Dr. Thomas Szasz notes:

"Between January 1942 and June 1945, out of approximately fifteen million examinations for induction into the Armed Services, nearly two million individuals were rejected for neuropsychiatric disability; that is, 12 percent of those examined were rejected for mental illness. Actually, the rate had been 9.7 percent in 1942, and rose to 16.4 percent in 1945. Moreover, out of every one hundred rejections for all causes, an average of

39.1 percent were for neuropsychiatric disability. This proportion rose from a low of 28.4 in 1942 to a high of 45.8 in 1944. Despite this screening—or possibly because of it, since it authenticated mental illness as so acceptable a ground for separating men from the Service—37 percent of all medical discharges from the Armed Forces were on the grounds of neuropsychiatric disability." [19]

Menninger would eventually become a president of the American Psychiatric Association, and, as part of the "Young Turks" of psychiatry (as they called themselves), he organized The Group for the Advancement in Psychiatry in 1946, which was "determined to capture control and to use APA as one of their instruments in spreading the influence of psychiatry into the nooks and crannies of American life." [20]

Menninger hints at eugenical views of his own in a paper he wrote a year later:

"One of the essential rôles of psychiatry must lie in the field of prevention of mental ill health. If we continue to confine ourselves to treatment only, it is inconceivable that we could ever meet the obligation." [21]

FRANCIS BRACELAND (1901-1985)

Dr. Braceland's major contributions to the growth of psychiatry began in 1942, when he became Special Assistant to the Surgeon General, U.S. Navy and wartime chief of its psychiatric section, rising to the rank of Rear Admiral of the U.S. Navy Medical Corps. He would later serve as personal physician to President Franklin D. Roosevelt. Like Menninger, he too was actively involved in the Selective Service.

Braceland was highly active in promoting psychiatry as the solution to many of the internal problems of the American military. According to *The New York Times*, before the Senate Subcommittee on Wartime Health and Education in 1944, "the Army and Navy medical psychiatrists…showed by their testimony that conditions of modern war confronted the country with a serious problem in the treatment, training and readaptation of many victims of wartime mental and emotional disturbances. Colonel W.C. Menninger, director of the division of neuropsychiatry of the Army Medical Corps, and Comdr. Francis J. Braceland, of the Navy's division of neuropsychiatry, stressed the need for more psychiatrists with the armed forces." [22]

Also during this time, Braceland, Menninger, and Robert Felix, a prominent psychiatrist in the U.S. Public Health Service, appeared before Congress to lobby for the passage of the National Mental Health Act. Their efforts helped create the National Institute of Mental Health (NIMH) in 1949, a federally funded psychiatric research center which was placed under the administrative structure of the National Institutes of Health (NIH).

After his service in the military, Braceland became the first psychiatrist ever at the Mayo Clinic and taught psychiatry at the University of Minnesota's graduate school, before becoming a clinical professor of psychiatry at Yale University and a lecturer at the Harvard Medical School. Like Menninger, Braceland also served a term as president of the American Psychiatric Association in 1957.

DANIEL BLAIN

Born in China to Presbyterian missionaries, Daniel Blain graduated among the top six doctoral candidates at the Vanderbilt University School of Medicine in 1929. After years of clinical work, Blain was accepted into the U.S. Public Health Service as a medical officer eight months after the U.S. entered World War II. In 1942, he was appointed to head up the psychiatry program at the War Shipping Administration (a precursor to the Merchant Marines), where he worked in conjunction with the United Seamen's Service on the establishment of rest homes for the treatment of 30 to 40 merchant marines suffering from war neuroses, the purpose of which was to return them to active duty as quickly as possible.

Daniel Blain—Psychiatrist at the U.S. War Shipping Administration (now the Merchant Marines), and Medical Director of the American Psychiatric Association from 1948 to 1958. One of psychiatry's most influential lobbyists.

In 1945, Blain was appointed director of Neuropsychiatric Services in the Department of Medicine and Surgery of the Veterans Administration. During this time he was able to expand greatly psychiatry's position there, earning the praise of the American Psychiatric Association, which successfully lobbied Congress for increased appropriations to the medical program Blain was running.

In 1948, Blain resigned to assume the newly created position of Medical Director for the American Psychiatric Association. For the next ten years he would use his authority to form alliances between the psychiatric community, the government and private individuals and groups to eliminate any other mental health alternative other than psychiatry.

On May 17, 1953, *The New York Times* ran a story with the headline "Curbs on Treating Mental Ills Urged." The story said, in part:

"The American Psychiatric Association issued a statement today warning against state laws that licensed any profession other than the medical profession to treat mental ailments.

"Dr. Daniel Blain, medical director of the American Psychiatric Association, said that medical practice laws of most states were passed before the tremendous advances of recent years in the diagnosis and treatment of mental illness and before the increased recognition of the interrelationship [sic] of physical and mental illness.

"He asserted that to include mental as well as physical conditions in state medical practice laws would rule out more so-called 'quacks' than any number of licensing laws."[23]

In not-so-subtle fashion, Blain was attempting to shut out the opposition and establish psychiatry as government's best and only friend in the treatment of mental health. It didn't seem to matter that psychiatric cures were not forthcoming—which leads one to wonder just who the quacks really were—as long as the coffers were filling up with government contributions. Then, as now, the general public wasn't willing to pay for their services, but the government and the military were.

Blain went on to have a long career as an apologist for and supporter of psychiatry, much of which would involve such dubious projects as the training of seminary students in psychiatry and the attempted implementation of the controversial Siberia Bill, both of which will be discussed in a later chapter.

PSYCHIATRY AND ITS EXPANDING ROLE IN AMERICAN MILITARY INTELLIGENCE

Winfred Overholser, in his capacity as chief psychiatrist for the U.S. Army Medical Corps, was one of the major factors in psychiatry's increas-

Winfred Overholser—Superintendent of St. Elizabeth's Hospital in Washington, D.C. He conducted experiments on soldiers at St. Elizabeths for the OSS and later for the CIA.

ing infiltration of the intelligence community. During the war he collaborated with his friend "Wild Bill" Donovan in prewar experimentations with truth drugs and hypnosis. These tests were conducted at the request of the British M5's Psychological Warfare Board to see if these drugs could be used to get information out of enemy prisoners of war during interrogations. This psychiatric drug and hypnosis testing, shrouded as it was by its cloak of secrecy, would soon take on all the colors of a renegade operation when the supervision of intelligence operations was taken away from the Joint Chiefs of Staff.

There were, however, other forces at work, notably powerful and well-financed elements of international commerce.

As was true in the case of the Rockefellers' relationship with the German chemical company I.G. Farben, prior to the Second World War—oil and chemicals are natural commercial partners—international commerce was an avenue of influence as well as exchange. Oil and chemicals were not, however, the only businesses operating cooperatively in this sphere. Banking interests were also represented in many of the important commercial centers of the world.

Prior to the Second World War, Allen Dulles, who would later work for the OSS and head the CIA, sat on the board of directors of Schroder, the powerful, international German bank. Not coincidentally, his brother John

Foster Dulles (later the Secretary of State under Eisenhower) was the leading attorney at Sullivan and Cromwell, an international law firm, based in New York, that represented Stein Bank, another German bank with ties to Schroder. Just prior to the outbreak of the war, Allen Dulles joined Sullivan and Cromwell and was immediately sent to Berlin to consult with German industrialists who were very concerned that the United States government would seize their American holdings should war be declared.

Allen Dulles was successful in working out legal strategies for the formation of various corporate covers and secret agreements which would protect the assets of the German companies. One of these agreements involved I.G. Farben, which had contracts with the Rockefellers' Standard Oil empire. Needless to say, the Rockefellers were very concerned, because they stood to lose a lot of money if war intervened in their business dealings. Dulles' success meant that the money flow between the two companies would continue unmolested throughout the wartime period.

It also meant that I.G. Farben could take advantage of the political climate in Germany to expand its activities to include the setting up of a plant near Auschwitz. Using concentration camp prisoners as slave labor, Farben manufactured Zyklon B, the poison gas that would ultimately be used against their own work force.

Appropriately enough, the I.G. Farben offices in Frankfurt became the headquarters for the Allied Reconstruction Forces after the war, when the Marshall Plan became the operating program for the reconstruction of Germany. According to the plan, German industry would be the first area addressed. During the next four years, billions of American dollars flowed overseas—to the same industrialists who had been protected and profiting during the war.

In this political climate, psychiatrists like Overholser found that they could receive massive amounts of government defense funding to fight an enemy that provided them not only with the inspiration for their own calling, but with an immense influx of "experts" fleeing Germany. It was one nation inspired by a psychiatric frenzy fighting another. Either way, the psychiatrists couldn't lose.

In the race for supremacy in psychological warfare, the use of drugs became a rapidly growing new field. One of the prime locations for research was St. Elizabeth's Hospital, which was used for testing of marijuana and other drugs. OSS documents have reported that in its findings that test subjects, after smoking a mix of tobacco and marijuana, exhibited a "state of irresponsibility, causing the subject to be loquacious and free in his impartation of information." [24]

Overholser, as superintendent of the hospital and a member of the OSS' Truth Drug Committee, was prominently involved. At the request of the Military Intelligence Services Psychological Warfare Branch, in October 1942, he worked with George Hunter White in the development of truth serums. During this time, he also worked with OSS psychologist R.C. Tyron on the "Morale Project." This project, originated by Overholser himself, was not designed to address "morale" at all—it was devoted to the subject of Mind Control.

In a letter to Harry Steckel, a fellow military psychiatrist, Overholser wrote:

"It is possible indeed that this division may develop into just the sort of thing we have been hoping for, namely one which will not only know something about morale but do something about it. Dr. Tyron the other day at my suggestion recommended a medical set-up in his division to be in [the] charge of a psychiatrist...." [25]

Mind control experiments were begun and a new and fearful psychiatric era was underway.

Alarmed by the covert and somewhat criminal activities of the OSS (particularly since they were reticent about telling him what they were doing), President Harry Truman dissolved the agency after the war, saying he was "concerned about 'building up a gestapo.'" [26]

However, the fallout of World War II was intense distrust and sometimes paranoia. The new world power America enjoyed, combined with Cold War fears, formed an antagonistic suspicion of anyone who might be perceived as an enemy bent on world domination. The flames of these fears were certainly fanned by the intelligence community, particularly Donovan and his predecessor at the OSS, Allen Dulles, who lobbied feverishly for the National Security Act of 1947. As the former head of the European branch of the OSS during the war, Dulles was very familiar with German intelligence programs and personnel. As a result, he placed a high priority in "mind control" technology, which would flourish under the CIA. He was so convinced of this necessity that he recruited the unlikeliest of bedfellows—Reinhard Gehlen, the head of the Nazi Intelligence network under Hitler and an expert on the Soviet Union, whom Dulles absorbed into the CIA along with the rest of Gehlen's cohorts, collectively known as the "Gehlen Organization."

The National Security Act of 1947 created not only the CIA but the National Security Council (NSC) and the National Security Agency (NSA), which would form the basic military intelligence structure of the Cold War. Donovan was picked to serve as the CIA's first head and many former OSS military psychiatrists were transferred into the fledgling intelligence super-agency. Later on President Truman claimed that "the CIA was set up by me for the sole purpose of getting all the available information to the President. It was not intended to operate as an international agency engaged in strange activities." [27]

But this is not what happened. The Act went beyond separating the intelligence community from the direct supervision of the military. It granted the National Security Council "sweeping and virtually unlimited powers to integrate all policies of government and coordinate all agencies, both foreign and domestic." [28]

Eventually, Allen Dulles would become the head of the CIA. He placed a premium on using psychiatry for the purpose of "mind control," the experiments of which have not ceased even up to the present day.

THE COSMO AND CENTURY CLUBS

There were two prominent social clubs originally established in the early 1900s that came to flourish as meeting grounds for those that were involved in the government, military, and psychiatric mind control arenas. While this motion may at first seem trivial, the significance of these clubs to this examination should not be ignored, for it was here that the major players in these areas met, socialized and formed personal and political alliances. Here was classic backroom politics in action, where favors and business deals were sealed with a handshake and other people's futures were shaped.

The Cosmo Club was located in Washington, the center of American government, and New York, the financial center of the United States and the world—as well as the seat of the American Psychiatric Association—was the site of the Century Club.

Over the years, members of the Cosmo Club included:

Daniel Blain, medical director of the APA and a military psychiatrist

Winfred Overholser, a top military psychiatrist and superintendent of St. Elizabeth's Hospital

Zigmond Lebensohn, who worked on mind control experiments at St. Elizabeth's with Overholser and trained psychiatrists in military intelligence

Robert T. Mores, a military psychiatrist and Commissioner for Mental Health in Washington

Harold Stevens, a psychiatrist at St. Elizabeth's and the Veterans Administration

Adolf Meyer, German psychiatrist who became known as the "Father of Modern American Psychiatry" and who founded the APPA (American Psychopathological Association)

William "Wild Bill" Donovan, head of the OSS and first director of the CIA

Dr. Charles H. Judd, a psychiatrist and pupil of Wundt

John Dewey, a pupil of Wundt most responsible for making psychology part of the American school systems

G. Stanley Hall, Wundt's first American pupil and the top psychologist at Columbia University's Teachers College

Nelson and Laurence Rockefeller, John D. Rockefeller, Jr.'s sons who carried on the family business and philanthopy. Nelson later entered politics, becoming the Governor of New York and Vice President of the United States under President Ford

E. L. Thorndike, another of Wundt's pupils involved in the push to get psychology into American schools

Henry Kissinger, Secretary of State under President Nixon

Noteworthy members of the Century Club included:

Allen Dulles, who worked in the OSS and later became head of the CIA, especially interested in the field of psychiatric mind control

John Foster Dulles, whose law firm negotiated deals to protect certain German industries during the war. He later was appointed Secretary of State under Eisenhower and the Washington, D.C., international airport was named after him

G. Brock Chisholm, the top Canadian military psychiatrist, founder of the World Health Organization, and co-founder of the World Federation for Mental Health

Adolf Meyer, also of the Cosmo Club

Lawrence Kolb, head of the U.S. Division of Mental Hygiene, a fore-runner of the National Institute of Mental Health (NIMH), and a military psychiatrist

Nicholas Katzenbach, former U.S. Deputy Attorney General

James Cattell, Wundt's assistant for three years, and prominent American educational psychologist

James E. Russell, child psychiatrist

E.L. Thorndike, educational psychologist

John D. Rockefeller and his three sons John D. III, David, Laurence and his grandson David, Jr.

THE AMERICAN PSYCHOPATHOLOGICAL ASSOCIATION

Like the Cosmo and Century Clubs, the membership roster of the APPA was rife with military psychiatrists, which gave them ample opportunity to mingle and form key alliances and networks. Here is just a portion of the APPA's 1952 membership:

Leo Alexander, German-born American military psychiatrist and apologist at Nuremberg for Nazi military psychiatrists

Daniel Blain, medical director of American Psychiatric Association

Francis Braceland, top psychiatrist in the U.S. Navy

D. Ewen Cameron, Canadian mind control psychiatrist who undertook projects for the CIA

G. Brock Chisholm, top psychiatrist for the Canadian Armed Forces and co-founder of the World Federation for Mental Health

Robert Felix, director of NIMH

Paul Hoch, German psychiatrist at the New York Institute for Psychiatry and CIA experimenter with LSD

Lothar Kalinowsky, proponent and importer of ECT into the U.S.

Franz Kallmann, German psychiatrist who popularized schizophrenia in North America as a diagnosis

Lawrence Kolb, military psychiatrist and director of the U.S. Narcotics Division, which became the Division on Mental Hygiene, a forerunner of NIMH

William Menninger, top Army psychiatrist and co-founder of the

Group for the Advancement of Psychiatry

Winfred Overholser, top military intelligence psychiatrist and superintendent of St. Elizabeth's Hospital in Washington, D.C.

John Whitehorn, CIA psychiatrist from Johns Hopkins, served as a front man for funding CIA experiments

In 1961, the membership list included these members:

Alexandra Adler, whose father Alfred Adler, a famous Austrian psychiatrist, came to the U.S. after the war

Lauretta Bender, LSD experimenter on autistic children

Jacques Gottlieb, psychosurgery advocate who proposed brain surgery for blacks who participated in the race riots in Detroit in the 1960s

Zigmond Lebensohn, military psychiatrist at St. Elizabeth's under Overholser

Sandor Rado, German-trained psychiatrist who emigrated to the U.S. before the war and served on the Selective Services Board during World War II

Howard Rome, director of the psychiatric department at the Mayo clinic

Harry C. Solomon, lobotomist

Harvey Tompkins, member of the Joint Commission on Community Mental Health Centers and a member of GAP (Group for the Advancement of Psychiatry)

Louis J. "Jolly" West, a military intelligence psychiatrist and CIA LSD experimenter

HOW AMERICAN INVOLVEMENT HELPED THE NAZI PSYCHIATRISTS ESCAPE PUNISHMENT AFTER THE WAR

After the war, psychiatrists were assigned to help the Allied troops find those responsible for the Nazi atrocities in Germany and bring them to justice at the Nuremberg Trials.

One of these psychiatrists was Austrian-born Leo Alexander, who was trained in Germany and had worked as a psychiatrist at the Kaiser Wilhelm Institute. A staunch supporter of eugenical and biological psychiatry, he had moved to Boston before the war, where his "prestigious" German background and training enabled him to become the Associate Director of Research at the Boston State Hospital and Instructor in

Psychiatry at nearby Tufts University.

Alexander later worked for the United States Secretary of War (now Secretary of Defense) and became the psychiatrist at the Federal Office of the Chief Counsel for War Crimes in Nuremberg from 1946 to 1947. It was Alexander's responsibility to go to Germany, interview the Nazi psychiatrists and investigate the research and experimentations in the concentration camps.

His 1945 investigation of Nazi war crimes was declassified the following year by the Army and Navy Office of the Publication Board "with the hopes that it will be of direct benefit to U.S. science and industry." [29] It proved instead to be of direct benefit to some of the men behind Hitler.

In his report, Alexander admits that psychiatrists played a role in the Nazi extermination, but lays much of the blame on only four people. Professor Heyde, he characterized as "an SS man...[who] also held the position of so-called 'psychiatrist to concentration camps.'" [30] Carl Schneider was "a great scientific supporter of the sterilization law." [31] Hermann Pfannmüller was "a brutal fellow who actually enjoyed to dispatch patients to their death...[was] most directly responsible" for the killings at the Eglfing-Haar asylum, "although he acted in the name of the Bavarian Ministry of the Interior." [32] Ernst Rüdin, he states, had fled the Kaiser Wilhelm Institute before the arrival of Allied troops "because of the part he had played in the program of killing the insane." [33]

Toward the rest of the psychiatric community Alexander is most forgiving. In an earlier paper on July 20, 1945, he reports that while working as Rüdin's assistant at the Kaiser Wilhelm Institute in Munich between April 1944 and April 1945, a neurologist named Dr. F. Jahnel performed psychiatric examinations on 7,750 patients, of whom 5,000 were soldiers, 170 prisoners of war, and the rest civilians. The neuroses he encountered were "solved by means of suggestive treatment with the aid of painful electric currents, as well as by the policy of not letting the patients attain the goals which the illness served." [34] By the time Alexander's report came out, Dr. Jahnel had become the director of the Institute and was allowed to keep his job and continue his work, never to worry about any of his war crimes.

Under the cover of objective reporting, Alexander sympathetically quotes psychiatrists throughout his piece who intimate that the Nazi psychiatrists were a historical anomaly, rather than representatives of the eugenical philosophy they practiced:

"Professor Bumke stated that [the Nazi extermination] was a tragic crime. The mistrust of the public against psychiatrists had been gradually stilled through faithful public service on the part of psychiatrists extending over about 100 years, but this policy of killing the mentally ill has stirred up all that old mistrust again. 'Psychiatrists, as you know, were always suspected of 'putting people away,' and now they were not only suspected of putting them away, but there was real evidence that they were actually killing them. That was the tragedy.'" [35]

He then dismisses Hitler's own psychiatrist, Dr. Theodor Morell, as "something of a quack and faker" who "treated Hitler mainly with hormones," and quotes Bumke's "expert diagnosis" of Hitler as "a hysterical psychopath, with excessive need for recognition and with traits of genius." [36]

Alexander's willingness to accept such historical revisionism smacks of a fellow psychiatrist—a bedfellow in training and philosophy—allowing his colleagues to close ranks. His scapegoats, naturally enough, were Hitler and the "large SS staff required for the mass killings...." [37] In a 1948 article in a psychiatric journal aptly entitled "Sociopsychologic Structure of the SS: Psychiatric Report of the Nuremberg Trials for War Crimes," Alexander lays the bulk of the blame of the Holocaust on the SS, then attempts to rationalize their behavior:

"The master crime to which the SS was committed was the genocide of non-German peoples and the elimination by killing, in groups or singly, of Germans who were considered useless or disloyal....

"One of the most sinister traits of the Hitler regime was that it utilized a craving for irrelevant excitement by these personalities with weak ego in its system of seduction already described.... It was, apparently, a function of the more spectacular atrocities in concentration camps, especially in Auschwitz, to provide this type of excitement. The most spectacular of the mass atrocities were called Sonderaktionen ("Special Actions"). One of these, practiced particularly in Auschwitz, was the burning of live prisoners, who were often children, in pits... on piles of gasoline-soaked wood." [38]

Throughout this article, Alexander never once mentions the role psychiatrists played in the instigation of and participation in the mass experimentations and murder of millions of people during the Holocaust.

Despite this, he published papers promoting the use of data gathered during Nazi experimentation on prisoners in concentration camps. One of his papers, entitled "The Treatment of Shock from Prolonged Exposure to Cold, Especially in Water" was based on "a wealth of most revealing material"—SS Chief Heinrich Himmler's papers, found in a salt mine in Austria. One of the Nazi experiments tested to see how long a person could survive in icy water, and for those who survived, how long it would take to return their body temperature back to normal without permanent damage. As the *Los Angeles Times* reported later, "Alexander carefully gleaned all the data he could from the Nazi experiments" because they were "too valuable to be buried." [39]

Alexander was not the only psychiatrist passionately defending the criminals within his profession. This only made sense; if psychiatry should share equal blame for the mass exterminations of the Holocaust, their practitioners would suffer the same fate as the Nazis.

Francis Braceland came to the Nuremberg Trials to serve as a special witness, where he testified that Rudolf Hess, Hitler's devoted "deputy Führer" responsible for all Nazi party matters, was not feigning insanity, thus helping to save Hess' life. Tavistock psychiatrists J.R. Rees and H.V. Dicks, along with Canadian psychiatrist D. Ewen Cameron had also examined Hess, and likewise found him insane. This was an interesting twist, psychiatrists now coming forward as experts declaring as insane those who could have exposed their profession. It doesn't require a cynic to spot the irony in that scenario.

Historian Müller-Hill notes:

"Almost no one stopped to think that something could be wrong with psychiatry, with anthropology, or with behavioral science. The international scientific establishment reassured their German colleagues that it had indeed been the unpardonable misconduct of a few individuals, but that it lay outside the scope of science. The pattern of German anthropology, psychiatry and behavioral science continued essentially unchanged, and it will continue so, unless a substantial number of scientists begin to have doubts and to ask questions." [40]

The cover-up and the spin control has successfully continued to the present day. Psychiatrist Robert Jay Lifton, in his book *The Nazi Doctors*, repeatedly refers to the Nazi psychiatrists as "physicians," and rationalizes the role played by psychiatry during the Third Reich. Instead of admitting that his own profession spawned and executed Hitler's genocidal programs, Lifton attempts to convince us that the psychiatrists of the Third Reich were somehow "used" by the Nazis. The failure of Leo Alexander and the Americans to bring the Nazi psychiatrists to justice at the Nuremberg Trials therefore receives Lifton's scant attention.

Even the American, Canadian and English psychiatrists who personally knew Rüdin and his racial theories (like Rees, Chisholm and others) remained silent about his and psychiatry's role. Instead, they successfully swept everything under the carpet, and went on to become prominent within their respective governments and among their colleagues. In doing so, they were able to carry forward their agenda to expand the reach of mental health into all sectors of society—after all, Germany was just an example of a world gone mad, and they were the ones who could make things right.

MILITARY PSYCHIATRY AND "MIND CONTROL" EXPERIMENTATION

As we have mentioned earlier, after the war, the intelligence community, (particularly Allen Dulles at the CIA) was particularly interested in the field of mind control. Many of the leaders of their experiments were German-born psychiatrists who had come over to the United States before the war.

One of them, Dr. Erich Lindemann, was trained in Cologne and Heidelberg, but emigrated to the United States in 1927 to teach and research psychiatry at the University of Iowa. In 1934 he received a Rockefeller Fellowship in psychiatry at Harvard, where he became a professor of psychiatry in 1937.

Lindemann experimented for the military by giving his test subjects "truth drugs" and then interrogating them in both threatening and non-threatening environments. It was in the non-threatening environments where the normal subjects reported a general sense of euphoria, ease and confidence, and where they exhibited a marked increase in talkativeness and communicability. [41]

British psychiatrist William Sargant, an ardent supporter of electroshock and drug therapy from London's Maudsley Hospital, went a step further, pioneering the way for the psychiatric implantation of false memories. At a U.S. Senate hearing, Sargant recommended "that the therapist deliberately distort the facts of the patient's life-experience to achieve heightened emotional response and abreaction. In the drunken state of narcoanalysis, patients are prone to accept the therapist's false constructions."[42]

After the Second World War, the threat of Communist invasion, widely promoted by the military and intelligence leaders such as Donovan and Dulles, was used to justify the continued experimentation in the use of mind control to handle people, crowds—even whole populations. The real purpose, of course, was to learn how to control anybody the government wanted to, whenever it wanted to.

Some of these experimenters were:

D. Ewen Cameron, who worked for the CIA in the 1950s at the Allen Memorial Institute of McGill University in Montreal. One of his pet projects involved the use of drugs, electric shocks and hypnosis to wipe out a person's memory and to implant new ones.

Martin Roth, a British psychiatrist and visiting professor of psychiatry at McGill who worked under Cameron as Director of Experimental Therapeutics, where he conducted LSD experiments on twenty-four different patients. Roth was a close associate of Eliot Slater, a psychiatrist who had studied in Germany under Rüdin and had written many articles and books on his research into the genetics of schizophrenia. Two of these books were co-written by Roth and William Sargant.

Zigmond Lebensohn interned and did his residency in psychiatry under Overholser from 1934 to 1937. After a stint as a professor of psychiatry at Georgetown University, Lebensohn returned to St. Elizabeth's, where he trained Navy psychiatrists and experimented under Overholser from 1941 to 1945. He was also a consultant to the Walter Reed Army Hospital, NIMH and the U.S. Information Agency. In 1959, Lebensohn was appointed to the American Medical Association's new Committee on the Medical Use of Hypnosis.

Paul Hoch, a Hungarian-born psychiatrist trained at the University of Goettingen in Germany. In 1933, he emigrated to the United States to become the Senior Clinical Psychiatrist at the Rockefeller-supported New York State Institute for Psychiatry at Columbia. In the early 1950s, Hoch led a research project on LSD for the CIA. In 1953, in a terrible instance of an experiment gone wrong, professional tennis player Harold Blauer died shortly after receiving an injection of MDA (known on the streets as "the love drug"). All seemed forgiven, however, when Hoch was later appointed to the position of Commissioner of Mental Hygiene for the state of New York by then Governor Nelson Rockefeller, and soon became Rockefeller's leading expert on mental health.

LSD AND THE PSYCHIATRIC EXPERIMENTS BY THE CIA

In 1953, the CIA approved experimental programs for the "...covert use of biological and chemical materials..." to investigate whether and how it was possible to modify an individual's behavior."[43] Using various private foundations such as the Josiah Macy, Jr. Foundation and the Geschicher Foundation, the CIA covertly channeled funds to a small army of psychiatrists dedicated to this mission. Among this network of LSD experimenters were Harold Abramson, Paul Hoch, Frank Fremont-Smith (the head of the Macy Foundation), D. Ewen Cameron, Milton Greenblatt and Louis J. ("Jolly") West.

Research was extensive. In 1954, the CIA hired Eli Lilly & Company of Indianapolis to manufacture LSD so that it could buy locally in tonnage quantities and avoid having to rely on a foreign company for its product.

Greenblatt was the Research Director of the Boston Psychopathic Hospital (now called the Massachusetts Mental Health Center, a much more euphonious name), a pioneering mental health institution affiliated with Harvard University. It was here that Viennese doctor Otto Kaunders came in 1949, looking for money for research on an experimental new drug called lysergic acid diethylamide (or "LSD"), manufactured by the Swiss pharmaceutical company Sandoz. Greenblatt became very interested. "We were very interested in anything that could make someone schizophrenic," he was quoted as saying.[44] Using LSD, Greenblatt hoped to induce a model psychosis, which they then could find the antidote for, thereby finding a cure for schizophrenia.

With the director of Boston Hospital's Drug Unit, Dr. Lester Grinspoon (a German-born psychiatrist who came to the United States after the war), Greenblatt first tested LSD on volunteer staff members. The first was Robert Hyde, the hospital's number-two man:

"Hyde drank a glass of water with 100 micrograms of LSD in it....Hyde became 'quite paranoic, saying we had not given him anything. He also berated us and said the company had cheated us, given us plain water. That was not Dr. Hyde's normal behavior; he is a very pleasant man.'"[45]

Several years later, Hyde would become a secret CIA consultant.

Greenblatt and his fellow researchers also tested LSD on student volunteers from Harvard and Radcliffe.

One of the volunteers was Timothy Leary, a professor of clinical psychology at Harvard whose experiments and personal use of LSD are legendary. Inspired by an experience with hallucinogenic mushrooms in Mexico, Leary found in LSD a powerful means of changing one's way of living. His famous slogan "turn on, tune in, drop out" was coined in the mid-sixties, and inspired a whole generation of college students to experiment with LSD and other psychedelic substances:

"Through magazine interviews, television appearances, movies, records and books Leary projected himself as a culture hero of a new generation which was fighting for an individual's right to alter his own consciousness—a right which Leary maintained was guaranteed by the Constitution of the United States." [46]

He and an associate, Walter Pahnke, then a doctoral candidate at Harvard, conducted an experiment on Good Friday with ten theology students, who would experience a deep "religious" experience while under the influence of LSD. This widely promoted study inspired other psychiatrists to suggest using LSD for religious studies and ceremonies.

Just as Timothy Leary was promoting LSD on the East Coast, psychiatrist Louis J. "Jolly" West, chairman of the Department of Psychiatry at the University of Oklahoma, was deeply involved in LSD work as part of his research experiments for the CIA. West is notorious in psychiatric circles for killing an elephant after injecting it with a massive overdose of LSD. West and other CIA colleagues rented an apartment in the Haight-Ashbury section of San Francisco to test the potential of mind-altering drugs on hippies:

"They had administered the drug to test subjects and watched unperturbed as the toughest of specimens were reduced to quivering jelly, their confidence and poise demolished under the impact of the hallucinogen. No doubt about it—LSD was a devastating weapon." [47]

At the suggestion of Aldous Huxley, the author of *Brave New World*, West hypnotized his subjects prior to administering the LSD in order to give them "post-hypnotic suggestions aimed at orienting the drug-induced experience in some desired direction." [48] This was an idea that had originally been discussed in 1959 at the First International Congress on Hallucinogenic Drugs, sponsored by the Macy Foundation and Sandoz.

Another key CIA researcher was Dr. Harris Isbell of the Kentucky Addiction Research Center in Lexington, a division of the U.S. Public Health Service Hospital. Despite its name, the Center was actually a penitentiary for heroin addicts, sexual deviants and the mentally ill. It was also the place the CIA sent new drugs to be tested (along with fourteen other secret penal and mental institutions). Like the Nazi psychiatrists of World War II, Isbell used his prisoners as guinea pigs, experimenting with over 800 compounds the CIA sent him over the course of ten years. Also like Nazi Germany, these prisoners were largely members of minority groups—only in this case, they were almost exclusively African-American. In exchange for their cooperation, Isbell would give his "patients" as much heroin or morphine as they wanted. In fact, "it became an open secret among street junkies that if the supply got tight, you could always commit yourself to Lexington...."[49]

The CIA was not even above testing LSD on each other. In one three-day retreat, a CIA scientist pulled a prank by spiking after-dinner cocktails with LSD. One researcher, Dr. Frank Olson, a biological warfare specialist who had never taken LSD before, had a bad reaction and immediately slid into a deep depression. Alarmed, the CIA sent him to Dr. Harold Abramson, the chief of the allergy clinic at Mount Sinai Hospital and one of the CIA's top LSD researchers. While waiting a transfer to a Maryland sanitarium, Olson checked into a 10th-story room at the Statler Hilton and threw himself out the window and onto the pavement below.

As a result, the CIA began an elaborate cover-up and Allen Dulles, the head of the CIA, ordered a temporary stop to the in-house testing until the investigation was completed. In the end, the scientists involved were given what amounted to a slap on the wrist.

LSD experimentation was also popular among so-called "legitimate" researchers. Lauretta Bender, a psychiatrist at Creedmore State Hospital in New York, tested the effects of LSD on autistic and schizophrenic children. In a workshop organized by the Psychopharmacology branch of the National Institute of Mental Health in January 1969, Dr. Bender delivered a speech entitled "LSD and Amphetamine in Children," which stated in part:

"We gave this [LSD] first to young, autistic children, and we found we were able to get an improvement in their general well-being, general tone, habit patterning, eating patterns and sleeping patterns.... We also tried LSD on two adolescent boys who were mildly schizophrenic.... They became disturbed to the extent that they said we were experimenting on them....

"We used LSD on 89 children from January 1961 to July 1965.... We hope to go back to using LSD because we have found that it is one of the most effective methods of treatment we have for childhood schizophrenia."[50]

By 1968, LSD, marijuana and cocaine were available on street corners and schoolyards throughout the country. The CIA, alarmed at the fact that the "psychedelic revolution" was "tuning people out" to such a degree that they were actively protesting the Vietnam War and demanding social reforms, eventually withdrew the "real" LSD and all its derivatives completely from the market thereby showing what a government can do when it really decides to put a halt to drug use. But just as the LSD supply vanished, the market became mysteriously glutted with heroin. The American drug culture was now firmly established.

"The CIA knew that heroin causes no 'consciousness expansion.' It brings on a physical feeling, a warm, glowing 'highs' and then dullness and insulation. But the government was interested in behavior control, and heroin, like LSD, was an important tool in gaining such control."[51]

Twenty years of experimentation convinced the CIA that LSD could be used to manipulate large crowds and create psychotic reactions indistinguishable from schizophrenia, one of its original goals. These drug reactions were then used by the psychiatric community to demand more and more money to subsidize "treatment" for the burgeoning drug culture.

Jolly West, after twenty years of brain-damaging research, sometimes on unwitting subjects, wrote in 1975 that "LSD therapy has been tried for alcoholism, narcotic addiction, homosexuality, criminal behavior, various neurotic symptoms, psychoses and resistance to psychotherapy. However, its efficacy remains uncertain."[52]

What is certain is that a culture dedicated to the taking of mind-altering drugs was developed in America and elsewhere in the 1960s, and has been steadily expanding to this day, along with a corresponding rise in crime and violence.

This drug culture opened up a new market for psychiatrists—the rehabilitation of drug addicts. This necessitated more facilities, more research—and much more money. After all, panic-stricken Americans demanded it; now there were "drug crazies" everywhere who had previously been hidden behind the doors of large mental institutions. Now any normal-looking person could suddenly go psychotic at any time—and drugs and addicts were everywhere on the streets. Taking advantage of the situation, the psychiatric community could now attempt to handle the "runaway insanity" to which they had contributed so richly. "Give us your money," they said in essence, "and we will make it go away."

BLUEBIRD AND MKULTRA

The CIA did not go out of the mind control experiment business altogether. They only became more secret. Two such projects were nicknamed BLUEBIRD and MKULTRA. These tests were conducted primarily on unsuspecting human guinea pigs, including Army soldiers, drug addicts in the U.S. Public Health Service, and civilians.

MKULTRA was a brainchild of Richard Helms, later the head of the CIA under President Nixon, who proposed it to Allen Dulles. In 1963, Helms would say, "In sum, if we are to continue to maintain the capability for influencing human behavior, we are virtually obligated to test on unwitting humans. The best method for conducting these tests securely is our relationship with the Bureau of Narcotics, an arrangement which has stood up through eight years of close collaboration." [53]

MKULTRA was originally designed, according to its head Sid Gottlieb, "to investigate whether and how it was possible to modify an individual's behavior by covert means." [54]

From the beginning, the project was concerned mainly with LSD testing. Its operatives included Hyde's group at Boston Psychopathic Hospital, Harold Abramson at Mount Sinai, Carl Pfeiffer at the University of Illinois Medical School, Harris Isbell at the Kentucky Addiction Research Center, and Jolly West at the University of Oklahoma. D. Ewen Cameron tested PCP—known on the streets as "Angel Dust"—on psychiatric patients at Allan Memorial Institute in Montreal. PCP was later stockpiled by the CIA as a "nonlethal incapacitant," although high dosages, according to the CIA's own report, could "lead to convulsions and death.".[55]

In 1956, Harris Isbell began to experiment with LSD as a potential serotonin stimulator, a brain transmitter chemical which affects the mood of a person, making him calm, relaxed and restful. This is the natural substance that puts us to sleep—bananas, turkey and milk are rich in serotonin. Psychiatric experimentation on this project continued into the 1970s, when commercial drug companies began official research of their own into drugs to find serotonin-producing drugs, but without the disastrous side effects of LSD. The first such commercial drug, Prozac (fluoxetine), was introduced in 1987, and carries it's own potentially dangerous side effects. In the early 1990s it was followed by Zoloft (sertraline), Effexor (venlafaxine) and Paxil (paroxetine).

A chilling result of the CIA's mind control experiments was elucidated by Dr. Wayne Evans, a military psychologist and former director of the Military Stress Laboratory of the U.S. Army Research Institute of Environmental Medicine, and drug specialist and a consultant to pharmaceutical companies. In 1971, he wrote:

"If we accept the position that human mood, motivation, and emotion are reflections of a neurochemical state of the brain, then drugs can provide a simple, rapid, expedient means to produce any desired neurochemical state that we wish. The sooner that we cease to confuse scientific and moral statements about drug use, the sooner we can rationally consider the types of neurochemical state that we wish to be able to provide for people.... We are on the edge of a 'choose your mood' society. Chemicals which affect the mind, as pollutants, prescribed or 'over-the-counter' drugs, foods and beverages and even 'incapacitating' chemical warfare agents are every where, used by every one, every day." [56]

It is not hard to see how this "choose-your-mood" drug society would have fulfilled Professor Wundt's fondest dream.

"We can therefore justifiably stress our particular point of view with regard to the human psyche, even though our knowledge be incomplete. We must aim to make it permeate every educational activity in our national life...."

> Colonel J.R. Rees
> Military psychiatrist

PROJECT PAPERCLIP AND THE PSYCHIATRIC PERMEATION OF AMERICAN SOCIETY AFTER WORLD WAR II

Even before the end of World War II, when German defeat seemed imminent, the OSS, then run by "Wild Bill" Donovan, began a top-secret operation to smuggle prominent Nazis, a large number of whom were implicated in war crimes, into the United States for the purpose of using their skills and inside information. Reinhard Gehlen, the Third Reich's top intelligence official for Russia and his entire spy team was one notable example.

As early as 1952, this became public knowledge. The Joint Chiefs of Staff revealed that there was a:

"[P]ostwar movement of German and Austrian scientists and engineers to the military installations, industrial laboratories and universities of the United States....Between May 1945 and December 1952 the United States government imported 642 alien specialists under several programs known collectively by the code-name 'Paperclip.'"[1]

The U.S. government claimed that Paperclip's sole purpose was to raid the immense scientific talent that Germany possessed so that Russia would not get them. The famous rocket scientist Werner von Braun's arrival in the United States was a widely publicized example. Until it finally ended in 1973 (the government claimed that the project ended in 1947), over sixteen hundred scientists and researchers were brought over to the United States, and hundreds of others went to work for defense and intelligence agencies.

As promised in their early conferences, psychiatrists have succeeded in getting into and controlling most every aspect of American life. This is all the more frightening when one realizes that the declining quality of life in America is parellel in time with the massive infiltration of psychiatry into the American society.

PSYCHIATRY AND POLITICS

Like the men behind Hitler, the leaders of the American psychiatric movement understood that if they could achieve legitimacy through legislation, they could then implement their objectives on a far-reaching basis, and receive considerable government funding for it. It is not surprising, therefore, that they moved close to powerful politicians and those near to them as advisors and personal physicians.

In 1937, when President Franklin D. Roosevelt was suffering from fatigue and loss of appetite, Francis Braceland was one of the experts called in to treat him.

At the height of the drug culture in the early 1960s, John F. Kennedy was treated to shots of "vitamins" by his personal physician Max ("Dr. Feelgood") Jacobson "that left JFK flushed and excited, leading some to speculate that the shots included methamphetamine and/or cocaine."[2] This would not be out of character for Jacobson, whose celebrity clientele also included such celebrities as Elizabeth Taylor, Eddie Fisher, Andy Warhol, Johnny Mathis, Truman Capote, Otto Preminger, Anthony Quinn, Tennessee Williams and Robert Kennedy (who would receive the same chemical combinations as his brother).

Debbie Reynolds, who was married to Fisher at the time, told the *San Francisco Chronicle* in a 1989 interview that Fisher "had deep mood swings that confused me; he had depressions. I didn't realize what was wrong or what his going to Max Jacobsen [sic]—the 'speed' doctor who was always ready to give celebrities their shots—would lead to. 'Dr. Needles,' I called him."[3]

As President Kennedy's attending physician, "Dr. Needles" was in a unique position to influence the course of world events—with a quick injection. As Stanford University's Dr. Herbert Abrams, also a member of the University's Center for International Security and Arms Control, wrote:

"Kennedy's need for the lift provided by injections from Dr. Max (Dr. Feelgood) Jacobson, which apparently contained amphetamine, illustrated how a President could easily obtain secret, and possible dangerous, treatment by circumventing the official physician."[4]

The true danger of such injections cannot be understated. According to a 1995 article in the *Los Angeles Times*:

"President John F. Kennedy was given injections by his personal physician before important summit meetings, according to Ronald K. Siegel, a UCLA psychopharmacologist who has studied methamephetamine.

"Methamphetamine usually is prescribed by doctors for treatment of narcolepsy, obesity and attention-deficit disorder....

"'Initially, methamphetamine creates feelings of euphoria, energy and confidence. Continued use leads to depression, sleepiness and tolerance to the drug, sparking even greater use and leading to a third stage,' he explained.

"'Meth also creates hypersexuality,' Siegel said, 'but in time, the user may prefer meth to sex altogether,' he said."[5]

Not the best of side effects, considering that Dr. Feelgood's visits were occurring during the Cuban Missile Crisis showdown with Soviet President Nikita Krushchev!

As if that weren't enough, consider also that the German-born Dr. Jacobson graduated in 1927 from Kaiser Wilhelm University—a breeding ground for the Nazi psychiatrists in prewar Germany. The state of mind of the most powerful man on the planet was being manipulated by a medical doctor whose training was at the feet of those who would become the men behind Hitler!

JFK and his brother Robert (who was the Attorney General at the time of his "vitamin" injections) were not the only members of the family to be treated by psychiatrists. Sen. Edward Kennedy's wife Joan was treated for alcoholism several times at the Silver Hill Foundation, a private Connecticut psychiatric hospital. Rosemary Kennedy, JFK's sister, was born retarded and would frequently embarrass the family with violent outbursts:

"In Rose Kennedy's memoirs, published in 1974, she described how the girl had become violent. Eminent medical specialists were consulted, and the advice was that the girl should undergo 'a certain form of neurosurgery.'[6] Rose Kennedy left no doubt as to what that 'certain form' was, when she described Rosemary as having become 'permanently incapacitated,' with no chance of ever living a normal life."

One of the experts the Kennedys consulted was Walter Freeman, a Georgetown University psychiatrist who had studied with Antonio Egas Moniz and was the first person to perform a lobotomy in the United States. Freeman's tireless promotion of lobotomy as a surgical procedure inspired approximately 100,000 such operations worldwide. It was Freeman, incidentally, who is credited with the lobotomy of Frances Farmer, a vastly talented 1930s Hollywood starlet whose downfall was tragically chronicled in the movie "Frances."

Rosemary Kennedy's mental condition was one of the reasons the psychiatric lobby, led by William Menninger, was able to get JFK to endorse and sign into law the 1963 Mental Retardation Facilities and Community Mental Health Centers Construction Act, which included large grants for research into the cause of mental retardation. According to the National Institutes of Health, the bill "began a new era in federal support for mental health services."[7]

Just as frightening as the treatment of President Kennedy by Dr. Jacobson was Richard Nixon's relationship with his personal physician, the Austrian-born Arnold Hutschnecker. Like Jacobson, Hutschnecker was trained at Kaiser Wilhelm University in Berlin, where he received his diploma in 1924. In 1936, he was licensed in the United States, and his interest shifted to the field of psychosomatic medicine. He began to practice psychotherapy in 1955.

According to *The Washington Post*, Nixon started seeing Hutschnecker in 1952[8] while serving as Eisenhower's Vice President. Syndicated columnist Jack Anderson adds that:

"An unnamed source close to Nixon told *The New York Times* that the then-Vice President, exhausted after a foreign trip, went to Dr. Hutschnecker for treatment and was given 'some pills.'"[9]

Anderson goes on to quote Harriet Van Horn, a newspaper columnist and neighbor of Hutschnecker's who witnessed many of Nixon's visits, which continued up until the early 1960s:

"'When I lived next door to Dr. Hutschnecker, for example, I occasionally saw [Nixon's] grim visage passing under the next canopy. Nagged by the curiosity that nags all journalists, I once asked a building employee, 'Does Mr. Nixon visit friends at 829?'

"'Naw,' came the reply, 'He comes to see the shrink.'"[10]

Nixon is said to have referred then House Minority Leader Gerald Ford to Hutschnecker:

"In 1965, at his friend Nixon's suggestion, Gerald Ford also began seeing Hutschnecker during a particularly trying period as House Minority Leader. Eight years later, during the confirmation hearings on Ford's vice presidential nomination, the doctor was called to testify in closed-door session."[11]

Ford had "categorically" denied the charges, asserting that he "dropped by Hutschnecker's office once...but that he went there merely to say hello..."[12] When Hutschnecker appeared, he confirmed "that Ford visited his office once for social conversation...."[13] Echoing Nazi psychiatrist Hans Bürger-Prinz, who had called for "silence with respect to everything," Hutschnecker lamented that:

"[O]ne thing made perfectly clear in Senate committee hearings on the nomination of Rep. Gerald Ford to be Vice President is that a consulting psychiatrist or psychotherapist is still an unforgivable sin for an American politician."[14]

Hutschnecker's prior influence upon Nixon, however, had been great. In 1970, Hutschnecker wrote a memo to the Nixon White House, which advocated "mass psychological testing" of six- to eight-year olds "to detect the children who have violent and homicidal tendencies." On a compulsory basis, those who were found to be "severely disturbed" would then be assigned to "camps with group activities." There, they would learn "more socially acceptable behavior patterns."[15]

This proposal attracted the interest of Nixon's advisor John Ehrlichman, who forwarded the letter to the Department of Health, Education and Welfare, requesting an opinion "on the advisability of setting up pilot projects embodying some of these approaches."[16] HEW rejected the idea outright, calling it "most unfavorable." In defense of the idea, Hutschnecker insisted that it was a "personal suggestion meant for the President, a plan to cut down on crime..."[17] As informal as the idea may have been, there are remarkable comparisons to a 1943 memo from the Gestapo's Crimino-Biological Institute: "The task is to identify as early as possible the criminally inclined person. Those with continual character failures who are fully capable of work will be put into a youth protection camp."[18]

Richard M. Nixon—A patient of German-born psychiatrist Arnold Hutschnecker

The failure of Hutschnecker's proposal did nothing to hurt him. In 1971, he was appointed by President Nixon to be a consultant on a new drug abuse prevention center being established in Washington. From this position, Hutschnecker was able to propose the training of social workers and teachers in certain psychiatric techniques on a national basis without governmental interference, including:

"[R]ole playing, during which children, free from criticism and reassured of no judgmental treatment, could act out their feelings, impulses, thoughts, fears, angers, etc. The basic idea was that not teachers but the children themselves would be the therapists."[19]

Hutschnecker proposed a $3 billion budget for this program, which was to be implemented nationwide within ten years. But again, he failed—the plan was jettisoned after Nixon became implicated in the Watergate scandal and later resigned. Other versions, however, were to follow.

Nixon's final days in the White House were characterized by near-dementia and drug use. In a 1992 article in the *Australian Financial Times*, Benjamin Stein, then a speechwriter for President Nixon, recalls an incident in 1974:

"I walked into the office of the White House physician, next door to the White House. As I asked for some anti-allergy medicine, I noticed a surgical, steel tray laden with filled syringes, their needles dripping. Next to them was a vial of potent chlorpromazine tranquillizer. I knew the corpsman who was loading the tray and I asked him what it was all about. He said it was for someone 'over there,' jerking his thumb toward the White House. He would not tell me who was getting shots of tranquillizer in those final days at the Administration. He said only that it was 'someone who needs to have his head clear and won't.'"[20]

In their book *The Final Days* which chronicles the end of the Nixon presidency, Woodward and Bernstein detail his failing grip on reality, quoting Nixon's son-in-law Edward Cox as saying at one point, "The President was up walking the halls last night, talking to pictures of former Presidents—giving speeches and talking to the pictures on the wall...The President might take his own life."[21]

Despite the fact that they had not "cured" the most powerful man on the planet, but only driven him into a highly hallucinatory and suicidal state, the psychiatric community recommended that the only answer was "more psychiatry." Hutschnecker, in his book *Hope*, shamelessly asserted that:

"...it will be the job of physicians, especially those whose work concentrates on the functioning of the human mind, to develop methods of better prevention of illness (be it physical or mental)... As a result of my past studies about the mental health of political leaders I introduced a new term 'psychopolitics,' that was to widen our psychodynamic studies on the mental health of political leaders."[22]

The term "psychopolitics" may not yet have become a psychiatric catchword, but psychiatry's influence upon our political leaders has not abated.

In 1992 it was widely reported that President George Bush had been taking the prescription drug Halcion, a sleeping pill banned or restricted in eleven countries because possible side effects including confusion, anxiety, hostility, hallucinations, paranoia, seizures, hyperexcitability and dizziness. Former Nixon speechwriter Stein, described it as:

"[T]he most terrifying drug I have ever used.... People who have used heroin tell me Halcion is better for making bad thoughts simply disappear. The flip side is…it does not just do its magic and then disappear. Without it, sleep is almost impossible. I felt depressed and often suicidal for days after taking it and more or less permanently depressed if I took it continuously. It makes the user alternately supremely confident and then panicky with an unnameable dread. It causes intense, truly terrifying forgetfulness as well as a serene bliss about that forgetfulness.…Halcion is serious medicine."[23]

Bush's erratic behavior and fractured, nonsensical statements during the January 1992 campaign in New Hampshire incited much speculation about the effects of the drug on the President. For example, there is the following observation the President made in Dover: "I said to them there's another one that the Nitty Gritty Nitty Gritty Great Bird and it says if you want to see a rainbow you've got to stand a little rain. So don't cry for me, Argentina. We've got problems…and I am blessed by good health."

Syndicated columnist Donald Karl wrote:

"I'm getting a little worried about George Bush. Make that more than a little. He's been acting funny lately."[24]

Gossip columnist Liz Smith wrote:

"Watching the President of the U.S. recently in New Hampshire and…listening to everybody talk about how 'crazy' he has been acting, I found myself wondering: 'Can our Peerless Leader possibly be the victim of unwitting substance abuse?'"

Smith went on to suggest this might be linked to Halcion, "the drug of choice [which] was being taken in epidemic numbers on Air Force One by both an exhausted press and jet-lagged administration insiders."[25]

One of those "administration insiders" was Secretary of State James Baker, who, according to the *Miami Herald*, "sometimes takes Halcion when he is on the road. He jokingly refers to the pills as 'blue bombs,' a reference to the color and potency of the .25 milligram tablet, the largest dose available."[26]

Bush's successor, Bill Clinton, has also been under a psychiatrist's care. In the recent book *Clinton Confidential*, George Carpozi, Jr. reveals that the Clintons saw a University of Arkansas psychotherapist in 1985 in an attempt to save their failing marriage.

In a political climate where even the Head of State is routinely subjected to public (and private) psychiatric diagnosis (and sometimes, as we have seen, treatment), it should come as no surprise that the psychiatric community would attempt, as self-proclaimed experts, to make the final decision as to who is fit to govern and who isn't.

One example of this came in 1983, when the Group for the Advancement of Psychiatry (GAP) recommended that "a panel of qualified physicians, including psychiatrists, should examine top political leaders on an annual basis."[27]

In a 1989 article in *The Washington Post*, these calls were renewed. Julian Lieb and D. Jablow Hershman, co-authors of "The Key to Genius: Manic Depression and the Creative Life," theorize that "mild mania is almost a requirement to meet the physical and emotional demands of our marathon political campaigns." Their solution:

"Psychoanalysis—with its goal of permanent change, usually requiring years of treatment—offers no solution. Fortunately, a new branch of psychiatry, psychopharmacology, is appropriate for both crisis management and the treatment of chronic disorders such as manic depression.

"The psychopharmacologist is the specialist most conversant with the large and growing array of psychoactive medications provided by modern science. These drugs can treat symptoms ranging from confusion, indecision, lethargy and memory lapses to agitation, anxiety, paranoia and suicidal feelings. The White House physician cannot match the seasoned psychopharmacologist's experience with the adminsitration of these medications. To ensure that the president has available the best and most up-to-date care, a psychopharmacologist should be added to the White House staff."[28]

So far, the opposing view is still holding out. In response to this article, syndicated columnist Edwin Yoder, Jr. rebutted:

"The best way to assure sanity in presidents isn't to summon the psychiatrists to watch over them, it is to restore to parties and political professionals the screening function they once exercised."[29]

PSYCHIATRY AND EDUCATION

We have already seen how the early Wundtians and their disciples initially got involved in the American educational system. Figures such as William Welch and Adolf Meyer of Johns Hopkins University, and James Cattell, G. Stanley Hall and John Dewey of Columbia, backed by the

Flexner Report of 1909 were instrumental in ensuring that the psychological approach would dominate education to the exclusion of other approaches.

They were assisted by many others, most notably James Russell, a student of Wundt's who received his doctorate at Leipzig in 1894. For thirty years Russell was the Dean of Columbia University's Teachers College, which would become the largest and most influential training ground for educators in the world.

Another Wundtian making his mark on American education was Edward Lee Thorndike. Thorndike was especially interested in "animal psychology."

"As briefly stated by Thorndike himself, psychology was the science of the intellect, character, and behavior of animals, including man."[30]

After completing his graduate work, Thorndike was hired by Russell to experiment at Teachers College. Applying the "laws" of animal behavior to human children, Thorndike evolved a teaching philosophy, which he imparted to scores of teachers, who then went back to their classrooms all over the United States and implemented the new "educational" psychology.

Thorndike was a Wundtian in every sense of the term. In his 1906 book *The Principles of Teaching Based on Psychology*, Thorndike defined teaching as "the art of giving and withholding stimuli with the result of producing or preventing certain responses."[31] To Thorndike, a stimulus was anything external which might influence a person—a noise, something he sees or feels, even the air he breathes. A response was seen as the person's reaction to the stimulus—an emotion, an act, an opinion, and so forth. In considering the teacher as providing stimuli through which desirable social and behavioral response patterns could be engendered, Thorndike was dangerously close to suggesting the conditioning of schoolchildren by their teachers. His rationale can only be understood if one takes into account his stimulus-response philosophy:

"Education is interested primarily in the general interrelation of man and his environment, in all the changes which make possible a better adjustment of human nature to its surroundings."[32]

In the words of Paolo Lionni, the view of Thorndike and fellow Wundtians like Dewey was that "man is a social animal who must learn to adapt to his environment, instead of learning how to ethically adapt the environment to suit his needs and those of society. Individualism and the developing of individual abilities give way to social conformity and adaptation; the product of education becomes 'well-adjusted' [conditioned] children."[33]

This basic Wundtian philosophy, as flawed as it is, persists to this day, and is prominently on display in today's horrific "Outcome-Based Education," psychiatry's latest contribution to the American educational system.

CYRIL BURT AND THE "IQ" TEST

Underlying these attitudes are, of course, basic eugenical assumptions regarding the inferiority of certain types of individuals.

British psychologist Cyril Burt's father was a physician to the family of Francis Galton, and an ardent admirer of Galton's work. As a boy, Burt is said to have met Galton on several occasions, becoming extremely interested in his observations and theories. After completing his studies at Oxford University where he experimented in the measurement of intelligence, Burt went to Germany to study at Wurzburg, which had succeeded Leipzig as the focal point of German psychological research by the early 1900s.

In 1913, Burt was appointed to the position of "Educational Psychologist" by the London County Council—the first position of its kind in the world ever offered to a psychologist. During this time he turned out a prolific quantity of research on intelligence analyses. Among them was the English translation of the Binet-Simon test (known in the United States as the Stanford-Binet scale) as well as a battery of psychological "attainment tests" to be given to schoolchildren, published in his 1921 book *Mental and Scholastic Tests*. The Stanford-Binet test measured what Burt called the "Intelligence Quotient," or "IQ."

Using mountains of data he collected, Burt attempted to use statistical analyses to assess intelligence and predict future achievement. Underlying these "facts," however, were Burt's deep-seated eugenical beliefs. In his 1935 book *The Subnormal Mind*, he strongly emphasized genetic inheritance as a factor in the differences of intelligence levels between socioeconomic classes. In effect, Burt was trying to confirm Galton's theory that intelligence is controlled by a "general factor" determined by one's genes, combined with so-called "group factors" which were determined by one's environment and social background. In combining these two "factors," Burt created the equivalent of coupling eugenics and Wundtian stimulus-response reaction. This notion was widely embraced, nonetheless, by the psychological/psychiatric community, and persists to this day as the "nature versus nurture" debate.

Burt is also credited with the original idea for the Mensa Society, when he suggested during a 1945 radio broadcast that exceptionally intelligent people should be polled for their opinions on critical issues facing the world. The only criterion for membership in Mensa was that one had to have an IQ rating in the top 2 percent of the population of one's own country.

So far, it appears that the organization has had a decidedly eugenical orientation. In 1962, in the only such poll on record, over 1800 British Mensa members were consulted on what to do about unhealthy dependents. Of them, 47 percent recommended the legalized killing of "sufficiently unhealthy or subnormal infants."[34]

In 1994, Mensa published in its November newsletter articles written by some of its "exceptionally intelligent" members advocating the extermination of the homeless, retarded or elderly. The ensuing controversy resulted in the firing of its editor, proving that the top 2 percent may not be so smart after all.

Unfortunately, eugenical notions still permeate some schools of thought relating to IQs. As long ago as 1924, Burt's IQ test was used as the scientific justification for the U.S. Immigration Act, which succeeded in keeping non-English-speaking immigrants, such as Africans, Asians, Italians and Jews, out of the United States. But it would soon be used in the United States to attempt to justify even more nefarious purposes and prejudices.

In the winter of 1969, the *Harvard Educational Review* published a 123-page treatise by Professor Arthur R. Jensen entitled "How Much Can We Boost IQ and Scholastic Achievement?" Jensen, who had studied at the Institute of Psychiatry in London under the famous German-trained British psychiatrist Aubrey Lewis and had since become the Professor of Educational Psychology at U.C. Berkeley in 1961, was a passionate supporter of the validity of the IQ test and an admirer of Burt and E.L. Thorndike, whom he called "probably America's greatest psychologist."[35]

Basing his conclusions on the disproportionately lower IQ scores among African-Americans, Jensen adopted a firm eugenical stance that came to be known as "Jensenism." In a March 1969 article entitled "Born Dumb?," *Newsweek* summarized his philosophy:

"Dr. Jensen's view, put simply, is that blacks are born with less 'intelligence' than whites. The existing statistical evidence, he says, shows that blacks score some 15 points lower than most whites. The reason, he argues, is that intelligence is an inherited capacity and that since a prime characteristic of races is that they are 'inbred,' blacks are likely to remain lower in intelligence."[36]

Jensen's solutions are equally repugnant:

"Since intelligence is fixed at birth anyway, he claims, it is sensless to waste vast sums of money and resources on such remedial programs as Head Start which assume that a child's intellect is malleable and can be improved ('Compensatory education has been tried and it apparently failed,' he writes.) Instead, programs should concentrate on skills which require a low level of abstract intelligence."[37]

The blame for the failure of a psychiatric school system in an increasingly psychiatric society was being placed squarely on the shoulders of one's own genes. However, Jensen had an even grander vision. Toward the end of his tract, his true eugenical views came out into the open:

"Is there a danger that current welfare policies, unaided by eugenic foresight, could lead to the genetic enslavement of a substantial segment of our population? The possible consequences of our failure seriously to study these questions may well be viewed by future generations as our society's greatest injustice to Negro Americans."[38]

Jensen defended his views in his 1973 book *Educability and Group Difference*, when he theorized:

"The possibility of a biochemical connection between skin pigmentation and intelligence is not totally unlikely in view of the biochemical relation between melanins, which are responsible for pigmentation, and some of the neural transmitter substances in the brain. The skin and the cerebral cortex both arise from the ectoderm in the development of the embryo and share some of the same biological processes."[39]

Jensen's themes were echoed by fellow geneticists, like William Shockley of Yale University and Richard Herrnstein, professor and chairman of the

Harvard psychology department. Herrnstein had been publishing eugenical books and articles since his 1973 work *IQ and the Meritocracy*, in which he recommended that a meritocracy of genetically superior minds should replace the traditional democracy.[40] In 1994, Herrnstein would write an even more controversial book, *The Bell Curve*, in which he and co-author Charles Murray stated that African-Americans do worse than whites in intelligence tests because they are "genetically disabled."[41]

To this day, eugenical researchers continue to make fervent attempts to prove their misguided beliefs. It is quite likely that "brain wave tests" which measure "neural efficiency" will soon replace IQ tests in most American school systems. These tests have their own sets of dangers, for although they do measure the amount of electrical activity in the brain, their own inventor acknowledges that the raising and lowering of this activity can be caused by any number of outside factors:

"Just as deficiencies of certain vitamins and the presence of alcohol, tranquilizing drugs, and anaesthetics in the body systems cause a reduction of mental acuity, they also cause reductions of the neural efficiency measured...."[42]

MODERN AMERICAN "PSYCHO-EDUCATION"

Psychiatry's influence on modern education has not been confined only to analyses of schoolchildren's abilities. It has also covered the teacher's role, the curriculum—indeed, the entire approach to education—with disastrous results.

The basis of this particular push stems from a psychiatric philosophy articulated in 1946 by Dr. G. Brock Chisholm, psychiatrist and founding member of the World Federation for Mental Health:

"The reinterpretation and eventually eradication of the concept of right and wrong which has been the basis of child training...[is] the belated objectiv[e] of practically all effective psychotherapy.... If the race is to be freed from its crippling burden of good and evil it must be the psychiatrists who take the original responsibility."[43]

The plan was to replace academic-based education with mental health-based concepts. This was adopted by the 1950 White House Conference on Education which stated:

"...All schools should move as rapidly as possible toward adequate guidance and counseling services for all individuals at all age levels...."[44] Knowledge of how the child achieves internal security and balance will probably help us reduce mental illness and juvenile delinquency." In 1952, the National Training Laboratory (NTL) became part of the National Education Association (NEA). In 1968, it separated from the NEA but maintained the same purpose: to "change teachers' inflexible patterns of thinking."[45] In an essay in NTL's book *Issues in Human Relations Training*, author David Jenkins said NTL's laboratories emphasized that:

G. Brock Chisholm—Head military psychiatrist in Canada and co-founder of the World Federation for Mental Health

"The trainer has no alternative but to manipulate; his job is to plan and produce behavior in order to create changes in other people."[46]

The process to achieve this was dubbed "Sensitivity Training."

In 1955, the National Institute of Mental Health (NIMH) funded a five-year study on mental health which made recommendations for more psychologists and psychiatrists to be employed in schools. Not coincidentally, NIMH now spends $600 million a year on psychiatric and psychological research, some of which is carried out on children in schools.

The report of this study, "Action for Mental Health," was released in 1961 and said that the school curriculum "should be designed to bend the student to the realities of society, especially by way of vocational education ...the curriculum should be designed to promote mental health as an instrument for social progress and a means of altering culture...."[47]

As for teachers, the same report proposed "to create a new person carefully trained in psychotherapy but without the lengthy basic medical, general clinical, and advanced specialty training."[48]

The stage was set for a new leader in psychiatric education.

CARL ROGERS

Carl Rogers was a student of Dewey's most influential disciple, William Kirt Kilpatrick and truly a product of his time. A professor of psychiatry at the University of Wisconsin, he made a ground-breaking speech at a Harvard University conference, which he later published under the title *On Becoming a Person* in 1961. In it, he stated that "...anything that can be taught to another is relatively inconsequential, and has little or no significance..." and that "...the only learning which significantly influences behavior is self-discov-ered, self-appropriated learn-ing...[which] cannot be directly communicated to another."[49]

Carl Rogers—Educational psychologist who introduced psychological programs into the schools. He later recanted when he observed that these programs were, in fact, destructive.

Rogers concluded that given this, "...the outcomes of teaching are either unimportant or hurtful" and that "...such experience would imply that we would do away with teaching....examinations...grades and cred-its...[and] degrees as a measure of competence."[50]

In essence, Rogers' point was that since the process of learning is self-actualized, the indoctrination of names and dates into the minds of schoolchildren will do little or no good. Instead, teachers should become facilitators of their pupils' realizations about life.

Simply put, Rogers wanted to replace teaching with psychotherapy into the public schools.

The reverberations of this short speech were felt far and wide. The "humanistic" approach to education had never been tried before, and here was psychiatry's perfect opportunity.

In 1968, Rogers attended a symposium on American life in the 21st century called "USA 2000," where he suggested that education in the year 2000 would have five principal characteristics:

• Traditional subject matter would be very minor in importance.

• The emphasis on teaching would be replaced by an emphasis on facilitation.

• The ideal of lifelong learning would be promoted (and therefore students might never be graduated.)

• Exploration of feelings would replace intellectual discussions.

• Students would engage in self-pacing behavior—in other words, teachers would no longer give their students deadlines, encouraging them instead to go at their own pace.

Much of this would later show up in President Clinton's "Goals 2000" legislation, which included "Outcome Based Education."

Rogers (who would go on to become a president of the American Psychological Association) and his collaborator, William Coulson, would write voluminously about this new approach, only to have a change of heart. Rogers would later revise his book *Freedom To Learn*, adding a 25-page section repudiating his program as "a pattern of failure." Ironically, after his death in 1987, Rogers' publisher, Charles E. Merrill, came out with a third edition which eliminated the chapter recanting the thesis.

In 1993 Coulson would also disavow his life's work and take great pains to let the world know of his error.

By then, however, it was too late. The gears behind "Outcome Based Education" had already been set into motion.

"OUTCOME BASED EDUCATION"

The philosophical basis of "Outcome Based Education," or OBE, has been around since Rogers first gave his lecture at Harvard. The curricula and programs are not new—they have been hiding under other names since the 1960s: "Values Clarification," "Mastery Learning," "Higher Order Critical Thinking Skills," "Moral Reasoning," "Citizens and Charter Education," "Family Living," "Sex Education," "Death Education," "Problem-Solving Class," and "Decision-Making" are some of the terms.

OBE's roots lie in several key reports and pieces of legislation.

A year after Rogers spoke at Harvard, NIMH issued another report, "The Role of Schools in Mental Health," a chilling reminder of the psychiatric programs during the Nazi era:

"The school is the one place where all youth congregate and where it is thus feasible to detect, if not treat, [mental] illness. Many informed people, therefore, view the nation's schools as the most suitable place to begin reducing this burden. Their goal is to improve the health of the 'next generation'—children now in school."[51]

The following year, Congress passed and JFK signed into law the 1963 Community Mental Health Centers Act, which demanded that teachers obtain a "knowledge of mental hygiene" to be able to identify their students' "emotional problems" and to get "parents to overcome their fears of seeking help" for their children.[52]

By the 1970s, psychiatry's grip on children was almost proprietary. No longer were teachers facilitators—they were being asked to become the functional equivalent of parents as well. Psychiatrist Chester M. Pierce summed it up in a 1973 speech at a Childhood International Education Seminar:

"Every child in America entering school at the age of 5 is mentally ill because he comes to school with certain allegiances to our founding fathers, toward elected officials, toward his parents, toward a belief in a supernatural being.... It's up to you as teachers to make all these sick children well—by creating an international child of the future."[53]

Read the forgoing quotation again and shudder as you realize that this sort of eugenical thinking was the theoretical foundation of "Outcome Based Education."

OBE is a federal program which gives sizable block grants to states to develop educational programs which require its students to attain certain outcomes before they are allowed to graduate. These outcomes are not academic in nature, but are oriented much more around the changing of behavior, attitudes and feelings. Since a student cannot graduate without having conformed (and thus be effectively shut out of the job market), it would behoove his parents to know just what the government intends him to learn.

The frightening possibilities are elucidated in a keynote speech at the 1989 Governors' Conference on Education by Shirley McCune, the senior director of the government-funded Mid-Continent Regional Educational Laboratory and a passionate supporter of the program, sometimes referred to as the "high priestess of OBE":

"When you walk in the building, there's a row of offices. In one are drug counselors, one is for social security...schools are no longer in the schooling business, but rather in the human resource development…we have an opportunity to develop the kind of society we want."[54]

In effect, what McCune is so ardently espousing is government appropriation of the responsibility for the total social and academic education of youth. In his article "Parents as Teachers, or Teachers as Parents," Christopher Corbett writes:

"As one former U.S. Health Department consultant put it, 'Both parents are [periodically] evaluated…. The child is given a personal computer code number by which he can be tracked for the rest of his life. There are twelve computer code definitions which label a child 'at risk.' Since the expectation is that every child will be found 'mentally ill,' there is no code for normal.'"[55]

The state now becomes the parent—and the parents are relegated to the status of "breeders and supervised custodians."[56]

As a logical consequence, it is the government that assumes the responsibility for the "development of personality":

"The phrase 'development of personality' also has a special meaning in hygienist discourse…. [It] is a shorthand notation for a cluster of systematically related assumptions, attitudes and concepts which includes the following essential elements: personality maladjustments are the cause of individual mental disorder and social problems of all sorts; childhood is the critical period in the development of personality; children are extremely vulnerable to personality disorders; the school is the strategic agency to prevent, detect and 'adjust' problems in the child's personality development; and finally, the personality development of children must take priority over any other educational objective."[57]

Another aspect of OBE is its reliance upon computers as teaching tools. In time, every student in America will be given two computer portfolios from which to work. The first is a "working portfolio," where students store their best work for viewing by the teacher/facilitator. The other is an "electronic portfolio," a vast database containing personal details such as medical records, psychological reports, personal and family information and disciplinary history, which can later be furnished to the federal government, state agencies or prospective employers. Gone are the days when a person can put his best foot forward in a job interview—the government has already created his or her life's resume.

In his book *Understanding the Truth about Education Reform*, former

Oregon state legislator Ron Sunseri quotes some test questions designed to provide data for the electronic portfolios of his state's OBE program (bear in mind that the students taking these tests are high school students):

"• I care what my parents think about the things I do. (Y/N)

• I love my parents. (Y/N)

• When you have sex, how often do you and/or your partner use a birth control method such as birth control pills, a condom (rubber), foam, diaphragm or IUD? (multi-choice).

• I respect my father and mother. (Y/N)

• My parents expect too much of me. (Y/N)

• My family life is happy. (Y/N)

• How many times in the last month have you had a good conversation with one of your parents that lasted ten minutes or more? (multi-choice)

• In the last year, how often, if at all, have you thought about killing yourself? (multi-choice)

• It is against my values to have sex while I am a teenager (multi-choice)

• Children have a duty to obey their parents at all times. (multi-choice)" [58]

Given that OBE's own proponents have a stated desire to "develop the kind of society we want," it would be logical to assume that students giving "unacceptable" answers to these and other questions would be remanded to psychiatric or psychological treatment (as even now they can be, and in many states, without their parents' consent).

The fact that the "values" against which the students' answers are judged are also developed by psychiatrists and psychologists has led Sunseri to call OBE "unabashed brainwashing."

The furor over OBE is far from over. This is a program whose aims and goals are very reminiscent of Thorndike's ideal of teaching: "to produce desirable and prevent undesirable changes in human beings by producing and preventing certain responses." In this case, it is government, not the teacher, which is telling its citizens what and how to think, essentially to "adapt" to a uniform environment. Those who don't cannot receive educational accreditation from the government and are forced to take menial or lower-paying jobs.

Over all of this is a government with access to its citizens' electronic portfolios. Big Brother isn't just watching you—he's teaching you, too.

PSYCHIATRY AND THE U.S. COURT SYSTEM

For years, psychiatry had been trying to get into the courts, but to no avail. In fact, it was in the 1929 Conference on Mental Health sponsored by the National Council on Mental Hygiene and the Tavistock Clinic that the idea was first formally proposed:

"...Children's courts should no longer be courts of criminal jurisdiction, but places, rather, for the diagnosis and prevention of crime...."[59]

The 1954 *Durham* decision changed all that. In his landmark ruling, Judge David Bazelon of the U.S. Court of Appeals in the District of Columbia changed the criteria for the traditional "insanity defense" forever. No longer should the courts be the ones to determine the sanity of the individual, he decided; it was now a "medical question," to be left to the "experts." Bazelon's decision was a logical outcome of the massive psychiatric permeation of society during this time, for he was said to have had some psychoanalysis, and was thus favorably inclined toward psychiatry.*

The effect of his decision was the birth of forensic psychiatry, a new application of psychiatry in courts of law. The insanity defense quickly gained a following among attorneys looking for a way to exonerate otherwise guilty clients. There was no problem finding a psychiatrist with a favorable diagnosis—since insanity as a condition was so poorly defined (if it was at all), opinions were as varied as the experts who made them.

Bazelon himself would soon "become disenchanted with the performance of psychiatrists in the court room under the Durham rule procedures."[60] Eventually he became quite critical of psychiatric labels, believing that they concealed rather than revealed the underlying problem.

In the 40 years since psychiatry first entered the American court system, very little positive has occurred. The lack of results psychiatry has experienced in their attempts to cure the patients remanded to their care is glaring. In 1976, the *Rutgers Law Review* reported:

"Recent studies...have found that for certain serious crimes the arrest rate for ex-mental patients exceeds the rate for the general population...in 1976, Zitrin *et al.* found that the arrest records for rape, aggravated assault, and burglary for a group of discharged mental patients were higher than

---

* For more information on psychiatry's influence on the insanity defense and the U.S. court system from the 1954 *Durham* decision to present day, see *Psychiatry—The Ultimate Betrayal,* by Bruce Wiseman.

those of the general population in their community."[61]

Unlike general medical doctors, who are expected to cure their patients' physical illnesses, psychiatrists have failed in their duty, not only by failing to cure their patients, but by creating repeat offenders. What is especially galling is the claim that what is needed is "more therapy." Per a 1962 report in *The Northwestern Law Review*:

"It is equally fallacious to give the impression that all that is needed is more psychiatrists providing more treatment, implying that therapy invariably gets good results. The hard fact remains that, unlike other medical specialties, psychiatry lacks adequate statistics and follow-ups, because psychiatrists have not seriously attempted to check on their methods and results in the way other medical doctors regard as their scientific duty."[62]

Others like psychiatrist Alfred K. Baur go so far as to state that psychiatrists have no business judging insanity:

"…The term insanity is used synonymously with criminal irresponsibility. The concept of responsibility has its roots in religion, morality and culture. I thoroughly agree with Roche, who states, '…no psychopathology can calibrate moral responsibility, that moral reponsibility is not a measurable objective mental phenomenon but merely a symbol which mediates a group attitude about deviant behavior.'"[63]

Baur goes even further:

"Another major difficulty in the determination of criminal irresponsibility resides in the field of psychiatry itself. Psychiatrists have a similar tendency to give names to concepts and then deal with them as if they were 'things.' This is true of most psychiatric diagnostic categories. Such terms as 'psychosis,' 'psychoneurosis,' and 'sociopath' are essentially indefinable, and if defined, the definitions will not be generally accepted for the simple reason they do not exist."[64]

PSYCHIATRY AND RELIGION

From what we have seen so far in the basic tenets behind the theories of eugenics and mental hygiene, it would at first appear that psychiatry's greatest enemy might be religion.

It has been led by people who believe in eradicating notions of right and wrong. Its leading proponents have been the supposed justification for actual participants in the largest-scale mass murder in recorded history.

After all, psychiatry sprang from people who believed that man had no spirit and was nothing more than a stimulus-response animal. As we have seen, this is certainly true of Wundt, whose experiments in conditioning prefigured the mind control programs that were to follow. This was so much that case that:

"It was the boast of Wundt's [psychology] students, in 1869 [in Leipzig, Germany], when the first psychological laboratory was established that psychology had at last become a science without a soul."[65]

Sigmund Freud was likewise a strong opponent of religion. In his 1928 book *The Future of an Illusion*, he wrote several passages invalidating religion as a legitimate social institution:

"[Religious ideas] which profess to be dogmas, are not the residue of experience or the final result of reflection; they are illusions, fulfillments of the oldest, strongest and most insistent wishes of mankind; the secret of their strength is the strength of these wishes...."

"[A] poor girl may have an illusion that a prince will come and fetch her home. It is possible; some such cases have occurred. That the Messiah will come and found a golden age is much less probable; according to one's personal attitude one will classify this belief as an illusion or as analogous to a delusion.

"Thus religion would be the universal obsessional neurosis of humanity. It, like the child's, originated in the Oedipal Complex, the relation to the father. According to this conception one might prophesy that the abandoning of religion must take place with the fateful inexorability of a process of growth, and that we are just now in the middle of this phase of development."

And finally:

"[T]he true believer is in a high degree protected against the danger of certain neurotic afflictions; by accepting the universal neurosis he is spared the task of forming a personal neurosis."[66]

Given such violent anti-spirituality at the core of its belief system, it is little wonder that a 1986 survey published by *The American Journal of Psychiatry* found that 95 percent of psychologists and the majority of psychiatrists acknowledge they are atheists or agnostics, compared to 90 percent of the general public who do believe in God.[67]

In view of this, we can see why Jesus Christ would be the subject of psychiatric attack from the very beginning. After 1907, when Freud described an obsessive neurosis as a "private religious system and religion as a universal obsessional neurosis,"[68] many other early psychologists jumped on the bandwagon:

In his 1910 book *La Folie de Jesus* (*The Madness of Jesus*), Charles Binet-

Sangle wrote, "In short, the nature of the hallucinations of Jesus, as they are described in the orthodox gospels, permits us to conclude that the founder of the Christian religion was afflicted with religious paranoia."[69]

In 1912, American psychiatrist William Hirsch said about Jesus Christ: "Everything that we know about him conforms so perfectly to the clinical picture of paranoia that it is hardly conceivable that people can even question the accuracy of the diagnosis."[70]

Of course, attacking Jesus Christ has never been a very smart political move. In 1923, in his book *The Dance of Life*, the

J.R. Rees—British military psychiatrist and director of the Tavistock Clinic, and co-founder of the World Federation for Mental Health

famous English psychologist Havelock Ellis tries to have it both ways, by attempting to merge his own eugenical beliefs with Christian doctrine:

"...we are constantly reminded of the profound truth which often lay beneath the parables of Jesus, and they might well form the motto of any treatise on eugenics...He proclaimed symbolically a doctrine of heredity which is only to-day beginning to be formulated: 'Every tree that bringeth not forth good fruit is hewn down and cast into the fire.' There was no compunction at all in his promulagtion of this radical yet necessary doctrine for the destruction of unfit (racial) stocks...."[71]

Ellis understood that the general public would never tolerate an outright assault on their church or their religious beliefs. A new, much more subtle plan had to be drawn up.

The plan was first elucidated in a speech by J.R. Rees, which later appeared as an article entitled "Strategic Planning for Mental Health," which appeared in a psychiatric journal in October 1940:

"If we are to infiltrate the professional and social activities of other people, I think we must imitate the totalitarians and organize some kind of fifth column activity.*

"…We have made a useful attack upon a number of professions. The two easiest of them naturally are the teaching profession and the church: the two most difficult are law and medicine.

"Let us not speak in terms of 'mental hygiene,' but in terms of 'mental health'…Let us all therefore very secretly be fifth columnists."[72]

Rees, we may well recall, began running the Tavistock Clinic in 1934, which trained not only British and American military intelligence in psychiatric techniques, but schoolteachers as well. His colleague, Brock Chisholm, who had called for the "reinterpretation and eventually the eradication of the concept of right and wrong," wrote that this concept deprived the human race of "its natural capacity to enjoy the satisfaction of its natural urges."[73] We can only assume that by this he means "wrong" urges, since there are no religious or moral laws against "right" urges.

It is not surprising, of course, that Chisholm recommends mental hygienists for this "reinterpretation," because: "the fact is that most psychiatrists and psychologists and many other respectable people have escaped from these moral chains and are able to observe and think freely."[74]

Thus:

"Psychiatry must now decide what is to be the immediate future of the human race. No one else can. This is the prime responsibility of psychiatry."[75]

WOLVES IN SHEEP'S CLOTHING

In the coming years, psychiatry would begin to carry out the strategies outlined by Rees and Chisholm.

The first major step was taken in 1946 by another co-founder of WFMH, British psychiatrist Percy Backus. Backus joined forces with Rev. Leslie Weatherhead, a minister trained in psychology, to form the Society

---

* According to the *Oxford Concise Dictionary*, the expression "Fifth Column" means: "organized body sympathizing with and working for the enemy within a country at war, etc."

313

for Medical and Pastoral Psychology. This organization attempted to combine psychiatry with religion, and strongly supported the idea that all ministers should also be trained in psychology in order to detect early signs of mental illness.

Five years later, Weatherhead authored the book *Psychology, Religion and Healing*, which advocated the establishment of clinics where parishioners would be treated both by a minister and a "sympathetic doctor"— meaning a mental hygienist. Such a clinic, which was intended to provide "spiritual, psychological and medical aid,"[76] would also subject its patients to shock treatment, lobotomies and tranquilizers, presumably as adjuncts to a Christian catechism.

An even stronger and certainly more permanent effort was made in 1947, by the Group for the Advancement of Psychiatry (GAP). During a conference in Minneapolis, all 100 members of the group unanimously approved the following press statement in which they attempted to convince their audience that psychiatry and religion were not only related but had similar aims. To any man of the cloth who didn't understand their underlying intentions, these pronouncements might seem very reasonable:

"For centuries, religion and medicine have been closely related. Psychiatry as a branch of medicine has been so closely related to religion that at times the two were almost inseparable. As science developed, however, medicine and religion assumed distinctive roles in society, but they continued to share the common aim of human betterment. This also holds true for that method of psychiatry known as psychoanalysis.

"We, as members of the Group for the Advancement of Psychiatry, believe in the dignity and integrity of the individual. We believe that a major goal of treatment is that progressive attainment of social responsibility. We recognize it as of crucial significance, the influence of the home upon the individual and the importance of ethical training at home. We also recognize the important role religion can play in bringing about an improved emotional and moral state.

"The methods of psychiatry aim to help patients achieve health in their emotional lives so that they may live in harmony with society and with its standards. We believe that there is no conflict between psychiatry and religion. In the practice of his profession, the competent psychiatrist will therefore always be guided by this belief."[77]

In addition to the GAP statement, four prominent Catholic psychiatrists, Edward Strecker (a CIA experimenter), Leo Bartemeier (a military psychiatrist), Frank Curran (a child psychologist and professor) and Frank J. Gerty (a psychiatrist at NIMH), released a joint statement which specifically addressed the relationship between psychiatry and Catholicism:

"We take issue with the recent series of public statements attacking psychiatry attributed to Monsignor Fulton J. Sheen of Catholic University of America, Washington, D.C. These statements have been widely interpreted as charging that the science and practice of psychiatry is irreligious.

"It is a fundamental tenet of the Catholic Church that there can be no conflict between true science and religion. We wish to state our empathetic agreement with this principle.

"Psychiatry is a recognized medical specialty dedicated to the diagnosis and treatment of the mentally and emotionally sick. It occupies the same position in the field of medicine as does surgery or any other specialty concern with the relief and care of human suffering.

"The Catholic Church has sponsored and supported the teaching of psychiatry at the Catholic University of America, at the Church's five medical schools, and in its numerous hospitals. At the present time, a number of Catholic priests who are physicians are being trained in psychiatry with the approval of the Catholic Church."[78]

By the 1950s psychiatry was increasingly usurping a role traditionally served by religion—the counselor. Here, of course, scripture was usurped by the soulless conditioned-reflex attitudes of the psychiatric eugenicists. Even divinity schools, former bastions of religious inspiration and training, added psychology to their curriculum. The first was Fuller Theological Seminary in Pasadena, California in 1950, where its course in "Pastoral Counseling" had as its course description: "...Physical illness; symptoms of nervous and mental need; balanced and unbalanced personalities; findings of contemporary psychiatry and their evaluation in terms of evangelical Christianity...."[79]

That same year, the magazine *Pastoral Psychology* was first published. On its editorial advisory board were such notables as Carl Rogers, Daniel Blain and William Menninger. By 1969, the board had changed to include Robert Felix, the head of NIMH from 1948 to 1964, and Margaret Mead, a prominent and influential anthropologist who studied many of the same subjects as psychologists of her era.

Rees' psychiatric "fifth column" was well on its way to becoming a reality.

In 1954, the Academy of Religion and Mental Health was chartered, with a membership that included clergymen of many diverse faiths along with psychiatrists and psychologists. On its Board of Trustees were such key psychiatrists as Francis Braceland, Daniel Blain, Leo Bartemeier and Frank Fremont-Smith, as well as Mrs. Godfrey S. Rockefeller. Its own statement of purpose said that the organization:

"...would create opportunities for clergymen of all faiths to extend their understanding of the respective roles of religion and medicine in the maintenance, restoration, or increase in the health of individuals and groups. Similarly, it would create opportunities for the psychiatrist and behavioral scientist to increase their understanding of the role of religion in restoring human beings to total health."[80]

The Academy sponsored programs such as conferences on "religion in the developing personality...psychological testing for ministerial selection, [and] healthy and unhealthy religion,"[81] as well as formal "clinical" (i.e., psychological) pastoral training for the clergy. Fellowships and grants to clergymen and seminarians were "awarded with the support of the Smith Kline & French Laboratories,"[82] a large American pharmaceutical company. By 1961, between 8,000 and 9,000 clergymen had taken such courses.

By 1956, divinity school curricula became even more psychologically oriented. Fuller Theological Seminary expanded its Pastoral Theology curriculum to include four new psychologically-based courses: "Practicum in Practical Care," "The Psychology of Behavior Disorders," "Problems in Pastoral Counseling," and "Personality Development and Dynamics." In the same year, NIMH launched a five-year "pilot program" intended to incorporate "behavioral sciences" into the theological programs at Loyola University, Harvard Divinity School and Yeshiva University.

Despite the massive government support, psychiatry was not winning over parishioners. A 1960 report submitted to Congress by the Joint Commission on Mental Illness and Health (which will be covered in depth later) included surveys which showed that of those Americans who sought help for their problems, 42 percent consulted clergymen, 29 percent consulted with physicians in general, and only 18 percent went to psychiatrists or psychologists, with 10 percent going to social agencies and marriage clinics.[83]

Nevertheless, the report arrogantly and falsely argues that clergymen were not a good resource because "few [parishioners] were prepared to be told that they must accept at least a share of the responsibility for their problems and that they must change themselves accordingly. That is why so many chose the clergymen and the physician over the more searching, difficult and prolonged therapy offered by the psychiatrist."[84] Never mind that the church preaches responsibility and expects its parishioners to atone for their wrongdoings, or that the "therapy offered by the psychiatrist" makes no distinction between right and wrong. Difficult and prolonged though it may be, psychotherapy has been unworkable, expensive and in many cases harmful.

Undeterred, mental hygienists redoubled their efforts to displace religion. Hand in hand with their cohorts in government, psychiatrists were shockingly successful in perverting religion's goals.

In May 1965, and with the funding of the CIA (through the Josiah Macy, Jr. Foundation, its cover organization), the Second International Congress on LSD was held in the United States, chaired by Dr. Frank Fremont-Smith, a past president of both the Macy Foundation and the World Federation for Mental Health. American psychiatrist Walter Pahnke presented a paper at this congress called "The Contribution of the Psychology of Religion to the Therapeutic Use of the Psychedelic Substances." Pahnke, who had conducted the "good Friday" LSD experiment with Timothy Leary on ten theology students, concluded that:

"I feel that this area of psychology and religion is an area for serious scientific study, especially with these drugs. I feel that my experiment was only a first step. Who knows what the implications might be just for the one discipline that was mentioned—the training of ministers?"[85]

The assault on religion continued, this time with direct hits on its institutions. In 1967, psychologist William Coulson, working under the auspices of Carl Rogers, introduced humanistic psychology and "nondirective counseling" to some two dozen religious orders. The result of his "research" was the complete destruction of the religious order of the Sisters of the Immaculate Heart of Mary and their 59 schools in less than a year and a half.

In 1993, Coulson, realizing the evil he had caused, recanted his psychiatric philosophy and confessed his sins in a statement to the press:

"We corrupted a whole raft of religious orders on the West Coast in the '60s by getting nuns and priests to talk about their distress....The IHMs (Sisters of the Immaculate Heart of Mary) had some 60 schools when we started; at the end, they had one. There were some 560 nuns when we began. Within a year after our first interventions, 300 of them were petitioning Rome to get out of their vows. They did not want to be under anybody's authority, except the authority of their empirical inner selves.

"We did similar programs for the Jesuits, for the Franciscans, for the Sisters of Providence of Charity, and for the Mercy Sisters. We did dozens of Catholic religious organizations.

"We provoked an epidemic of sexual misconduct among clergy and therapists....

"The net outcome of sex education, styled as Rogerian encountering, is more sexual experience.

"Humanistic psychotherapy, the kind that has virtually taken over the Church in America...dominates so many forms of aberrant education like sex education, and drug education...."[86]

This psychiatric search and destroy mission is only made more heinous by the fact that NIMH had provided the grant for Coulson's research, either oblivious or unconcerned with the constitutional separation of Church and State.

The advent of the community mental health centers (CMHCs) in the 1960s and 1970s further uprooted the clergy from their role as spiritual counselors, forcing them increasingly to be a part of mental health education. Yet psychiatry continued its onslaught. GAP published a report in 1968 which stated: "The contents and psychodynamic influences of religion appear relatively frequently in the manifestation of mental illness."[87]

The following October, Paul Pruyser, a clinical psychologist and Director of the Department of Education at the Menninger Foundation wrote:

"The word soul has lost its meaning and even its plausibility...

"Men and animals...are now more likely to be seen as continuous with each other than as categorically distinct.

"Faith, hope and love can no longer be seen simply as virtues or graces; they are processes in flesh and blood.

"…theological education has greatly felt the impact of the psychological disciplines, particularly psychiatry.

"…referrals for psychiatric evaluation and treatment are being made with increasing frequency from the ranks of the clergy and the religious." [88]

It was in this social climate that the Academy of Religion and Mental Health and the American Foundation of Religion and Psychiatry merged to form the Institutes of Religion and Health (IRH). Their self-described purpose was to be a "non-profit, tax-exempt psychiatric counseling center that prepares clergy and members of other helping professions as pastoral counselors, marriage and family counselors and instructs men and women working in a religious environment in the skills of parish counseling. Techniques of group therapy are taught." [89]

Included in the agenda of a 1977 brochure was a $556,000 grant from NIMH providing seed money for the establishment of ten pastoral counseling centers around the country. Community-based seminars and school programs included such topics as "Schools Without Failure Seminar" and "Death and Dying." The latter program, nicknamed "Death Education" by its critics, was strongly attacked in Congressional Hearings in 1984 for such questionable practices as having children write their own obituaries or deciding which would be their preferred method of dying. Attributed to this program at these hearings was the escalating suicide rate of school-aged children.

In the last twenty years or so, we have seen a greatly expanding role psychiatry has played in religion. The late 1970s brought us the chain of "Christian" Minirth-Meier psychiatric clinics, founded by psychiatrists Paul Meier and Frank Minirth, which from 1977 to 1986 had grown from one clinic to 25 clinics with an increase of staff from 38 to 315.

Other programs which gained steady growth and acceptance during the 1980s were the RAPHA "Christian Counseling Center," opened in St. Mary's Hospital in Galveston, Texas. By 1991, RAPHA operated 32 psychiatric in-patient programs in 17 hospitals.

In 1991, Charter Hospital corporation launched a pilot program in Houston called "Kairos" for in-patient psychiatric hospitalization especially for Christians. Such rapid growth would not have been possible without government help—during the 1980s and early 1990s, many states mandated insurance coverage for mental health.

While much of religion has seemingly opened its arms to psychiatry, the reverse is not true. At the core of its beliefs, psychiatry harbors a deep-seated antipathy for all things spiritual, since it never has acknowledged the existence of a human soul. Any "conversion" on the part of psychiatry, therefore, should be viewed with suspicion.

In a book entitled *Religion May Be Hazardous to Your Health*, psychiatrist Eli S. Chesen wrote:

"Religion is actually a kind of consumer good that is without question potentially harmful to the user's mental health.... I am not espousing atheism or any other religious stance. I am merely setting down a series of conclusions based upon the observations of case histories.... There is a common, close association between religion and psychotic disorders.... There is absolutely no question in my mind that many ultrafundamentalist preachers are themselves suffering from a schizophrenic psychosis."[90]

Of course, the word "schizophrenia" and other such diagnoses were widely used in Germany by the early psychiatrists immediately prior to the rise of the Nazis to power. It has since been used as a "miscellaneous" category which has never been (and, in fact, cannot be) adequately defined. As we have seen, however, the power of certain labels like these to oppress and control people has been handed down from generation to generation of psychiatrists since it was first used in the racial purity programs designed by the men behind Hitler.

Religion is currently under a direct assault by the "mental hygiene" movement, which seeks to label religious conviction as a "psychiatric illness" so that they can then treat it and ultimately eradicate religion altogether.

If you doubt this, read the latest edition of the *Diagnostic and Statistical Manual*, the psychiatric "bible" which categorizes mental disorders. The new edition, which contains more "illnesses" than ever, was published in 1994. Under the category "Other Conditions That May Be a Focus of Clinical Attention" is listed a disorder called "Religious or Spiritual Problem":

"This category can be used when the focus of clinical attention is a religious or spiritual problem. Examples include distressing experiences that involve loss or questioning of faith, problems associated with conversion to a new faith, or questioning of spiritual values that may not necessarily be related to an organized church or religious institution."[91]

For thousands of years, it was the pastor who ministered to the spiritual needs of his parishioners. A cursory glance through the words and deeds of Wundt, Freud, the men behind Hitler and their students, protégés and followers—the "mental hygiene movement," in a word—will quickly demonstrate a committed, long-term desire to destroy religion in the name of "materialistic humanism."

Any religion, therefore, which teaches the existence of God or the immortality of the soul will recognize psychiatry for what it is and realize that any "reconciliation" will come at their peril.

"I swear…to keep according to my ability and my judgment the following Oath:…I will prescribe regimen for the good of my patients according to my ability and my judgment and never do harm to anyone.… If I keep this oath faithfully, may I enjoy my life and practice my art, respected by all men and in all times; but if I swerve from it or violate it, may the reverse be my lot."
Hippocratic Oath

PSYCHIATRY GETS INTO THE MEDICAL PROFESSION

Central to the ideology of the psychiatrists that inspired and supported Hitler before and during the days of the Third Reich was the idea that mental illness was inherited through defective genes, and any cure could only be effected through the elimination of those genes. As we have seen, the end result of this sort of thinking was the sterilization of hundreds of thousands of mentally retarded and handicapped Germans, cruel experimentation on live human prisoners of concentration camps, and the systematic murder of millions of "genetic inferiors."

Needless to say, these practices fell quickly into disfavor after the war. Those who had gotten away with their part in the Holocaust were not about to try it again.

But that didn't mean that their ideology had changed. In fact, it has continued right up to the present day. Hereditary research is anything but a thing of the past.

As mentioned earlier, the term "schizophrenia" was coined in 1908 by the Swiss psychiatrist Eugene Blueler after being inspired by Kraepelin's research into hereditary factors in illness. The first true genetic psychiatrist was Ernst Rüdin, an enthusiastic believer of hereditary schizophrenia who served on the Task Force of Heredity Experts, the panel which drew up the German sterilization law of 1933. The Task Force was headed by Heinrich Himmler, the chief of the Gestapo and later commander of the Nazi concentration camps. Schizophrenia research on twins continued throughout the war, most cruelly and grotesquely in the psychiatric experimentation of Mengele and Hallervorden.

Rüdin's student Franz Kallmann came to the United States in 1937 and continued his research, popularizing schizophrenia as a diagnosis in the English-speaking psychiatric community. Since then, psychiatrists have maintained a fervent interest in schizophrenia research, even though an accurate definition of the term has never been formulated.

It is this elusive definition which puzzles critics of psychiatry such as psychiatrist Thomas Szasz:

"Schizophrenia is defined so vaguely that, in actuality, it is a term often applied to almost any kind of behavior of which the speaker disapproves. It would therefore be as impossible to review the phenomenology of schizophrenia as it would be to review the phenomenology of heresy. It is possible, however, to...show that not only does it not identify any demonstrable disease, it does not even point to any objectively demonstrable referent."[1]

The basic problem, according to Szasz, is that schizophrenia "does not explain what is wrong with the alleged patient, but justifies what 'his' psychiatrist does to him..."[2]

It is for this reason that diagnoses of schizophrenia are decidedly unscientific, depending instead on the bias of the diagnostician:

"Many contemporary psychiatrists recognize, and acknowledge, that the referent to which the term 'schizophrenia' points is uncertain and variable...It is not possible to validate a diagnosis of schizophrenia. There is no test which can independently confirm that the individual so designated is, in fact, schizophrenic."[3]

Because there is no current scientific or even particularly workable definition of schizophrenia, there is no evidence that such a phenomenon exists in and of itself. Diagnoses can be as varied as the people who give them. Standard scientific experimental control mechanisms that eliminate bias (such as so-called "single blinds" and "double blinds") have been nonexistent in schizophrenia research, and therefore there is no uniformity in diagnosis or application. Simply put, the term schizophrenia can be applied to just about anybody behaving "abnormally," since the term itself has never been defined. Worse, the inscrutable, almost mystical quality of the word confers a great deal of power upon those who are in a position to diagnose it.

In summary, Dr. Szasz writes:

"It is, in my opinion, simply pointless to continue to treat the term as if it were the name of a disease whose biological character is exactly like that of any other "organic" disease. Nevertheless, according to the official—medical, psychiatric, legal, scientific—view, the proposition that schizophrenia is a disease is now a foregone conclusion."[4]

As more or less a catch-all phrase, schizophrenia is the most popular diagnosis by psychiatrists today. A study of the history of schizophrenia research in the United States after its introduction from Germany yields some interesting parallels.

The first major research center for schizophrenia in the United States was installed at the Washington University School of Psychiatry in St. Louis in the 1940s, under Dr. Edwin Gildea:

"…This department was distinguished by its insistence on treating mental disorders as brain diseases—then an innovative idea. Gildea encouraged biochemical and pharmacological studies of the brain when Freudian theory reigned supreme and was seldom questioned in American psychiatry."[5]

Eli Robins succeeded Gildea in 1963. By that time, the psychiatry department had added a "family studies" section which sifted through family histories in an attempt to discover evidence of the transmission of specific psychiatric disorders. One of its researchers was Samuel Guze, a well-known psychiatrist and professor at Washington University, who considered such evidence proof of "a valid clinical entity."[6]

Believing that "genetics is a factor in every recurrent or chronic form of mental illness,"[7] Guze, along with Robins and George Winokur, tried to apply a scientific approach to mental illness through biochemistry, pharmacology and long-term genealogical studies. By 1970, mainstream psychiatric research had shifted to biological psychiatry, even though Guze would admit in a 1988 lecture at London's Maudsley Hospital:

"There is no such thing as a psychiatry that is too biological…I say this even though I believe that we know still too little about the physiology of the brain in most psychiatry conditions."[8]

A breakthrough (at least from a public relations point of view) on schizophrenia research occurred in 1972 when the University of Minnesota published the famous Gottesman-Shields Twin Study. Written by psychiatric researchers Irving Gottesman and James Shields, the book *Schizophrenia and Genetics: A Twin Study Vantage Point* offered what it considered definitive proof that schizophrenia is a real disease that is genetically transmitted. The authors acknowledge a debt to Ernst Rüdin for his 1916 schizophrenia study. Their bibliography lists a number of other Nazi-era psychiatrists and researchers such as Edith Zerbin-Rüdin (Ernst's daughter), Manfred Bleuler, Franz Kallmann, Eugen Kahn and Hans Luxenberger. The Nazi eugenical journal "Archiv für Rassen- und Gesellschaftsbiologie" ("Archive for Racial and Social Biology") is also blatantly cited.

It is also no coincidence that the University of Minnesota is connected with a publication of this study. The University's Dight Institute is one of the top research labs in human genetics in the country. Its founder, Charles Dight, was one of America's most energetic Nazi ideologists in the 1920s and 1930s. In a letter to the editor of the *Journal* (New Ulm, MN) in July 1933, Dight wrote:

"The report consistently comes from Berlin that congenital feeble-mindedness, insanity, epilepsy, and some other serious conditions that are inheritable are to be stamped out among the German people. Adolf Hitler is having broad and scientific plans formed for this. If carried out effectively, it will make him the leader in the greatest national movement for human betterment the world has ever seen. The world's two great needs are cooperation in industry for social good and biological race betterment through eugenics."[9]

Later that summer, an inspired Dight wrote a personal letter to Hitler on Minnesota Eugenics Society stationary:

"Chancellor Adolf Hitler

Berlin, Germany

Honorable Chancellor:

I inclose (sic) a clipping from the *Minneapolis Journal* of Minnesota, United States of America, relating to, and praising your plan to stamp out mental inferiority among the German people.

I trust you will accept my sincere wish that your efforst (sic) along that line will be a great success and will advance the eugenics movement in other nations as well as in Germany.

Sincerely,

C. F. Dight, M.D.

President Minnesota Eugenics Society"[10]

In 1938, the University of Minnesota Board Of Regents accepted the terms of Dight's will, in which he donated $150,000 to be used to establish a center "...for the rating of people, 1st, as to the efficiency of their bodily structure, 2nd, as to their mentality, 3rd, as to their fitness to marry and reproduce."[11]

The result was the Dight Institute, which worked with the University's psychiatry and psychology departments to become America's and perhaps the world's leading eugenics research organization. It was the Dight Institute that received (and still holds) all of the eugenics records of Charles Davenport's Eugenics Record Office: hereditary data, eugenical sterilization legislation and litigation and all actual eugenical sterilization operations. Today the Institute is devoted to "the study of genetically-linked behavior disorders and disease,..."[12] unmistakedly a different phrasing of the same old eugenics strategy.

Despite the lack of evidence that "schizophrenia" even exists as a separate and distinct disease, the claims of the Gottesman-Shields Twin Study legitimized its further study and diagnosis. It also legitimized further funding from official sources.

One of these sources is The National Alliance for Research on Schizophrenia and Depression (NARSAD), a tax-exempt alliance of private individuals, researchers and drug companies that funds psychiatric research and activities, much of which involves the corporately financed development of new psychiatric drugs. Some of the members of NARSAD's advisory board are Julius Axelrod of NIMH, Herbert Pardes (a Columbia University psychiatrist and former president of the American Psychiatric Association), Frederick Goodwin (former head of NIMH), Eli Robins and Samuel Guze of Washington University, Nina Schooler (a member of the FDA drug advisory committee) and Jack Barchas and Daniel X. Freedman, UCLA psychiatrists and colleagues of Jolly West.

In 1990, one of their researchers, Philip S. Holzman, wrote an article in the NARSAD Research Newsletter called "The Genetics of Schizo-phrenia," in which he asserted:

"Hardly any responsible scientist today disputes that schizophrenia is a genetic disorder. Scientists do, however, dispute how much influence genes exert, how the disease is transmitted, and whether we can now locate the gene. Systematic genetic studies of schizophrenia have been carried out for over 80 years, but a radical shift in the direction of those studies now promises answers to those unresolved questions."[13]

Is there any hope that they might come up with a cure within the next eighty years? Not likely, as schizophrenia has never even been proven to exist as a disease. Nor have Wundtian theories, based as they are on the premise that man is an animal composed of a body, a brain and a nervous system, ever been proven to cure mental illness, a hard fact purchased at the cost of a few million brain cells in countless patients.

This "radical shift" promises a continuation of the same sort of research that has been followed for the past eighty years, for which millions of tax dollars will be spent in the vain hope that an answer can be found. But searching for a cure for schizophrenia is like tilting at windmills, a fruit-less fight against an imaginary foe.

PSYCHIATRY AND DRUG ABUSE TREATMENT

Another quite separate sphere of medicine indulged in by psychiatrists is the treatment of drug abuse, opiates in particular.

Opiates are a class of drugs producing sleep, sluggishness or stupor which includes morphine, codeine, heroin and perhaps its most misunder-stood member, methadone. Currently methadone is used in the treatment of heroin addicts, but its history goes back a long way.

For more than a century, physicians have been trying to cure drug addiction by substituting other, less "harmful" drugs. More often than not, this has not only failed miserably, but led to a new, even worse addiction causing further personal and societal decline.

The daisy chain begins in the late 1800s, when morphine was pre-scribed as a solution to alcohol abuse. In 1889, the *Cincinnati Lancet-Clinic* editorialized:

"Is it not the duty of physician when he cannot cure an ill, when there is no reasonable ground for hope that it will ever be done, to do the next best thing—advise a course of treatment that will diminish to an immense extent great evils otherwise irremediable?... The use of morphine in the place of alcohol is but a choice of evils, and by far the lesser."[14]

By the turn of the century, physicians were quickly realizing that morphine carried with it an immense addictive power of its own—far worse than alcohol. And so, a suitable replacement for morphine had to be found.

In the summer of 1901, Dr. Maurice B. Ahlborn wrote an article in the *New York Medical Journal* advocating morphine's successor:

"Heroin will take the place of morphine without its disagreeable qualities. There seems to be no craving for the heroin awakened by its continual use, as the subsequent gradual withdrawal after its substitution has been attended with no particular craving."[15]

Results, of course, proved otherwise. Heroin is highly addictive, and the solution seemed to be yet another substitute drug. That drug was methadone.

Methadone was developed during World War II by the German chemical company I.G. Farben as a synthetic painkiller, the same I.G. Farben that used Jewish slave labor to produce lethal gas for concentration camp prisoners.

After the war, American pharmaceutical companies became interested. According to the testimony of Dr. Michael Smith, the head of the Lincoln Detox Program in South Bronx, New York before the National Hearings on the Heroin Epidemic in 1976:

"Immediately after World War II in Europe, [an Eli Lilly & Co.] research chemist named Dr. Ervin C. Kleiderer joined the Technical Industrial Intelligence Committee of the State Department, which was investigating Nazi drug companies. Kleiderer's team brought methadone to this country. Two years later, Lilly marketed Dolophine cough medicine, retaining the Nazi brand name for methadone, which had been chosen to honor Adolf Hitler."[16]

In 1947, researchers at the Drug Addiction Committee of the National Research Council found that there was "absolutely no doubt that methadone is a dangerous and addicting drug."[17]

A year later, anesthesiologist Henry Knowles Beecher of Massachusetts General Hospital completed a three-year study funded by the Army, concluding that "milligram for milligram, these substances are the exact equivalent of morphine, both in pain-relieving power and in bad side effects.".[18] Beecher's subsequent experiments in the use of methadone in Army hospitals as a cheap substitute during heroin withdrawal resulted in approval of the Office of the Surgeon General in 1951.

In 1963, the husband and wife team of Dr. Vincent Dole, an internist, and Dr. Marie Nyswander, a psychiatrist, began a study to see if large doses of methadone could be effective in reducing a craving for heroin. Their method differed widely from earlier research in that they were prescribing 80 to 120 milligrams per day, four to five times the dosage used earlier. Taken in such high doses, methadone creates such a high level of tolerance to heroin that it would be prohibitively expensive for an addict to achieve a heroin "high." On the other hand, methadone supposedly gives its user a feeling of well-being and clear mind without causing him to become "strung out."

The only problem with all of this is that methadone is itself highly addictive. If a drug user stops using it, the craving for heroin quickly returns. Typically, heroin addicts receive methadone in gradually increasing doses, up to 100 to 120 milligrams per dose. A single dose is cheap—about ten cents (the medication was nicknamed "orange handcuffs" because it could be taken orally in an orange-flavored liquid). Methadone patients, as they are euphemistically known, are also required in many states to undergo psychological counseling during the years of their withdrawal from heroin. This counseling and treatment is recognized as an approved medical expense by G.I. insurance and many state medical insurance plans.

This adds up to an enormous cash cow for psychiatrists and the pharmaceutical companies—without freeing a single addict.

Dole and Nyswander admitted their less than spectacular results in 1976, after more than ten years of the most heavily funded government drug program in U.S. history:

"The projections of ten years ago were overly optimistic...The great majority of heroin addicts remain on the streets and the programs have lost their ability to attract them to treatment."[19]

In 1979, Michael Smith added that methadone was five times as deadly as morphine and that:

"Withdrawal from Methadone addiction is a long, drawn-out, brutal experience....There is not a two-to-five day crisis of vomiting and tremors as with heroin....(Methadone withdrawal symptoms) occur for weeks and usually months on end." [20]

This is corroborated by an anonymous former methadone addict in a letter to the editor of the *Newport (R.I.) Mercury*:

"After eight months of methadone, I finally demanded a 28-day detox. I knew somehow there was another way. Toward the end of the detox, I was extremely ill and ended up on the eighth floor of the Newport Hospital for three weeks with acute anxiety..." [21]

Adding that for her "the effect of another drug is enhanced while on methadone," she continues:

"Life on methadone is a half life at best—you are constantly drugged and in the ozone. The pupils are constantly dilated and the addicts look high. I didn't even feel alive.

"I feel that methadone only prolonged my dependency. The counseling that my husband and I went to at the clinic lasted for one hour each week. We read *High Times* with the therapist." [22]

The effectiveness of methadone clinics to get patients off of heroin has never been questioned. However, its effectiveness to render them drug-free is practically nonexistent. In a 1987 interview, the director of a methadone program in Columbus, Ohio, Ron Pogue, admitted:

"How many people walk away from our program and never pick up drugs again? Less than one percent. I know a couple of people who have been gone from this program for eight years and have never been back to this program. If you were to ask me, 'Do I know they have never used drugs since they left here?', I doubt that.

"They've been able to manage their lives in a responsible enough fashion so that they were not forced to come back into this treatment program.

"That, for us, is a cure. We don't get a lot of those." [23]

Not only is there no evidence to suggest that methadone addicts ever get off methadone, but the National Institute on Drug Abuse, in a paper studying 1,544 cases from the National Drug/Alcohol Collaborative Project, found that:

"Regular users of illegal methadone appear the most involved with other drugs in that some 91.3 percent are also regular users of heroin; more than half are also regular users of cocaine, alcohol, and marijuana; and more than 40 percent are also regular users of other opiates and barbituates."[24]

The study goes on to identify illegal methadone users as most likely (55 percent) to commit crimes to feed their habit. Like heroin and morphine before it, methadone is now a highly addictive black market street drug.

According to the *International Journal of Pharmacology* in 1975:

"It must not be forgotten that methadone is a powerful narcotic analgesic (slightly more powerful than heroin) with an addiction liability all its own.... In fact, some addicts readily admit that they prefer methadone as their drug of abuse."[25]

Stephen Langer, the medical director of California's Contra Costa County's drug abuse program agrees:

"Keeping people on long-term methadone...is totally bankrupt in the long run. It's a way to sweep the problem under the carpet; it is in no way going to curb the desire for drugs. We had people who were taking methadone and shooting heroin at the same time."[26]

Worse, the effects of years of methadone use and abuse eventually exact a physical toll on its takers. Joan Matthews-Larson, M.D., founder and executive director of the Minnesota-based Health Recovery Center, talked about her personal observations of methadone programs:

"But after seeing it up close, it isn't the end at all. They're on another drug; their nervous system and the damage that's been done from their drug addiction are still causing them a lot of misery. They're not stable; there's been no repair at all."[27]

Currently, another link in the chain is being forged, as a drug substitute for methadone (as well as for heroin and cocaine): Ibogaine.

Iboga is a West African plant which was used in religious rituals dating back to 1864. In 1901, two pairs of European scientists isolated ibogaine, iboga's principal alkaloid (a nitrogen-based component of a vegetable usually used as a drug, e.g., quinine, morphine or strychnine).

The first experimentation with ibogaine in the United States was performed in 1955 by MKULTRA psychiatrist Dr. Harris Isbell of the Addiction Research Center of the U.S. Public Health Service Hospital in Lexington, Kentucky. As part of his secret CIA-funded drug experiments, Isbell gave ibogaine to eight former morphine addicts to compare its hallucinogenic effects with those of LSD.

By the 1960s, ibogaine had slipped out onto the streets of San Francisco and New York and had become very popular, forcing the federal government in 1967 to classify it as a Schedule 1 drug, meaning an illegal drug with no medicinal value and a high potential for abuse. That is a distinction ibogaine shares with LSD, for example.

According to its supporters, however, ibogaine completely halts any craving for heroin, methadone and cocaine without any of the common withdrawal symptoms such as shakes, chills, depression or diarrhea. The only problem, they say, is that it puts its users on a 25-hour drug trip.

But there are many other problems.

Even ibogaine's advocates admit that the drug may not work for everyone nor may its benefits be permanent. "Backslides" are not uncommon, and ibogaine users may be required to take another dose every three to six months.

Nor, according to psychiatrists themselves, has ibogaine ever been adequately tested. Dr. Herbert Kleber, a Yale psychiatry professor who later became President George Bush's deputy drug czar, complained that "There are no double-blind controlled studies that say it works in humans."[28]

The most major objection to ibogaine is that it causes brain damage. In September 1993, the *Orlando Sentinel* reported that:

"At the Johns Hopkins School of Medicine, two scientists have found evidence that ibogaine causes physical changes in the brain that interrupt the cycle of addiction.

"After giving rats high doses of ibogaine, Dr. Mark Molliver and Dr. Elizabeth O'Hearn analyzed the animals' brains. They found dead cells in a portion of the cerebellum that ordinarily controls repetitive tasks."

From there, the article takes a decidedly Wundt-inspired psychiatric spin:

"One theory is that the same brain cells that control repetitive tasks also control obsessive-compulsive behavior—the mental disorder that can send someone into endless handwashing or eyebrow-plucking. If this is true, the drug might sever pathways into the brain that keeps addicts reaching for their needles.

"'We don't like brain damage—we need every nerve cell we've got,' Molliver said, 'But we have to wonder: Could you compensate? And maybe the [cell] degeneration we're seeing is responsible for the anti-addictive effect of ibogaine.'"[29]

In his statement, Molliver basically throws up his hands and admits that he has no solution short of the destruction of brain cells—not a solution at all. In true psychiatric fashion, a destructive act—the intentional disabling of a part of the brain of a human being—is endorsed as a "solution" to an existing problem. This, of course, will yield new problems in time, but to Wundtians, positive solutions are unobtainable, just as they were during the Third Reich when "life unworthy of living" was sterilized or exterminated.

The fact remains that ibogaine is a dangerous drug. According to Carlo Contoreggi, medical officer of the Addiction Research Center in Baltimore:

"Ibogaine is this weird, complex alkaloid...with all sorts of different facets, and all these facets have very potent chemical actions—not only in the brain, but in the heart, the blood vessels, the liver. We don't know how it works, we don't know if it does work."[30]

Currently ibogaine is legal only in the Netherlands, where treatment is overseen by a psychiatrist. In August of 1993, the U.S. Federal Drug Administration approved the first ibogaine experimentation on humans, to be conducted at the University of Miami. It is an interesting commentary on the research team when one of them, pharmacologist Deborah Mash, also seems to have given up on anything other than a chemical "solution":

"Addiction in our society is not going to go away....We need a magic bullet. Is ibogaine the magic bullet? I don't know, but it's something that should be looked into."[31]

Yet research continues, with such possibilities as LAAM, a type of longer-lasting methadone, and an ibogaine analogue that would eliminate its hallucinatory effects. The theory behind these drugs, however, remains the same as in the theories underlying electroshock and brain surgery: "Cures" can only be accomplished by the use of methods that destroy brain cells and reprogram brain function.

The lead researcher of the University of Miami's ibogaine experiment, Juan Sanchez-Ramos, admitted this in a 1993 interview with the *San Diego Union-Tribune*:

"Some people don't understand a therapy that would use a drug to eliminate a drug dependence, but it's the same approach used in depression, treating a chemical imbalance with anti-depressants."[32]

Never mind that no one knows how the brain as an organ functions, or that chemical imbalances have never been proven to exist. And never mind that there are indeed very damaging long-term side effects of psychotropic drugs. With the current psychiatric influence within the medical community, drug addiction treatment, as well as mental health care in general, will continue to be driven down this road, an endless concatenation of problems and pseudo-solutions. Not that this doesn't benefit the psychiatric community—as long as there are no permanent solutions, the dollars will keep rolling in, and in ever-increasing amounts.

THE CREATION OF NIMH, PSYCHIATRY'S JUGGERNAUT

Perhaps the chief reason behind the failure of modern society to find solutions to drug addiction and mental illness and its chasing of such psychiatric butterflies as "schizophrenia" lies in the entrenched psychiatric viewpoint in this country. Psychiatry did not catch on because it was effective or popular with the general public. It caught on because of certain wealthy backers (as in education, with the Rockefeller and Carnegie Foundations) and by passing favorable legislation.

The first major piece of legislation occurred in 1929, when the U.S. Congress established a Narcotics Division within the Public Health Service, specifically to treat drug addiction. By 1930, the name of this division was changed to the Division of Mental Hygiene. In its ensuing years, it was headed by psychiatrist Lawrence C. Kolb, who maintained a quiet but determined lobby with Congress to get this agency into the mainstream.

In 1940, Kolb attempted to establish a federally funded National Neuropsychiatric Institute under the U.S. Public Health Service which would conduct basic psychological research into mental disorders and provide support to other more specific psychiatric study. Although the onset of the Second World War scuttled these plans, Kolb was appointed to an even more important position, Commander in the Medical Corps of the Navy Reserves, a post he held from 1941 to 1946 (Kolb would also go on to serve as president of the American Psychiatric Association from 1968 to 1969).

As in the case of the men behind Hitler, in 1944, the Second World War, with its steady influx of "shell-shocked" soldiers returning stateside, presented Kolb's successor, Robert Felix, with a unique opportunity to expand his influence. William Menninger, then chief of Army neuropsychiatry, called for federal action to resolve the shortage of "professional mental health personnel" to handle this problem. (Felix, by the way, had served as a psychiatrist at the Addiction Research Center prior to his appointment, the same facility Isbell would later lead during his LSD research for the CIA).

"World War II proved the critical catalyst for change. The thrust toward medical specialization accelerated; new structural relations were forged

Robert Felix—First director of the National Institute of Mental Health (NIMH) and a key lobbyist for the psychiatric industry, shown demonstrating the organizational and financial lines of NIMH.

among the agencies of the federal government, physicians and medical institutions; federal funding for research increased; and the role of the Public Health Service expanded dramatically."[33]

Felix envisioned a network of outpatient community clinics that would replace the state hospitals in both preventive and therapeutic services for the mentally ill. In other words, the federal government was now going to take over the states' traditional roles in providing care and treatment for the mentally ill, a broad stroke that would eliminate a system that was not working all that poorly and replace it with a uniform, national system. Felix wanted to ensure that "…the national government—precisely because of its dominant position in the political system and access to seemingly inexhaustible resources—would have a significant voice in the formulation and implementation of policy."[34]

To that end he conceived of what would be known as the National Mental Health Act of 1946:

"He not only wrote the legislation; he also orchestrated its movement through both houses of Congress. One of the shrewdest and most effective federal bureaucrats of his generation, Felix...redefined mental disorders in public health terms."[35]

This legislation was so radical that not even the American Psychiatric Association had thought to lobby for anything like it. The Act had three separate goals:

"...first, to provide federal support for research relating to the cause, diagnosis and treatment of psychiatric disorders, second, to train mental health personnel by providing federal fellowships and institutional grants, and third, to award federal grants to the states to assist in establishing clinics and treatment centers and to fund demonstration studies dealing with prevention, diagnosis and treatment."[36]

Part of this legislation also included the establishment of the National Institute of Mental Health (NIMH), which Felix convinced the Surgeon General to place within the National Institutes of Health, positioning it alongside such mainstream research agencies as the National Cancer Institute. NIMH replaced the Division of Mental Health and Robert Felix was appointed its head, a job he would hold for the next fifteen years.

The establishment of NIMH and its positioning within the National Institutes of Health had a tremendous impact on forwarding the goals of psychiatry:

"Its officials would have the capacity to speak to a national constituency—a power that transcended the divergent interests of 48 states. As the federal agency most directly involved with mental health, the NIMH could frame a national agenda and employ fiscal resources that were not committed to any institutional system. Its identification with medical science and psychiatry only enhanced the authority of its staff. Close ties with congressional leaders of both parties, moreover, permitted NIMH officials to provide the data that would ultimately reshape policy. In short, the very existence of the agency gave individuals both within and without the federal government a powerful instrument with which to promote innovation."[37]

Thanks to the lobbying of Felix—with able assistance from his fellow government psychiatrists Daniel Blain, Francis Braceland and Jack

Ewalt—government funding of NIMH grew from $300,000 to $50 million in 1959, and by 1964 it had ballooned to $89 million.

Besides the enormous changes caused by its energetic introduction and promotion of psychiatry into society and society's resultant changes (which will be explored in depth in the next chapter), NIMH has been very active in backing studies and programs which follow psychiatric principles. Examples of this include:

1956: A $12 million appropriation from Congress for the establishment of the Psychopharmacology Research Center for research into the clinical and basic aspects of psychopharmacology.

1966: The establishment of another sub-section to handle alcohol abuse, the National Center for Prevention and Control of Alcoholism. By 1970, it attained the status of "division", and eventually became an "institute" in 1970 (The National Institute of Alcohol Abuse and Alcoholism)

1966: Also established was the Center for Studies of Narcotic and Drug Abuse. It would also become a division in 1968, and an institute in 1972.

1970: The FDA approves the use of lithium as an "anti-manic," based upon NIMH research.

1978: Dr. Solomon Snyder, an NIMH grantee, wins the Albert Lasker Award in Basic Medical Research for "…identifying the opiate receptors, and the demonstration of their relation to the enkephalins, natural chemicals released by the brain which have the effect of relieving pain and influencing emotional behavior."[38]

1980: The Epidemiologic Catchment Area (ECA), a massive five-year, 20,000-person study to get an "accurate picture of rates of mental and addictive disorders" is launched.

1989: "Congress passed a resolution and President Bush signed a proclamation establishing the 1990s as the "Decade of the Brain." NIMH continued its strong emphasis on its research into the basic functions of the brain and their relationship to mental illness."[39]

It is sad to note that the hundreds of millions of dollars of research have not resulted in a society with decreases in the rates of alcohol and drug abuse and an increase in sanity. That was, after all, the mission of NIMH. And yet, as a result of almost fifty years' work, the rates of alcoholism, drug abuse, insanity and suicide continue to skyrocket. The history of NIMH is a history of abject failure.

Evidence of underlying medical illness and a lack of proof of any such syndrome as schizophrenia have hardly deterred the psychiatrists and researchers inspired by the early eugenicists. Currently the National Institutes of Health and the U.S. Department of Energy are financing what is known as the Human Genome Project, a coordinated effort which is touted as the genetic equivalent to the Manhattan Project or the Apollo moon landing.

The goal of this project is enormous: the "mapping" out of all of the estimated 50,000 to 100,000 human genes (i.e., finding their location on the human chromosome), and sequencing the approximately 3 billion DNA base pairs that make up the human genome.* As an illustration of the magnitude of this work, three billion letters end to end would fill a million-page book. The work on this project, which is employing more than 2000 scientists at a total cost of $3 billion,[40] is estimated to be completed by September 20, 2005. Ironically, the first three annual meetings on genome mapping took place in Cold Spring Harbor, New York, the site of Davenport's Eugenics Record Office.

Its proponents hope that by creating a genetic "map," birth defects or diseases such as diabetes, sickle cell anemia and Huntington's or Alzheimer's Disease can be predicted, thus enabling doctors to perform pre-emptive treatment. While this might be fine medically, psychiatrists are already licking their chops. Psychiatrist Nancy C. Andreason writes:

"Molecular genetics and molecular biology offer the second major advance in modern scientific psychiatry by exploring the way in which abnormalities in genes can cause mental illness.... Most mental illnesses, including depression, anxiety, schizophrenia, alcoholism, and even criminality, run in families. Scientific studies, using techniques such as evaluating twins, have confirmed that many of these problems also have a genetic component."[41]

There is every reason to fear the Human Genome Project will be misused. Joe E. Smith, director of Pharmacy at Thomas Jefferson University Hospital in Philadelphia writes:

"As our ability to detect propensities toward illness increases, so too does the ability to discriminate. Genetic testing may become widespread in schools and the workplace—where it is already being used in limited ways.

---

* The word "genome" refers to the total genetic endowment of the chromosomes of a human cell.

One day schools, employers, the government, and insurers might be able to obtain a complete genetic profile from the blood drawn from a finger during a regular physical examination. This profile might include an individual's susceptibility to…manic depression and schizophrenia…such information presents the same potential for stigmatization and exclusion that genetic disease itself does." [42]

Looked at in historical perspective, the Human Genome Project is yet another classic attempt at eugenics. All of its potential benefits aside, it must be regarded with a clear eye and an acute sense of wariness, especially when embraced by those who claim to specialize in the workings of the human mind. Unless guarded against, history can and does repeat itself, as we shall see in the next chapter on the "ethnic cleansing" carried out in Bosnia.

Paramount is a respect for individual human rights, even those of the mentally ill. University of South Carolina Professor J. David Smith writes:

"…even when the 'felt necessities of our times' seem to urge so compellingly for society to act quickly and efficiently, this must be true. The ethical foundations of human life are to be found in human sources. The eugenicists looked to evolutionary theory and Mendelian genetics for moral truths. They felt that natural selection and Mendelian gene distributions could provide models for social ethics. The failure of this approach was evidenced in the needless institutionalization of those deemed to be 'unfit' for the social 'struggle,' in the sterilization of people inaccurately assessed to be the carriers of defective genes, and in the moral horrors of the Holocaust." [43]

Given this, what basis do we have for trusting the "doctors of the soul?" Their past record does not inspire confidence. Nor is there any evidence that this is about to change. In over 100 years of trying to treat psychiatric illness, very few advances have been made, save in techniques designed to relieve the symptoms by destroying a part of the brain.

And they freely admit it, too. In April 1995, the head of the National Institute of Mental Health, Rex Cowdry, admitted in hearings before a Congressional subcommittee of the Committee on Appropriations:

"We do not know the causes. We don't have methods of 'curing' these illnesses yet. All we have are ways to reduce symptoms in a majority of individuals with these illnesses." [44]

Are these the people we should be trusting with our genes?

"We do not know the causes. We don't have methods of 'curing' these illnesses yet. All we have are ways to reduce symptoms in a majority of individuals with these illnesses."

Rex Cowdry, Acting Director
of NIMH, April 1995

LIFE IN THE MODERN AMERICAN "AGE OF PSYCHIATRY"

Day-to-day life in the United States is becoming increasingly dangerous and difficult. Taxes are high, corruption abounds, drugs proliferate, crime is rampant and our moral institutions are decaying. Despite increased police presence, we seem to be turning into a criminal society.

Never before has there been a greater psychiatric influence on society, either. A coincidence?

We know this much for sure: psychiatric programs have been completely unable to do anything about these recent trends. Proponents of psychiatry argue that this is ample reason for an increase in psychiatric programs, since psychiatry simply can't keep up with the insanity rate of present-day society. However, as we shall see, there is a direct correlation between psychiatry and rapid increases in drug abuse, crime, suicide and illiteracy.

Psychiatry is intimately linked to the decline of the quality of life in our society, and, indeed, the world.

NIMH AND THE COMMUNITY MENTAL HEALTH CENTERS

In the preceding chapter, we saw the birth of NIMH under Robert Felix, and its subsequent growth as a major funding source for psychiatric studies and programs. Research, however, was not NIMH's only activity—Felix also envisioned psychiatry assuming an integral part in the daily life of every American.

In 1953, Kenneth Appel, a psychiatrist at the University of Pennsylvania and president of the APA, first raised the idea of creating a Flexner-type report for the national mental health industry. Taking their cue from Appel, Felix, Daniel Blain, Francis Braceland and Jack Ewalt joined in, trumpeting mental illness as a growing national crisis and successfully lobbying Congress for the passage of the National Health Study Act in 1955, which provided $1.55 million for a five-year research project into the matter.

Concurrent with the study were the efforts of the National Advisory Mental Health Council to convince state governors to pass favorable mental health legislation. New York was the first state to pass the so-called "Community Mental Health Services Act," which mandated the installation of psychiatric clinics throughout the state, at a ratio of one per 50,000 people. Twelve other states quickly followed suit before 1963, when the federal government got involved.

Also while the Joint Commission was hard at work coming up with their recommendations, another, far more ominous piece of legislation was being drafted.

THE "SIBERIA BILL"

In 1949, the National Mental Health Council of the U.S. Public Health Department wrote a model law called "The Draft Act Governing Hospitalization of the Mentally Ill." Winfred Overholser, the head psychiatrist at the Public Health Department's St. Elizabeth's Hospital in Washington and a member of the Council, was also heading a committee to study the possibility of developing a model mental health plan in Alaska that could be used throughout the United States.

In 1956, when the result of Overholser's work, the Alaska Mental Health Bill, was presented to Congress, Alaska had not yet achieved statehood. As a federal territory, the bill had to be sent to federal lawmakers in Washington in lieu of the state legislature, as any other similarly proposed law would go. The psychiatrists behind the Alaska Mental Health Act knew that passage by Congress would give the bill sufficient national stature and prestige to inspire similar legislation in the 48 states.

The bill earmarked $6 million for one million acres of land in Alaska to be fenced off and set aside to build a mental facility where any person could be committed involuntarily by a psychiatrist. It also provided for contractual agreements with other states, allowing them to commit their mentally ill directly to Alaska. Treating psychiatrists of other states could also transfer their existing patients to Alaska if they deemed it to be in their patient's best interest.

Section 103(b), of the Bill provided:

"That 'any individual' may be 'admitted' into the asylum upon (a) a written application of an 'interested party,' (b) by health or welfare officer, (c) by the Governor, or (d) by the head of an institution in which the individual may be, if the application is accompanied by a certificate of a licensed physician that on the basis of an examination such individual is, in his opinion, mentally ill and is therefore likely to (1) injure himself or (2) injure others if at liberty, or being in need of care or treatment lacks sufficient insight or capacity to make application in his own behalf."[1]

Section 102 granted the authority to institutionalize to "any health, welfare, police officer, or any person deputized by a United States Commissioner...upon endorsement of the certificate by the Governor or a Commissioner to physically take the individual into custody and forthwith transport him to the mental institution."[2]

To say that the Alaska Bill violated rights guaranteed to all American citizens under the United States Constitution is an understatement of epic proportions.

Judge Joseph Call of Los Angeles made the following comparison between the bill and the Sixth Amendment of the U.S. Constitution:

ALASKA	SIXTH AMENDMENT
1. It permits no examination of any type.	1. The right to a speedy and public trial.
2. No statement of probable cause needs to be filed under oath to support the issuance of a warrant for arrest or apprehension.	2. The right to be informed of the charge preferred against him.
3. No judge or magistrate need issue a warrant of arrest.	3. The right to be represented by an attorney at all stages of the proceedings.
4. No examination is permitted of the patient by the patient's own physician.	4. The right to trial by an impartial jury.
5. No examination is provided for by any physician.	5. The right to be confronted by the witnesses against him.
6. No trial is permitted by a judge.	6. The right to subpoena witnesses in his own behalf for his own defense.
7. No trial is permitted by a jury."[3]	

The bill, nevertheless, passed quickly in the House.

However, the issue was quickly picked up in the press, which dubbed it "Siberia U.S.A." A huge public outcry ensued, resulting in its defeat in the Senate on the grounds that it violated the civil rights of the people it was supposed to help. For years afterward, however, psychiatrists still referred to the language of the "Siberia U.S.A." bill as their preferred model legislation for involuntary commitment.

The Senate defeat did not seem to deter the psychiatric community. In a 1957 speech to the World Federation for Mental Health entitled "Growing Up in a Changing World," G. Brock Chisholm rallied its members to the cause and called for them never to give up:

"When now we also have to recognize that neuroses propagate themselves and affect whole families, we may well begin to speculate on the advisability that psychiatrists, once the necessary one or two or three millions of them are available, should be trained as salesmen and taught all the techniques of breaking down sales resistance. Should not the prospective groups of psychotherapists employ advertising and sales organization in order to drag in customers? Isn't this the expressed desire of the Joint Commission on Mental Illness and Health to the Congress of the U.S.?..."

"Should attempts be made by the profession to induce governments to institute compulsory treatment for the neuroses as for other infectious diseases?"[4]

Winfred Overholser, appearing as an expert witness before a congressional committee (as he regularly did) in 1961, echoed Chisholm's sentiments:

"I am glad to say that today no State requires a jury trial for admission to a mental hospital, although in a number of states such a trial is available upon the demand of the patient or someone on his behalf.

"There is, of course, under the U.S. Constitution, no right to a jury trial for this purpose..."[5]

Clearly the psychiatric community was not about to roll over and die.

"ACTION FOR MENTAL HEALTH"

In 1961, the Joint Commission on Mental Illness and Health completed its investigation and submitted its report, entitled "Action for Mental Health," calling for the establishment of federally-funded community health centers around the United States. Massive training of personnel would be needed to staff these centers, and a broad public information campaign would be needed to enlighten the public to recognize mental illnesses and support a national program of prevention and treatment. The recommended financial outlay was also striking. Federal funding for mental health was to double in five years and triple in ten.

The Joint Commission's report had its critics, led by Robert Felix, who thought that the report was too general and aimed too much to please; Felix would shortly come up with a plan of his own.

His persistence was rewarded after the inauguration of President John F. Kennedy, who appointed him to a highly influential position on an interagency task force to consider the recommendations of the Joint Commission. Needless to say, the task force almost completely ignored the recommendations of the Joint Commission, and strongly supported large cutbacks in the state asylum system in favor of federal "community-centered mental health programs."[6] Critics, some within NIMH itself, charged that this plan ignored the everyday realities faced by those whom the programs were supposed to help, since 1960s demographic data showed that 48 percent of mental patients were unmarried, 12 percent widowed and 13 percent divorced or separated—hardly the kind of people likely to be rehabilitated in loving and supportive homes as outpatients.

Yet Congress passed the new legislation supported by Dr. Felix and his task force, with little opposition in either the House or Senate. President Kennedy signed the bill into law in October 1963, just over a month before his assassination.

Robert Felix had not only succeeded in establishing the community mental health plan, he also wrote the regulations governing its operation. Those regulations essentially left state hospital facilities out of the community mental health center plan, leaving them to fend for themselves.

This is not surprising, since in Felix's mind, the two systems served vastly different clientele. State asylums were for the severely and chronically mentally ill; community health centers could be defined in public health terms, where preventative mental health care could be provided to the public at large. No doubt Felix envisioned a society where visits to the psychiatrist were as common as a visit to the general practitioner. The community clinics, therefore, were oriented more toward marital and family difficulties, children's emotional problems, juvenile delinquency and substance abuse. Little attention was paid to the seriously mentally ill, who were shuffled off to the state institutions.

The amendments to the Social Security Act in 1965 that created Medicare (which provided hospital insurance for the elderly) and Medicaid (which gave money to the states to provide medical care for the poor), plus the growth in such federal entitlement programs as welfare payments to discharged psychiatric patients, hastened the exodus from state asylums to community health centers. Under Medicare many of the elderly who had been in state institutions could now be moved to community nursing homes. The community centers could also now receive funding for the treatment of the indigent.

As a result, by the late 1960s, state mental patients flooded out into society and into the community mental health center system. Deinstitutionalization was in full swing.

In order to cope with this massive influx of outpatients, the federal government initiated sweeping social welfare legislation. Some of this public assistance included federal housing projects, food stamps, the expansion of disability insurance and the creation of supplemental income programs. By 1977, the General Accounting Office found that Medicaid was "one of the single biggest purchasers of mental health care and the principal Federal program funding the long-term care of the mentally disabled" and the most significant "federally sponsored program affecting deinstitutionalization."[7]

Plainly stated, the results of the community mental health system were devastating to the country. Psychiatrists had established themselves as powerful, self-anointed experts in virtually every facet of American society—education, the family (through marriage and family counseling), the court system (in juvenile courts as delinquency counselors), medicine, and drug rehabilitation.

The irony is that just as during the days of the Third Reich, psychiatry would never have survived without government support because among the ordinary citizenry, it was largely distrusted and ignored.

THE ELEMENTARY AND SECONDARY EDUCATION ACT

Prior to 1965, most American public schools were funded by state and local governments, with very little federal assistance or intervention.

However, the passage of the Elementary and Secondary Education Act changed all that. Backed by the National Education Association (NEA), an educators' union with pro-psychiatry leanings, the Act provided funding to "...local educational agencies serving areas with concentrations of children from low-income families to expand and improve their educational programs by various means (including preschool programs) which contribute particularly to meeting the special educational needs of educationally deprived children."[8]

The legislation also called for the "...the establishment, maintenance and operation of programs...designed to enrich the programs of local elementary and secondary schools and to offer a diverse range of educational experience...such as...comprehensive guidance and counseling...psychological and social work...."[9]

With the Act also came certain highly lucrative "special education" programs. Under these programs, school districts were paid a set amount per child by the government, thus giving them a financial incentive to label as many children as possible "educationally deprived."

Ten years later, Congress passed the Education for All Handicapped Children Act. Although this Act was intended to provide equal education to children with handicaps such as blindness, cerebral palsy and multiple sclerosis, language was inserted into the bill which provided also for "children with specific learning disabilities."[10] This was enough of an opening for the psychiatric community, which now had a brand new educational cash cow. Labels such as "mentally retarded," "seriously emotionally disabled," or "learning disabled" were soon invented. The numbers of children being diagnosed as "learning disabled" skyrocketed. In a 1984 article in *Education Week*, it was reported that:

"Since the enactment in 1975 of the federal law guaranteeing handicapped children the right to an education, the number of learning-disabled students receiving special services in the nation's schools has risen by 948,658 children to 1.7 million, a 119 percent increase over a seven year period. During that same time, overall enrollment in public schools dropped by about 11.5 percent, according to federal statistics."[11]

Naturally, psychological counselors were on hand in the schools to "help" the children so labeled, more often than not by referring them to psychiatrists for drugs to modify or control the child's behavior.

PSYCHIATRY AND RACISM

Despite psychiatry's successful infiltration into virtually every phase of modern American life, life has gotten worse, not better.

Nowhere is this more true than in the inner cities. From these community mental health centers, poor people—primarily African-Americans—were introduced to a whole new level of mind-altering—but legally permissible—drugs. This, of course, ushered in a new wave of drug addiction, followed by an escalating crime rate that shows no signs of relenting. Today, single parent families are not the exception, but the rule.

As was the case in the Nazi era in Germany, the underclasses of the United States are and have been targeted by the psychiatrists as being somehow "inferior" to the rest of society. According to a 1922 study, African-Americans were more than twice as likely to be diagnosed as "retarded" as whites, with American Indians ranking a close second to African Americans. Those so diagnosed are often put into special classes and prescribed psychiatric drugs, many of which, as we have seen, have horrific side effects, and thus a cycle of drug addiction begins, followed shortly by the continual downward spiral of a culture. Incredibly, this continual degradation doesn't make psychiatrists feel culpable—it makes them feel right.

Racism in psychiatry goes back a long way. In 1797, Benjamin Rush, the "father of American psychiatry," contended that a genetic condition similar to leprosy called "Negritude" afflicted all dark-skinned races by causing their skin to turn brown. He had no cure for the "disease," but advised strongly that:

"First, whites should cease to 'tyrannize over them,' for their disease 'should entitle them to a double portion of our humanity.' However, by the same token, whites should not intermarry with them, for this would 'tend to infect posterity' with the 'disorder'…. Finally, attempts must be made to cure the disease."[12]

In the early part of the 20th century, further attempts were made to stigmatize certain races deemed to be "inferior." American eugenicist Paul Popenoe, following the ideological trend that cast blacks as lower in intelligence and therefore unfit for mainstream society, completed a study called "Intelligence and Race: A Review of Some of the Results of the Army Intelligence Tests—The Negro." Right up front he gives us an astonishingly unprovable scientific warning:

"...it must be borne in mind that the showing of the negroes is improved by the presence of much white blood in many of them; and that to get at the real ability of the black man one would have to subtract no small amount from all of the scores to be mentioned."[13]

He concludes his treatise by declaring:

"...it may be taken as certain that the negro is, as measured by intelligence tests, markedly inferior to the white men among whom he lives...the negro's low mental state is irremediable...the negro race is germinally lacking in the higher developments of intelligence.... The negro is mentally, therefore eugenically inferior to the white race."[14]

Popenoe was not just picking on one race. In an earlier footnote, he prefaces his study by saying:

"Apparently the same holds good for American Indians...."[15]

Attacks from modern-day eugenicists have never stopped. We have already seen the use of the IQ test to support claims by psychiatrists Arthur Jensen and Richard Herrnstein that African-Americans are natively less intelligent than whites.

We have also seen the use of drug addicts and convicts, most of whom were African-American, as human guinea pigs for CIA drug experiments under Dr. Harris Isbell at the Kentucky Addiction Research Center. Can this be any different from the cruel human experimentation performed by Mengele at Auschwitz?

In case there still is doubt, consider the psychosurgery experimentation conducted in the mid-1950s in New Orleans by Robert Heath, a psychiatrist from Tulane University, and Australian psychiatrist Harry Bailey. Heath and Bailey implanted electrodes into the brains of African-American convicts. During a lecture to a nursing class twenty years later at Tulane, Bailey would brag that it was cheaper to use Niggers than cats because they were everywhere and cheap experimental animals.[16]

Heath himself would go on to perform CIA-funded drug experiments, using African-American prisoners from Louisiana State Penitentiary. LSD and other strong hallucinogens were used to see whether they could cause (as one memo put it):

"...loss of speech, loss of sensitivity to pain, loss of memory, loss of will power and an increase in toxicity in persons with a 'weak type of central nervous system.'"[17]

THE VIOLENCE INITIATIVE

Under this onslaught from the outside, it would not be unreasonable for a group of people to become quite angry. After all, there is only so much drugging, so much experimentation, so little good education and so many times a person is told he is stupid and inferior before he is prone to rebel against his oppressor.

In response to this, the NIMH funded a vicious series of campaigns against African-Americans, which have gone under many names, the most recent being the "Violence Initiative."

The first known version of a violence program occurred in 1968 at the Boston Violence Center under neurosurgeons Vernon Mark and William Sweet, and psychiatrist Frank Ervin, who had been a student of Robert Heath's at Tulane. Inspired perhaps by Arnold Hutschnecker's failed proposal to perform psychological testing on children six to eight years of age to detect future criminality, Mark conducted an experiment in which he implanted electrodes in his patient's temporal lobes in an attempt to monitor his moods, and thus determine when he might become violent. Despite Mark's declarations that his first experiment was a great success, his first patient sued him, charging "great pain of body and mind" and the permanent loss "of his earning capacity and his ability to work."[18]

That same year, Sweet testified before the New York state legislature that those involved in the inner-city riots during the civil rights movement were suffering from "psychomotor epilepsy" (a type of brain disease), clearly implying that psychiatric drugs and/or brain surgery would be all that would be needed to solve the problems of the ghetto.

Encouraged, Sweet, Mark and Ervin appealed directly to Congress for further funding, and were rewarded with a $500,000 grant from NIMH in 1971, and a supplemental grant from the U.S. Justice Department. The purpose of this money was to investigate the causes of violence with specific reference to the role of genes, and examine into possible treatment methods, such as brain surgery. Once revealed, however, the public outcry forced the withdrawal of the grants. However, the "new idea" that violence could be genetically caused was now invading the psychiatric mainstream.

The race riots in Detroit in 1972 served as the inspiration and the justification for state funding for psychiatric research into the control and management of violence. Dr. Ernst Rodin, head of the neurology department of the Lafayette Clinic in Detroit and the leader of this project, suggested the use of "medical technology"—i.e., psychosurgery and castration—in a speech before fellow psychiatrists. In his judgment, children of "limited intelligence" are inclined to become violent if treated as "equals" with other children and thus should be subjected to an "authoritarian lifestyle." The "dumb young males who riot" should be castrated, said Rodin, for "the castrated ox will pull his plow" and "human eunuchs, although at times quite scheming entrepreneurs, are not given to physical violence.[19] Our scientific age tends to disregard this wisdom of the past...." Needless to say, Rodin's recommendations recall all too vividly the sterilization measures of Nazi Germany conducted under Ernst Rüdin, the architect of the Holocaust, whose name his closely resembles.

The second major violence program was put together in the wake of the Watts riots of the 1960s by psychiatrist and CIA mind control experimenter Jolly West of UCLA's Neuropsychiatric Institute (NPI). In the early 1970s, West submitted a proposal to the State of California and the U.S. Law Enforcement Assistance Administration (LEAA) for millions of dollars to establish the Center for the Study and Reduction of Violence in an abandoned Nike missile silo in the Santa Monica Mountains just north of Los Angeles. The Center's research primary function was to test inner city youth, primarily Latino and African-American, for violent behavior and then to propose solutions. Needless to say, West's solutions were less therapeutic than punitive—psychotropic drugs, brain surgery and castration.[20]

Rather than resort to physical castration, however, West advocated doing it chemically. In a proposal entitled "The Sexually Violent Male," using cyproterone acetate as his medium and state prisoners as his "subjects," West also believed that "Appropriate non-institutionalized clinical subjects suffering from violent sexual behavior must be identified,"[21] but did not elaborate on who those subjects would be or who would pick them. Further research on women, and autistic or retarded children was considered, as well as experimental treatments involving the implantation of electronic monitoring, or homing devices, in the brain of the subject. As with Mark, Sweet and Ervin, West's ideas generated fierce state-wide protests, which resulted in the suspension of state and federal funding for NPI in 1974.

Unfortunately, eugenics tends to be more or less a crusade to its supporters, who truly believe that they know best, while the rest of the world is mired in ignorance and superstition. This may well be why eugenical ideas have been with us since Benjamin Rush at least, and have appeared continuously in one form or another, more often than not under a differ-

Louis Jolyon West—Psychiatrist who experimented with LSD for the CIA. Former head of Neuropsychiatric Institute at University of California Los Angeles (UCLA)

ent name and in packaging that is "new and improved" and public relations friendly.

On February 11, 1992, Frederick K. Goodwin, the head of the Alcohol, Drug Abuse and Mental Health Administration and top-ranking psychiatrist in the Bush Administration, spoke to the National Health Advisory Council on the unveiling of the National Violence Initiative, a proposal which had already enjoyed strong support from Louis Sullivan, the Secretary of Health and Human Services (HHS) and was slated to become NIMH's number one funding priority by 1994: "If you look, for example at male monkeys, especially in the wild, roughly half of them survive to adulthood. The other half die by violence. That is the natural way of it for males, to knock each other off and, in fact, there are some interesting evolutionary implications of that because the same hyperaggressive monkeys who kill each other are also hypersexual, so they copulate more and therefore they reproduce more to offset the fact that half of them are dying.

"Now, one could say that if some of the loss of social structure in this society, and particularly within the high impact inner city areas has removed some of the civilizing evolutionary things that we have built up and that maybe it isn't just the careless use of the word when people call certain areas of certain cities jungles, that we may have gone back to what might be more natural, without all of the social controls that we have imposed upon ourselves as a civilization over thousands of years in our own evolution...." [22]

Only two weeks later, Goodwin appeared before the Mental Health Leadership Forum to apologize for his "inadvertent" remarks. According to Eli Newberger, President of the American Orthopsychiatric Association:

"After characterizing his earlier remarks as inadvertent and misunderstood, Dr. Goodwin responded to a question about his approach to the problems of urban violence by reiterating his views in essentially the same terms, shorn only of references to jungles and monkeys. At this moment of heightened sensitivity, in the immediate aftermath of his personal apology, Dr. Goodwin elaborated on his position by outlining his proposed federal program for dealing with violence among inner-city adolescents. The plan calls for establishing biological markers for the early identification of conduct-disordered youngsters. It aims to predict by the age of five—and at that point to intervene with—those children most likely to become disruptive and violent in adolescence."[23]

The Washington Post adds that Goodwin also said in the February 25 speech:

"Further down the line, somebody may come up with some interesting hypothesis that allows the adjunctive use of biological, medical interventions, but I think that is still quite experimental."[24]

Quite aside from the "monkey" references, part of the shock registered by Congress concerned how little they had known about the Violence Initiative, which NIMH had characterized as "disease prevention." John Conyers, a Democratic congressman from Michigan, a leading member of the Congressional Black Caucus (CBC), charged that HHS did not "supply us with the paper work on this initiative and the two African-American members of the Mental Health Advisory Panel were unfamiliar with the program."[25]

Simply put, the Violence Initiative would use genetic researchers to find biochemical "markers" to "identify" children as young as five as potentially violent. Much of the emphasis seems to be placed on the presence of serotonin in the brain—the more serotonin, the less violent a person will be. Naturally, the psychiatric and pharmaceutical communities are high on the idea, as several different drugs which promote the production of serotonin in the brain are currently on the market (the first and most well-known of which, the controversial antidepressant Prozac, is the pharmaceutical industry's biggest money-earner). Many more are waiting for approval from the U.S. Food and Drug Administration.

For his gaffe, Goodwin was "demoted" to the position of head of NIMH, a small slap on the wrist, to be sure.

That summer, the National Institutes of Health became embroiled in another controversy when it provided a $100,000 grant to the University of Maryland for a conference to take place the following October entitled "Genetic Factors in Crime: Findings, Uses and Implications." In its brochure promoting the event, the University's Institute for Philosophy and Public Policy promised that:

"...genetic research holds out the prospect of identifying individuals who may be predisposed to certain kinds of criminal conduct, of isolating environmental features which trigger those predispositions, and of treating some predispositions with drugs and unintrusive therapies....Genetic research also gains impetus from the apparent failure of environmental approaches to crime—deterrence, diversion and rehabilitation." [26]

African-American leaders in particular were outraged—after all, this type of project could very easily turn into cultural genocide. The protest which followed caused NIH to withdraw the funds, thus killing the conference. It did not, however, kill the resolve of the modern eugenicists to press on with their research.

In 1993, the *Chicago Tribune* reported that NIMH was still promoting its program, "to raise the hope that violent behavior eventually can be curbed by manipulating the chemical and genetic keys to aggression...anti-violence medications conceivably could be given, perhaps forcibly, to people with abnormal levels." [27]

In response, the director of the group Network Against Coercive Psychiatry, Dr. Seth Farber said:

"Just like the Nazis...what [psychiatrists] want to do is scapegoat African-American youth, put them on drugs and take away the rights of their parents. It is an outrageous, racist and oppressive plan." [28]

Despite the fact that the Initiative has been temporarily quelled, whether by accident or design, its completely unproven theories have managed to creep into society. In explaining his decision in a 1990 custody suit between the genetic parents of a child and its surrogate mother, a California Superior Court judge said, "We know more and more about traits now, how you walk, how you talk, and everything else, all sorts of things that develop out of your genes, how long you're going to live, all things being equal, when your immune system is going to break down, what diseases you may be susceptible to...."

Citing a very controversial and unreplicated twin study at the University of Minnesota which asserted a direct link between intelligence and genes, the judge added:

"They have upped the intelligence ratio of genetics to 70 percent now."[29]

What is notable about this decision was not the awarding of the child to his biological parents, but that the judge based his ruling on genetic theories that have never been proven, and indeed, may never be. Wheeler notes that:

"...Critics say a new and virulent form of biological determinism that takes much of its cue from genetics is having pervasive effects on court rulings, philosophical notions of free will and proposed government programs intended to reduce inner-city violence. Genetics and neuroscience, say some scholars, are being used to shift the blame for problems such as poverty from society to the individual."[30]

The fact remains that "biological determinism," or the idea that your abilities and inclinations are fixed and predetermined by your genetic make-up, has never been proven. Nor has it ever been shown that one's upbringing is completely, or even predominantly responsible for one's situation. Each side of the "nature versus nurture" argument is fatally flawed, as it assumes man is a stimulus-response mechanism, buffeted helplessly by environmental stimuli. By blaming outside forces for one's condition in life, it eliminates the one factor that gives a person a feeling of importance and self-respect: responsibility for oneself and one's fellow man.

We have mentioned earlier that it is standard scientific research procedure to have a successful experiment replicated by an independent source before announcing the findings. This has never been true of the psychiatric community. Robert N. Proctor, associate professor of history at Penn State University, says:

"People talk about the social power of biological information, but they don't talk about the social power of misinformation. There will be front-page stories that a math gene has been discovered, and then a footnote four weeks later that there were problems with the study. This goes on and on."[31]

The real problem with the Violence Initiative and projects like it is that it plays upon the fears of the general public. Having sold the crime rate through the media as a crisis of mammoth proportions, psychiatrists have neglected to mention what they themselves know—that much of the crime and violence are side effects of years of psychiatric treatment and drugs. Comparisons with Nazi Germany are inevitable.

The most frightening part of this is that grant money from NIMH to study inner-city violence continues to flow into the coffers of psychiatry. Now, however, the words on their proposals have changed. Experiments in "at-risk behavior" (currently the preferred term) continue, less advertised than ever. It is urgent, however, that they are promptly noticed and recognized for what they are: thinly disguised eugenical racism under scientific cover, whose roots go directly back to Wundt and Galton.

PSYCHIATRY'S WORLDWIDE INFLUENCE

No one should get the mistaken impression that psychiatry's tentacles have only invaded the United States and Germany. Its influence, in fact, is felt throughout the world.

Upon his appointment by the United Nations' Interim Preparatory Commission to establish the World Health Organization in 1946, Canadian psychiatrist G. Brock Chisholm had a brilliant idea. Together with fellow psychiatrists J.R. Rees, George Stevenson, Charles Hinks and Arthur Ruggles, he organized the World Federation for Mental Health (WFMH) to coordinate and control the activities of various national mental health associations throughout the world (to Rees, this was no doubt another one of his "fifth column" activities).

The WFMH was officially born in 1948 at the Third International Congress on Mental Health in London, the theme of which was "Mental Health and World Citizenship." Rees was elected its President with the stated objective: "[The] principles of mental health cannot be successfully furthered in any society unless there is progressive acceptance of the concept of world citizenship. World citizenship can be widely extended among all peoples through the applications of the principles of mental health."[32] At a major turning point in world history there is an obligation on social scientists and psychiatrists to attempt this new formulation.

Noble sentiments, perhaps, until we realize that this is the same profes-

sion documented as already being deeply involved in eugenical sterilization movements, military espionage and OSS and CIA drug experimentation, all in the preceding dozen years. In this light the concept of "world
citizenship" takes on a different meaning. World citizenship implies world
government—under whom?

As if this weren't enough, here is a brief list of some of WFMH's other
founding members:

Frank Fremont-Smith, psychiatrist and director of the Josiah Macy, Jr.
Foundation, which covertly funded CIA experimental projects

Werner Villinger, T4 psychiatrist who escaped justice after the war

Friedrich Mauz, Nazi psychiatrist who became German delegate to the
WFMH

Other officers and senior committee members included:

Leo Bartemeier, American military psychiatrist

H.V. Dicks, Senior Psychiatrist at the Tavistock Clinic

Otto Klineberg, German-trained psychiatrist at Columbia University

Margaret Mead, cultural anthropologist from New York

Louis J. "Jolly" West, of CIA research

In a 1953 letter, Daniel Blain, medical director of the APA and member of WFMH wrote to J.R. Rees about a recent grant from the
Rockefeller Foundation for a communications system that would "give us
an opportunity to communicate with all hospitals in the world and will
assist in financing our other plans...."

Blain goes on to reveal a psychiatric "work in progress" which would fit
in nicely with their planned "world citizenship":

"We have by no means given up the idea of the International Mental
Hospital Service.... This Rockefeller Grant, as I mentioned above, will be
a great boon towards a communicating system."[33]

The "International Mental Health Service," which would have brought
all of the mental health facilities in the world under one umbrella, did not
come to pass—at least, not yet. It does, however, provide us with some very
frightening insights into psychiatry's ambitions.

PSYCHIATRIC INFLUENCE ON AMERICAN GOVERNMENT TODAY

In 1982, new legislation changed funding procedures for community
mental health centers from federal grants to states for specific programs (a

bureaucratic nightmare if the states didn't spend the money as earmarked) to "block grants," where the states would spend the money as they saw fit. Concurrent with this was the reclassification of many of these centers as "multi-service centers," which provided two or more services, thus making them eligible for the new funds. The net result was just what the APA lobbyists in Washington had hoped—more money for more facilities providing more services to a larger and larger patient base.

At the same time, psychiatrists in various states began lobbying for legislation to include mental health coverage in all medical insurance coverage. Again, they met with success: 30 states now have statutes making mental health coverage a mandatory part of every health insurance plan.

In recent years, psychiatrists backed by the APA and NIMH heavily lobbied Congress for mandated mental health coverage under President Clinton's proposed health care reform. Their objective was to guarantee mental health care for every American. Tipper Gore, the wife of the Vice President and the holder of a master's degree in psychology, served as the spokesperson for the movement.

Fighting against public perception of psychiatric therapy as the "Woody Allen Syndrome," in which a patient undergoes fifty years of costly psychotherapy and comes out the same, Gore pushed hard for a $6.5 billion annual package to treat what she estimated as 24 million adults and 12 million children who had severe mental disorders.

Her leading professional ally was Dr. Bernard Arons, an NIMH psychiatrist and clinical professor of psychiatry at George Washington University. According to the *Psychiatric News*, Arons "…he was chief clinical advisor at St. Elizabeth's Hospital in Washington, D.C. in the mid-1980s. His interest—and participation—in deinstitutionalization first whetted his appetite for broader policy issues affecting the mentally ill."[34]

Under the Clinton Plan, the federal government would have guaranteed 60 days of inpatient psychiatric hospital care and up to 30 psychotherapy visits. However, by the year 2000, there would be no limits on the amount or duration of mental health services, leaving employers and taxpayers to foot the bill all by themselves.

The proposed health care plan was defeated in Congress as too costly, a move that sank some of the fondest hopes of psychiatrists who had hoped to inflict universal mental health care upon every American.

PSYCHIATRY AND "ETHNIC CLEANSING" IN BOSNIA

The extent of present day psychiatry as a destructive influence is nowhere more real than in the current "ethnic cleansing" program being carried out in Bosnia-Herzegovina. What is especially chilling about the bloodshed is how closely it resembles the mass extermination of German minorities by Hitler and his Nazi psychiatrists.

Far from being a civil war, the conflict is actually a one-sided holocaust perpetuated by ethnic Serbs against Croats and Muslims, according to a recent CIA report. *The New York Times* reported that:

"In what is believed to be the most comprehensive United States assessment of atrocities in Bosnia, the Central Intelligence Agency has concluded that 90 percent of the acts of "ethnic cleansing" were carried out by Serbs and that leading Serbian politicians almost certainly played a role in the crimes....

"The report...also contains specific evidence that some Bosnian Serb leaders—including Radovan Karadzic—knew of the concentration camps through which many Muslims and Croats who had been evicted from their homes in 1992 were processed."[35]

Radovan Karadzic, incidentally, is a practicing psychiatrist and Serb leader, who began his 25-year doctor/patient relationship with Serbian president and strongman, Slobodan Milosevic, when he treated him for depression in Sarajevo.

The events leading up to the events in Bosnia begin at the death of Marshal Tito in 1980 and the subsequent breakup of the Yugoslav republic. Jovan Raskovic, a psychiatrist and friend of the then-President of the Federal Republic of Yugoslavia, Dobrica Cosic, was a frequent guest on political programs on Belgrade television, where he began to give vaguely Hitlerian speeches full of nationalistic and psychoanalytical overtones.

In 1986, Raskovic joined the Academy of Sciences of Serbia, where he became deeply involved in drawing up the infamous Memorandum of the Serbian Academy of Sciences, which advocated the creation of a "Greater Serbia." This document outlined the state of Yugoslavian society in the 1980s and blamed the poor economic and cultural conditions on the Croatian and Slovenian peoples:

"Serbia's position must be examined in the context of Croatia and Slovenia's political and economic domination, a situation at the origin of all of the changes up to this moment....Culture is becoming more and more regional; its Yugoslavian and universal meaning is shattering, and it is being used chiefly by the republics and the autonomous provinces in their hopes to become their own masters even in this domain. This general provincialization of culture lowers the standard of value and allows for a much larger social affirmation on the part of the least-talented creators."[36]

Radovan Karadzic—Sarajevo psychiatrist who became head of the SDS, the ruling Serbian political party, and one of the main instigators in the war in the former Yugoslavia.

Casting the Serbs as martyrs for World War II atrocities committed against them by Croat fascists, Raskovic attracted growing crowds of avid followers drawn to his rhetoric, and quickly became a dominant figure in Yugoslavian politics. Raskovic was the voice of supremacy to his fervent listeners advocating that they, the Serbs, because of their psychological superiority, should dominate the Croat and Muslim minorities and be the only ones to hold power:

"In my practice, having worked for almost thirty-five years at the border of three republics with Serbian, Muslim and Croatian populations, I was able to identify the different compositions of my patients' personalities....

"I noticed that the majority of the Serbian...exhibited signs of an Oedipal personality, which is to say a moderate dose of aggressivity accompanied by submission...Therefore, Serbs by nature would possess the qualities of authority with certain aggressive and open elements.

"I have noted that Muslims are fixated on the anal phase, and this phase is characterized by being received, which is part of their character. This character tends to appropriate things, dominate like a boss, value people by their possessions, their money, their social position, etc.... I have not obtained these ideas of fixation and cleanliness from the Koran but from my own experience and certain social and psychological characteristics...."

As for the Croats, "the character of castration is closed and hermetic. It is under perpetual influence of fear of castration, losing something that belongs only to oneself...afraid of being abused, of being treated without dignity."[37]

Because of these traits, Raskovic concluded, Serbs alone understood authority and leadership and must therefore exercise it over all the other peoples of Yugoslavia.

In 1990, Raskovic formed a political party in Croatia called the Serbian Democratic Party (SDS). This party counted among its members many of Raskovic's own patients, most notably the Minister of the Interior of the self-proclaimed Serbian Republic of Krajinia, Milan Martic. Later that year, the SDS would become directly responsible for inciting a civil war in the region.

In an interview with the newspaper *Nedjelna Dalmacija*, Dr. Boris Zmijanovic of Raskovic's former psychiatric clinic in Dalmatia declared:

"Without scruples, Dr. Raskovic used his patients for his political ends. He manipulated them. It is very interesting to note that the first leaders of the Serbian Democratic Party of Croatia were also Raskovic's patients."[38]

Raskovic also continued to manipulate the passions of the general Serbian public toward support for acts of genocide, all the while giving ample, but distinctly Nazi-like, justification for their actions:

"The Serbian people...have awakened. No one can do anything against you now.... If there is a civil war, and our heads and those of the Croatians fall—and it is certain that the heads of those currently in power in Croatia will also fall—defend yourself but do not provoke since we are a peace-loving people, we have never committed genocide, the way the Croatians have done against us."[39]

After successfully implementing his ethnic cleansing program in Croatia, Raskovic moved to Sarajevo, in Bosnia-Herzegovina, to do the same. In 1991, he appointed his devoted student of ten years, Sarajevo psychiatrist Radovan Karadzic, to lead the SDS in Bosnia. The appointment was not accidental, considering one of Karadzic's current patients was the Serbian President Milosevic.

Soon the mass extermination of Croats and Muslims was in full swing. By January 1992, Raskovic withdrew, confessing publicly on state television:

"I feel responsible because I made the preparations for this war, even if not the military preparations. If I hadn't created this emotional tension in the Serbian people, nothing would have happened. My party and I myself lit the fuse of Serbian nationalism not only in Croatia but everywhere else in Bosnia and Herzegovina. It's impossible to imagine an SDS in Bosnia and Herzegovina or a Mr. Karadzic in power without our influence. We have driven this people and we have given it an identity. I have repeated again and again to this people that it comes from heaven, not earth."[40]

Six months later, Raskovic was dead, a victim of a massive heart attack. Yet he did not take his policies of "ethnic cleansing" with him to his grave; Karadzic and Milosevic continued on, heedless of the import of his public confession.

The war crimes perpetrated by the Serbs against the Croats and Muslims are truly horrifying. A tribunal set up by the United Nations Security Council in February 1993 to look into war crimes in the former Yugoslavia found evidence of "150 mass graves, 900 prison camps and 90 paramilitary groups, mostly Serb...The Bosnia government alone has forwarded evidence about 42 mass murders, 20 mass graves and 5000 alleged war criminals."[41] In one instance, Serbian irregulars killed between 2000 and 3000 Muslim men, women and children.

In 1992, the world learned of "rape camps" that had been established in Bosnia-Herzegovina where "Serbs are raping captured women...In many cases the victims become pregnant and are held so they can no longer have an abortion." Bosnia's foreign minister said that "some women, girls and children spoke about that in such a way that it is quite clear that a part of their personality has been destroyed forever."[42]

German journalist Alexandra Stiglmayer, in the November 1992 issue of *Der Stern* magazine, reported that:

"The figure of 50,000 women raped—given by the Bosnian government, is certainly exact. These rapes are a tactic of war rather than simple amusement for the soldiers; when Karadzic's troops take a village, full-scale rape begins, and continues in subsequent prisoner camps."[43]

In January 1993, Amnesty International reported that "Muslim women have been the chief victims and the main perpetrators have been members of the Serbian armed forces." [44]

Panic-stricken Croats and Muslims are pouring into refugee camps too small to accommodate all of them. The U.N. Deputy Commissioner for Refugees Douglas Stafford appealed to the U.N. to give further aid:

"These people have been beaten, tortured and have experienced atrocities of the worst kinds. They are in need of immediate protection." [45]

By the end of 1992, more than 1.5 million people were displaced by the war, including an estimated one-half of the Muslim population, according to the annual human rights report of the U.S. State Department. It went on to say:

"The policy of driving out innocent civilians of a different ethnic or religious group from their homes, so-called ethnic cleansing, was practiced by Serbian forces in Bosnia on a scale that dwarfs anything seen in Europe since Nazi times." [46]

The slow response by western nations has made the ethnic Croats and Muslims' chances appear exceedingly dim in the face of a Hitleresque onslaught with a psychiatric heritage. In an April 1995 report, Tadeusz Mazowiecki, Special Rapporteur to the United Nations' Commission on Human Rights, reported that Karadzic and Milosevic's ethnic cleansing programs have had their desired effect:

"According to the prewar 1991 census, the territory of what is now northern Bosnia and Herzegovina had a population of 625,000 Serbs, 356,000 Muslims and 180,000 Croats. Estimates made by the Office of the United Nations High Commissioner for Refugees place the total number of Serbs now at some 719,000, while Muslims number about 37,000 and Croats 30,000—signifying a reduction by some 90 per cent of the local Muslim population and by 85 per cent of the Croat population since the beginning of the war." [47]

Mazowiecki goes on to report that "Bosnian Serb authorities consistently refuse access by human rights monitors to territories controlled by them...[and] have never implemented the commitments that they have undertaken...Access to medical care is reported to be difficult for non-Serbs...." [48]

The most recent news is even more dismaying. On August 11, 1995, the *Los Angeles Times* reported that:

"U.S. Ambassador Madeleine Albright showed the U.N. Security

Council photographs...that she said depicted mass graves in Bosnia-Herzegovina that hold the bodies of as many as 27,000 civilians murdered by Bosnian Serb forces after two U.N. "safe areas" were overrun last month....

"She said the photos, combined with eyewitness accounts, provide a 'compelling case that there were wide-scale atrocities committed...against defenseless civilians.'

"A senior U.S. official said later that 2,000 to 2,700 Bosnians, mostly Muslim men and boys, were machine-gunned by nationalist Serb troops after the insurgents overran the Muslim enclaves of Srebrenica and Zepa.

"'There were high-level Bosnian Serb military people present,' Albright said....' This is clearly a case that needs to be investigated further by the war crimes tribunal.'" [49]

Any argument that Raskovic, Karadzic and Milosevic represent the "lunatic fringe" of psychiatry completely misses the point. If anything, the two Serb leaders are classic examples of eugenicists who use psychiatry to assume leadership positions and make blanket statements about minorities to justify their suppression and mass extermination. The fact that they are obvious about it does not make them lunatics—it only makes them obvious.

The atrocities of the Nazi era, with its scapegoating of religious and ethnic minorities and its widespread use of starvation, rape and torture on its political prisoners, is an exact parallel. Inspired by its psychiatrically based eugenical notions of "racial purity," this is ample proof that a holocaust can, indeed, happen again—for it already has in Bosnia-Herzegovina.

Far more subtle forms of these ideas continue to abound, and may always be with us. Although concealed behind the banner of "scientific progress," they are just as dangerous and destructive in their results. We can see the early beginnings of these "results" every day on Main Street, U.S.A.: the drugging of our children in the name of "mental health"; the search for criminal predispositions or a never-proven "criminal gene" (which, of course, would be spotted early by the government and "handled" by psychiatrists); the Big Brotherism of Outcome Based Education; drug-based "mind control" experimentation on the part of military psychiatrists, designed to make its opponents (including any American citizens who object) compliant and malleable; "world citizenship" under psychiatry's watchful eye.

The latest U.S. statistics bear this out.

• The violent crime rate known to police has escalated from 150 crimes per year per 100,000 people in 1960 to 750 in 1992.[50]

• The estimated number of arrests for possession of drugs has gone from 360,000 in 1980 to over 700,000 in 1992. For the sale or manufacture of drugs, the figures are parallel: 100,000 in 1980 to 338,000 in 1992.[51]

• The divorce rate in the United States has skyrocketed from 395,000 in 1950 to just under 1.2 million in 1994.[52]

• The number of illegitimate births to girls aged 15 to 19 has risen from 8.6 percent in 1960 to 36 percent in 1991. For girls under 15, from 4.6 per thousand in 1960 to 11.0 per thousand in 1991.[53]

• Meanwhile, the suicide rate for 15- to 25-year-olds has gone from 4.8 per 100,000 people in 1955 to over 12.0 in 1982. For 5 to 14 year olds, from 2.0 per million people in 1958 to 6.0 in 1982.[54]

Contrast this to the enormous increases in federal funding for programs claiming to combat these trends:

• In 1967, there were 1,447 community mental health centers in the United States. By 1990, there were over 2,250.[55] Total expenditures have risen from $500 million in 1970 to $6.5 billion in 1990.[56]

• In 1963, about $50 million in research grants were awarded by NIMH. Today, that total is over $475 million.[57]

• The federal education budget has ballooned from $9 billion in 1976 to over $30 billion in 1995.[58]

In any place that these ideas have taken root and been practiced, progress and well-being have steadily declined. The example of the men behind Hitler is reason enough to become extremely vigilant against any infiltration of these ideas into any part of society, and justification to stamp it out where it currently exists.

True scientific progress is measurable. In its experimental phases, the scientific results are uniform—there is no place for fudging, other results, or professional opinion. The application of a true science always results in more healthy people in a better society. The discoveries of the polio and smallpox vaccines are examples. Furthermore, a true science resolves the actual cause of an existing illness—it does not attempt to destroy human tissue or body organs (like the brain) using drugs or scalpels in the name of "relief" in order to make the subject manageable, and thus more convenient to his caretakers. Any such "therapy" that does this as part of its regular practice is not a therapy; any "science" that advocates such practices is not a science. Psychiatry so practices and so advocates—it is merely a technology of torture.

A FUTURE WITHOUT PSYCHIATRY?

There is hope. Psychiatry, as we have mentioned earlier, is not very popular with the general public. It is not even all that popular in the real medical community. With a costly and destructive "therapy" that can go on with little result for years, the psychiatric community knows that its only hope lies with the governments of the world, some of whom have supported them since the turn of the century. Withdrawal of government support would be catastrophic to them.

Even its own practitioners admit that psychiatry is a dying industry. As early as 1972, Dr. Vivian Rackoff spoke before the Ontario Psychiatric Association's annual conference, characterizing psychiatrists as "pill-givers, others as arrogant, and still others as gurus" with no "market for their products."[59]

More recent is an article in the June 1993 issue of the *Psychiatric Times*, where Dr. Paul Genova stated that psychiatry is a "rotting ship" which has "lost its own integrity."[60] That same month, the *Los Angeles Times* reported a steady decline in graduates from American medical schools who were specializing in psychiatry.

It might be interesting to see psychiatry take stock of itself and recognize the harm that its programs have wrought upon society; psychiatry is fast becoming the cause of its own extinction. An ideological "housecleaning" would be a good start—but it may be too late for that. The psychiatric community must begin to do something it has heretofore been incapable of doing—looking at itself objectively and assessing its true impact upon society rather than loudly condemning its critics in its own stimulus-response fashion and labeling them with the brain pathology-of-the-month.

Until then, it is quite possible that they will drag the rest of the civilized world down with them—not a very appetizing option.

The solution rests with the citizen. Vigilance is, of course, essential; active participation in democracy even more so. The purse-strings of psychiatry are held by government, just as they were in Nazi Germany. In those days, however, the German people were left woefully ignorant of what Hitler and his henchmen were doing. This doesn't have to happen today. The example of the men behind Hitler gives us the ability to spot others who might try to follow in their ideological footsteps. Despite all that they profess otherwise, their psychiatric ancestors are always recognizable by their words and deeds.

Good standard medical care, religious values that emphasize the spiritual nature of man, an educational program that stresses the application of basics and encourages individuality and exciting new ideas, and a justice system that relies on the discovery of the truth and demands the assumption of personal responsibility by each and every one of its citizens—these are the qualities of a thriving culture. It is not wishful thinking to believe that this can take place—it can happen if we make it so.

A prerequisite to a society like this, of course, is the cleaning up of the field of mental health and ensuring that reforms are made which prevent any future eugenical or euthanistic "solutions." As long as a psychiatric pseudoscience masquerading as "therapy" continues to use coercion and brutality on its patients, no society can truly be free.

It is up to you to help.

CHAPTER 6

"Bitter fruit does not become sweet, even if it is smeared with honey."

Bidpai, *"Das Buch der Beispiele alter Weisen" ("The Book of Examples by Wise Old Sages")*

PSYCHIATRY, YESTERDAY AND TODAY

The conclusion of this book should be the dawn of new and better research, because, to a very significant degree, the men behind Hitler were psychiatrists and one of the lingering scandals of the Nazi era is that theoretically, ideologically and therapeutically, almost nothing has changed since Hitler euthanised himself in a bunker. His ideological comrades-in-arms within psychiatry were able to continue to practice their eugenical ways unmolested, refining their therapies and training new generations of disciples and advocates of repackaged Third Reich-style brutalities.

It is actually amazing that so much of this story has been so badly publicized. In that darkness and occasional twilight, the original psychiatric ideology has survived virtually intact in its antisocial glory. Students of the men behind Hitler and their protégés have professorships in universities and hold important political positions in the mental health arena. The power of psychiatry simply has never waned. It possesses its own influential lobby, it possesses an almost unlimited decision-making power over minor and legally incapacitated patients, and it is also able to victimize people because of its clout and control.

Has psychiatry become more humane? Yes and no.

Yes, because some conditions in psychiatric clinics have certainly improved. To a large degree, this was brought about by increased pressure from an enlightened public as well as vigilant and reactive pressure groups, law enforcement and legislatures.

No, because it remains inhumane in many particulars and even inhuman in others. Because it has embraced rather than renounced many aspects of its barbarous, Nazi-influenced heritage. Because its arrogance shelters and coddles monsters in its midst. Because it resists encroachment from those who elevate man and spirit above their idea of science.

"The fact is, the men behind Hitler *were* psychiatrists. And the symbiotic relationship that existed between them was possible only because both Nazism and psychiatry are limbs that have grown from the same diseased ideological tree. For this reason it is certain that human experiments will continue to be performed, patients will be tortured and unwilling patients will be forced to submit to what passes for treatment.

The following appeared on April 1, 1993 in the *Münchner Merkur*:

"Researcher in search of 4,000 pairs of twins."

"Psychologist Alois Angleitner of the University of Bielefeld, who is involved in the study, hopes, according to his own words, to find out if the temperament of people is established at birth. This could be investigated easily through studies of twins. According to Angleitner, there has not been much twin research in Germany for over fifty years."

The old research methods have never died. Old ideologies are still taught too, albeit with a new look and new labels. Behind mellifluous cover words, psychiatry still follows its traditional view of man as a beast devoid of spirit, unworthy of basic dignities.

The message has not been fully learned or understood.

On February 9, 1993, the Dutch parliament officially legalized a euthanasia policy that would exterminate hundreds of thousands of mentally and physically ill patients who have been deemed not worthy of living. The Dutch have, in effect, declared the killing by physicians as permissible—an incredible turnaround.

The new law permits lethal injection "under heavily controlled circumstances." The guidelines for these "circumstances" follow a 28-point checklist covering such points as whether the patient is incurably ill, suffers unbearable pain or has asked repeatedly for a mercy killing.

The new law, which became effective in early 1994, demands that physicians report every case of euthanasia. Justice Minister Ernst Hirsch-Ballin says the law will now bring mercy killing into the open so that it can be "regulated" instead of remaining a common practice and a well-kept secret.

Prior to this, the only European nation ever to legalize the practice of euthanasia was Germany, during a time most people like to pretend is gone.

So is the future one of "never again" or is it to be "one more time?"

In this book, we have seen many psychiatric methods follow a trail to human degradation and murder. To suffering and pain. To racism, violence and euthanasia. To a mirror of the ideology of the Third Reich.

With all this is mind, we have to preserve the rights of all individuals. These rights were shamelessly abrogated in the 1930s and 1940s. It is not much different today. Once committed, a person is helplessly delivered into the machinery. Efforts to escape torture will be used against him and characterized as part of his syndrome. The scenario is a nightmare for those affected who are helpless, and those who dare resist the treatment are condemned to even more of it.

With remarkably flexible diagnoses and ambitious programs for "community-oriented psychiatry," psychiatry is currently striving to expand its patient base to include as many people as possible. In the not-too-distant future, anybody may become a psychiatric patient, to be delivered defenseless into the potentially despotic hands of the heirs to a history of horrors.

One thing is certain: Psychiatrists have never demonstrated either the ability or the willingness to police themselves. In the past thousands of them have stood silently by—in Germany, in the United States, in Britain and elsewhere—while monsters among their peers stripped individuals of dignity, sanity and even life. Therefore, like any other group in society, if the psychiatric community cannot maintain its own ethical standards then the appropriate authorities must enforce those standards of society. Governments are, however, slow to act—until the people they govern urge them to do so. It is our fervent hope that the truth about the men behind Hitler will prompt well-meaning people everywhere to raise their voices and demand that no longer may human rights be subverted by those who would operate under the authoritarian cloak of a pseudoscience.

Our personal freedoms are, after all, too easily lost and too hardly won.

REFERENCE NOTES

Part I—Chapter 1
THE MISSING PIECE
OF THE PUZZLE

1. *See* Adolf Hitler, *Mein Kampf*, Munich 1936, where he describes the Jews and other minorities as a "race of rats, bloodily fighting each other"
2. H. Picker, *Hitlers Tischgespräche*, publ. by P.E. Schramm, 1963
3. *See* Gebhardt, *Handbuch der Deutschen Geschichte*, volume IV/2 Stuttgart 19789, p. 548
4. *See* Degesch—proceedings, assize court in Frankfurt 1949, criminal case Peters (managing director of Degesch), assize court Frankfurt 1955. Quoted in Gebhardt, *op. cit.*, p. 550
5. *See* Gebhardt, *op. cit.*, p. 550
6. *See* Joachim C. Fest, *Hitler*, Frankfurt, Berlin 1992
7. *See* Wilfried Daim, *The Man Who Inspired Hitler*, Berlin, Vienna 1985

Part I—Chapter 2
THE HISTORY OF THE
POLITICS OF HATE

1. Population theories actually go much farther back than that. The first documented population theory was formulated by Giovanni Botero in 1589, but it was Malthus who disseminated and popularized his variation.
2. *See* Will Durant, *Die Napoleonische Ära*, Frankfurt, Berlin 1982, p. 91
3. False notions and incorrect assumptions abound in Malthus' thesis. For example, during Malthus' lifetime, the populations of Europe, China and India doubled—and were better nourished than ever. The same held true for the United States, where even fewer farmers netted rich agricultural surpluses for export.
4. Will Durant, *op. cit.*, p. 93
5. Charles Darwin, *Die Abstammung des Menschen* (translated by Heinrich

Schmidt and prefaced by Gerhard Heberer), Stuttgart 1966
6. Compare: Christoph Mai, *Die Zwillingsmethode, Zur Geschichte eines humangenetischen Forschungskonzeptes bis 1945*. Diss. med. Hamburg 1988, p. 461
7. Charles Darwin, *Die Abstammung des Menschen und die geschlechtliche Zuchtwahl*, Part I, Stuttgart 1871, 146.
8. *See* H.M. Peters, *Soziomorphe Modelle in der Biologie*, in: Ratio 1 (1960), pp. 22-37. Also: *Historische, soziologische und erkenntniskritische Aspekte der Lehre Darwins*. In: H.-G. Gadamer, P. Vogler (Publ.): *Neue Anthropologie*, Vol. 2, *Biologische Anthropologie* (Part 1), Munich and Stuttgart 1972, pp. 326-352
9. W. Schallmayer, Vererbung und Auslese in ihrer soziologischen und politischen Bedeutung, Jena 1910
10. *See* Gisela Bock, *Zwangssterilisation im Nationalsozialismus. Studien zur Rassenpolitik. Opladen*, 1986, pp. 28-76
11. Jürgen Kroll, *Zur Entstehung und Institutionalisierung einer naturwissenschaftlichen und sozialpolitischen Bewegung. Die Entwicklung der Eugenik/Rassenhygiene bis zum Jahre 1933*, Tübingen 1983, p. 18
12. "Here is an insight, which has been formulated by me for the first time: that there are no moral truths at all…Morality is only an interpretation of certain phenomena, or, more precisely, a misinterpretation." Friedrich Nietzsche, book III, *op. cit.*, p. 425
13. Friedrich Nietzsche, book V, publ. by Karl Schlechta, Munich 1965, p. 91: "The world—including mankind—as it 'truly' is, is without any purpose, and is nonsense!"
14. Friedrich Nietzsche, book II, *op. cit.*, p. 589

15. Nietzsche wrote: "They are always looking for an enemy. In some of them there is a hatred at first sight...They love peace as a means toward new wars, and they love a short peace more than a long one."

16. Friedrich Nietzsche, book III, *op. cit.*, p. 428

17. *Ibid.*, book III, p. 67

18. *Ibid.*, book II, p. 182

19. Friedrich Nietzsche, book II, *op. cit.*, p. 182: "Cross bred races are also cross bred cultures and cross bred moralities: Most of the time they are malevolent, gruesome and unstable."

20. Friedrich Nietzsche, book III, *op. cit.*, p. 93

21. Friedrich Nietzsche, book III, *op. cit.*, p. 624

22. Friedrich Nietzsche, book IV, *op. cit.*, p. 430

23. Original title: "Essai sur e'ingalite des races humaines"

24. *See* Joachim Fest, *op. cit.*, p. 81

25. *See* Gerhard Schmidt, "Vom Rassenmythos zu Rassenwahn und Selektion," in: *Der Nervenarzt* (56) 1985, p. 337

26. *See* Joachim Fest, *op. cit.*, p. 82

27. The race theories of Gobineau were further amplified by the Frenchman G. Vacher de Lapouge (1854-1936). Lapouge advanced the idea of the superiority of the "Aryan race" in 1889 while lecturing at the University of Montepellier.
cp: Lapouge 1939, Günter Bausler and (publ.) Eugenth. *Entstehung und Gesellschaftliche Bedingtheit,* Jena 1984, p. 26

Part I—Chapter 3
A SHORT FOCUSED HISTORY OF PSYCHIATRY IN GERMANY

1. *See* Peter Lehmann, *Der chemische Knebel*, Berlin 1990

2. *See* Ingo Steudel, *Die Innovationszeiten von Prüfungsfächern in Deutschland und ihre Bedingtheiten. Diss. med. Kiel*, 1973

3. For a history of psychiatry, see especially: A.A. Roback, *Weltgeschichte der Psychologie und Psychiatrie, Olten im Breisgau,* 1970

4. Lenzmann, Julius (1843-1906), from a speech at the German Reichstag on January 16, 1897

5. Krafft-Ebing, speech of Gerichtliche Psychopathologie, Stuttgart 1892, Vol. 3

6. L. Löwenfeld, *ber den Nationalcharakter der Franzosen und dessen krankhafte Auswüchse, Wiesbaden* 1914

7. W. Fuchs, "Kriegspsychologisches," in: *Münchner Medizinische Wochenschrift* 1916, pp. 565-566

8. Johannes Bresler, "Betrachtungen ber geistige Prophylaxe (Schlua)," in: *Münchner Medizinische Wochenschrift* 1926, pp. 285-288

9. Max Nonne, *Anfang und Ziel meines Lebens*, Hamburg 1971, pp. 177-178

10. The "traumatic neurosis" was considered an organic change caused by a traumatic experience, which triggered a mild psychological disturbance. Not everyone agreed. For example, the director of the Tübingen medical clinic, Prof. Naegeli, called "traumatic neurosis" a simulated "new illness" that only arose because of benefits in the German health insurance system (Naegeli, "Zur Frage der Krankengeldauszahlung an erkrankte und verwundete Kriegsteilnehmer," in: *Ärztliches Vereinsblatt*, No. 1019 of 04.20.1915, p. 156

11. Karl Heinz Roth, *Die Modernisierung der Folter in den beiden Weltkriegen*, in "1999" (*Zeitschrift für Sozialgeschichte des 20. und 21. Jahrhunderts*) 2 (1987), 8-75, 16 and Ewald Stier: "Psychiatrie und Heer," in: *Der Deutsche Militärarzt* 1 (1936), 17. Quoted by: Riedesser, Peter und Verderber, Axel: *Aufrüstung der Seelen, Militärpsychologie und Militärpsychiatrie in Deutschland und Amerika*, Freiburg 1985, p. 11

12. Georg Wohlmuth: Feinstrom, Gavanisatoren, catalogue 1929, p. 8

(StaHH 352-3, 10 1-60). In as far as these electrodes had actually been used in military psychiatry could not be elicited to this day with certainty.

13. Fritz Kaufmann: "Die planmäßige Heilung komplizierter pscyhogener Bewegungsstörungen bei Soldaten in einer Sitzung." In: *Münchener Medizinische Wochenschrift*, vol. 1916, *Fachräztliche Beilage* No. 22. cp: *M. Raether: ber die Heilung von funktionellen psychischen Störungen nach der sog. Kaufmann-Methode*. In: *Neurologisches Centralblatt 37* (1918), p. 163. Dr. M. Raether was the head doctor of the Provinzial-Heil—und Pflegeinstitut in Bonn. At the annual conference of the Gesellschaft Deutscher Nervenärzte in Bonn on September 29, 1917, Raether gave a lecture which included a demonstration of "Kaufmann Cure" (see also Peter Riedesser and Axel Verderber: *Aufrüstung der Seelen. Militärpsychologie und Militärpsychiatrie in Deutschland und Amerika*. Freiburg 1985, pp. 15-17)

14. Max Nonne: Therapeutische Erfahrungen an den Kriegsneurosen in den Jahren 1914 -1918. In: Karl Bonhoeffer: "Über die Bedeutung der Kriegserfahrungen für die allgemeine Psychopathologie und Ätiologie der Geisteskrankheiten." In: of same (publ.): *Geistes—und Nervenkrankheiten* (handbook of medical experiences in the world war, vol. 4). Leipzig 1922, p. 105

15. Professor Wagner von Jauregg was heavily involved in the development of shock therapy, and even received the Nobel Prize for his work on "malaria therapy." The various shock therapies of the '30s came straight from the basic theories of "malaria therapy," which involved the use of insulin, Cardiazol and electroshock.

16. Sigmund Freud, quoted by Rene Gicklhorn: "Sigmund Freud ber Kriegsneurosen, Elektrotherapie und Psychoanalyse." In: Psyche 26 (1972), pp. 944-945

17. Emil Kraeplin, *100 Jahre Psychiatrie*. In: Z. Neur. 63 (1918), pp. 161-275

18. *See* Ingo Steudel: *Die Innovationszeit von Prüfungsfchern in der medizinischen Ausbildung in Deutschland*. Disseration, Kiel 1973

19. C. Wernicke: *Zweck und Ziel der Psychiatrischen Kliniken*, 1889

20. Otto Wuth to Oswald Bumke dated 2.5.1943: BA/MA (Bundesarchiv/Militärarchiv Freiburg) RH 12-23 H20/504. It becomes very clear how much clinical psychology was hated and dispised by neuropsychiatrists in the correspondence of the top consulting psychiatrist in the German army, Otto Wuth and the Munich psychiatric consultant Oswald Bumke. In 1943 Wuth recommended that any wounded soldier whose brain damage caused trembling and other such symptoms should not be allowed to be treated by psychologists and other such quacks but with "proven methods" like operations on the larynx, treatments with electric current and the injection of "indifferent liquids" in order to remove the symptoms. Naturally, this was not therapy, but little more than torture.

Part I—Chapter 4
THE SECRET PACT WITH THE DEVIL: THE ALLIANCE BETWEEN RACIAL THEORISTS AND PSYCHIATRY

1. *See* Gustav Liebermeister: *Über die Behandlung von Kriegsneurosen*, Halle a.d.S. 1917, pp. 7-8

2. Alfred Ploetz: *Die Tüchtigkeit unserer Rasse und der Schutz der Schwachen*, Berlin 1895, p. 225

3. K. Hintze: "Staatssozialismus oder soziale Fürsorge auf genossenschaftlicher Basis?" In: *Ärztliches Vereinsblatt* 1924, p. 163 (private archive doc.

15/W1)

4. Walther Auer: "Zu dem, Aufruf an die deutsche rzteschaft" des Herrn Reg.-Med.-Rat Dr. Boeters." In: *Ärztliches Vereinsblatt* of 01/23/1924, p. 28

5. Gustav Aschaffenburg was the director of the "department of the mentally insane" in Lindenthal, where his main interest was in the psychiatric effects of various medicines. He developed theories on the phenomenon of "delirium tremens," "the delusion of the grouch," and "diminished responsibility," among others. His published works include "Das Verbrechen und seine Bekämpfung," Heidelberg 1906; "Die Sicherung der Gesellschaft gegen gemeingefähliche Geisteskranke," Berlin 1912; "Lokalisierte und allgemeine Ausfallerscheinungen nach Hirnverletzungen" (article), Halle 1916; "Psychiatrie und Strafrecht," Cologne 1928. He was the publisher of the "Handbuch der Psychiatrie," Leipzig and Vienna 1911-1928, which dealt with the general symptomatology of psychoses. Quoted by: August Hirsch (publ.): *Biographisches Lexikon der hervorragenden Ärzte aller Zeiten und Völker*, Berlin and Wies 1934, p. 42

6. Fritz Lenz: "Die soziologische Bedeutung der Selektion." In: *Schranitz and Herberer* (publ.): *100 Jahre Evolutionsforschung*, Stuttgart 1960

7. Jürgen Kroll: *Zur Entstehung und Institutionalisierung einer naturwissenschaftlichen und sozialpolitischen Bewegung: Die Entwicklung der Eugenik/Rassenhygiene bis zum Jahre 1933*. Soc. dissertation—Wiss., Tübingen

Part I—Chapter 5

HOW PSYCHIATRIC IDEAS INFILTRATED SOCIETY

1. Source: Alfred Hoche: Jahresringe. *Innenansicht eines Menschenlebens.* Munich and Berlin 1937

2. *Ibid.*, p. 290

3. quoted by Klee, *op. cit.*, p. 20ff

4. quoted by Klee, *op. cit.*, p. 24

5. Prof. Dr. Max von Gruber, *Docent Dr. Ernst Rüdin*, Fortpflanzung, Vererbung Rassenhygiene. Munich 1911

6. *Ibid.*, p. 91

7. *Ibid.*, p. 163 following pages

8. *Ibid.*, p. 279f.

9. *Gesetz zur Verhülung erbkranken Nachwuchses vom 14. Juli 1933*, adapted and explained by Dr. Arthur Gött, Dr. Ernst Rüdin & Dr. Falk Ruttke. Munich 1934, p. 5

Part I—Chapter 6

THE SECRET ACTIVITIES OF THE THIRD REICH: T4—THE KILLERS GO TO WORK

1. Gotz-Aly, (publ.), *Operation T4 1939—1945: The "Euthanasia" Headquarters of Tiergartenstrasse 4*, Berlin 1989, p. 56

2. Klee, *"Euthanasie" im NS-Staat*, Frankfurt am Main 1989, p. 86

3. quoted by Klee, *op. cit.*, p. 60

4. quoted by Klee, *op. cit.*, p. 61

5. *Ibid.*, p. 64

6. *Ibid.*, p. 78

7. *See* Alfred Hoche on the appointment of a "commission" for the selection of victims for "euthanasia." In: Karl Binding and Alfred Hoche: *Die Freigabe der Vernichtung lebensunwerten Lebens. Ihr Maaß und ihre Form.* Leipzig 1920, p. 51

8. Klee, *op. cit.*, p. 101

9. from: Ernst Klee Archive

10. quoted by Klee, *op. cit.*, p. 106

11. eyewitness report of August Becker

12. Aly among others, *Aktion T4*, p. 11

13. Klee, *Dokumente zur Euthanasie*, Frankfurt am Main 1985, p. 100

14. Klee, *"Euthanasie" im NS-Staat*, p. 120/121

15. testimony of an eyewitness, (Mauthe) on October 18, 1948, quoted by Klee, *op. cit.*, p. 101

16. This data is contained in an investigation by Gerhard Schmidt of over 2000 patients. Quoted by Klee, *op. cit.*, p. 122

17. *Ibid.*, p. 123
18. *Ibid.*, p. 123
19. *Ibid.*, p. 184
20. Eyewitness account of Maximilian L., custodian at Hadamar, April 6, 1946 (4aJs/45 StA Ffm)
21. Klee, *"Euthanasie" im NS-Staat*, p. 241
22. *Ibid.*, p. 251
23. All of the film footage was to be destroyed in 1945. Luckily, however, a cameraman who had taken part on the production of the T4-movies secretly filmed a second copy. It was discovered in a STASI-archive in the former GDR in 1991—a historic documentation of the horror.
24. statement of Mennecke. Open session of the Eichberg proceedings on December 3, 1946. Quoted by Ernst Klee: *"Euthanasie" im NS-Staat*. Ffm 1985, p. 340
25. report of Dr. Bischoff on 10/12/1945. In: Poltrot, 57. Quoted by Klee: *"Euthanasie" im NS-Staat*. Ffm 1985, p. 341
26. *Ibid.*, p. 345
27. From the records of Rudolf Hoess, quoted by Kaden and Nestler, *Documents of Crime: From the Files of the Third Reich*, Vol. 3, Berlin 1993, p. 40
28. From a sentencing of a Nazi criminal, Gustav Münzberger. Quoted by: Klee, *"Euthanasie" im NS-Staat*, p. 378
29. *Ibid.*, p. 371
30. quoted by Robert Jay Lifton, *The Nazi Doctors*, Basic Books, 1986, p. 170
31. *Ibid.*, pp. 184-185
32. from Dr. Johannes Schottky, on 02/26/1971 (OT4Z). Quoted by Klee: *"Euthanasie" im NS-Staat*. Ffm 1985, p. 341
33. *Ibid.*, p. 342
34. *Ibid.*, p. 62

Part II—Chapter 1
HOW THE TRANSITION WAS ENGINEERED

1. quoted by Ernst Klee, *"Euthanasie" im NS-Staat*, p. 385f.
2. *Ibid.*, p. 414
3. quoted by Klee, *Was sie taten—Was sie wurden. Ärzte, Juristen und andere Beteiligte am Kranken—oder Judenmord*, Frankfurt 1988, p. 146
4. "Viele Nazi-Richter bernommen," *Frankfurter Rundschau*, May 4, 1992
5. Spiegel-series 1988: "Die Mörder sind noch unter uns," issue 25, p. 116
6. *Ibid.*, pp. 115-116
7. Hendrik van den Bussche (publ.): *Medizinische Wissenschaften im Dritten Reich. Kontinuität, Anpassung und Opposition an der Hamburger Medizinischen Fakultät (Hamburger Beiträge zur Wissenschaftsgeschichte, vol. 5)*. Berlin and Hamburg 1989, p. 427
8. *Ibid.*, p. 427
9. StA HH, HW-DPA, IV 166, *Degkwitz an den Hohen Senat der Hansischen Universität*, 06/16/1948. Quoted by Hendrik van den Bussche, *loc. cit.*, p. 428
10. Spiegel-series 1988: "Die Mörder sind noch unter uns," issue 25, p. 116
11. Munziger-Archive delivery 21/64 of 05/23/1964
12. Fabian von Schlabrendorff, *Begegnungen in fünf Jahrzehnten*, Tübingen 1979, p. 368ff
13. Klee, *Was sie taten, was sie wurden, op. cit.*, p. 139ff
14. Werner Villinger and Hermann Stutte: "Zeitgemaße Aufgaben und Probleme der Jugendfürsorge," *Der Nervenarzt*, paper 6, June 1948, pp. 249-254
15. G. Kloos, *Grundria der Psychiatrie und Neurologie*, edition 1968 (first edition 1944), p. 461
16. Hendrik van den Bussche, *op. cit.*, p. 431, footnote 64

Part II—Chapter 2
GERMAN PSYCHIATRY AFTER THE WAR: ECHOES OF THE PAST

1. quoted by Thom, et. al., *Medizin unterm Hakenkreuz, VEB Verlag Volk und Gesundheit* 1989, p. 69
2. Max Weinreich, *Hitler's Professors*, New

York 1946, p. 33

3. Ernst Rüdin at the 5th annual assembly of the Gesellschaft Deutscher Neurologen und Psychiater in Wiesbaden, March 1939

4. Munzinger Archive of 3/28/1964, No. 1313

5. Kretschmer, Konstitutionslehre und Rassenhygiene in Rüdin: *Erblehre und Rassenhygiene im völkischen Staat,* Munich 1934, p. 185

6. *Ibid.,* p. 186

7. Hans-Ludwig Siemen, "Menschen blieben auf der Strecke…" *Psychiatrie zwischen Reform und Nationalsozialismus.* Gütersloh 1987

8. Ernst Klee, *Was sie taten—was sie wurden, op. cit.,* p. 172

9. Thom, et. al., *Medizin unterm Hakenkreuz, VEB Verlag Volk und Gesundheit* 1989, p. 165

10. Ernst Kretschmer, *Mensch und Lebensgrund. Gesammelte Aufsätze,* Tübingen 1966, p. 145

11. *Ibid.,* p. 149

12. *Ibid.,* p. 160

13. Kurt Novak: *"Euthanasie" und Sterilisierung im "Dritten Reich."* Göttingen 1978, p. 106

14. Benno Müller-Hill: *Tödliche Wissenschaften,* Reinbek 1984, p. 35

15. See Ernst Klee: *Was sie taten—was sie wurden, op. cit.,* p. 171

16. Werner Villinger and Hermann Stutte: "Zeitgemaße Aufgaben und Probleme der Jugendfürsorge," *Der Nervenarzt,* H 6, June 1948, pp. 249-254

17. *See* the descriptions in: Hendrik van den Bussche, *Medizinische Wissenschaft im "Dritten Reich." Kontinuität, Anpassung und Opposition an der Hamburger Medizinischen Fakultät (Hamburger Beiträge zur Wissenschaftsgeschichte, Vol. 5).* Berlin and Hamburg 1989, p. 431, footnote 64

18. Hendrick van den Bussche (pub), *op. cit.,* p. 431

19. StA HH (State Archive Hamburg), Uni 1, A 1608, p. 1

20. *Der Spiegel,* No. 19/1961, *Ärzte—die Kreuzelschreiber*

21. *Der Spiegel,* No. 23/1961

22. quoted by Klee, *"Euthanasie" im NS-Staat,* p. 397

23. *Der Nervenarzt* 51 (1980), pp. 503-504

24. Klee, *"Euthanasie" im NS-Staat,* p. 227

25. *Münsterische Zeitung* of May 17, 1980

26. Ernst Klee, *Was sie taten—was sie wurden. Ärzte, Juristen und andere Beteiligte am Kranken- und Judenmord, op. cit.,* p. 239

27. in *Der Spiegel* No. 25/1988, p. 115

28. Klee, *"Euthanasie" im NS-Staat, op. cit.,* p. 101

29. *Ibid.,* p. 146

30. *Ibid.,* p. 146

31. The infamous Auschwitz doctor Josef Mengele, an assistant physician to Dr. Otmar Freiherr von Verschuer, (the director of the institute for genetics and racial study in Frankfurt) was also an admirer of twin research. His cruelty and brutality is well known. For example, it is said that he had drawn a straight line on the wall 1.56 meters off the floor. Whoever was shorter had to go in the gas chamber; whoever was taller was experimented on with brain operations, injections of the various experimental solutions, etc., and following that murdered (if they hadn't already died on the dissecting table). On one occasion, he had a pair of twins shot and then opened up their chests just to prove to his colleagues that his diagnosis was correct (he was wrong). Mengele fled after the war to Argentina, where he supposedly drowned in 1978, during a swim in the ocean.

32. *See* Fiat Review of German Science 1939-1946, Wiesbaden 1948, p. 260

33. from: *Psychiatrie und Gesellschaft,* 1958, p. 162

34. *Der Nervenarzt,* vol. 26, 1955, p. 386

35. *Der Spiegel* of April 24, 1980—"Aus der

Fassung." Quoted from: Keppler, Mehler, *Der sanfte Schrei*, Munich 1989

36. Friedrich Panse: "Das Schicksal von Renten- und Kriegsneurotikern nach Erledigung ihrer Ansprche," *Deutsche Zeitschrift für Nervenheilkunde*, vol. 88, Leipzig 1926, p. 233

37. Peter Riedesser and Axel Verderber: *Aufrüstung der Seelen, Militärpsychologie und Militärpsychiatrie in Deutschland und Amerika*. Freiburg 1985, p. 32

38. "1999" (Zeitschrift für Sozialgeschichte des 20. und 21. Jahrhunderts) 2 (1987), pg. 8-75, (note 9), pp. 42-45 Also cp. Roth 1987 Roth, Karl Heinz: *Die Modernisierung der Folter in den beiden Weltkriegen*.

39. Dr. Helmuth E. Ehrhardt, "Beitrag zur elektrischen Erregbarkeit des Nerven unter der Einwirkung von Narkoticis," Inaugural Dissertation, Breslau 1940, chapter Lebenslauf

40. published in: *Deutsche Zeitschrift für Nervenheilkunde*, vol. 159, 1948, pp. 75-80 (under Villinger)

41. *Der Nervenarzt*, 19. year 1948, edition 1, pp. 37-42

42. Weingart , et. al., Rasse, Blut und Gene, *Geschichte der Eugenik und Rassenhygiene in Deutschland*, Frankfurt am Main 1988, p. 589f

43. quoted by Klee, *Was sie taten—was sie wurden, op. cit.*, p. 171

44. *Deutsches Ärzteblatt* of January 27, 1977

45. Helmut E. Ehrhardt, Euthanasie und Vernichtung 'lebensunwerten' Lebens, in: *Forum der Psychiatrie*, publisher Hans Bürger-Prinz, Hamburg 1965, p. 34

46. *Ibid.*, p. 42

47. Prof. Helmut Selbach was on the staff of the Kaiser-Wilhelm-Institute for Brain Research in Berlin under Spatz in the 1940s. Spatz worked very closely with Julius Hallervorden, the director of the institute's neuropathological department, who procured 500 brains of euthanized mentally ill. Selbach published articles on brain research under Spatz and de Crinis.

48. Excerpt from a six page research application addressed to the Federal Department of Civil Defence. The applicant was "Prof. Dr. Hippius, neurological clinic of the University of Munich."

49. *Wirtschaftswoche* No. 34, vol. of 8/18/1989

50. *See*: AZ 123 js 3115/90 from the district court of Munich I of March 21, 1991

51. *See* "Klinische Erfahrungen mit dem Rauwolfia-Alkaloid Reserpin in der Psychiatrie" by J. Hiob and H. Hippius. *German Medical Weekly*, No. 41 of October 14, 1955, p. 1499

52. *SPEKTRUM der Psychiatrie und Nervenheilkunde* 2/1989

53. document of the office of the Chief Council for War Crimes, document # L0170

54. *Münsterische Zeitung* of May 17, 1980

55. *Die Tageszeitung*, July 1, 1982, p. 9, "Herr Professor Helmchen und das Menschenexperiment"

56. *Der Nervenarzt*, year 38, vol. 5/1967, p. 219

57. H. Helmchen, "Delirante Abläufe unter psychiatrischer Pharmakotherapie," in: archive for psychiatry and periodical for all of neurology. vol. 202/1961, p. 399, quoted in *Die Tageszeitung* (TZ) of July 1, 1982, p. 9

58. H. Helmchen, "Probleme der Therapieforschung in der Psychiatrie," *Der Nervenarzt*, No. 53/1982, p. 378

Part II—Chapter 3

THE REMARKABLE SECRET CONNECTIONS OF GERMAN CHILD AND ADOLESCENT PSYCHIATRY

1. *Deutsches Ärzteblatt* from January 27, 1977

2. *Zeitschrift für Kinderforschung*, published by Reiter, Villinger, Hoffmann and Zutt, vol. 49, issue 1, publishing house J. Springer, Berlin 1941, p. 1

3. *Ibid.*, p. 14
4. *Ibid.*, p. 18
5. *Ibid.*, p. 21
6. *Ibid.*, p. 21
7. *Der Spiegel*, No. 23/1961
8. source: Götz Aly (pub.), *Aktion T4*, p. 130
9. *Zeitschrift für Kinderforschung, op. cit.*, p. 93
10. *Ibid.*, pp. 111-112
11. *Ibid.*, p. 113
12. *Ibid.*, p. 81
13. source: Klee, *Dokumente zur Euthanasie*, p. 249
14. *Zeitschrift für Kinderforschung, op. cit.*, p. 82
15. *Ibid.*, pp. 85-86
16. *Der Nervenarzt*, No. 41/1970, pp. 313-314
17. *Münchener Medizinische Wochenschrift*, 1933, p. 1007
18. source: Klee, *Dokumente zur Euthanasie*, p. 237
19. Hermann Stutte, "30 Jahre Deutsche Vereinigung für Jugendpsychiatrie," *Der Nervenarzt*, No. 41/1970, p. 314
20. *Die Zeit*, No. 38/1992
21. Dr. Paul Schröder, *Kindliche Charaktere und ihre Abartigkeiten, with illustrated examples from Dr. Hans Heinze*, Breslau 1931
22. *Ibid.*, p. 15
23. "Among the members of the child euthanasia committee were Hitler's personal physician Karl Brandt, the ophthalmologist Dr. Helmut Unger,…pediatrician Dr. Ernst Wentzler (…), Dr. Hans Heinze…and Professor Werner Catel…" (Ernst Klee in *"Euthanasie" im NS-Staat*, p. 77)
24. quoted by Klee, *Was sie taten—was sie wurden, op. cit.*, p. 136
25. *Ibid.*, p. 136
26. Götz Aly among others, Reform und Gewissen—*"Euthanasie" im Dienst des Fortschritts*, Berlin, 1985, p. 64
27. Thom, *Caregorodcev, Medizin unterm Hakenkreuz*, Leipzig 1989, p. 144
28. Klee, *Was sie taten—was sie wurden, op. cit.*, pp. 136-137
29. *Der Spiegel*, issue 25/1988, *Die Mörder sind noch unter uns*, p. 119
30. source: Ernst Klee: *Sichten und Vernichten*. In: *Die Zeit*, issue 38 of September 11, 1992
31. in the place cited in the text
32. *See* also the article of Carola Bollmann and Ulrike Wittich: "Hermann Stutte und das Unerziehbarkeitsdogma in der deutschen Psychiatriegeschichte," in the magazine *Behindertenpädagogik*, year 22, issue 2/1983, p. 107-123 and the letters to the editor in the periodical *Behindertenpädagogik*, year 23, issue 1/1984, pp. 44-48 as well as the answer from Carola Bollmann published in the same periodical, p. 50
33. *Die Zeit, loc. cit.*
34. "In memoriam Hermann Stutte," *Der Nervenarzt* (1982) 53, p. 492, "
35. *Die Zeit, loc. cit.*
36. Prof. Manfred Müller-Kppers, *modern erziehen, Grundlagen—Probleme—Lösungen*, Munich 1972, p. 263
37. Rudolf Degkwitz (pub.), *Hundert Jahre Nervenheilkunde*, Stuttgart 1985, p. 95
38. *Die Zeit, op. cit.*
39. *Deutsches rzteblatt* 84, issue 28/29, from July 1987, p. 1215
40. rztezeitung, February 19, 1988, p. 1
41. *Leipziger Volkszeitung* from 10/13/91: "SS-Vergangenheit von Prüfer entlarvt—Professor Harrer verlat Waldheimer Untersuchungsausschau"
42. Nissen, Eggers, Martinius, Kinder—*und jugendpsychiatrische Pharmakotherapie in Klinik und Praxis*, Berlin, Heidelberg, New York Tokyo 1984
43. *Ibid.*, p. 83
44. *Ibid.*, p. 84
45. *Ibid.*, p. 83
46. *Ibid.*, p. 89
47. *Denkschrift zur Lage der Kinder—und Jugendpsychiatrie in der Bundesrepublik Deutschland*, published by the board of directors of the German Society for

Child and Youth Psychiatry in March 1984, new edition from July 1990. Publisher Prof. Dr. Dr. H. Remschmidt and Prof. Dr. M. H. Schmidt, p. 9

48. *Ibid.*, p. 11

Part II—Chapter 4
RESEARCH AND GENETICS:
AN OLD PRODUCT IN
A NEW PACKAGE

1. Document of the Office of the Chief Council for War Crimes, document # L-170, from July 20, 1945

2. *See* article in *Frankfurter Rundschau* from May 20, 1985, Dr. Klaus-Dieter Thomann, "Rassenhygiene und Anthropologie"

3. *Gruber, Rüdin: Fortpflanzung, Vererbung, Rassenhygiene*, Munich 1911

4. "25 Jahre Kaiser Wilhelm Gesellschaft," vol. 1, Berlin 1936

5. Max-Planck-Gesellschaft, *Berlichte und Mitteilungen*, issue 2/92, p. 13f

6. Ernst Rüdin, "20 Jahre menschliche Erbforschung an der Deutschen Forschungsanstalt für Psychiatrie in München," Kaiser-Wilhelm-Institut; pub. in archive for racial and social biology including racial and social hygiene, Munich 1938, vol. 32, issue 3, p. 193

7. The Max Planck Institute for Psychiatry is the successor organization of the Kaiser Wilhelm Institute for Psychiatry. Their names are identical with the German Research Institute in Munich, whose name has never been dropped and is currently being used as a second name.

8. *See:* Aly Götz, Karl Friedrich Masuhr, Maria Lehmann, Karl Heinz Roth, Ulrich Schultz, Reform und Gewissen—*"Euthanasie" im Dienste des Fortschritts. Beiträge zur national-sozialistischen Gesundheits- und Sozialpolitik: 2*, Berlin 1985, p. 64 and p. 73

9. *Yearbook of the Max-Planck-Gesellschaft zur Förderung der Wissenschaften e. V.* 1961, part II, Göttingen 1961, p. 670

10. Act for the prevention of a genetically sick rising generation, worked on by Gütt, Rüdin and Ruttke. Munich 1934, p. 5

11. *Ibid.*

12. *Ibid.*, p. 55

13. source: *MPG, Berichte und Mitteilungen* 2/92, p. 21

14. Aly, et al., *op. cit.*, p. 64ff.

15. source: Klee, *Dokumente zur Euthanasie*, p. 248

16. Aly et al., *op. cit.*, p. 66

17. *Ibid.*, p. 67f.

18. Jahrbuch 1940 of the *Kaiser-Wilhelm-Gesellschaft for Promotion of the Sciences*, p. 25

19. Fritz Lenz: "Die soziologische Bedeutung der Selektion," Schranitz and Herberer (pub.): *100 Jahre Evolutionsforschung*, Stuttgart 1960

20. Dr. O. Freiherr von Verschuer, *Erblehre des Menschen*, Berlin 1934, p. 29

21. Dr. Klaus-Dieter Thomann, "Rassenhygiene und Anthropologie: Die zwei Karrieren des Prof. Verschuer," article in the *Frankfurter Rundschau*, May 20, 1985

22. Dr. Miklos Nyiszli, Auschwitz—A Doctor's Eyewitness Account, New York 1960, p. 174ff.

23. *Frankfurter Rundschau* #115, May 20, 1985, Dr. Klaus Dieter Thomann, "Rassenhygiene und Anthropologie: Die zwei Karrieren des Prof. Verschuer"

24. Today, the Max Planck Institute for Psychiatry (DFA) consists of a clinical and a theoretical institute. The theoretical institute, based in Martinsried near Munich, performs "basic research," while the clinical institute still lies in the Kraepelinstrasse in Munich.

25. *See Psychologie Heute*, year 17, # 8/1990, "Alle psychiatrischen Erkrankungen haben eine genetische Grundlage," pp. 61-65

Part II—Chapter 5
"MENTAL HYGIENE"—
WHAT DOES IT REALLY MEAN?

1. *See* O. Bunke, G. Kolb, H. Roemer, E. Kahn (pub.): *Handwörterbuch der psychischen Hygiene und der psychiatrischen Fürsorge*. Berlin and Leipzig 1931, pg. 296ff. Cp. also: H. Schulte: *Geschichte und Aufgaben der Mental hygiene in Deutschland*. In: Helmut E. Ehrhardt (pub.): *Psychiatrie und Gesellschaft*. 1958, pg. 156-166, as well as the essay of the Viennese psychiatrists H. Hoff and W. Spiel: "Bedeutung und Grenzen der psychischen Hygiene für Psychiatrie und Psychotherapie." pg. 175-183. Cp. also Hans Roemer: *Die rassenhygienischen Aufgaben der praktischen Psychiatrie unter besonderer Berücksichtigung der offenen Fürsorge.* In: Ernst Rüdin: *Erblehre und Rassenhygiene im völkischen Staat*. Munich 1934

2. H. Schulte: "Geschichte und Aufgaben der Mental hygiene in Deutschland," Helmut E. Ehrhardt (pub.): *Psychiatrie und Gesellschaft*. 1958, p. 160

3. *Roemer in the Zeitschrift für Psychische Hygiene*, vol. 2, issue 1, 1928. Quoted by H. Schulte: "Geschichte und Aufgabe der Mental hygiene in Deutschland," *Psychiatrie und Gesellschaft*, Helmut E. Ehrhardt (pub.): 1958, p. 158

4. Hermann Stutte, *Kinderspychiatrische Beiträge zur Mental hygiene*, Alma Mater Philippina (University of Marburg), 1973

5. *Zeitschrift für psychische Hygiene*, # 1/1928, p. 11

6. Hans-Ludwig Siemen, *Menschen blieben auf der Strecke. Psychiatrie zwischen Reform und Nationalsozialismus.* Gütersloh 1987

7. Rüdin among others, *Erblehre und Rassenhygiene im völkischen Staat*, Munich 1934, p. 120ff.

8. Benno Müller-Hill: *Tödliche Wissenschaft. Die Aussonderung von Juden, Zigeunern und Geisteskranken 1933-1945*, Reinbek near Hamburg 1984, p. 130

9. The William Alanson White Memorial Lectures. Second Series in: *Psychiatry, Journal of the Biology and Pathology of International Relations*. Vol. 9, # 1, February 1946

10. H. Schulte, "Geschichte und Aufgabe der Mental hygiene in Deutschland," Helmut E. Ehrhardt (pub.): *Psychiatrie und Gesellschaft*, 1958, p. 161

11. H. Ehrhardt, D. Ploog, H. Stutte (pub.): *Psychiatrie und Gesellschaft, Ergebnisse und Probleme der Sozialpsychiatrie*, (to the 60th birthday of Werner Villinger), Bern and Stuttgart 1958, p. 160

12. *Ibid.*, p. 176

13. *Ibid.*, p. 176

14. *Ibid.*, p. 165

15. Dr. Mabuse, Zeitschrift im Gesundheitswesen, year 11, April 1986, "Humangenetische Beratung," p. 30

16. *Ibid.*, p. 30

17. *Ibid.*, p. 30

Part II—Chapter 6
"OPERATION MENTALLY ILL":
THE NEW STRATEGIES OF THE
MENTAL HYGIENE MOVEMENT

1. Rüdin, *Erblehre und Rassenhygiene im völkischen Staat*, Munich 1934, p. 123

2. Hans Roemer, "Die rassenhygienischen Aufgaben der praktischen Psychiatrie unter besonderer Berücksichtigung der offenen Fürsorge," from Ernst Rüdin, *Erblehre und Rassenhygiene im völkischen Staat*, Munich 1934, p. 120

3. Walter Schultze, "Die Bedeutung der Rassenhygiene für Staat und Volk in Gegenwart und Zukunft," in: Ernst Rüdin, *Erblehre und Rassenhygiene im vlkischen Staat*, Munich 1934, p. 3

4. The periodical *Der Nervenarzt* reminds us of the case of psychiatrist Gottfried Ewald, who had left the preliminary inquest into the T4 out of protest. He then wrote to the Reich's Minister of Health: "Fear and mistrust will take hold of the population...it will now be said: Whoever goes into a sanatorium

will be killed." (J.E. Meyer, "Gnadentod für behinderte Kinder, für Demente und chronisch Geisteskranke—Die neuesten Zielvorstellungen der Euthanasie," *Der Nervenarzt* Nr. 48, 1977, p. 565.—This case shows us that not only was it possible for psychiatrists to distance themselves from their own acts, but also to justify their behavior by claiming to have only acted on orders

5. Gütt, Rüdin, Ruttke, *Gesetz zur Verhtung erbkranken Nachwuchses*, Munich 1936, 2nd edition, p. 60

6. Gütt, Rüdin, Ruttke, *Ibid.*, p. 61

7. Klaus Dorner (pub.), *Fortschritte der Psychiatrie im Umgang mit Menschen: Wert und Verwertung des Menschen im 20. Jahrhundert, 36. Gütersloher Fortbildungswoche 1984, Veranst. Landschaftsverb. Westfalen-Lippe*, Rehburg-Loccum 1985, pp. 211-216. The original memorandum is located in the federal archives.

8. According to investigations by *Der Spiegel*, Manger-König was obviously on the payroll of the pharmaceutical industry (*Der Spiegel*, # 27/1985, pg. 29.) According to this issue, Manger-König received a remittance of 10,000 DM from Hoechst AG in December 1978 for "his support and understanding, that has proved advantageous during the last year."

9. *Der Nervenarzt*, 35, year 1964, p. 224

10. Klaus Dorner (pub.), *Fortschritte der Psychiatrie im Umgang mit Menschen: Wert und Verwertung des Menschen im 20. Jahrhundert, 36. Gütersloher Fortbildungswoche 1984. Landschaftsverb. Westfalen-Lippe*, Rehburg-Loccum, 1985, pp. 211-216

11. *Deutscher Bundestag*, 6th legislative period, *Drucksache* VI/474 Sachgebiet 212

12. *Ibid.*

13. *Ibid.*

14. *Aktion Psychisch Kranke*, minutes of the 1st general members' meeting on January 18, 1971—2 p.m., Bundeshaus

15. Statutes for the Aktion Psychisch Kranke, Vereinigung der Reform der Versorgung psychisch Kranker e.V.; authenticated copy of July 9, 1971

16. Walter Picard, a member of the German parliament, was the first petitioner for the inquiry. Picard was a professional political propaganda expert and accomplished lobbyist. *Der Spiegel* reported on December 4, 1972 that Picard belonged to the "Studiengesellschaft für staatspolitische ffentlichkeitsarbeit" ("Research Organization for Public Works Concerning National Policy"). The address "P.O. Box 1" served as a cover address for anonymous election campaign advertisements which engaged in heavy mudslinging against the sitting SPD government. In one instance, full page advertisements screamed that a SPD government was incapable of guaranteeing "safety for our Jewish citizens too." However, only two days prior to this in the anti-Semitic newspaper *National Zeitung*, Picard's party had called to "arms all those who think and feel German." (*Der Spiegel*, Nr. 50/1972, pg. 38ff)

17. Dr. Caspar Kulenkampff (born 1921) is a vehement advocate of electroconvulsive therapy (see *Der Nervenarzt*, 30th year, issue 2, pg. 66ff.); director of the health care department for the Landschaftsverband Rheinland. Under his authority was the Brauweiler state hospital whose "climbing scandals" (escapes of patients) caused such a scandal that the hospital's director was brought to court. In 1982, a punishment order was issued on Kulenkampff during preliminary proceedings by the City of Cologne. Kulenkampff also oversaw the Rheinische Landesklinik Bonn, whose director, Huhn, (see below) led a life riddled with scandals. Kulenkampff himself conceded (regret-

tably too late) that the clinic was extremely poorly run. Starving patients, as well as several tragic accidents, some resulting in death, had brought the clinic to the attention of the press. It should also be mentioned in passing that Kulenkampff belonged to the previously mentioned "Action Committee for the Improvement of Care for the Psychologically Ill" in 1959.

18. Prof. Dr. Med. Albert Huhn (born 1923), a neurologist and psychiatrist. On February 22, 1980, the newspaper *Kölner Stadt-Anzeiger* reported that charges had been brought against Huhn by a Cologne lawyer for bodily injury resulting from the application of electroshock without permission.

19. Prof. Heinz Häfner (born 1926), a psychiatrist at the University of Heidelberg, was awarded his doctorate in 1950 in Munich under Kretschmer. The director of the Zentralinstitut für Seelische Gesundheit (Central Institute of Psychological Health) of the University of Heidelberg, Häfner is a strong advocate of electroshock. There are two milestones in particular which mark Prof. Häfner's career as a researcher: his discoveries in the field of brain surgery and his research into the "psychiatry of the persecuted," which critically examined Nazi persecution and its end results. The "material" that was being investigated (the language of psychiatry is marked by a tendency to talk about human beings as if they were "matter") consisted of about 700 patients who were victims of Nazi persecution. Originally, the investigation was supposed to see if those persecuted by the Nazis were entitled to legal compensation. Of course, the central role of psychiatry in all of these events, which certainly was known by the authors, was noticeably absent. Häfner's co-author, W. Ritter von Baeyer, was, after all, a student of Rüdin's. Many other psychia-

trists of the Nazi era such as Bürger-Prinz, Hoff, Kretschmer and Panse were also named in the bibliography. A thorough historical revisionism permeates this psychiatric document; but what can you expect from "expert testimony" about the victims of the authors' academic mentors? The conclusion of the research, of course, was that victims of "legally performed compulsory sterilizations" had no claim for compensation—not a peep about how Rüdin and other psychiatrists had been the main culprits in the sordid affair. (by Baeyer, Häfner, Kisker, *Psychiatrie der Verfolgten*, Berlin, Göttingen, Heidelberg 1964)

20. Prof. Dr. Med. Joachim-Ernst Meyer (born 1917) studied under both the T4 consultant, Friedrich Mauz, in Königsberg and Max de Crinis, the T4 psychiatrist, in Berlin. In 1949, he was awarded his doctorate for a thesis quoting the "very important realizations" of Hallervorden's brain research [Hallervorden was the psychiatrist who had procured over 500 brains from the killing institutes of the mentally sick]. In 1975, Meyer strongly criticized the push in the United States for the "mercy killing" of handicapped children and demented and chronically mentally ill patients.

21. Dr. Walter Theodor Winkler (born 1914) was awarded his doctorate in Marburg under Kretschmer in 1939. Another of his teachers was the Nazi psychiatrist Mauz. He was a member on the scientific advisory board of the federal medical society from 1962 to 1972. In 1970, he wrote a commentary on a just-passed law establishing preventive measures for psychological illnesses (*Der Nervenarzt*, year 41, issue 11, 1970, pg. 548ff.). In it, psychotropic drugs and electroshocks could be used on compulsorily hospitalized patients without their consent under legally permitted measures. The objective of the

law was an "adjustment to society," because "new combinations of events will develop to which the individual will have to adjust to if he wants to co-exist with and within the society."

22. *Drucksache # 7/1124* of the Bundestag

23. psychiatric memorandum from 1943, Federal Archive Koblenz

24. "Die Rolle der Vererbung im menschlichen Verhalten," Neue Anthropologie 2/74, p. 29

25. *Drucksache 7/4200*, Deutscher Bundestag, 7th legislative period, preamble

Part II—Chapter 7
FROM SOCIAL DARWINISM
TO HUMAN GENETICS:
RESEARCH IN THE
NAZI TRADITION

1. *American Journal of Psychiatry* 1968, vol. 125, No. 6

2. *See* interview with Prof. Bernd Klees (criminal lawyer). In: Thomas Weidenbach and Gerd Weiss: *Die Gen-Jäger. Biologen zwischen Wahn und Wissenschaft. Eine Gerd Weiss Filmproduktion*, Cologne 1990, source: B.O.A. Archiv No. 3018.0001: WDO-WCM 8/22/90, West 3. WDR 1990

3. Thomas Weidenbach and Gerd Weiss: *Sie Gen-Jger, op. cit.*, p. 4

4. The acronym FISH stands for "Fluorescent In-Situ Hybridization." For an in-depth explanation of the process, see Rolf H. Latusseck, "Neue Verfahren bringen rasche Gewissheit, Wie sich Erbkrankheiten sicher erkennen lassen," in *Die Welt,* No. 263, 1991, p. 21. See also *"Science"* magazine, vol. 254, p. 378

5. *Zeitschrift für Kinderforschung*, pub. von Reiter, Villinger, Hoffmann and Zutt, vol. 49, issue 1, Berlin 1941, p. 113

6. Interview with Prof. Bernd Klees (criminal lawyer), quoted in: Thomas Weidenbach and Gerd Weiss: *Die Gen-Jäger. Biologen zwischen Wahn und Wissenschaft. Eine Gerd Weiss*

Filmproduktion. Cologne 1990, source: B.O.A. Archive No. 3028.0001:WDO-WCM 8/22/90. West 3. WDR 1990

7. Dr. Mabuse, *Zeitschrift im Gesundheitswesen*, year 11, 1986, No. 41, p. 32

8. Allen R. Utke: Der Bioschock. Neue Biologie im Verhör. Munich 1980, p. 71

9. *Ibid.*, p. 71

10. Benno Müller-Hill: *Tödliche Wissenschaft. Die Aussonderung von Juden, Zigeunern und Geisteskranken 1933-1945.* Reinbek near Hamburg 1984, p. 7

Part II—Chapter 8
THE NAZI TRADITION IN
PSYCHIATRIC THERAPY

1. Peter Lehmann, *Der chemische Knebel*, p. 13ff.

2. quoted by Lehmann, *op. cit.*, p. 14, Reil, Johann Christian, *Rhapsodien ber die Anwendung der psychischen Curmethode aus Geisteszerrttungen*, Halle 1803

3. *Ibid.*, p. 18f.

4. *Ibid.*, p. 15f.

5. *Ibid.*, p. 15f.

6. *Ibid.*, p. 17f.

7. Kretschmer. In: *Nonne 1922* (annotation 209), pg. 108. Quoted by Hans-Ludwig Siemen: *Das Grauen ist vorprogrammiert. Psychiatrie zwischen Faschismus und Atomkrieg.* Gieaen 1982, pp. 19-20

8. "Cerletti was born on September 26, 1877, in the Italian town of Cornigliano and died on July 25, 1963, in Rome. He studied medicine in Turin and Rome and passed his medical examination in 1901 in Rome. He first performed a special assignment in histopathology and neuropathology, then studied clinical psychiatry under Kraepelin, whom he admired greatly. After his appointment to the position of professor for psychiatry at the University of Rome, Cerletti began his experiments with artificially produced seizures in 1935. He later developed the first electroshock apparatus and in April

1938 he performed the first (…) electroshock on human beings." (Thomas Szasz, *Wem dient die Psychiatrie? Vom Schlachthaus zum Irrenhaus*. In: Basaglia, Franco and Franca Basaglia-Ongaro (pub.): *Befriedigungsverbrechen. ber die Dienstbarkeit der Intellektuellen*. Ffm. 1980, p. 241). It is interesting to note that slaughterhouses and psychiatry actually have more in common than meets the eye. The Scottish psychiatrist Mowbray reports that in 1958 a Danish slaughterhouse contacted a psychiatrist to find out "if his most recently concocted physical therapy…would be of value to the humane killing of pigs." The "therapy" consisted of the inhaling of carbon monoxide until unconsciousness sets in. (reported by Peter Lehmann, Der chemische Knebel, Berlin 1990, p. 67)

9. *See*: Keppler, Mehler: *Der sanfte Schrei*. Munich 1989, p. 85

10. source: Aly, *Aktion T-4*, p. 159

11. Keppler, Mehler, *op. cit.*, p. 86

12. *Anklage der Wiener Staatanwaltschaft*, p. 25

13. *Wiener–Archive*, pg. 25, quoted by Klee, *op. cit.*, p. 438

14. *See* M. Daum: *Arbeit und Zwang, das Leben der Hadamarer Patienten im Schatten des Todes*. In: Dorothee Roer, Dorothee and Dieter Henkel (pub.): *Psychiatrie im Faschismus*. Bonn 1986, pg. 184ff. Also cp: *Fachschaft Medizin an der Universität Köln* (organizer) among others: *Heilen und Vernichten im Nationalsozialismus. Der Katalog zur Ausstellung*. Cologne 1985, p. 154ff

15. Ernst Klee: "…wie ein Hammer auf den Kopf. Behandlung mit Elektroschocks führte in Frankfurt zu einem Psychiatrie-Streit," from *Die Zeit*, 2/18/1977

16. *See Psychologie Heute*, June 1977, p. 34

17. *See Psychologie Heute*, June 1977, p. 34

18. *See Psychologie Heute*, June 1977, p. 34

19. Jules H. Masserman and Mary Grier Jacques "Effects of cerebral electroshock on experimental neuroses in cats," *The American Journal of Psychiatry*. Vol. 104, No. 1, (1947), p. 97

20. *See* Bernhard J. Alpers and Joseph Hughes: "Changes in the brain after electrically induced convulsions in cats," *Archives of Neurology and Psychiatry*, Vol. 47 (1942), pp. 385-398. Hans Hartelius: "Cerebral changes following electrically induced convulsions. An experimental study on cats," Copenhagen 1952

21. *See* Hermann Keppler and Ha. A. Mehler, *op. cit.*, p. 87-88

22. Hans Göppinger: "Muß vor einer Elektroschockbehandlung der Kranke auf mögliche körperliche Schäden hingewiesen werden?" *Deutsche Medizinische Wochenschrift H 45*, year 80, 1955, p. 1667. Dr. Hans Göppinger of the Psychiatric and Neurological Clinic of the University of Heidelberg

23. Keppler, Mehler, *op. cit.*, p. 86

24. Klaus Heim: "Behandlung aus der Steckdose. Therapie oder psychiatrischer Mythos?" *Deutsche Zeitung*, 3/11/1977

25. Keppler, Mehler, *op. cit.*, p. 86

26. Ernst Klee: "…wie ein Hammer auf den Kopf. Behandlung mit Elektroschocks führte in Frankfurt zu einem Psychiatrie-Streit," *Die Zeit* from 2/18/1977

27. *See* First European Symposium on ECT, March 26-29, 1992, Graz, Austria, *Abstractbook*, pp. 18-25

28. *Der Nervenarzt*, year 41, issue 3, March 1970, p. 105

29. transcript of the press conference regarding the ECT-Workshop, October 16, 1992, auditorium of the TU Munich, p. 16

30. A. E. Hotchner: *Papa Hemingway*, Munich 1966, p. 346. A. E. Hotchner was a longtime friend of Hemingway.

31. *See* also an article in *Der Spiegel*, "Brandherd im Gehirn. Die

Elektroschock-Therapie findet auch in deutschen Kliniken wieder Befürworter," *Der Spiegel*, No. 3, 1991, p. 178

32. *See* Ruth Kuntz-Brunner: *Psychotherapie. Streit um die richtige Methode.* In: *Deutsche Universitäts-Zeitung (DUZ)*, issue 7, 1992, pp. 26-28

33. *Der Spiegel*, No. 24, 6/9/1986; quoted by Keppler, Mehler, *op. cit.*, p. 77

34. *Ibid.*, p. 78

35. *Fortschritte der Neurologie, Psychiatrie und ihrer Grenzgebiete*, year 15, 1957, Stuttgart, issue 4, p. 240/241

36. University of the Saarland, *Forschungsbericht* 1977, p. 158

37. *Aktuelle Neuropädiatrie, 2. Jahrestagung der Gesellschaft für Neuropädiatrie* Kiel 1976, pub. H. Doose, Stuttgart 1977, p. 151

38. *National Observer*, August 3, 1974

39. *AZ Munich* from July 4, 1980, p. 29

40. *Der Stern*, No. 33 from August 7, 1980, p. 26

41. *Der Spiegel*, 26/1990, p. 66

42. *Blick*, March 28, 1991

43. *Blick*, March 12, 1991

44. "Approximately 6.7 percent of all patients receive medications that could cause addiction under certain circumstances. Therefore, over a long period, a danger for developing an addiction does exist. We are talking here about mind altering, or so-called psychotropic medicine." see: "Suchtgefahr bei Langzeit-Einnahme," *Frankfurter Rundschau* No. 15 of 1/18/1992, p. 9. Too many medications in too large dosages are being prescribed, particularly for older people. "From the prescribed psychopharmaceuticals, over two-thirds of the sleeping and sedative medication ends up in the hands of those over sixty." This was the result of a study by the Allgemeine Ortskrankenkasse (AOK = Germany's general health insurance company), commissioned by the health minister of North-Rhine-Westfalia. (*See* also:

Ältere Menschen erhalten zuviel Pillen. In: *Westdeutsche Allgemeine* of 11/27/1991). Cp also Thomas Szasz regarding the dangers of psychopharmaceutical addiction, *Das Ritual der Drogen.* Vienna 1979

45. *Hamburger Morgenpost*, 1/9/1992, p. 7. For more about the horrifying side effects of psychoactive medication, see also Peter Lehmann: *Der chemische Knebel.* Berlin 1990

46. *See* Langbein among others, *Bittere Pillen*, Cologne, 1993, 65, p. 131.

47. The trade names of neuroleptics are, to name a few: Haldol, Mellaril, Stelazine, Thorazine, Prolixin, Trilafon, and others.

48. *See*: Heinz E. Lehmann, "Therapeutic Results with Chlorpromazine," *Canadian Medical Association Journal*, vol. 72/1955, pp. 91-99.

49. *See* Langbein among others, *Bittere Pillen*, op. cit., p. 133ff.

50. Langbein, Martin, Weiss, *Bittere Pillen, Nutzen und Risiken der Arzneimittel*, Cologne 199365, p. 86

51. "The Rise of Senseless Violence in Society: Psychiatry's Role in the Creation of Crime," published by the Citizen's Commission on Human Rights, Los Angeles 1992

52. *Ibid.*

53. reported in *Der Stern* magazine issue 43, 10/17/1991

54. Prof. Dr. F. Reimer, German psychiatrist, in *Spektrum* 5/1989, p. 195

Part III—Chapter 1

THE BEGINNINGS OF PSYCHIATRIC INFLUENCE IN THE UNITED STATES

1. quoted by Wolfgang G. Bringmann, Norma J. Bringmann and William D.G. Balance, *Wundt Studies: A Centennial Collection*, (Toronto: C.J. Hogrefe, Inc., 1980), p. 13

2. Thorne Shipley, ed. *Classics in Psychology* (New York: Philosophical Library, 1961), pp. 52-3, extracted from *Wundt,*

Wilhelm Contributions to the Theory of Sensory Perception, trans. from *Beiträge zur Theorie der Sinneswahrnehmung* (Leipzig: C.F. Winter, 1862)

3. Wilhelm Wundt, *Lectures on Human and Animal Psychology*, (New York: MacMillan & Co., 1894), pp. 5-6

4. Paolo Lionni, *The Leipzig Connection* (Sheridan, Oregon: Delphian Press, 1980), p. 9

5. William James, *Letters*, vol. 1, 1920, p. 263; quoted by Robert J. Richards, *Wundt Studies: A Centennial Collection*, *op. cit.*, p. 42

6. Duane P. Schultz, *A History of Modern Psychology*, 6th edition, (New York: Harcourt Brace, 1972), p. 45

7. Edna Heidbreder, *Seven Psychologies*, (New York: D. Appleton-Century Publishing Co., Inc., 1933), p. 94

8. Gardner Murphy and Joseph Kovach, *Historical Introduction to Modern Psychology*, 6th ed., (New York: Harcourt Brace, 1972), p. 175

9. Paolo Lionni, Paolo, *op. cit.*, pp. 18-19,

10. quoted in Gary Allen, "Hands Off Our Children," *American Opinion*, XVIII, No. 9, (October 1975), p. 3

11. Rudolph Pintner, et. al., *An Outline of Educational Psychology*, (New York: Barnes & Noble, 1934), p. 14

12. Prof. J. McVicker Hunt, as quoted by Allan Chase, *The Legacy of Malthus*, (New York: Alfred A. Knopf, 1975), p. 229

13. quoted by Allan Chase, *The Legacy of Malthus*, *op. cit.*, p. 14

14. *Ibid.*, p. 14

15. quoted by C. P. Blacker, "Galton's Outlook on Religion," *The Eugenics Review*, July 1946, p. 73

16. Chase, *op. cit.* pp. 57-58

17. Alexander Thomas, M.D., and Samuel Sillen, Ph.D., *Racism and Psychiatry*, (New Jersey: The Citadel Press, 1972), p. 3

18. Chase, *op. cit.* p. 229

19. Chase, *op. cit.*, p. 229

20. Rudolph Flesch, *Why Johnny Can't Read*, (New York: Harper & Row, 1955), p. 12

21. Adolf Meyer, "In Memoriam: Emil Kraepelin," Supplement to the *American Journal of Psychiatry*, Vol. 151, No. 6, June 1994

22. Victor H. Bernstein, "The Man Who Created Nazi Murder Science," *P.M. Daily*, August 21, 1945, p. 5

23. *Ibid.*, p. 7

24. *Ibid.*, p. 7

25. Ibid, p. 7

26. Ernst Rüdin, "Rassen—und Gesellschaft Biologie," 10 January 1943, p. 321

27. "Proceedings of the First International Congress on Mental Hygiene," lecture translated by Dr. B. Liber, published by The International Committee for Mental Hygiene, Inc., New York, 1932, pp. 485-486

28. Meyer, "In Memoriam: Emil Kraepelin," April 1927, reprinted in *The American Journal of Psychiatry* Sesquicentennial Supplement, June 1994, p. 143

29. Meyer, "A Short Sketch of the Problems of Psychiatry," *The American Journal of Psychiatry* Sesquicentennial Supplement, June 1994 p. 43

30. Peter Collier and David Horowitz, *The Rockefellers*, (New York: Holt, Rinehart and Winston, 1976), pp. 72-73.

31. Abraham Flexner, *Medical Education in the United States: A Report to the Carnegie Foundation for the Advancement of Teaching*, (New York: 1910), p. 151

32. *Ibid.*, p. 158

33. *Ibid.*, p. 180

34. W.A. Evans, *Journal of the American Medical Association*, Sept. 16, 1911

35. Thomas Malthus, *Essay on the Principle of Population*, 6th edition, 1826, quoted by Chase, *op. cit.*, p. 6

36. *Ibid.*, p. 6

37. quoted by Allan Chase, *op. cit.*, p. 14

38. *Ibid.*, p. 114

39. *Ibid.*, p. 115
40. *Ibid.*, p. 112
41. Charles Davenport, letter to Francis Galton, Oct. 26, 1910
42. Allan Chase, *op. cit.*, p. 125
43. *Ibid.*, p. 125
44. *Ibid.*, p. 133
45. *Ibid.*, p. 133
46. *Ibid.*, pp. 133-134
47. *Ibid.*, p. 134
48. Hitler, *Mein Kampf, op. cit.*,1925. Translation quoted from Blacker, *op. cit.*, p.44, and English language edition (New York: Reynal & Hitchcock, New York, 1941), p. 608
49. Allan Chase, *op. cit.*, p. 233

Part III—Chapter 2
NAZI PSYCHIATRISTS ENLIST IN THE AMERICAN MILITARY

1. Alexis Carrel, *Man the Unknown*, (New York: Harper & Brothers, 1935) p. 291
2. *Ibid.*, p. 299
3. *Ibid.*, p. 319
4. quoted by R.C. Lewontin, Steven Rose and Leon J.Kamin, *Not in Our Genes*, (New York: Pantheon Books, 1984), p. 208
5. Richard Abrams, "Interview with Lothar Kalinowsky, M.D., October 8, 1987, *Convulsive Therapy*, Vol. 4, 1988, p. 28
6. Report of the Proceedings of the Conference on Mental Health, (London: Adlard & Sox, Ltd., 1929), p. 1
7. *Ibid.*, p. 28
8. *Ibid.*, p. 69
9. *Ibid.*, p. 14
10. "Proceedings of the First International Congress on Mental Hygiene," (New York: International Committee for Mental Hygiene, Inc., 1932), pp. xv-xvii
11. "Report of the Programme of the Second Biennial Conference on Mental Health," 1931, p. 1
12. *Ibid.*, p. 14
13. *Ibid.*, pp. 14-16
14. *Ibid.*, p. 17

15. H.V. Dicks, "Fifty Years of the Tavistock Clinic," (London: Routledge & Kegan Paul, 1970), pp. 306-307
16. J.R. Rees, "Strategic Planning for Mental Health," article in "Mental Health," Vol. 1, No. 4, Oct. 1940, p. 104
17. Arvilla Merrill, "Winfred Overholser— A Biographical Sketch," *The American Journal of Occupational Therapy*, Sept.-Oct. 1949
18. *Ibid.*, p. 3
19. Thomas Szasz, "The Manufacture of Madness," (New York: Harper & Row, 1970), p. 39
20. Robert L. Robinson, "Robinson Remembers 30 Years of the APA," *Psychiatric News*, November 16, 1979
21. William Menninger, "The Role of Psychiatry in the World Today," Sept. 1947, reprinted in *American Journal of Psychiatry*, June 1994 Sesquicentennial Supplement, p. 79
22. "Urge All Doctors to Aid Mental Ills," *New York Times*, July 12, 1944.
23. "Curbs on Treating Mental Ills Urged," *New York Times*, May 17, 1953
24. John Marks, *The CIA and Mind Control: The Search for the Manchurian Candidate*, (New York: McGraw-Hill, 1980), p. 6
25. Letter from Overholser to Steckel, October 1942
26. Sallie Pisani, *The CIA and the Marshall Plan*, (University Press of Kansas: 1991), p. 58
27. Papers of Harry S. Truman, Post-Presidential Files, Box 4, in a letter from Truman to William B. McArthur of *Look Magazine*, 10 June 1964
28. Walter Bowart, *Operation Mind Control*, (New York: Dell Publishing Co., 1978), p. 279
29. Barry Siegel, *Los Angeles Times*, "Nazi Data: A Dilemma for Science" Oct. 30, 1988
30. Leo Alexander, "Public Mental Health Practices in Germany: Sterilization and

Execution of Patients Suffering From Nervous or Mental Disease," p. 29

31. *Ibid.*, p. 7
32. *Ibid.*, p. 9
33. Leo Alexander, "Neuropathology and Neurophysiology, including Electro-Encephalography, in Wartime Germany," July 20, 1945, p. 42
34. *Ibid.*, pp. 41-42
35. Leo Alexander, "Public Mental Health Practices in Germany: Sterilization and Execution of Patients Suffering From Nervous or Mental Disease," p. 30
36. *Ibid.*, p. 30
37. *Ibid.*, p. 43
38. Leo Alexander, "Sociopsychologic Structure of the SS: Psychiatric Report of the Nuremberg Trials for War Crimes," *Archives of Neurology and Psychiatry Journal*, 1948, p. 625
39. Barry Siegel, "Nazi Data: A Dilemma for Science," *Los Angeles Times*, Oct. 30, 1988
40. B. Muller-Hill, "Murderous Science: Elimination by Scientific Selection of Jews, Gypsies and others, Germany 1933-1945," (New York: Oxford Press, 1988), p. 87
41. From the Joint Hearing before the Select Committee on Intelligence and the Subcommittee on Health and Scientific Research of the Committee on Human Resources, United States Senate, Aug. 1977
42. *Ibid.*
43. John Marks, *The Search for the Manchurian Candidate, The CIA and Mind Control*, (First McGraw-Hill paperback edition, 1980), p. 57
44. *Ibid.*, p. 53
45. *Ibid.*, p. 54
46. Bowart, *op. cit.*, p. 79
47. Martin A. Lee and Bruce Shlain, *Acid Dreams*, (New York: Grove Press, Inc., 1985), p. 190
48. *Ibid.*, p. 48
49. *Ibid.*, p. 24
50. Lauretta Bender, "LSD and

Amphetamine in Children," from *Psychotomimetic Drugs*—Proceedings of a Workshop Organized by the Pharmacology Section, Psychopharmacology Research Branch, National Institute of Mental Health Held at the University of California, Irvine, on January 25-26, 1969, Daniel H. Efron, ed., (New York: Raven Press, 1969), pp. 269-270
51. Bowart, *op. cit.*, pp. 82-83
52. edited by R.K. Siegel and L.J. West, Hallucinations—Behavior, Experience, and Theory (a Wiley Biomedical Publication with 21 color illustrations), p. 295
53. "Memorandum to the D/Director of the CIA, Re: Testing of Psychochemicals and Related Materials," 17 December 1963, p. 2, #7
54. John Marks, *op. cit.*, p. 57
55. Lee and Shlain, *op. cit.*, p. 188
56. Wayne O. Evans, Ph.D., *Psychotropic Drugs in the Year 2000, Use for Normal Humans*, Charles C. Thomas, Springfield, Illinois, 1971, pp. 42, 158

Part III—Chapter 3
PROJECT PAPERCLIP AND THE PSYCHIATRIC PERMEATION OF AMERICAN SOCIETY AFTER WORLD WAR II

1. Joint Chiefs of Staff, "Statistical Report of Aliens Brought to the United States under the Paperclip Program." OTS (Washington, DC: Office of Technical Services, Dept. of Commerce, Dec. 1, 1952)
2. Lee and Shlain, *op. cit.*, p. 102
3. Marian Zailian, "Good Ship 'Molly Brown': Debbie Reynolds Unsinkable in Role as Determined Survivor," *San Francisco Chronicle*, Dec. 3, 1989, p. 19
4. as quoted by Pamela Warrick, "If the President Can't Lead," *Los Angeles Times*, May 17, 1992, p. E-2
5. Tom Gorman, article: "Powerful People Have Been Users of Dangerous Drug," *Los Angeles Times*, March 13, 1995, p.

A-15.

6. Martin Porter, "Night of the Human Tomatoes: Why is Washington Pushing the New Lobotomy?," *High Times,* March 1979, pp. 64-65

7. *NIH Almanac,* 1993-1994, Bethesda, MD: National Institutes of Health, Sept. 1994, p. 72

8. Nancy Collins and Haynes Johnson, "Nixon on TV Wednesday—And the Traps Are Laid," *Washington Post,* May 1, 1977

9. Jack Anderson, "Democrats Point Out Nixon Saw Shrink Too," *The New York Times,* July 1, 1969

10. *Ibid.*

11. Dick Russell, "The Unsavory Business of Mind Control," *Argosy* magazine, Nov. 1975, p. 30

12. *New York Times,* Oct. 17, 1973, p. 29. col. 1

13. *New York Times,* Nov. 21, 1973, p. 1, col. 1

14. *New York Times,* Nov. 20, 1973, p. 39, col. 1

15. Russell, "The Unsavory Business of Mind Control," *op. cit.,* p. 30

16. *Ibid.,* p. 30

17. *Ibid.,* p. 30

18. *Ibid.,* p. 31

19. Arnold Hutschnecker, *Hope: The Dynamics of Self-Fulfillment,* (New York: G.P. Putnam's Sons, 1981), p. 249

20. Benjamin Stein, *Australian Financial Times,* Jan. 24, 1992, p. 12

21. Bob Woodward and Carl Bernstein, *The Final Days,* (New York: Simon and Schuster, 1976), p. 395

22. Hutschnecker, *op. cit.,* p. 246

23. Stein, *op. cit.,* p. 12

24. Martin Merzer, "Halcion and Bush-Speak: A Link?," *The Miami Herald,* Feb. 2, 1992, pp. 1-2

25. quoted by Merzer, *op. cit.,* p. 2

26. *Ibid.,* p. 2

27. quoted by Milton Greenblatt, "Power and the Impairment of Great Leaders," a lecture at the American Psychiatric Association Annual Meeting, May 2, 1983, New York.

28. Lieb and Hershman, "Should There Be A Shrink In The White House? When a President is Troubled, a Psychiatrist—not a Chief of Staff—is What's Needed," *Washington Post* National Weekly Section, Feb. 20-26, 1989

29. Edwin Yoder, Jr., "When Presidents Act Weird," *Tampa Tribune,* Feb. 22, 1989

30. Lawrence A. Cremin, David A. Shannon and Mary Evelyn Townsend, *A History of Teachers College,* Columbia University, (New York: Columbia University Press, 1954), pp. 46-47

31. Edward L. Thorndike, *The Principles of Teaching Based on Psychology,* (New York: A.G. Seiler, 1925), pp. 7-8

32. *Ibid.,* p. 3

33. Paolo Lionni, *The Leipzig Connection, op. cit.,* p. 35

34. quoted by J. David Smith, "Perspectives: Reflections on Mental Retardation and Eugenics, Old and New: Mensa and the Human Genome Project," article in Mental Retardation, June 1994, p. 236

35. quoted in *The Legacy of Malthus, op. cit.,* p. 357

36. *Ibid.,* p. 469

37. "Born Dumb?," *Newsweek,* March 31, 1969, p. 84

38. *Ibid.,* p. 84

39. Allan Chase, *op. cit.,* p. 476

40. Richard Herrnstein, "IQ," *The Atlantic Monthly,* Sept. 1971, Vol. 228, No. 3., p. 58

41. Richard Herrnstein and Charles Murray, *The Bell Curve: Intelligence and Class Structure in American Life,* (New York: Free Press, 1994)

42. Allan Chase, *op. cit.,* p. 610

43. G. Brock Chisholm, "The Responsibility of Psychiatry," William Alanson White Memorial Lecture, Oct. 23, 1945, Washington, DC, published in *Psychiatry,* February 1946

44. Edward A. Richards, ed., "Proceedings of the Midcentury White House

Conference on Children and Youth, Dec. 3-7, 1950" (Raleigh, NC: Health Publications Institute, Inc., 1950), p. 177

45. Bill Jasper, *The New American*, August 1993, p. 4

46. quoted by Dennis Laurence Cuddy, "Chronology of Education," (Highland City, FL: Pro Family Forum, 1994), p. 35

47. "Action for Mental Health," Final Report of the Joint Commission on Mental Illness and Health, (New York: John Wiley & Sons, 1961), p. 124

48. *Ibid.*, p. 125

49. Carl Rogers, "On Becoming a Person," (Boston: Houghton Mifflin Co., 1961) p.276

50. *Ibid.*, pp. 276-277

51. *"The Role of Schools in Mental Health,"* National Institute of Mental Health, 1962, p. 4

52. "Community Mental Health Centers Act,"

53. *Ibid.*

54. Videotape of speech, Shirley McCune, Governors' Conference on Education, Kansas City, Mo., 1989 quoted by Ron Sunseri, Understanding the Truth About Education Reform, (Sisters, Oregon: Multnomah Books, 1994) p. 62

55. Christopher Corbett, "Parents as Teachers, or Teachers as Parents," *Freedom Club Report*, Aug. 1992

56. *Ibid.*

57. Sol Cohen, "The Mental Hygiene Movement, The Development of Personality and the School: The Medicalization of American Education," *History of Education Quarterly*, Summer 1983, p. 124

58. Sunseri, *op. cit.*, pp. 85-86

59. "Report of the Proceedings of the Conference on Mental Health," edited by J.R. Lord, (London: Adlard & Son, Ltd., 1929), p. 34

60. Robert Robinson, *op. cit.*, p. 2

61. Joseph C. Cocozza and Henry J.

Steadman, "The Failure of Psychiatric Predictions of Dangerousness: Clear and Convincing Evidence," *Rutgers Law Review*, Late Summer 1976, p. 1088

62. Melitta Schmideberg, "The Promise of Psychiatry: Hopes and Disillusionment," *Northwestern Law Review*, March-April 1962, p. 21

63. Alfred K. Baur, M.D., "Legal Responsibility and Mental Illness," *Northwestern Law Review*, March-April 1962, pp. 12-13

64. *Ibid.*, p. 14

65. John B. Watson and William McDougall, *The Battle of Behaviorism—An Exposition and an Exposure*, (London: Kegan Paul, Trench, Trubner & Co., Ltd., 1928) p. 14

66. Sigmund Freud, *The Future of an Illusion*, (New York: W.D. Robson-Scott, 1953) pages as noted

67. David B. Larson, et al., "Systematic Analysis of Research on Religious Variables in Four Major Psychiatric Journals, 1972-1982, published in *The American Journal of Psychiatry*, Vol. 143, No. 3 (March 1986) pp. 329-334

68. quoted from "Psychiatry and Religion: A Variable History," *Journal of Religion and Health*, Vol. 13, No. 2, 1974, p. 139

69. quoted in Thomas Szasz, *The Manufacture of Madness, op. cit.*, p. 311

70. William Hirsch, *Conclusions of a Psychiatrist*, quoted in Szasz, *op. cit.*, p. 312

71. Havelock Ellis, *The Dance of Life*, Grosset & Dunlap, New York, 1923, pp. 339-340

72. J.R. Rees, "Strategic Planning for Mental Health," from Mental Health, Vol. 1 No. 4, Oct. 1940, pp. 103-106

73. G. Brock Chisholm, "The Responsibility of Psychiatry," *op. cit.*, p. 8

74. *Ibid.*, p. 9

75. *Ibid.*, p. 11

76. FDA Drug Review, Postapproval Risks 1976-1985, United States General Accounting Office, Washington, DC, April 26, 1990, pp. 1-4, 24-32, 74-78.

77. William C. Menninger and Henry W. Brosin, *Religion and Psychiatry*, 1947

78. *Ibid.*

79. *Fuller Theological Seminary*, catalog number 4, 1950-51, Pasadena, California, pp. 22-23, 37-38

80. "Serving Troubled Mankind: A Collaborative Program for a Healthier Nation," Academy of Religion and Mental Health, New York, 1969, p. 1

81. *Ibid.*, p. 6

82. *Ibid.*, p. 7

83. "Therapeutic Revolution," *Christianity Today*, May 17, 1993, p. 29

84. "Action for Mental Health," Final Report of the Joint Commission on Mental Illness and Health 1961, *op. cit.*, p. 103

85. "Franchising Hope," *Christianity Today*, May 18, 1992, p. 24

86. William Coulson, "How I Wrecked the I.H.M. Nuns," *The Latin Mass*, Special Edition, pp. 12-16

87. "The Interface of Psychiatry and Religion: A Program for Career Training in Psychiatry," *Journal of Psychology and Theology*, Vol. 10, No. 1, p. 22

88. *Pastoral Psychology*, Oct. 1968, pp. 21-32

89. IRH brochure, circa 1977

90. quoted by Thomas Szasz, "Insanity, The Idea and its Consequences," New York, 1987, p. 68

91. *Diagnostic and Statistic Manual IV*, American Psychiatric Association, 1994, p. 685

Part III—Chapter 4
PSYCHIATRY GETS INTO THE MEDICAL PROFESSION

1. Thomas Szasz, *Schizophrenia: The Sacred Symbol of Psychiatry*, Basic Books, Inc., New York, p. 87

2. *Ibid.*, p. 90

3. *Ibid.*, p. 115

4. *Ibid.*, p. 90

5. Marion Hunt, "Genetics in Psychiatry: An Essential Tool," *NARSAD Newsletter*, Winter 1990, p. 1

6. *Ibid.*, p. 1

7. *Ibid.*, p. 1

8. *Ibid.*, p. 3

9. *The Journal*, July 28, 1933

10. photocopy of letter on file

11. Marc Kimball, "Institute May Be Renamed Due To Benefactor's Beliefs," *Minneapolis Daily*, May 2, 1985

12. *Ibid.*

13. Philip S. Holzman, "The Genetics of Schizophrenia," *NARSAD Research Newsletter*, Winter 1990, p. 3

14. quoted in Max Ben, "Pharmacotherapy: Millions Spent, Little Gained," *Professional Counselor*, Dec. 1992, p. 46

15. *Ibid.*, p. 46

16. Milton Moscowitz, Michael Katz, Robert Levering, *Everybody's Business*, San Francisco: Harper & Row, 1980), p. 228

17. *Freedom* magazine, October 1988, p. 21

18. "Methadone for Pain," *Newsweek*, Jan. 8, 1951, p. 48

19. *Freedom* magazine, *op. cit.*, p. 22

20. *Ibid.*, p. 22

21. letters to the editor, *Newport (RI) Mercury*, April 14, 1989

22. *Ibid.*

23. Ray Belew, "Methadone 'Victory' Rate: 1 percent," *The Columbus Dispatch*, July 2, 1987, p. 1-A

24. Max Ben, *op. cit.*, p. 46

25. *Ibid.*, p. 46

26. *Ibid.*, p. 47

27. *Ibid.*, p. 47

28. Spencer Rumsey, *Newsday* (Nassau and Suffolk edition), November 19, 1992, p. 68 (Correct though he may be, Kleber has his own interests in the matter. He is the co-developer of a rival substance, buprenorphine, which also claims to cure drug addiction. Buprenorphine is also an opiate which "blocks" the euphoric effects of heroin use, but sup-

posedly with milder withdrawal symptoms—yet another link in the chain.)

29. "Drug's Side Effect: Blocking of Addiction, Some Users Claim," *The Orlando Sentinel*, Sept. 5, 1993, p. A-12

30. *Newsday*, Nassau and Suffolk edition, Nov. 19, 1992, p. 72

31. *Ibid.*, p. 68

32. Nancy McVicar, "Safety Tests Proposed for Anti-Cocaine Medicine," *San Diego Union-Tribune*, August 28, 1993, p. A-19

33. Gerald N. Grob, "Government and Mental Health Policy," *The Milbank Quarterly*, Sept. 22, 1994, p. 471

34. *Ibid.*, p. 471

35. *Ibid.*, p. 471

36. *Ibid.*, p. 471

37. *Ibid.*, p. 471

38. *NIH Almanac* 1993-1994, p. 72

39. *Ibid.*, pp. 72-73

40. *See* Joe E. Smith, "Ethical Issues raised by the Human Genome Project," *American Journal of Hospital Pharmacy*, Vol. 50, Sept. 1993, p. 1945

41. Nancy C. Andreasen, M.D., "Brave New Brain," Vogue, January 1990, p. 198

42. Joe E. Smith, *op cit.*, p 1948

43. J. David Smith, "Reflections on Mental Retardation and Eugenics, Old and New: Mensa and the Human Genome Project," *Mental Retardation*, Vol. 32, No. 3, June 1994, p. 238

44. Hearings Before a Subcommittee of the Committee on Appropriations, House of Representatives, One Hundred Fourth Congress, First Session, (Washington, DC: U.S. Government Printing Office, 1995), p. 1205

Part III—Chapter 5
LIFE IN THE MODERN AMERICAN "AGE OF PSYCHIATRY"

1. McClay, *Bats in the Belfry*, (Los Angeles: Rosewood Publishing Company, 1964), p. 163

2. *Ibid.*, p. 163

3. Address of Judge Joseph Call, "Constitutional Threats in the Alaska Mental Health Act," May 1956

4. quoted by McClay, *op. cit.*, p. 162

5. Senate Hearings, *Constitutional Rights of the Mentally Ill*, March 1961

6. "Action for Mental Health," Final Report of the Joint Commission on Mental Illness and Health 1961, (New York: John Wiley & Sons, 1961), p. viii

7. H.H. Goldman, N.H. Adams, and C. Taube, General Accounting Office, "Returning the Mentally Ill to the Community: Government Needs to Do More," Washington, 1977

8. Elementary and Secondary Education Act of 1965, "Laws of the 89th Congress, First Session," April 11, 1965, p. 29

9. *Ibid.*, p. 45

10. Education for All Handicapped Children Act of 1975, Subchapter I, General Provisions, Section 1401, Definition 1

11. *Education Week*, April 24, 1984, quoted by Samuel L. Blumenfeld, "NEA: Trojan Horse in American Education," (Boise, Idaho: The Paradigm Company, 1984), p. 128

12. Thomas Szasz, *The Manufacture of Madness*, (New York: Harper & Row, 1970), p. 156

13. Paul Popenoe, "Intelligence and Race," The Journal of Heredity, Vol. XIII, No. 7, July 1922, p. 295

14. *Ibid.*, p. 298

15. *Ibid.*, p. 295

16. "Harry Bailey: A Sadist Dressed Up as a Doctor, or Just Insane?" *The Sydney Morning Herald*, Aug. 6, 1988

17. Alan W. Scheflin and Edward M. Opton, Jr., *The Mind Manipulators*, (New York and London: Paddington Press Ltd., 1978), p. 150

18. *Ibid.*, pp. 288-295; *The New York Times*, February 10, 1979

19. quoted by Gerald Horne, "Race Backwards: Genes, Violence, Race and Genocide," Covert Action, Winter

1992-93, p. 32

20. Linda King, "The Brain Eaters: Psychosurgery at UCLA," *Los Angeles Free Press*, March 15, 1974, p. 15

21. *The Journal for Personal Freedom*, Vol. 1, Issue 3, p. 3

22. partial transcript of Feb. 11, 1992 meeting of the National Health Advisory Council

23. Eli Newberger, MD, letter to Louis W. Sullivan, MD, Secretary, Department of Health and Human Services, March 11, 1992

24. Lynne Duke, "Controversy Flares over Crime, Heredity," *The Washington Post*, August 19, 1992

25. Letter to the Editor, *Wall Street Journal*, April 1, 1992

26. quoted in Gerald Horne, *op. cit.*, p. 31

27. "Tracking down the monster within us—'Genes of Agression' Found," *Chicago Tribune*, December 12, 1993

28. "Genetic Screening Program Threatens Inner City Youth," *Louisville Defender*, August 20, 1992, p. A9

29. quoted by David L. Wheeler, "Debate Over Studies Linking Biology and Behavior," *The Chronicle of Higher Education*, June 24, 1992, p. A-7

30. *Ibid.*, p. A-7

31. quoted by Wheeler, *Ibid.*

32. J.R. Rees, "Mental Health and World Citizenship," International Congress on Mental Health, London, 1948

33. Letter from Daniel Blain to Dr. John Rees, July 2, 1953

34. "Psychiatrist Heads Tipper Gore's Staff on Mental Health Reform," *Psychiatric News*, April 16, 1993, p. 18

35. "Rockefeller Promises to Fight for MH Care in National Reform Plan," *Psychiatric News*, March 5, 1993, p. 1

36. Roger Cohen, "CIA Blames Serb Forces for Atrocities," *Detroit Free Press*, March 9, 1995

37. Memorandum of the Serbian Academy of Arts and Sciences, as quoted in "War of Aggression in Ex-Yugoslavia" by

CCHR, 1993

38. "Oedipean and Castrated: Academy Prof. Jovan Raskovic on Ethnic Characteristics," *Intervju*, Sept. 15, 1989

39. "SDS Leaders—Patients of Dr. Raskovic!" *Nedjeljna Dalmacija*, Oct. 17, 1991

40. "War of Aggression in Ex-Yugoslavia," by CCHR, Feb. 1993, p. 7

41. "Jovan Raskovic on the psychiatric couch," *Vjesnik*, Jan. 24, 1992

42. "The Hunt for the Killers of Bosnia," *U.S. News & World Report*, April 10, 1995, p. 53

43. "U.S. urged to stop Serb 'rape camps,'" *Associated Press*, quoted in *Rocky Mountain News*, Dec. 11, 1992

44. Alexandra Stiglmayer, "Vergewaltigung auf Befehl," *Der Stern*, Nov. 26, 1992, p. 4

45. "Bosnia Herzegovina: Rape and sexual abuse by armed forces," Amnesty International, January 1993 p. 1

46. J. T. Nguyen, "Legal Experts Named to Balkans War-Crimes Panel," *UPI Newswire*, Oct. 26, 1992

47. "Serbian Cruelty Is the Worst Since Nazis, U.S. Asserts," *International Herald Tribune*, Jan. 20, 1993.

48. Tadeusz Mazowiecki, "Situation of Human Rights in the Territory of the Former Yugoslavia, published by the United Nations Economic and Social Council, November 6, 1992, p. 2

49. *Ibid.*, pp. 2-4

50. Norman Kempster, "Photos Show Mass Graves of Civilians From 'Safe Areas,' U.S. Tells U.N.," *Los Angeles Times*, August 11, 1995, p. A-12

51. Sourcebook of Criminal Justice Statistics 1993, Bureau of Justice Statistics, Dept. of Justice, table 3.107

52. BJS Data Report, 1989, 1994, U.S. Department of Justice, Office of Justice Programs, Bureau of Justice Statistics

53. Statistical Abstract of the United States, Bureau of the Census, U.S. Dept. of

Commerce, (1974), p. 51, 66, (1994) p. 102, 105; The World Almanac and Book of Facts 1995, Funk & Wagnall's Corporation (1994), p. 957

54. Statistical Abstract of the United States, 1940 through 1985 (various years) 1988, 1990, 1994, 1995

55. Mental Health, United States 1985, National Institute of Mental Health, Alcohol, Drug Abuse and Mental Health Administration, Public Health Service, U.S. Dept. of Health and Human Services, p. 150; Additional for 15-19 year old data: Statistical Abstract of the United States, Bureau of the Census, U.S. Dept. of Commerce, (1988), p. 82, (1990) p. 86

56. "Expenditures in Mental Health Organizations by Type of Organization: United States, 1990," Center for Mental Health Services, Public Health Service, U.S. Dept. of Health and Human Services; Mental Health, United States, Center for Mental Health Services and National Institute for Mental Health, U.S. Dept. of Health and Human Services, (1992) p. 21; National Data Book, January 1980, Alcohol, Drug Abuse and Mental Health Administration, U.S. Dept. of Health, Education and Welfare, p. 25

57. "Expenditures in Mental Health Organizations by Type of Organization: United States, 1990," Center for Mental Health Services, Public Health Service, U.S. Dept. of Health and Human Services; Mental Health, United States, Center for Mental Health Services and National Institute for Mental Health, U.S. Dept. of Health and Human Services, (1992) p. 46 (1987), p. 56

58. Mental Health Research Grant Awards, fiscal year 1972 National Institute of Mental Health, Public Health Service, U.S. Dept. of Health, Education and Welfare; Alcohol, Drug Abuse, Mental Health, Research Grant Awards, fiscal

years 1973, 1974, 1975, 1978, 1979, 1981, 1982, 1983, 1984, 1985, 1986, 1987, 1988, 1990, National Institute of Mental Health, Alcohol, Drug Abuse and Mental Health Administration, Public Health Service, U.S. Dept. of Health and Human Services, (U.S. Dept. of Health, Education and Welfare 1973-1978), Budget Office, National Institute of Mental Health, U.S. Dept. of Health and Human Services, 1995

59. U. S. Dept. of Education computer file, obtained from the Internet; URL:gopher: //gopher.ed.gov; Statistical Abstract of the United States, 1980, 1988, 1994

60. Leone Kirkwood, "Psychiatrist analyzes colleagues, diagnoses a messiah complex," *Globe and Mail*, Toronto, February 1, 1972

61. Paul Genova, "A Good Good-bye: Is American Psychiatry Terminally Ill?" *Psychiatric Times*, June 1993, p. 19

Part III—Chapter 6
PSYCHIATRY, YESTERDAY
AND TODAY

1. *Münchner Merkur* from 4/1/1993, *Forscher auf der Suche nach 4000 Zwillings-Paaren*

INDEX

MORE INFORMATION CARD

YES, I would like to receive more information (FREE OF CHARGE) on:

❏ PSYCHIATRIC VIOLATIONS OF HUMAN RIGHTS AND WHAT CAN BE DONE TO ELIMINATE THEM.

I am also interested in receiving more information on the specific subjects of:

❏ PSYCHIATRY'S ROLE IN THE CREATION OF CRIME
❏ PSYCHIATRIC HEALTH CARE FRAUD
❏ PSYCHIATRY'S DESTRUCTION OF EDUCATION
❏ PSYCHIATRIC ABUSE OF THE ELDERLY
❏ PSYCHIATRIC RAPE

Call 1-800-307-1211
or fill out and mail in the following form.
Please mail information on the items checked above to:

NAME: _____

ADDRESS: _____

CITY: _____ STATE: _____ ZIP: _____

TELEPHONE NUMBER: _____ FAX: _____

ORDER FORM

IS THERE A SINGLE SOURCE BEHIND SOCIAL CHAOS?

Our cities didn't become lawless battlegrounds ruled by criminal gangs without a reason.

FIND OUT THE REASON.

ORDER THIS CHILLING NON-FICTION EXPOSÉ TODAY!

Psychiatry—the Ultimate Betrayal by Bruce Wiseman

Call 1-800-307-1211 or fill out and mail in the following form:

NAME: _____

ADDRESS: _____

CITY: _____ STATE: _____ ZIP: _____

TELEPHONE NUMBER: _____ FAX: _____

❏ Please send me _____ copies of *Psychiatry—the Ultimate Betrayal.*

PSYCHIATRY—THE ULTIMATE BETRAYAL: $24.95

I am enclosing $_____ (includes postage and handling costs*)

I am making my payment by: ❏ check** ❏ credit card
❏ Amex   ❏ Visa   ❏ M/C   ❏ Discover

Card # _____ Expiration Date _____

* Add $1.75 per item for shipping and handling. California residents add 8.25% sales tax. ** Please use envelope.
ORDERS SHIPPED WITHIN 24 HOURS OF RECEIPT.

❏ I would like to order _____ additional copies of *Psychiatrists—the Men Behind Hitler.*
at $24.95 each, plus shipping and handling.

BUSINESS REPLY MAIL
FIRST CLASS MAIL   PERMIT NO. 70527   LOS ANGELES, CA

POSTAGE WILL BE PAID BY ADDRESSEE

CITIZENS COMMISSION ON HUMAN RIGHTS
6362 HOLLYWOOD BOULEVARD, SUITE B
LOS ANGELES, CA 90028

NO POSTAGE
NECESSARY
IF MAILED
IN THE
UNITED STATES

BUSINESS REPLY MAIL
FIRST CLASS MAIL   PERMIT NO. 70527   LOS ANGELES, CA

POSTAGE WILL BE PAID BY ADDRESSEE

CITIZENS COMMISSION ON HUMAN RIGHTS
6362 HOLLYWOOD BOULEVARD, SUITE B
LOS ANGELES, CA 90028